CAROLINE MOOREHEAD

Caroline Moorehead is the b̶i̶ of Bertrand Russell, Freya Stark and Martha Gellhorn. Well work in human rights, she history of the Red Cross and refugees, *Human Cargo*. Her bi of Lucie de la Tour du Pin, *Dancing to the Precipice*, was shortlisted for the Costa Biography Award in 2009. Caroline's most recent book was *A Train in Winter*. She lives in London.

ALSO BY CAROLINE MOOREHEAD

Fortune's Hostages

Sidney Bernstein: A Biography

Freya Stark: A Biography

*Beyond the Rim of the World: The Letters of
Freya Stark* (ed.)

Troublesome People

Betrayed: Children in Today's World (ed.)

Bertrand Russell: A Life

The Lost Treasures of Troy

*Dunant's Dream: War, Switzerland and the
History of the Red Cross*

Iris Origo: Marchesa of Val d'Orcia

Martha Gellhorn: A Life

Human Cargo: A Journey Among Refugees

The Letters of Martha Gellhorn (ed.)

*Dancing to the Precipice: Lucie de la Tour du Pin
and the French Revolution*

*A Train in Winter: A Story of Resistance,
Friendship and Survival*

CAROLINE MOOREHEAD

Village of Secrets

Defying the Nazis in Vichy France

VINTAGE

1 3 5 7 9 10 8 6 4 2

Vintage,
20 Vauxhall Bridge Road,
London SW1V 2SA

Vintage is part of the Penguin Random House group of companies whose
addresses can be found at global.penguinrandomhouse.com.

Penguin
Random House
UK

Copyright © Caroline Moorehead 2014

Caroline Moorehead has asserted her right to be identified as the author of
this Work in accordance with the Copyright, Designs and Patents Act 1988

First published by Vintage in 2015

(First published in Great Britain by Chatto & Windus in 2014)

www.vintage-books.co.uk

A CIP catalogue record for this book is available from the British Library

ISBN 9780099554646

Printed and bound by CPI Group (UK) Ltd, Croydon CR0 4YY

Penguin Random House is committed to a sustainable future for our
business, our readers and our planet. This book is made from Forest
Stewardship Council® certified paper.

MIX
Paper from
responsible sources
FSC
www.fsc.org   FSC® C018179

To Anne and Annie, companions on my travels

The memory of the world is not a bright, shining crystal, but a heap of broken fragments, a few fine flashes of light that break through the darkness.

Herbert Butterfield

In searching for an explanation of the motivations of the Righteous Among the Nations, are we not really saying: what was wrong with them? Are we not, in a deeper sense, implying that their behaviour was something other than normal? . . . Is acting benevolently and altruistically such an outlandish and unusual type of behaviour, supposedly at odds with man's inherent character, as to justify a meticulous search for explanations? Or is it conceivable that such behaviour is as natural to our psychological constitution as the egoistic one we accept so matter-of-factly?

Mordecai Paldiel

Contents

Principal characters

The pastors

André and Magda Trocmé and their children Nelly, Jean-Pierre,
  Jacques and Daniel in le Chambon
Edouard and Mildred Theis in le Chambon
Daniel Curtet in Fay-sur-Lignon
Roland Leenhardt in Tence
Marcel Jeannet in Mazet

The rescuers

Mireille Philip, who ran the network taking children to Switzerland
Georgette and Gabrielle Barraud, owners of the Beau Soleil
Dr Le Forestier, the doctor of le Chambon
Miss Maber, an English teacher at the Ecole Nouvelle Cévenol
Oscar Rosowsky, medical student and master forger
Mme Déléage, placer of children for the OSE
Mme Roussel, Catholic who concealed Jews in le Chambon
Pierre Piton, boy scout who guided Jews to Switzerland
Emile Sèches, proprietor of Tante Soly
August Bohny, Swiss director of La Guespy, L'Abric and Faïdoli
Daniel Trocmé, director of Maison des Roches
Charles Guillon, mayor of le Chambon
Roger Darcissac, teacher in le Chambon
Marie Exbrayat, proprietor of an ironmonger's shop in Fay
Lulu Ruel, proprietor of a café in Mazet, and her daughter
  Lucienne
Dorcas Robert, proprietor of a café in Yssingeaux
Virginia Hall, SOE and OSS agent

Léon Eyraud, organiser of the Maquis

Jean, Eugenie, Roger and Germain May, proprietors of the Hôtel May

Jean Deffaugt, Mayor of Annemasse

The children

Hanne Hirsch and Max Liebmann

Simon and Jacques Liwerant

Jacques and Marcel Stulmacher

Genie, Liliane, Ruth and the girls from Roanne

Pierre Bloch

Gilbert Nizard and his brothers and sisters

Madeleine Sèches of Tante Soly

The Justes

Abbé Glasberg, rescuer at Vénissieux

Père Chaillet, of Amitié Chrétienne

Madeleine Barot, general secretary of Cimade

Joseph Bass, of the Service André

The Jewish rescuers

Madeleine Dreyfus, of the OSE

Georges and Lily Garel, of the OSE's Circuit B

Liliane Klein-Liebert, social worker with the OSE

Georges Loinger, conveyer of children to Switzerland

Andrée Salomon, of the OSE

Germans and collaborators

Inspector Praly, policeman in le Chambon

Major Schmähling, commander of German garrison in Le Puy

Robert Bach, prefect of the Haute-Loire

René Bousquet, Vichy chief of police

Chronology

1939

1 September	Germany invades Poland
3 September	Great Britain, New Zealand, Australia and France declare war on Germany
26 September	French government outlaws Communist Party

1940

29 February	Ration cards introduced
21 March	Reynaud replaces Daladier as prime minister
13 May	German army crosses Meuse and enters France
18 May	Reynaud appoints 84-year-old Pétain deputy prime minister
24 May	British Expeditionary Force falls back on Dunkirk
10 June	French government leaves Paris. Italy declares war on France and Britain
14 June	Germans enter Paris
16 June	Reynaud is replaced by Pétain
22 June	Franco-German armistice signed at Rethondes
23 June	Hitler visits Paris. Laval becomes deputy prime minister
1 July	Pétain's government moves to Vichy

22 July	Vichy government begins to review citizenship
13 August	Freemasons banned from many professions
27 September	Germany demands census of Jews in occupied zone
3 October	First Statut des Juifs, defining Jewishness and banning Jews from certain occupations
22 October	Jews in Baden and the Palatinate rounded up, deported to France and interned
24 October	Pétain meets Hitler at Montoire
5 November	Creation of Nîmes Committee

1941

March	Vichy sets up the Commissariat Général aux Questions Juives (CGQJ) under Xavier Vallat
14 May	First *rafle* of Jews in Paris
2 June	Second Statut des Juifs
22 July	Vichy law authorises confiscation of Jewish property and enterprises
29 November	Vallat sets up the Union Générale des Israelites de France (UGIF), supposedly to let Jews manage their own affairs
11 December	Germany declares war on USA

1942

20 January	Wannsee meeting commits Reich to Final Solution
4 February	Formation of the Service d'Ordre Légionnaire, predecessor to the Milice
1 March	Start of Allied bombing of France
19 March	Vallat sacked from CGQJ, replaced by Darquier de Pellepoix
27 March	First train of Jews leaves Drancy for Auschwitz

29 May	Jews over the age of six in occupied zone ordered to wear a yellow star
30 June	Eichmann arrives in Paris to implement Final Solution
16–17 July	*Rafle* of Jews in Paris, *Opération Vent Printanier*. 12,884 people arrested
5 August	Start of deportations of Jews from southern zone
10 August	Lamirand visits the Plateau Vivarais-Lignon
13 August	Switzerland closes its borders to Jewish refugees
August	Letters of protest from French prelates
September	Pastor Marc Boegner directs Protestants to save Jews
8 November	Allied landings in North Africa
11 November	Germans invade southern zone

1943

January	Combat, Libération-Sud and the FTP join forces as the Mouvements Unis de la Résistance (MUR)
18 January	Siege of Leningrad lifted
24 January	Germans destroy Vieux Port of Marseilles
31 January	Milice founded, with Darnand as secretary general
16 February	Service du Travail Obligatoire (STO) introduced
9 July	Allies reach Sicily
25 July	Mussolini replaced by Badoglio
8 September	Germans take over Italian-occupied *départements* in southern France
13 October	Italy declares war on Germany

1944

22 January	Allies land at Anzio
6 June	D-Day landings

7–10 June	German massacres at Tulle and Oradour-sur-Glane
15 August	French and Allied troops land in Provence. Progressive liberation of France by Allies, French armies and Resistance begins
17 August	Last train of Jews leaves Drancy for Auschwitz
24–25 August	French forces enter Paris. Germans surrender
1 September	French troops reach le Chambon
23 October	Britain, USA and Canada officially recognise de Gaulle's government

France in 1942

Land occupied by Italy until 1943

Vichy France

French land occupied by the Nazis

■ Internment camps

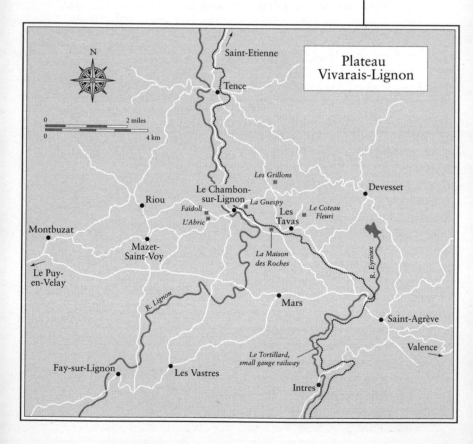

Paris

FRANCE

Lyons

N

Saint-Etienne

Tence

Plateau
Vivarais-Lignon

0   2 miles
0   4 km

Les Grillons

Le Chambon-
sur-Lignon   *La Guespy*   Devesset

Riou   *Faïdoli*   Les
           L'Abric   Tavas   *Le Coteau
Fleuri*

Montbuzat

Mazet-
Saint-Voy   *La Maison
des Roches*

Le Puy-
en-Velay   *R. Eyrieux*

R. Lignon   Mars

                                            Saint-Agrève

                                            Valence

Fay-sur-Lignon   Les Vastres   *Le Tortillard,
small gauge railway*

Intres

Foreword

In the spring of 1953, *Peace News*, a fortnightly magazine aimed at America's pacifist community, carried an unusual story. It was about a half-French, half-German Protestant pastor called André Trocmé who, between the arrival of the Germans in Paris in May 1940 and the liberation of France in the summer of 1944, helped save some 5,000 hunted communists, Freemasons, resisters and Jews from deportation to the extermination camps of occupied Poland.

Posted to the remote parish of le Chambon-sur-Lignon, high in the mountains of the Eastern Massif Central, Pastor Trocmé, as *Peace News* told it, so inspired his Protestant parishioners with his absolute faith in pacifism that, lit up by a 'conspiracy of good', they took in, hid, fed and smuggled to safety in Switzerland those whose names appeared on Nazi death lists. Many of those rescued were children.

As the Cold War was beginning and fears of global conflict were spreading, here was proof that Gandhian non-violence could work. More than that, the story was a perfect weapon in the struggle to find meaning for the Vichy years, by minimising collaborators and celebrating resisters. In the same way that the plateau of Vercors, where the Maquis briefly established a free government, became a symbol of heroic resistance, le Chambon could become one of selfless morality. In this *'pays de grand silence'*, where generations of Huguenots had kept quiet when it was dangerous for those who were not Catholics to speak out, 'non-violent resistance to the Hitler–Pétain system was born'. A complaisant regional prefect and a good German officer, along with a number of feisty but not always prudent local inhabitants,

9

completed the cast of characters. It was not long before people began using the phrase 'banality of good' to describe the modesty and ordinariness of the Chambonais, in counterpoint to Hannah Arendt's overused words about evil. In the wake of the *Peace News* story came eulogies, newspaper articles, memoirs, documentaries and films, and they have never stopped coming. In 1988, le Chambon became the only village in the world to be honoured by Yad Vashem as Righteous Among the Nations. A myth was born.

There is one problem: all was not quite as it seemed.

Many Jews and resisters were indeed saved – but certainly not 5,000; and they had been saved not by non-violence but by a remarkable adventure in imagination and cooperation. It was not the only adventure of its kind, but the area's very remoteness and the tacit support of almost every one of its inhabitants makes it stand out. There was a fairly decent prefect and a less than murderous German officer, but neither could be described as good. There was not just one village, le Chambon, but half a dozen others across the whole plateau of the Vivarais-Lignon, as well as many outlying hamlets, and not one Protestant pastor but 24, along with members of other Protestant faiths, like the Darbyists and the Ravenists, descendants of followers of the Plymouth Brethren, as well as Catholics and many who professed no religious faith at all. Doctors, teachers, university professors, students and a large number of boy and girl scouts all played key parts. And André Trocmé himself was a far subtler, more troubled and doubting man than the myth suggested. Hero to some, mythomane to others, Trocmé, who died in 1971, has become a figure of renown.

As ever, the truth, inasmuch as it can be established 70 years after the event, is considerably more interesting. The myth has much diminished reality. It has also given rise to an unceasing flow of feuds, jealousies, backbiting, calumnies, hearsay, claims and counterclaims and prejudice, pitting Catholics against Protestants, armed resisters against pacifists, civilians against Maquisards, believers against agnostics, those who seek glory against those who wish to remain silent. To this day the topic is as heated as it was in the years in which it first turned into an explosive mixture of local politics and historical rivalry. Nor did it help when, in 2004, President Chirac called le Chambon '*la conscience de notre pays*'.

What actually took place on the plateau of the Vivarais-Lignon during the grey and terrifying years of German occupation and Vichy rule is indeed about courage, faith and morality. But it is also about the fallibility of memory.

Part One

Escaping

CHAPTER ONE

Mea Culpa

When Aaron Liwerant brought Sara, his fiancée, to Paris from her parents' house in Warsaw in the summer of 1926, France was a good place for refugees. The French government was welcoming, granting naturalisation to the many Poles, Russians, Galicians and Romanians who came to fill the jobs in industry and mining left vacant by the high number of French casualties in the Great War. The international bookshop on the Left Bank sold books and papers in Russian and Polish. The French proved welcoming too to the Germans, Austrians, Italians and Spaniards arriving in the wake of the rise to power of Hitler, Mussolini and Franco, and some of the refugees went off to work in agriculture in the south.

Aaron was a leatherworker, and Sara covered the clasps he brought home from the workshop with silk, and sometimes with leather. Their first child, Berthe, was born in April 1927; a son, Simon, followed in November 1928. Though Aaron and Sara occasionally talked of the day they would be able to go back to Poland, they naturalised the two children and made them French citizens.

The Liwerants occupied two rooms, with no bathroom and a shared lavatory, in Belleville, which, along with the Marais and the 11th, 12th and 18th arrondissements, was home to most of the foreign immigrants in Paris, and particularly to the Jewish families like theirs working in fur and textiles. Aaron's sister had also settled in France and she too had French citizenship, but neither she nor Aaron and Sara saw themselves as observant. To be Jewish in France in the 1920s and 1930s was to enjoy the legacy of the French Revolution, which had conferred equal rights on all the country's religious minorities at a time when such

VILLAGE OF SECRETS

tolerance was shared only by the new United States of America. The Liwerants thought of themselves as equals, loyal citizens of a strong, emancipated republican state.

Aaron and Sara Liwerant, with their children

Though the family spoke Yiddish at home, Berthe and Simon were bilingual in French. France was their home; neither had known any other, though they listened with interest to the stories of their grandparents in Poland and of the pogroms that had driven their mother and father into exile. After school, Simon helped his mother cover the clasps for Aaron's leatherwork, and with the one-franc coins she gave him, he bought stamps, usually of aeroplanes.

The elections of 1936 had brought Léon Blum, a Jew and a socialist, to power with the Front Populaire, which welcomed immigrants and did much to improve conditions for French workers, but also sparked off strikes and violent confrontations. By now, France had a greater percentage of foreigners than any other country, including the United States. And when the world economic recession, which came relatively late to the country, brought high unemployment to French industry, workers began to feel hostility towards the very men and women they had so warmly welcomed not long before.

Simon was 10 when Léon Blum's government fell in 1938, amid much rhetoric about the perils of world Jewry and personal slander against the Jewish Blum, a Proustian figure with floppy straight dark hair, a neat moustache and spats, who was referred to by some as a parasite and a vagrant, a pervert and underminer of 'healthy male virility'. Searching for culprits for the country's ills, some of the French began to see in the three million foreigners, and especially the foreign Jews, the perfect scapegoats; the river of anti-Semitism and xenophobia that poured out in pamphlets, books and articles peddling rumours of secret societies, satanic rituals and fifth columnists, and which so many believed to have vanished for ever in the post-Dreyfus years, was suddenly turning out to have merely gone underground. The words of the elderly former prime minister Raymond Poincaré, 'After the Dreyfus affair, anti-Semitism will no longer ever be possible again in France', began to sound a little foolish.

It was somehow more seductive, though alarming, to listen to the royalist intellectual Charles Maurras announce, in the right-wing, nationalist *L'Action Française*, that 'One thing is dead: it is the spirit of semi-tolerance accorded to the Jews . . . a formidable *à bas les Juifs* is smouldering in every breast and will pour forth from every heart', or to follow the spiteful attacks of his colleague, the scruffy, rodent-like Céline, the specialist in children's diseases. Maurras himself was a short man, with a stutter and a neat goatee; his young activists, the Camelots du Roi, were thugs.

France, the two men agreed, had for too long been exploited and betrayed by internal enemies, in numbers they likened to a tidal wave. Their undoubted verbal brilliance lent their ideas a certain legitimacy. When, in May 1939, Edouard Daladier's new government spoke of 'ferreting out, identifying and expelling' the illegal foreigners, there were many happy to listen to him. A leading member of the radicals, Daladier had been moving steadily towards the right. Jewish immigration had reached 'saturation point'. Ten thousand Jews should be sent 'elsewhere'. In Belleville, the Liwerants and their

Jewish neighbours lay low, hoping that such sentiments would pass, as they had done before. The declaration of war in September 1939 did not trouble them greatly, nor did the *drôle de guerre*, the phoney war, even if the Catholic writer Georges Bernanos observed, before emigrating to South America, that it really was not *drôle* at all, but mournful. Some 40,000 Jewish men had enlisted in the French army. In March, while the war seemed stalled, the government passed to a dapper barrister with a keen interest in sports called Paul Reynaud.

Simon was 12 when the Maginot line, France's impregnable barrier of cement and steel, was outflanked by the Panzers in May 1940. Within days, the German army was advancing on Paris, driving before it a wave of terrified citizens and defeated military recruits, while in Paris the government gathered in force in Notre-Dame to offer prayers for divine intervention. Sara had just given birth to her third child, a boy they called Jacques. Escape was not an option for her, but she persuaded Aaron to join the exodus south, the eight million people who fled from their homes before the German advance, to see for himself what possibilities existed for the family away from Paris. He was soon back, recounting how he had got as far as Orléans and that he had escaped attention from the military by putting his belongings in an abandoned pram and pretending that it contained a baby. For a while, as the German occupiers in Paris appeared to be behaving so correctly towards the country they had overrun, the Liwerants continued to feel safe, though they marvelled at the sight of the German women who arrived with the troops as secretaries and office workers, dressed like American airline hostesses, with their 'lumpy athletic figures'. They had changed the 'w' in their name to a 'v', which they thought made it sound more French.

Like the rest of France, Sara and Aaron felt reassured by the declarations of France's new leader, the elderly veteran of the Great War, 84-year-old Maréchal Pétain, the aloof and immaculate embodiment of the legacy of the great French victory at Verdun. Pétain had a neat little moustache, a soft belly, and pale blue eyes, and he held himself, as befitting an *ancien combattant*, very upright. They shared his desire for a new moral order, a National Revolution, in which fecund and stable families would redeem the Blum years of profligacy and too much liberty. It sounded comforting when he spoke of his 'beloved France' and his decision to bestow on its people 'the gift of my own person'; like naughty children, they would have to redeem themselves through pain and collective mortification. 'You have suffered . . .' he told them, 'you will suffer more . . . your life will be very hard.' The Liwerants liked the idea of a country in which people returned to the land they had abandoned in favour of city life and had more children, even if it seemed peculiar that the ills that had apparently caused the ignominious French defeat included paid holidays, Pernod, the white slave trade, strikes, gambling, bathing suits, democracy and the 'degrading promiscuity in work-shops, offices, factories . . .'

In the mea culpa that swept France in May and June of 1940, with its wild talk of 'libertine, enfeebling self-indulgence', it seemed to Sara and Aaron puzzling that no one seemed to question why, since the country was being punished by a vengeful God, He was at the same time choosing to reward Hitler and his Nazi ambitions. Collaboration had not yet acquired its overtones of treason, but was rather seen as a spur to changing the way the French were to be schooled, employed and governed, with discipline and a strengthening of national fibre. Tough new measures were to rescue the country from a 'republic of women and homosexuals'. On the wall of Simon's classroom hung a picture of the Maréchal, shouldering the burden of government when he should have been enjoying a well-earned retirement; his portrait was to be found on posters, postcards and coins. On stamps it had replaced that of the traditional Marianne. Not since the Second Empire had France had the effigy of a living ruler on its coins. In the cult of Pétain, to disobey was to betray. Jeanne d'Arc was also in evidence, another fine symbol of patriotism, piety and sacrifice. The ravings of men like Maurras and Céline, the Liwerants told themselves, hardly applied to them.

On 22 June, Pétain signed an armistice in a railway siding in the forest of Compiègne, cutting France into an occupied zone, governed by Germany, and an unoccupied zone, run by the French from the spa town of Vichy, and agreeing to terms not unlike those forced on the Germans at the Treaty of Versailles. It was Hitler's first visit to Paris, and he slapped his knee in delight at the country of which he was now master. Then, barely eight weeks later, the first signs of something new and ominous appeared: on 27 August, Pétain removed the penalties for anti-Semitic defamation. At this point, the Germans were not yet planning to make France in their own image of *Judenfrei*, free of Jews, but rather to turn the unoccupied part of France – the one third of the country that was to be ruled by the Vichy government, separated by a heavily guarded 1,200-kilometre demarcation line – into a reception centre for their unwanted Jews.

Forbidding those Jews who had fled south from returning to their homes in the north, the Germans started taking over the Jewish businesses abandoned during the exodus and ordering banks to open Jewish deposit boxes, from which they confiscated gold, foreign currencies and jewellery. Soon, 4,660 firms in Paris carried the yellow sticker of confiscation. On 3 October, after a census of the Jews in the capital and its suburbs, which put the number at 113,462, of whom 57,110 were French citizens and 55,849 foreigners, came the first Statut des Juifs from the Vichy government which would rapidly turn into a wholesale process of marginalisation and destitution. It was perfectly clear, announced Vichy, that the Jews had 'exercised an individualistic tendency which has resulted almost in anarchy'. They had to be curbed, punished. It was the speed with which all this happened that was so terrifying; and the spirit in which it was done, combining both a thirst for revenge and a sense of eager repentance. The Vatican, consulted, was acquiescent. For the Germans, it could not have gone better: they had found a country not merely resigned to defeat, but ready to blame itself for what had happened, and eager to accommodate and anticipate lest worse befall.

Jews, declared the Vichy government – in this as in much else going ahead of and beyond the German demands – would henceforth be banned from certain jobs and put on to quotas for others. A Jew, they decreed, was a Jew if he had three Jewish grandparents, or two if his wife was also Jewish. Civil servants, among them judges, clerks and teachers, began losing their jobs, along with lawyers, photographers, antiquarians, scientists, costume- and filmmakers, nurses and bookkeepers. Permission was given to regional prefects to intern 'foreigners of the Jewish race'.

To help the French better comprehend the virulent nature of the Jewish plague, a venomous anti-Semitic film, *Jew Süss*, was made, attracting many thousands of viewers, as did a supposed documentary about the Rothschild family, in which, at regular intervals, rats filled the screen, then seemed to overflow into the cinema. The Jew, as portrayed in the pages of the German scandal sheet *Der Stürmer*, introduced into France, was a small, fat, ugly, unshaven, drooling, bent-nosed man with pig-like eyes. In his school playground, Simon, one of a small group of Jewish children, was now fighting daily battles against bullying fellow pupils. Though he was small, and so short-sighted that he felt himself to be as blind as a mole, he was robust and did not lose many of his fights.

Not all the repressive measures were aimed at the Jews. One of the first edicts, on 13 August, had targeted Freemasons, and they too were now banned from much of French professional life. Sixty thousand Masons were investigated, and 15,000 Masonic dignitaries were sacked. After Ribbentrop and Molotov signed their Soviet–Nazi non-aggression pact in August 1939, many members of France's Communist party and former partners in the Front Populaire had been sent off to internment camps by Daladier's government. After the German invasion they had not been released but were kept there as troublemakers. Jews, Freemasons and godless communists, followers of Marx or Trotsky or Rosa Luxemburg and seen as part of a Judeo-Bolshevik conspiracy, dark forces of the 'anti-France', were all soon to be engulfed in a turbulence of fear and persecution. It was enough, now, to be foreign, to have a foreign accent, to be a suspect. The French, wrote the novelist Henri de Montherlant, were displaying their true colours: a mixture of inertia and moral cowardice.

And then, at the end of March 1941, the Vichy government, at the instigation of the Germans, who had decided that there was still no proper comprehension in France of the 'necessity for a full-scale purification of Jews', agreed to 'address the Jewish problem'. Pétain appointed a bullet-headed wounded veteran of the Great War called Xavier Vallat, a friend of Maurras, as director of the Commissariat Général aux Questions Juives – the CGQJ – with its headquarters in the seedy Hôtel Algeria in Vichy. Vallat had receding hair and heavy black eyebrows, and he wore a black eyepatch. He was a lawyer, a devout Catholic and an unashamed anti-Semite; he spoke of his anti-Semitism as '*de l'Etat Français*', state anti-Semitism inspired by Catholic doctrine. 'I have been anti-Semitic far longer than you,' he told Theo Dannecker after the 27-year-old German officer arrived in Paris to represent Eichmann, head of Jewish affairs for the Gestapo. Dannecker, it would be said, was not only vicious but insane. Jews, declared Vallat, were 'invariably dangerous' except in very small doses; and they were culturally unassimilable.

What had to be done was to confiscate – steal – their property and eliminate them from the economic, social and cultural life of France, while craftily funnelling their wealth into French rather than German hands. Vallat regarded himself, he declared, not as 'a butcher and certainly not as a torturer' but as a surgeon, brought in to cure a country 'stricken by Jewish brain fever', from which it had almost died. The anti-Semitic regime he envisaged would soon be the harshest in Europe, policed by a special force, the Police aux Questions Juives. Both Vichy and the Germans believed France's Jews to be fabulously rich.

Since his return to Paris, Aaron had continued to work with his old firm, bringing clasps and handles back to Sara in the evenings. Coming home one day in mid-May 1941, he heard that orders had gone out to 'invite' Jews to register with their local police stations. He thought it applied to everyone, French and foreigners alike, and went cheerfully, despite Sara's misgivings, taking his bicycle and saying that he would go straight from there to work. That evening, there was no sign of him. Instead, a policeman banged on the door and told Sara to pack a case for her husband and take it to the barracks at the Porte de Lilas. Thirteen-year-old Simon went in her place and learnt that his father was being sent, along with some 4,000 others, to an internment camp not far from Orléans, built to accommodate all the German prisoners the French army had confidently expected to capture. A few weeks later, Sara was allowed to take the three children to spend a Sunday with him.

It was not long before Aaron escaped. He arrived home late one night and was hidden by a French friend. He and Sara agreed that he would find a *passeur*, someone who, in return for money, would help him cross the demarcation line into the unoccupied zone, where, for the time being, Jews appeared to be relatively safe; from there he planned to make his way to Lyons, where the family had relatives. Once again, it was Sara who forced him to go, saying that men were far more at risk than women and children. In Belleville there was a lorry driver who used his truck to transport meat between the two zones. He was willing to hide Aaron in one of the two narrow boxes that ran along the chassis and in which blood from the carcasses normally collected. The crossing of the well-guarded border passed uneventfully, but once across, while looking for a bus to take him to Lyons, Aaron was stopped by the police. His only papers carried the clear stamp of '*Juif*'. This time, he was sent to one of the new work camps for Jews and internees in the south and trained as a woodcutter. Very occasionally he was granted leave to visit Sara and the children in Paris, where, all through 1941, further *rafles*, round-ups, were herding Jews into captivity.

For the first time, a small number of French Jews were also being picked up. Until this moment, many had continued to convince themselves that they were different in the eyes of the Germans from the foreign Jews, and that, providing they made no trouble, nothing bad would happen to them. As respected generations of French academicians, members of the bar, bankers and scientists, with impeccable French accents, how could any of this apply to them? As the writer and journalist Philippe Erlanger later described it, what was taking place was like an accident, a sort of calamity that happened to other people but not to you. On 12 December, 743 *notables*, distinguished French Jews, many of them doctors and lawyers, including Léon Blum's brother René, were arrested. And after an assassination attempt on a German officer, 100 hostages were shot, 1,000 Jews rounded up and the Jewish community in the occupied zone was fined a billion francs in reprisal. It was becoming horribly clear that the supposedly secular state, of which they felt themselves to be so viscerally a part, was no longer going to protect anyone.

Xavier Vallat, deemed too soft and lenient, was soon replaced by Darquier de Pellepoix, a man who had repeatedly spoken of the need to amputate the limb of Jewish plutocracy: no Jew, he said, should be shaken by the hand. Darquier was less tricky and more biddable than Vallat, a lazy, brutal, rapacious bon viveur who intended to carry out his task of executing the Nazis' anti-Semitic policies of 'economic Aryanisation' with verve and dedication, while personally profiting from them as much as possible. He forbade Jews the use of their first names – so that Aaron became 'le Juif Liwerant' – and set about doubling the staff of the CGQJ to 1,000 men and women. These were now put to plundering, spying and offering bribes to informers. As Darquier saw it, Jews were historical enemies whose racial characteristics were putting France in danger.

It was the yellow star that changed everything for Simon. Jews in Poland had been forced to wear identifying stars since 1939, and at the end of May 1942 came orders for this to be extended to all Jews in the occupied zone of France. The star, the size of a man's fist, was to be worn by every Jew over the age of six, placed somewhere visible on the left side on outer garments, paid for with one coupon of rationed clothing each. People of doubtful parentage were forced to sign certificates of 'not belonging to the Jewish race'.

Simon found the yellow star deeply upsetting, particularly after people started shouting *'sale Juif'* at him as he walked to school, so that he took to wearing it only when he could not avoid it, though he knew how dangerous this could be. He was top of his class, after a poor start before his teachers realised that he was profoundly short-sighted. Sara was just managing to bring in enough money to buy food, as the kindly workshop owner was continuing, despite the prohibitions on Jewish workers, to bring her clasps to cover. Restrictions were closing them all in. As a Jew, she could shop only between three and four in the afternoon, when the shops had emptied of most of their provisions, and on the Métro she could travel only in the last carriage. Music halls, theatres, cinemas, camping sites, public telephones were all out of bounds.

All over Paris, Jews were hungry and cold, living on their savings or the kindness of their French neighbours, themselves short of food, coal and clothing now that the Germans had turned much of French industry over to production for the Reich and trains full of loot of every kind were leaving most days from the Gare de l'Est for Berlin. At night, in the blacked-out capital, you could see the lights of bicycles shining like fireflies. Soon the French were down to a little more than a third of their pre-war coal. The winter of 1939 had been the coldest since Waterloo; those of 1940 and 1941 were little better. Even in Vichy there was very little fuel and Pétain's 30,000 civil servants lived in a permanent haze of woodsmoke from their makeshift stoves with pipes running out of the window. Coffee, of a kind, was being made from chestnuts, chickpeas, dried apples and lupin seeds; sugar from liquorice, boiled pumpkin and grape juice. In his father's absence, 13-year-old Simon felt responsible for the family, all the more so as Sara spoke French with a strong foreign accent. Her health had always been bad, and the birth of Jacques had further weakened her kidneys.

In November 1941, perceiving that it would be helpful if Jews could assist in their own destruction, Vichy had ordered the setting up of the Union Générale des Israélites de France – the UGIF – to coordinate all existing welfare organisations. These were now dissolved as separate entities. Some, sensing that this was merely a trap whereby Jews could be better identified and their addresses centrally registered, chose not to join and went underground; others accepted, believing that there was no other way to help the growing numbers of destitute people. Between them all they had some 40,000 people on their books. All Jews were now obliged to pay a tithe to the UGIF. Since the start of the hostilities, Jewish leaders had been protesting vigorously – and in vain – against the repressive measures. Long after evidence of Nazi planning and Vichy compliance seemed plain to everyone, many of these leaders continued to express their 'lucid desire to remain both an excellent Jew and an excellent Frenchman', but their intense wish to remain loyal to Pétain seemed to lock them into a vicious circle of docility and prudence. Others tried to flee. By now, some 35,000 Jews had applied to leave France, mainly for the United States, Latin America and China, but most were thwarted by the expense and the bureaucratic obstacles to obtaining visas.

Even as Darquier was taking over at the Commissariat in Vichy, in Berlin meticulous plans were advancing for the deportation of France's Jewish population. By now, Drancy, a disused housing estate on the outskirts of Paris, had become a way station for convoys of goods wagons bearing Jews to camps in the east, though these first departures were still shrouded in secrecy. In

April 1942, 57-year-old Pierre Laval, who had never made a secret of his desire for closer collaboration with Germany, had returned to power with the portfolios of the Interior, Foreign Affairs and Information, as well as the vice presidency of the Council, which effectively made him head of state. His reappearance signalled an end to most illusions about Vichy's intentions. Swarthy, stocky and shrewd, Laval was often to be seen wearing a tailcoat; he came from the Auvergne and his father was a butcher. Pétain, it was fast becoming clear, would no longer stand as a symbol of independence or protection against German demands.

Jews arriving at Drancy, c. 1942

A new German police chief, SS General Karl Oberg, had been appointed to France, and under him a clever young Nazi called Helmut Knochen. The two men were as one on the subject of the '*race maudite*', the cursed race of Jews. Knochen and Eichmann's representative Dannecker both had their offices in the Avenue Foch, the magnificent boulevard that runs from the Bois de Boulogne to the Arc de Triomphe. The French police were under ever stricter vasselage to their German counterparts, but René Bousquet, the hard-working, manipulative Gascon head of police in Vichy, remained for the moment unwilling to turn over French Jews. Instead he proposed including for deportation the foreign Jews from the occupied zone as well as the unoccupied zone, offering up all those Germans, Austrians, Poles, Letts, Czechs, Russians and Estonians who had entered France after 1 January 1936. At this point, Vichy did not seem to be intending to murder its 'undesirables', but it did want to get rid of them, though how much it knew about the Wannsee conference of January 1942 and the plans for a Final Solution for Europe's Jews is not clear. Oberg and Knochen observed with approval the way that Vichy was doing their work for them.

On 11 June 1942, a decision was taken in Berlin to deport 100,000 Jews from France, women as well as men, aged between 16 and 40, with exceptions for war veterans, unaccompanied minors under 18 and pregnant women. The costs of deportation – transport, blankets, clothes, food – were to be borne by the French. Bousquet and Oberg were juggling problems of their own: the Germans needed French help in carrying out the arrests, having only three battalions of police in France, while the French wanted an agreement to save French Jews. So a deal was made: some 3,000 French policemen would arrest 22,000 foreign Jews in Paris, and Bousquet would arrange for the delivery of similarly stateless and foreign Jews from the unoccupied zone. For the moment, overall numbers had been reduced, as there was not enough transport for them all.

On 30 June, six months after the Wannsee conference at which the fate of Europe's Jews was decided, Eichmann arrived in Paris to oversee the deportations. On 4 July, fearing a shortfall in numbers, Laval offered further concessions. He would also hand over to the Germans some of the stateless Jewish children, those who had come to France with their parents in the 1920s and 1930s. Women and children up to this point had not been regarded as fair game. Initial calculations that France contained some 865,000 Jews, a number inflated by the wild outpourings of journalists like Maurras and Céline, were now suspected to be grossly exaggerated. New calculations put the figure at more like 340,000. In theory, as naturalised French, Simon and Berthe were safe for the moment; but not Sara.

On 12 July, at one o'clock in the morning, the Liwerants' bell rang. Sara woke Simon and asked him to see who it was. Outside stood a police inspector in civilian clothing. 'You mustn't stay here any longer,' he told the boy quietly. 'Say to your mother that there is going to be chaos.' Next morning, Sara asked the concierge for permission to move from their first-floor apartment into an attic room on the sixth floor. Jacques was now two, and one of Simon's tasks was to collect the ration of milk for the baby every morning before going to school. As he reached the ground floor on the morning of 16 July, he was stopped by an inspector in plain clothes, accompanied by three uniformed policemen. '*Tiens, c'est un Juif*,' said the inspector, asking Simon where he was going.

Ordered to lead the policemen to his family, Simon unlocked the door to their flat on the first floor and pretended not to understand their questions about why it was empty. But then one of the men spotted that he had other keys in his hand. Marching him up before them, they climbed the building, floor by floor, trying each door until they reached the attic. There they found Sara and Jacques, but not Berthe, who had gone to stay with a friend. They were cowering under blankets. In spite of her poor French, Sara had the presence of mind to point out that the name on the list the police were carrying was not theirs – it had a 'w' rather than a 'v' – and that it must refer to another family. After much deliberation, the police agreed to check again at headquarters. When the three men in uniform were out of earshot, the inspector turned back. 'Let me give you some advice. Don't stay here. You won't get away with this twice.'

At four o'clock on the morning of 16 July 1942, just as it was getting light, the Vichy government launched *Opération Vent Printanier* – Spring Wind. Nine thousand French policemen, including cadets from the police academy and some 400 ultra-right volunteers, fanned out across the 3rd, 4th, 10th, 11th, 12th, 18th and 20th arrondissements in search of the 28,000 Jews they believed to be hiding there. There were no Germans among them, for Oberg and Dannecker had efficiently negotiated with Bousquet the use of France's large contingent of gendarmes, *gardes mobiles* and municipal police, men regarded as powerful, if incompetent, corrupt and partisan. The manhunt lasted until one o'clock on the afternoon of the 17th, but netted only a disappointing 12,884 people. They were taken to the Vélodrome d'Hiver, the winter cycling stadium on the Boulevard de Grenelle in the 15th arrondissement. Those unable to walk were carried on stretchers.

Twenty-four people, resisting arrest, were shot. Though the UGIF had hesitated to broadcast rumours of the impending raids, for fear of sowing panic, many ordinary French citizens and a few sympathetic and appalled French policemen, like the inspector who had warned Sara and the children, had combined to alert, then hide, the Jews.

As the days passed, conditions in the Vélodrome d'Hiver, where the blackout glass cast an eerie light, deteriorated to a nightmare of heat, smells and panic. It was extremely hot. On the fifth day, the men were transferred to Drancy, and, soon after, the women and children to the internment camps of Pithiviers and Beaune-la-Rolande. Trains carrying the first deportees to the east, to occupied Poland, started to roll before the end of the month.

There were terrible scenes when fathers who had miraculously obtained exemption as veterans went home to find that their children, who had been overlooked in the initial manhunt, had since been picked up and disappeared. On 20 July, Jewish mothers in Beaune-la-Rolande were loaded on to lorries to take them to Drancy. Fighting and screaming, they were bludgeoned into leaving their children behind; when these were sent on later to Drancy, their state was pitiful, and the smaller had long since lost the name tags that were to have identified them and restored them to their parents. The older children, those over 12, were initially kept back, but were then put into the cattle trucks in convoys that left between 31 July and 7 August; the younger followed on trains between the 17th and the 28th. Not one would return. No longer would it be possible for anyone to believe that those arrested were all workers destined for factories and industry in occupied Europe.

In their flat in Belleville, despite the odds, Sara and the children managed to avoid capture. Still believing that naturalisation would protect Berthe and Simon, Sara found a *passeur* to take herself and the baby across the demarcation line from occupied into unoccupied France, saying that she would send for the children when she reached Lyons. At Châlons, her *passeur* – one of a small but shameful breed of collaborating *passeurs* – handed her over to the Gestapo. Though she had time to destroy her papers, with the identifying word 'Juive' stamped on them, she fell and hurt herself. Her health had not been good since Jacques' birth. When she came to, she found herself in a hospital guarded by German soldiers; her bad French and foreign accent had told them enough about her origins. A friendly Red Cross nurse offered to take Jacques to her relations in Lyons.

In Belleville, Berthe and Simon, fearing every strange sound, every knock on the door, every distant noise of footsteps, seldom dared leave the flat. One day, a letter arrived; it was in Yiddish, which they could speak but not read, and they took it to their aunt to translate. In it, Sara explained what had happened, and said that they should lock up the flat, leave everything and join her in Chalôns. Simon thought it prudent to do only part of the journey by train, as the Germans were particularly vigilant at railway stations, and so at Beaune they changed to a bus. Somewhere along the route, SS officers got on board. Suspicious about the children's papers, they took them to the local *Kommandantur*, and put them into separate rooms, each guarded by a large Alsatian dog. They were told that if they moved, the dogs would bite them. Fifteen-year-old Berthe wet herself. At six that evening, a brusque Gestapo officer ordered them, on pain of arrest, to return immediately to Paris.

It was getting dark as the two children wandered the deserted streets of Châlons. A concierge in one of the town's smarter hotels finally took pity on them, but said that they would have to leave by dawn, when the German officer whose room he gave them returned from night duty. Soon after four, they were hustled out of the hotel. Crouching in the gateway of a private house, they spent the hours waiting for it to grow light and for the hospital to open. In their mother's ward were a dozen Jewish women who had been handed over to the Germans by the venal *passeurs*. Sara, whose fall seemed to have reduced her to a frail invalid, told the children that she had arranged with one of the nurses, a member of the Resistance, to get them across the demarcation line, here running parallel and through the river Saône, and into the unoccupied zone. They lived like hunted animals. Every evening, around six, they went to wait in a café for the sign that a boat had been found to take them across the water. Not many days later, a man wearing a helmet gave the signal for them to follow him. On the riverbank were a number of the Jewish women from their mother's ward. Sara was not among them.

Berthe and Simon crossed in a small boat, in a group of six; they slept the rest of that night in a farmhouse. Next day, Simon persuaded a reluctant Jewish refugee to let them share his taxi to Lyons, where they found Jacques and their cousins. There was no news of Sara.

Lyons, in the summer of 1942, was fast becoming unsafe for Jews, even those like the Liwerant children who had French citizenship. Berthe, who had already been learning her father's trade in Paris, was apprenticed to a sympathetic leatherworker. Simon was put in touch with the Organisation de Secours aux Enfants, the OSE. Their general secretary, Madeleine Dreyfus, a young woman from Alsace whose Jewish parents had come to France in the 1920s, with three children of her own, came to collect him. He was going, she told him, to a village in the mountains, where he would be safe; and he would take two-year-old Jacques with him.

There was another young boy, Jacques Stulmacher, whose story was leading in much the same direction. He was not quite nine when war was declared, living with his Russian father, Polish mother and younger brother Marcel in two small rooms in the 11th arrondissement in Paris. Their flat backed on to the Passage Alexandrine, and since most of the local inhabitants were Jews from Eastern Europe, they spoke in Yiddish to each other from their open windows across the narrow alleyway. Until he was three, and went to nursery school, Jacques did not know that any other language existed.

Jacques' father was an engineer by training. He had helped his own father run a factory making leather gloves until the Red Army had ordered them to produce boots instead and he was sacked for protesting that the leather was unsuitable. Jacques' grandfather claimed that he was too old to flee, but his father made his way through Turkey to Paris with his wife and young children and went to work for Citroën. He was active in the new trade union movement, and when hard economic times arrived he was one of the first to be laid off as a troublemaker. Jacques and Marcel were often hungry.

When the Germans broke round the Maginot line in the spring of 1940, the Stulmachers joined the frenzied exodus south, travelling in Jacques' uncle's ancient open touring car, seven of them crammed inside, his father riding on the running board. One night, as they sheltered in a hospice, German bombers strafed the building, apparently believing that government ministers who had passed this way not long before were still inside. Next morning, the bodies of those killed were laid out in neat rows in the court-yard. Jacques had never seen dead people before. The Stulmachers were unharmed.

They travelled on south, hoping to reach Bordeaux; whenever they heard the sound of bombers, they abandoned the car and hid in ditches or the forest. It was not fear of the bombs that worried her, said Jacques' mother, because bombs hit everyone impartially; it was anti-Semitism, which seemed to be aimed just at them. At Arès, they ran out of petrol. It was here that Jacques tasted his first oyster, though he was embarrassed when the waiter referred to them 'les huîtres' and his father thought they were called 'dix-huit', eighteen. Even though his father's French was distinctly better than his mother's, both his parents had strong accents.

The family soon returned to Paris, part of the vast wave of people going back to their homes in the north after the armistice was signed and fighting ceased. It was only now that Jacques discovered what it meant to be a Jew. For every misdemeanour, however small, the teacher who supervised the breaks at school punished the culprits by sending them to stand facing the wall, with their hands on their heads. But he seemed blind to the fact that the small group of Jewish children was continually attacked by older, stronger boys. Day after day, as break approached, Jacques thought of himself as a gladiator, facing the lions in ancient Rome. He also learnt his first lesson in decency. The day after the yellow star became mandatory, M Leflond, the head-master, assembled the entire school in the playground. 'I want you all to be particularly kind to the children wearing yellow stars. Neither for me, nor for any of the other teachers, is there any difference between any of you.' The supervisor from the playground mysteriously recovered his sight and there were no more attacks by bullies.

On his way home from school with his brother Marcel, Jacques would look at the shop windows that bore the sign 'No Jews and no dogs'. Sometimes passers-by shouted out 'Youpin' – Yid – at the two boys. There were not many places they could go now.

When, one day, a group of defiant young Jewish boys and girls, wearing their stars and singing, paraded down the Champs-Elysées, that too became closed to Jews. Every morning, the school sang 'Maréchal, nous voilà!', the new hymn to Pétain's glory. In the Passage Alexandrine, Jacques and his friends never played games: they talked. He no longer felt like a child, and childish games had lost their allure. He was 10.

It never occurred to his parents not to register themselves when ordered to do so; they came back from the police station with the words 'Juif' and 'Juive' printed in bold red letters on their identity cards. Even so, when Jacques' aunt came one day to warn them of rumours of a round-up of Jews, on 15 July 1942, and their neighbours exchanged frightened words from their windows in the Passage Alexandrine, the Stulmachers decided to go into hiding. A generous Portuguese couple in Saint-Ouen with a 13-year-old daughter were prepared to conceal all nine of them, both Jacques' family and his aunt's, in a wooden hut in the garden. Whenever neighbours came by, they had to remain absolutely silent, which was hard for Marcel, who had just turned six, and for their much younger cousin.

The news from Paris was grim. Jacques' best friend's father, picked up and taken to Drancy in an earlier round-up, was said to have been killed after he stole a carrot from the kitchens. His widow, ferocious in her attempts to save her three children, had struggled and fought when the French police arrived on the morning of 16 July. She had been unable to save any of them from being captured. Opération Vent Printanier had taken all the boys from the Passage Alexandrine.

For the time being, the Stulmachers were safe. But when life in the one room became intolerable, Jacques, Marcel and the small cousin were sent first to a family in Saint-Etienne de Rouvray for six months, then to an elderly couple in l'Aisne, who had a pig they called Adolphe. At the village school, Jacques would have skipped the weekly church service, except that on the first day, observing him leaving the line, an older and wiser child hauled him back. From then on, he never missed church; it didn't pay to stand out, even if only the elderly couple knew for certain that he was a Jew. He and Marcel had kept the name Stulmacher, saying that their family came from Alsace.

Seven months later, their father managed to make his way to Lyons, where he found work as a cobbler. Jacques' mother, still in hiding with the Portuguese family in Saint-Ouen, came to collect the children. They crossed the demarcation line by train at Vierzon, their *passeur* pretending to be the children's mother, while she sat somewhere else. There was an agonising moment in the middle of the night when two SS officers boarded the train and announced that there would be a check of documents, but something happened to move the train on and the danger passed.

No one thought it safe for the children to stay in Lyons. It was the OSE that, as with the Liwerant boys, stepped in to propose a hiding place in the mountains. The man who came to collect them, André Chouraqui, was adamant about one thing: there was to be no contact of any kind between parents and children, no letters and no visits. It all felt very bleak.

CHAPTER TWO

The camps of shame

On a plateau in south-west France covered in ferns and spiny acacia lies the hamlet of Gurs. In summer it is a pleasant spot, with a view across to the Pyrenees, their peaks covered in snow for much of the year. But in autumn, the rains turn the ground to mud, while winter brings bitter winds and biting cold to the exposed pastures. In early April and May 1939, 25,000 Spanish republicans arrived here, fleeing from Franco's army. They were housed in rectangular wooden barracks, 24 metres by 6, hastily erected in neat military rows on either side of a straight track. Not anticipating that the refugees would stay beyond the summer, the French authorities took no pains to make the huts warm or windproof. They used planks of raw uncured timber, which quickly shrank, leaving gaps, and put in no proper windows, only wooden shutters that could be raised a little way. The roofs were covered in bitumen.

By the late summer of 1940, the Spaniards were indeed long gone, either repatriated home, or sent to serve in work brigades or on the Maginot line. Some of the huts had been filled with communists, 'enemy aliens', those made stateless after Germany occupied their homelands, and 'foreigners of Jewish race', Vichy making use of laws put in place during the phoney war. But the camp at Gurs had room for many more when, at dawn on 22 October 1940, the gauleiters Joseph Bürckel and Robert Wanger began to round up 6,508 Jews in the territories of Baden and the Palatinate and, without consulting the French, dispatched them in sealed trains over the border into south-western France.

One of them was 15-year-old Hanne Hirsch, a tall, pretty girl with short fair hair parted at the side. Her father Max had been a portrait photographer and, after his sudden death in 1925, his wife Ella, who had been a concert pianist, had continued to run the studio in Karlsruhe in Baden. The business prospered, and once the Nazis came to power, Ella was kept busy producing photographs for the new ID cards, on which Jewish men and women still had the right to their own first names, but all took the second name Sara or Israel, indiscriminately. Karlsruhe had a close Jewish community of 3,000, though through the 1930s those who could leave did so; one of these was Hanne's elder brother, who was able to make his way to the United States.

On Kristallnacht, the night of 9 November 1938, when paramilitary soldiers from the SA attacked Jewish businesses, synagogues and buildings, the studio was ransacked and the glass cabinets smashed to splinters. The Jewish men arrested in Karlsruhe that night were sent to Dachau and Sachsenhausen, and when they came back later, they brought with them stories of brutality. Some were returned in coffins, and those of their families brave enough to do so opened the lids and saw signs of torture. From the balcony of her flat above the studio, Hanne and her friends watched the German soldiers marching in the streets below singing, 'When Jewish blood spurts from the knife, then things will go twice as well.' Ella was profoundly relieved that her son was safe in America.

While she was out shopping, very early on 2 October 1940, Ella was stopped by a policeman she knew from her precinct. Evidently somewhat embarrassed, he told her that the Jews were going to be deported, and that they had just one hour to pack a suitcase weighing no more than 30 kilos. Everything else was to be left behind. Ella sent Hanne to a Gentile friend with their remaining set of Bohemian glass for safe keeping. Most of the rest of their silver, porcelain and jewellery had long since been plundered by the Nazis. While she packed for herself and Hanne, taking warm clothes and a knife, fork, spoon, blanket and a little food for each of them, as instructed, Hanne packed for her 91-year-old grandmother Babette.

In the open lorries carrying them to the station were Ella's three sisters; Berta, the eldest, was diabetic, but robust. There had been rumours that they would be sent to Dachau, so there was much relief when the train crossed the frontier into France. They were cold, and had run out of food, because they had been forced to leave the luggage on the platform, to follow on a later train.

That day, seven trains set off for France; on Hanne's were Karlsruhe's remaining 950 Jews. The seats were wooden and there was no water. Many of those expelled were elderly; the oldest was 104. There were new babies and the inmates of a mental hospital, dragged from their wards. Since this sudden expulsion was in breach of the armistice terms between France and Germany, the trains continued to be shunted around the countryside while the government in Vichy protested. There had been plans to send the Jews from Baden and the Palatinate to Madagascar and turn the island into a vast ghetto, but they had come to nothing. Hanne's grandmother, who had been in excellent health, became confused, and a doctor on the train gave her a sleeping pill to calm her down. As the train passed Oloron-Sainte-Marie, the stationmaster reported hearing cries and moans. When the carriage doors were finally unlocked, 60 hours after leaving Karlsruhe, several people were found to have died. Babette appeared to have totally lost her mind.

They had left Germany in fine weather. In France it was raining hard, and by the time that Hanne, her mother and her aunts had trudged the 15 kilometres from the station to the camp at Gurs, they were soaked through and very cold. The huts they were put into had no beds or bunks, no mattresses or blankets. They felt relieved when Babette was taken away to a separate hut, for the very old and the sick, where she was put into a makeshift bed.

Internees at Gurs, 1941

37

The next day brought little comfort. The huts were grouped into '*îlots*', little islands of 25 barracks each, women and children separated from the men and boys over 14. They were surrounded by barbed wire. Hanne and Ella and her sisters were in *îlot* K, hut 13. Watchtowers and more barbed wire encircled the camp. The straight track that ran from one end of it to the other was almost two kilometres long. Bales of straw were handed out to act as mattresses, but there was too little of it to go around. Hanne and her family made a little encampment in one corner. Paper was stuffed into the cracks between the planks to reduce the draught, but even so the winds from the Pyrenees felt like ice to people so thinly dressed and so hungry. Each hut had a stove, but there was no wood, and it was almost entirely dark inside, the only light coming from two weak electric bulbs in the ceiling, and the doors at either end, kept shut against the cold. Their suitcases had finally been delivered, but everything inside was soaked through, having stood for several days in the rain.

The sandy clay soil of Gurs was impermeable, and there was no slope down which the rain could run away. The deep gluey mud, so thick that it was impossible to leave the hut without boots, never dried. There were just five taps for every *îlot*, and the water was only put on for a few hours each day. For the sick, the elderly and small children, the walk to the latrines, through ankle-deep mud, was an ordeal that led to frequent falls. The elderly broke bones.

What Hanne would remember all her life was the feeling of constant, insatiable hunger. There was very little to eat beyond ersatz coffee, coarse bread and watery soup made of root vegetables. The internees collected it in metal bowls, like prisoners, standing in a queue. Soon after the arrival of the Jews from Baden and the Palatinate, rations in Gurs were reduced. The internees were now losing weight steadily and beginning to show the first signs of malnutrition: loose skin, weakened muscles, trembling. The cold brought rheumatism. Fleas made people itch and scratch, their bodies covered with sores, eczema and impetigo. People lost their teeth. There were signs of rickets. A former prisoner in Dachau observed that the food there had been more plentiful. There were now some 50 to 60 deaths every week.

Writing to her brother-in-law in the US, Ella described Babette's 'terrible suffering', the ferocious cold, the incessant hunger. Begging him to send warm sweaters and stockings, as well as overalls for herself and Hanne, she wrote: 'I rely on your help and think that you will not desert us in our unspeakable misfortune . . . We need help immediately before we perish. Paper, toothpaste, skin cream, everything is welcome, even polish. Never in my life could I have imagined being in such a situation, as poor as beggars.' She asked him to pass the letter on to her brother, because she did not have enough money for two stamps.

Gurs was not the first of France's internment camps, of which more than 20 were dotted around the country, most of them in the unoccupied south, in disused army barracks, abandoned factories and prison buildings. But it was one of the worst. As the months passed, more and more people kept coming, stateless Germans and Austrians, communists, Freemasons, Gypsies, Jews, all Vichy's 'undesirables', from 59 countries. According to the German Kundt Commission, which carried out a series of inspections, looking for German dissidents to deport to face imprisonment or execution, there were already some 32,000 detainees in custody. And they kept on coming, from new *rafles*, police raids, and the ever more stringent policies to exclude more recent immigrants from the protection of French citizenship. Many spoke no French. All were fearful, depressed; the older among them were often silent and apathetic, traumatised by what had happened to them. Some, like Ella, kept busy, cleaning the huts, collecting and dividing up the rations of bread, according to ferociously monitored fairness. One of Hanne's aunts had been a seamstress in Karlsruhe, and she made a dress for her out of a petticoat and an apron.

Berta was growing sicker, her untreated diabetes beginning to affect her eyes; when there was light, Ella read aloud to her. Occasionally the women were allowed to visit their mother, still living in the hut for the very elderly. Hanne was with her one day when the old lady, in a rare moment of lucidity, asked where she was. Told that she was in a camp, she asked why. 'Because,' said Hanne, 'we are Jews.' What shocked her most was the way that every morning a man would push open the door to the hut and shout out: 'Have you got anything?' He was part of the burial detail, come to collect those who had died in the night, often of cold, having frozen to death in their sleep. She could not bear the heartlessness of it. All night she would listen to the groans and tears and the constant dripping of the rain on the bitumen roof.

When there was news of a fresh arrival of internees, people would hasten to the barbed wire to see if they included relations or friends. They stood in silence, staring. 'We had lost our pasts,' wrote one woman many years later. 'We no longer had a homeland. Over our future hung a black cloud.'

In November, Alex Cramer, a Swiss doctor with the rank of colonel with the International Committee of the Red Cross (ICRC) in Geneva, was finally allowed in to inspect three of the larger camps. One of these was Gurs. His report to Vichy was angry. There were no tables and no chairs, he wrote, the cold was ferocious and the elderly were dying. Rats were devouring the supplies and biting the small children, whose wounds grew infected. There were no special provisions for babies, though there were very few of these. The rudimentary hospital was lacking in medicines, disinfectants, equipment and linen. He had seen many people in rags, and children without shoes. The barbed-wire division between the *îlots* left no room for exercise, and the wire itself was being used, on the few sunny days, to dry the laundry. The situation in Gurs, he concluded, was 'very serious'; he recommended that it should be pulled down and the inmates either housed elsewhere or released. 'We are currently witnessing, impotent and appalled,' he wrote, 'the brutal expulsion of entire populations, who have been forced to abandon everything to invaders.'

The ICRC, allowed access by virtue of the Geneva Conventions, was in a weak position. War had been declared before it had been able to get through a new convention regarding the treatment of civilians in wartime, so that the delegates' jurisdiction covered only camps for prisoners of war. For civilians there was no protection. Cramer proposed asking the British to release the ships currently blocked in Dakar and Casablanca and allow them to be used to ferry the Jews to safety, but who would take them? How much notice Vichy accorded his report is unclear, even if, on one of his only visits to the camps, Pétain had conceded, with casual unfeeling, that the inmates were indeed 'emaciated, wan' and speculated as to how they might survive 'the winter and the hunger'.

There were people, however, who did pay heed to what Cramer had said.

It was by pretending to be the wife of a Protestant pastor that Madeleine Barot got into Gurs. Madeleine was the 31-year-old general secretary of Cimade, an association of mostly Protestant women drawing on a generation marked by the scouting and Christian youth movements of the 1930s and founded by Suzanne de Dietrich, herself a theologian and translator of Karl Barth. Cimade's first task had been to help refugees when Alsace-Lorraine fell to the Germans. Madeleine was a plump young woman with short brown hair; behind her seemingly easy-going manner lay tenacity and a fierce sense of justice. She had been working in Rome as an archivist at the French school, but with Italy's entry into the war in May 1940, she had returned to Paris and joined Cimade, soon taking over from its general secretary, Violette Mouchon, who moved up to become president. Madeleine's roots lay in Alsace and in her mother's strong feminism, and she felt considerable sympathy for the German Jews of the border provinces, expelled so ruthlessly from their homes. As a student in Paris, she had worked in the *bidonvilles*, the slums surrounding the capital, and had been much influenced by the theology of Karl Barth, the idea of total obedience to Jesus Christ, and the need to bear witness and speak out. In Gurs, she found her cause.

Having unexpectedly wormed her way past the guards and into the camp, Madeleine learnt that the officer in charge had just been informed that one of the new babies had died. He was a decent man and he lamented to Madeleine the lack of baby clothes and nurses. She offered to provide both. Installing herself in the nearby village of Navarreux, she recruited a nurse from Pau, Jeanne Merle d'Aubigné, who had been caring for her dying mother. Jeanne was a tall, strong woman who looked, said her friends, like a Valkyrie. A few days later, she reported to Madeleine that she needed help, desperately: there were more than 16,000 people in Gurs and many of them were ill. It was not enough, Madeleine realised, to visit the camps: you had to install yourself and live there. In ones and twos, Madeleine began to send in other young nurses and social workers. A small hut was taken over to act as headquarters. Though nothing was made official, the gates to Gurs had effectively been breached. Others stepped through.

One of the first of these was the OSE, the organisation to which Madeleine Dreyfus and André Chouraqui belonged and which was helping children like Simon Liwerant and Jacques Stulmacher get away from Paris. The OSE was an older organisation than Cimade. It had been founded in Russia on the eve of the Great War to help improve the health of destitute Jews, and later moved on to work in Romania, Poland and Latvia. In 1932, it had made Paris its headquarters; its president was Albert Schweitzer and one of its patrons Baron Robert de Rothschild. As German and Austrian families escaping the Nazis after Hitler's rise to power crossed into France, the OSE had set up children's homes. Never quite believing in the impregnability of the Maginot line, it had been one of the first organisations to go south, taking all the children to Montpellier and Lyons. And there it stayed, employing Jewish doctors as they lost their jobs under the Statut des Juifs and creating medical and social work programmes among the refugees.

Madeleine Dreyfus

It was in Lyons that Madeleine Dreyfus set up her office. She was a restless, conscientious woman and a natural organiser. Born Madeleine Kahn in 1909, she had worked as a bilingual secretary in an import-export business before discovering the surrealists and making friends with Cocteau and Breton. Through them she learnt of the work of Adler and began studying psychology. In 1933, she married Raymond Dreyfus, and after the birth of their two sons, Michel in 1934 and Jacques in 1937, the family moved to Lyons and Madeleine went to work as a psychologist with the OSE. Both Madeleines – Barot and Dreyfus – one Protestant, one Jewish, were now in Lyons, and both play a crucial part in this story.

Gurs having been breached by the welfare organisations, Madeleine Barot dispatched Ruth Lambert, a young French social worker, to join the team. Slowly, inching their way forward, the young women began to organise. Paradoxically, it was the very haphazard and unbureaucratic nature of the camps, the uncertainty about who was in charge, that made them susceptible to infiltration. The men sent in to run them in the early days were army officers, the guards often former policemen and soldiers disbanded after the fall of France; checked for alcoholism, criminal records and any hostility towards Vichy, they were left with surprising powers of initiative. Some were brutal; many were anti-Semitic.

The inmates in Gurs needed everything – food, medicines, blankets, hot water, books, religious services and distractions. Donald Lowrie, an American working for the YMCA, had become aware of conditions in the internment camps. He had been one of the founders of the Russian Student Christian Movement in France in the 1930s and spoke good French; he also had contacts in Vichy. As the US had not yet entered the war, Americans were still moving freely around the country, and Lowrie got permission to take books and musical instruments into Gurs. What seemed obvious to Madeleine Barot and Madeleine Dreyfus was the need for some sort of committee to coordinate relief for the camps. Lowrie put the idea to the Minister of the Interior in Vichy.

On 5 November 1940, 25 welfare organisations – Jewish, Protestant, Quaker and lay – met in Toulouse to decide on tactics. It was to be a 'complete and sympathetic collaboration of Christians and Jews'. From the first, however, not everyone present saw the situation the same way, some being more hesitant than others about what they considered should be the proper attitude towards the Vichy government. When Daniel Bénédite, from the American Welfare Committee, suggested stirring up a political scandal about conditions in the camps, there was an uneasy silence. Though cooperation with Vichy was still regarded by most organisations as the sole way forward, collaboration was beginning to ensnare people whose instincts might originally have caused them to act differently. A Service Social des Etrangers had been set up by Pétain, and its director, Gilbert Lesage, attended this first meeting; several of these present mistrusted him – unfairly, as it happened – suspecting him of having spies in the camps.

On one basic question they were all agreed: the need for immediate, concerted material aid, and a commitee to organise it. With France itself hungry and on ever-diminishing rations, and the Allied blockade preventing deliveries of anything that might be useful to the enemy war effort, the problem was where to find supplies. A recent medical report drawn up for the Committee had found that while the population of Marseilles was down to an average of 1,700 calories per day, the internees were getting just 832. The YMCA accepted the task of coordinating the work and Lowrie took on the role of president. The Hôtel Imperator in Nîmes – which gave its name to the new body – was chosen as the most convenient place for monthly meetings. The American Jewish Joint Distribution Committee, the JDC or Joint, consisting mainly of liberal Jews in the US, had been supporting French Jewish welfare organisations – the OSE among them – for some years. It now set about raising money and funnelling it towards the internment camps, some of it by borrowing francs from French Jews, against promissory notes to be redeemed after the war. Other money came in from Switzerland, smuggled over the border.

Because foreign organisations wishing to enter the camps were denied passes by Vichy – which had little desire to see its dirty linen paraded before the world – once news of Madeleine Barot's success reached Geneva, delegates from Swiss charitable groups became nominal workers for Cimade. In Geneva, a committee to coordinate funds and gather information was started at the World Council of Churches, under a German refugee called Dr Freudenberg. A 'Miss Lieven' turned up at the camp, bringing supplies in a Simca from the Quakers; she was in fact Princess Bernadotte of Sweden.

A 'commission for children and old people' was set up and arranged for deliveries of fruit, olives, jam, cereals, rice, milk products and, just occasionally, chocolate. A rota was established, providing extra meals to the most malnourished for a fixed number of weeks. Since the spot allocated for these meals lay at some distance from the children's huts, small figures could be seen wading through the mud, clutching their blankets around their shoulders, carrying the tins that served them as plates. Secours Suisse started a vegetable garden, but rats got into it before anything could grow. Groups of people from the surrounding countryside came together to 'adopt' those most in need, to whom they sent food and clothes. The Quakers got hold of some wool and gave it to the female prisoners to knit. The OSE managed to install some showers. A drainage system was dug, and the barracks were disinfected and whitewashed. Money was found for bicycles and a piano. The YMCA sent in footballs, chess sets and ping-pong. Cimade opened what it called the '*barraque de la culture*', where musicians could come to practise and books could be taken out on loan. Soon there were queues waiting for books every morning. Dr Cramer, who paid a return visit to Gurs, observed that 'many are the internees who are here finding a reason to live and to hope'.

They found some of it in the determination and cheerfulness of the young women from Cimade and the OSE, who became as subversive towards the authorities as they dared to be and who were often at odds with the guards; they saw themselves as 'civilian resistance'. They took to mocking the few nurses sent into the camp by Vichy as 'little dolls, artfully made up, with brilliant red nail varnish'. For their part, the authorities complained constantly that the young women were disrespectful.

For the adolescents, life in Gurs was bleak and confusing. Many parents seemed to have lost all sense of how to look after them and spent the days either agitating for release or sunk in apathy, crouching on their filthy straw mattresses in the almost totally dark huts. To see their mothers and fathers so reduced, so frightened, so lacking in resources, was terrifying. Hanne, who was strong and healthy and had just turned 16, longed for distraction. Having been forced by the Nazi laws in Karlsruhe to leave school at 14, she craved an education. She haunted the OSE's culture hut and volunteered to work in the camp office, where she ran errands and sorted the mail – the legitimate mail; the clandestine letters entered and left the camp with Jeanne or Madeleine, who wore loose-fitting clothes with baggy pockets.

It was in the office that Hanne met Max Liebmann, a studious 19-year-old from Mannheim, who had also arrived in Gurs on one of the trains bringing Jews from Baden, together with his mother and his aunt Jeanne. Passing through Lyons, where the French police were still desperately trying to make sense of this vast, unannounced influx from Germany, Max had acted as interpreter: his grandmother was a French citizen and he spoke both languages fluently. His father, who was a textile printer, had earlier been able to escape to Nice and had avoided the round-up.

Max was a musician, like his mother and grandmother, both of them concert pianists; he had played the cello until he was deported, taught by a brave Gentile despite the edicts forbidding such things. He too had found work in the camp office, having discovered that it provided him with a pass to visit his mother, segregated in one of the women's huts. One of Max's jobs was to keep a tally of the dead. When their turn came round for extra rations, Hanne and Max went together to collect their halva, milk and cheese. Through them, their mothers had become friends. A string quartet had been started with the instruments brought in by Donald Lowrie, and through the winter of 1940 it played its way through Beethoven's violin sonatas. One of the prisoners was the pianist Hans Ebbecke, the organist from Strasburg cathedral. He was a Christian, but had refused to be parted from his Jewish wife when she was interned.

On 6 January, Ella wrote again to her brother in America. This letter is full of lines that have been blacked out by the censor. 'Hanne,' she wrote, 'is always hungry . . . If possible, could you send some clothes and underwear, and also aprons, stockings, a corset for me and above all soap and powder for washing . . . I am very depressed by our present situation and realise how desperately poor and unlucky we are.' There were moves to obtain emigration visas, but Ella worried about who would pay for the tickets. 'And now, I come to the saddest part of my letter. Our dearest mother is so feeble, so shrunken, so very weak. There is no real name for her illness, just general decline, great pain and no possibility of relief.' She reported that she was able to visit Babette every day and that she had been bartering what little she had for some cognac and eggs. 'Everything is so unspeakably sad, I can't really describe it.'

The long, cold winter of 1940–1 was taking its toll. The rain never seemed to let up. A permanent smell of wet clay and urine hung over the camp. Early in the new year, Babette died. She had caught pneumonia, stopped eating and slowly starved to death. A nearby field had been turned into a cemetery and she was buried there, with Ella and her sisters and Hanne at the graveside. It had rained particularly hard the night before, and after the coffin was lowered into the earth, Hanne watched with horror as it came floating slowly back up again. Soon afterwards, Berta, whose untreated diabetes had been getting steadily worse, had a stroke that killed her. She was buried near her mother. The cemetery, on a gentle slope alongside the camp, with views across to the snowy Pyrenees, was filling up. In the five months since Hanne's arrival, there had been 645 deaths.

The cemetery at Gurs, 1952

Still hoping that visas might come through for herself and Hanne, Ella begged her brother 'urgently, not to desert us, but to help us out of this misery'.

*   *   *

All through that winter, a strong easterly wind blew through the camp for days on end, bringing flurries of snow from the Pyrenees. On the roofs of the barracks, the bitumen tore in the gales, letting in more rain. Unable to go outside, permanently damp, the inmates huddled close together; their faces were red and chafed, their hands and feet purple and covered in chilblains. Many had only cotton blankets. 'It is cold by day, it is cold by night,' reported one visitor, 'with no hope of getting warm before the arrival of the spring and the first fine day.' Scurvy, eye problems, diarrhoea, typhoid and tuberculosis spread around the camp. Doctors estimated that the inmates were receiving just two thirds of the calories they needed, and very few of the essential vitamins. When Jeanne Merle d'Aubigné did her rounds of the huts in the evening, after the lights had been switched out at eight o'clock, she could see the eyes of the people crouching along the walls shining like those of cats.

For those who had money, there was a black market in food, mostly run by the remaining Spanish republicans. The camp inhabitants would and did eat everything, including cats, dogs and rats, and the vegetable slops that normally went to pigs. When the rations shrank still further, Jeanne cycled frantically around the neighbouring farms in search of food. A local curé told her that he had nothing to give her. 'You have authority,' she said. The following Sunday he told his parishioners about the people starving in Gurs. The congregation gathered some food for the camp. Some of the the OSE girls were sent to Cannes and Nice to beg for money from the rich visitors to the grand hotels.

Even the special rations brought in for the most dangerously malnourished – hot chocolate, potatoes and turnips and sometimes a little meat by the Quakers; dates by the OSE; eggs by the Protestants; porridge and jam by the Swiss – seemed not to do enough to halt the steady daily decline in weight, though some of the children appeared to have lost their pinched and desolate look. Among the adults, the women survived longer, but what took everyone by surprise was the speed with which an apparently healthy man or woman could suddenly die. Fearing bad publicity in foreign newspapers, Vichy appointed a former prefect, André Jean-Faure, as inspector of camps – of which there were now 26 in the occupied northern zone, 15 in the Vichy south. He paid a visit to Gurs and came away appalled.

Conditions, he reported, were atrocious. They 'gravely impugned the honour of France'. (Somewhat more complacently, he observed that though it was indeed extremely cold in the camps, it was cold for everyone else in France too. He himself had caught flu in his own house, where temperatures had gone down to zero.) What was fast becoming clear to everyone was that, to save lives, people needed to leave Gurs.

Emigration was one obvious solution. The foreign Jews had lost their faith in France and longed to leave, preferably for the US or Palestine, but simply to get out of German-occupied Europe was enough. In principle, Vichy was pleased to see them go, but a combination of the extreme reluctance of other countries to accept them and a plethora of administrative complexities that made the much-derided bureaucracy of the Third Republic seem translucent in its simplicity meant that emigration became more and more impossible.

The British, pleading fears of alienating the Arabs, had all but sealed off entry to Palestine. The Jewish emigration organisation HICEM tried every loophole, drew up lists of possible candidates, helped individuals to take their cases to the foreign consuls in Marseilles, and gave people decent suits of clothes so that they would not look like beggars at their interviews. Anyone wishing to leave had to have an entry visa to a new country, a transit visa if passing through Spain or Portugal, and an exit visa from France, with a certificate of good morals from the police and a ticket paid for in American dollars. If going by ship, you needed to apply to the prefecture of the Bouches-du-Rhône for an allocated place; if heading to Shanghai, you needed a travel pass from the Ministry for the Colonies in Clermont-Ferrand. At every stage, the bureaucrats prevaricated. The prefect of the Bouches-du-Rhône did all he could to keep too many would-be emigrants out of Marseilles, while the individual camps dragged their heels about transferring people to Les Milles, the only camp in which they were permitted to complete the formalities. Since many of the affidavits, visas, passes and documents were only issued for a short time, the first had often long since expired by the time the last came through. Every day the rules seemed to change.

Even so, for a while at least, HICEM remained hopeful. Its director, visiting Gurs, spoke of 'enormous possibilities for immigration'. While these were shrinking by the day, Hanne's two aunts managed to get on the list for Cuba, and hoped to have their visas before too long.

An Emergency Rescue Committee had also been set up in New York in the summer of 1940 to help well-known political figures trapped in occupied France. With the intervention of Eleanor Roosevelt, 2,000 'danger visas' had been issued. Auctions – 'Who will bid me $500 for Marc Chagall?' – were held to raise funds. Once a decent sum had been raised, a young reporter with Foreign Affairs called Varian Fry, who looked a bit like a scholarly academic and who was bold and imaginative by nature, was sent to Marseilles with a list of 200 names. Most were Germans; on the list were Max Ernst and Heinrich and Golo Mann. There were no communists, they being as unwelcome to the Americans as to the French. In Marseilles, Fry was deluged by requests. And though he did indeed succeed in spiriting out a number of people who would undoubtedly have been arrested by Vichy or the Gestapo, not everyone got away. At Portbou, on the Spanish border, having successfully made his way over the mountains with a new manuscript, the philosopher Walter Benjamin was stopped by the police and told that, because he lacked a French exit visa, he would be sent back to France. He committed suicide instead. Not long before, he had written of 'the adventures of the external world, which, like wolves, appear at times'.

Eleanor Roosevelt had also been using her influence to arrange for visas for children whose relations in the US were able to pay the ever-escalating costs of travel. In 1939, passage by ship to New York had cost $80; now it stood at $500. HICEM, the American JDC and the OSE were able to secure 311 more visas for children with no families in the US. But for children as for adults, progress was agonisingly slow. After an incredible bureaucratic effort by the OSE, a first group of 60 children were gathered in Marseilles by the end of May 1941. A three-day leave was arranged for their mothers to see them off, in exchange for an absolute promise that they would return to their camps. Later, a second group left, bound for Cadiz. What made these departures so heart-rending was that some of the smaller children, who had been cared for outside the camps for some time, no longer recognised their mothers when they came to bid them farewell. Their

first language had become F...
hood had been forgotten. They ...
After they left, the mothers kept ...
the camps. None survived.

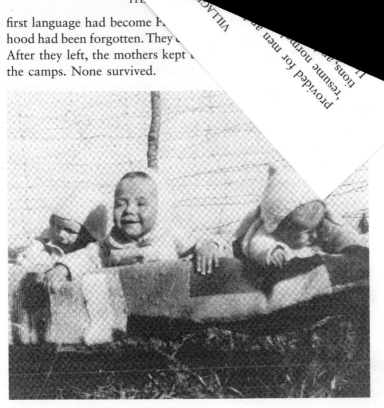

Three of the 5,000 children interned in the camps

The internment camps now held some 47,000 people, 40,000 of them Jews. They would have been even fuller had Vichy not decided to start placing fit 15–60-year-old men in compulsory work battalions, the Groupements de Travailleurs Etrangers, where they were treated harshly, and in conditions often little better than inside Gurs, except for the absence of barbed wire. There were also several schemes run by the various charitable organisations, under which the internees, 'on furlough, not to be released', could be freed and settled in 'assigned residence' from which they were allowed to stray no further than five kilometres. That these might soon become deathtraps, no one as yet perceived. One of these schemes, started under the auspices of the Nîmes Committee,

women aged between 20 and 45, able to
life' and work. Their keep was paid for by rela-
those with more money supported those who had none.
nder a new Direction des Centres d'Accueil, homes taking 50
to 60 people opened; others were set up by the Service Social des
Etrangers, and the Jewish scout movement. More could have been
established but for shortage of money. The JDC, which was paying
many of the costs, estimated that to free 1,000 people from the
camps would have taken 40 per cent of their entire annual budget.

There was also, of course, the possibility of escape. Getting out
of Gurs was not impossible, and some of the guards, increasingly
revolted by the system they were forced to administer, could be
persuaded to turn a blind eye. The problem, once outside the
fence, was how to survive. What did you do next if you had no
papers, no money and no French?

Early in 1941, there were estimated to be about 5,000 children
under 15 in the camps, approximately a third of them Jews from
Germany, Austria, Poland and the Baltic countries. Among the
adults, there was a small number of Gypsies, a few Spanish
republicans. Most were suffering painfully from the extreme cold,
the snow having lingered for many weeks on end; even in
Marseilles, the temperature remained below zero well into
February. To distract people from the horror of their daily lives,
the all-pervading stench of urine and excrement, and their acute
fears for the future, efforts were made in Gurs to lay on classes,
and Hannah Zweig, a relation of the writer Stefan Zweig, started
a theatre group. Vichy was supposed to send 80 teachers to the
camps, but only four showed up.

Fearing what the mud, lice and despair was doing to the children, the Nîmes Committee suggested to Vichy that if they would
not let everyone out and close Gurs down, then they should
consider freeing at least the children, under the auspices of the
welfare organisations, placing them where they could be properly
cared for and yet remain on the police register. There was as yet
no talk of hiding them, for at this stage they still seemed safe
from Nazi hands. Not all members of the Nîmes Committee
agreed, arguing that the money and time would be better spent
on improving conditions in the camps; in Gurs, in 1941 alone,
over 1,000 people had died.

The OSE became the leading partner behind the scheme, in the shape of an Alsatian doctor called Joseph Weill, and Andrée Salomon, a 31-year-old woman who had helped organise the main Jewish scouting movement in France, the Eclaireurs Israélites de France. Andrée looked a bit like a Gypsy, with long, untidy black hair and deep-set eyes that gleamed with defiance. She was much loved by everyone who came across her. The daughter of a Jewish ritual butcher from Alsace, she was trilingual in French, German and Yiddish. She was calm, smiled a lot, and possessed a strong nerve and a steely will. She did not give up, she would say about herself, and she did not cry. The OSE was already looking after 752 Jewish children, many of them orphans since the deportation of their parents, in homes and centres around the country. Andrée now set out around the various *départements* in the unoccupied zone to persuade the prefects to accept many more children, supervised by the OSE and placed in whatever school, convent or private home she could prevail on to take them. The OSE's team of young women followed her on their bicycles in search of havens. The JDC promised to provide the money.

Within the camps – now spoken of throughout France as *'les camps de la honte'*, the camps of shame – parents had to be persuaded to part with their children. The remaining Spanish republican families categorically refused to let their children leave; but the Jews, noted Andrée, accepted 'with great dignity and stoicism'.

In the summer of 1941, Ella was still hoping to get herself and Hanne to the US, or at least to Switzerland, where she had another sister and a cousin. An uncle who had got out of Dachau and emigrated in 1939 had raised enough money from friends and relations for their many permits and exit papers; but the days passed and no news of a possible departure came. Worrying constantly about Hanne, particularly now that TB, from which her husband had died, was spreading around the camp, she instantly agreed to the OSE's suggestion that Hanne should be one of the first children to leave Gurs. Hanne herself protested, not wanting her mother to find herself alone when her aunts left for Cuba. But Ella was adamant. She had been infuriated when a snide and gossipy neighbour had been heard to say that she believed Hanne to be pregnant, knowing full well that the girl's bloated stomach was due only to malnutrition. Max and Hanne had become inseparable and Hanne found it hard to leave him behind in Gurs. But as they agreed, the war could not last much longer, and they would soon all be together again.

Hanne Hirsch and Max Liebmann before the War

On 1 September 1941, Hanne and six other teenagers left Gurs. Like the three Parisian boys, Simon and Jacques Liwerant and Jacques Stulmacher, they knew only that they were bound for safety in the mountains. In Toulouse, where they stopped for lunch in a kosher restaurant in the old Jewish quarter, Hanne ate her first proper meal in almost a year. Later she would remember feeling disappointed that it included carrots, of which there had been far too many in Gurs. All seven teenagers left their mothers behind them. Hanne's parting from Ella was extremely painful.

The camp at Rivesaltes, some 400 kilometres to the east of Gurs, was a gentler place; at least at first. Originally built on a deserted field of abandoned vines on the plain between Narbonne and Perpignan, it had served as one of the main internment centres for the Spanish republican refugees before opening its gates to France's 'undesirables' in 1939. Originally there was no barbed wire, and no watchtower; the Canigou mountain peak rose like a Japanese volcano in the distance. Here the huts were built of cement, with brick roofs and a door at each end; there were small windows that shed a little light. On bright sunny days you could see the sea, glittering very blue to the west.

By the time another young Jewish boy, Rudy Appel, arrived in Rivesaltes in the winter of 1941, much had changed. The huts stretched as far as the eye could see across the sandy, treeless plain of stony red earth, over which blew constant strong winds, hot and full of dust in summer, sharp and biting in winter. Rivesaltes had 20,000 inmates, 5,000 of whom were under 15. On the model of the other camps, Rivesaltes had now been divided up into *îlots*, groups of huts separated from each other by barbed wire, on either side of which gathered men and women with swollen yellow faces, their muscles so shrunken that their bones stood out sharply. At night, searchlights bathed the camp in a ghostly yellow light. A suffocating stench rose from the latrines and a recent epidemic of gastroenteritis had killed 24 new babies. The straw for the mattresses had not been changed in six months; they were worn flat and were full of fleas. Blankets hung from the ceiling to give families a little privacy. Visitors to the camp reported seeing small children without shoes wandering between the huts, their feet bound up in cotton rags; it made them think of slums of an earlier age.

Rudy, the younger son of a distinguished judge in Mannheim, was 13, the same age as Simon, when in November 1938 Kristallnacht destroyed his home and took his father away. The Nazis who broke up the furniture, stole his mother's jewellery, and threw their books into the street below to be burnt on piles with other Jewish books, also arrested the judge and sent him to Dachau. For a while, however, the family felt almost fortunate. Good friends, luck and money rescued the judge and got him and Rudy's older brother to Philadelphia. After Rudy, as a Jewish child, was forced to leave school, his mother found a *passeur* to take him to Holland. Before he left Mannheim, she taught him to sew on a button, saying that he would have to learn to look after himself for a while. She stayed behind.

From his first school in Driebergen, Rudy, who was good at his studies and had always come top in Mannheim, was sent to a higher gymnasium in Rotterdam, spending his nights in an orphanage with Dutch children. He was not unhappy, and he felt safe, but he was uneasy about having so little control over his own life, others seeming to make every decision for him. His mother had managed to get herself out of Germany and into Belgium but was having trouble finding a safe passage on to Holland. She wrote to him twice a week, letters full of tenderness and instructions about how to behave, and she included in them a *coupon réponse*, a chit for a stamp, so that he could reply.

Rudy was in Rotterdam the day that the Allies bombed the docks. He sheltered in the basement of his school, listening to the noise of the explosions and smelling the acrid smoke from the burning machinery. Not long afterwards, he heard from his mother that he was to join her in Belgium. He had not seen her in two years. His father had sent word that they were to make their way to Marseilles and try to board a boat for the US, and another *passeur* was found to take them into France. The first journey passed without trouble. But crossing the demarcation line into unoccupied France near Limoges, pulling behind them the elderly Belgian woman who was travelling with them, they were stopped by the Vichy police. Rudy and his mother were taken to Rivesaltes. They were placed in separate *îlots*, and talked to each other across the barbed wire.

The camp was just entering its worst phase: rats, lice, epidemics, hungers; and all the symptoms of famine. They had not been there long when, on one of the blue-cold days of winter, a general disinfection was ordered. 'Skeletons covered in flabby and wrinkled skin stumbled out naked into the cold sun,' wrote Friedel Reiter, a young Swiss nurse, after the war, 'trembling, many hardly able to walk.'

Almost the worst thing about Rivesaltes, it would later be said, was the group of very small children, separated from their parents. Having arrived filthy and feral, they were liable to bite anyone who approached them. They seemed to have lost the ability to laugh or to play, and spent their days snivelling and whimpering. They had huge ballooning stomachs and suffered from eye infections. Those strong enough formed angry, rebellious packs. One little Polish girl, whose father had vanished and whose mother was thought to have gone insane, was described by a Quaker visitor as charming everyone with her blue eyes and curly brown hair. But her moods swung violently between 'serenity' and rage, when she stormed around for no apparent reason. Secours Suisse got permission to move the smallest of the children to a nursery in a deserted chateau near Perpignan. One camp worker, Mary Elms, abandoned all legality and smuggled some of the older ones out in her car. Every day now, German mothers came to her and said: '*Nehmen Sie mein Kind weg*' – take my child away.

HICEM and the OSE were continuing to do all they could to further emigration, and when Rudy and his mother got word that the judge had made some progress with visas for Cuba, Rudy was moved to Les Milles, the internment camp near Marseilles, which acted as a transit centre for potential candidates for emigration. Les Milles had been a brick factory before the war. While he was there, orders came that workers were being recruited for Germany. In the courtyard, as names were read out, he realised that although his surname began with an 'A', he had somehow been passed over. He then noticed that a blind veteran of the Great War had also been rejected. As he would say, many years later, 'It was as if someone tapped me on the shoulder.' He slipped across the courtyard and joined the other group whose names had been called. It was the correct thing to do. Though he did not know it at the time, it saved his life.

Soon afterwards, Rudy was returned to Rivesaltes: the visas had not come through and it now looked highly improbable that they ever would. His mother had been spirited out of the camp into a prison hospital in Perpignan by a doctor from Mannheim, a prisoner like themselves, who had told the authorities that she was very ill. The OSE and Secours Suisse were frantically doing all they could to remove children from the camp. Rudy had just turned 17, but he looked younger, a serious, sturdy boy, short in height, with a watchful expression and thick dark hair; Friedel Reiter managed to get the age on his papers altered to 15. Rudy thus became another of the adolescents, like Hanne, to leave internment for the safety of the mountains. Seven hundred and eighty children had now been rescued from the camps.

Just where they were going, however, and what they were leaving behind, was not yet clear to anyone.

CHAPTER THREE

Deportation fever

In the summer of 1942, something fundamental changed in France. It changed for the foreign Jews in the unoccupied zone of France, who would now be hunted down like animals, becoming the only Jews in Europe – other than those in Bulgaria – to be turned over to the Germans by a sovereign state. It changed for Jewish children, no longer under even nominal protection from Eichmann's men. It changed for the French Jews, who, after two years of self-delusion, began at last to perceive that the measures against foreign Jews would apply to them as well, though it would be a while before they were hunted with the same ferocity. Finally, it changed for a considerable number of ordinary French men and women, who, shaken out of their lethargy and complacency, took stock of what was happening in their country and decided they wanted no part in it.

On 27 June, a letter from a local official had reached the CGQJ in Vichy; it pointed out that something needed to be done to improve conditions in the internment camps before winter set in. The reply was brief and sinister: 'May I remind you that an operation is taking place which makes [any such action] at present absolutely unnecessary.' In Vichy, the German responsible for Jewish Affairs was overheard asking Laval whether he intended to apply to the Jews in Vichy France 'the same measures we are using in occupied France'. To which Laval apparently replied: 'The only Jews we have are your Jews. We will send them back to you any time you say.'

Events were indeed moving fast. On 29 June, Theo Dannecker, leader of the Judenferat, the 'Jew unit' in the German Security Service, the SD, in Paris, set out on a tour of inspection of the southern internment camps, in order to ascertain for himself the number of 'deportables'. There had been steady departures of trains for Auschwitz from the occupied zone: it was time to move south, into Vichy France. Disappointed to find that the numbers of Jews fell considerably below his earlier estimate of 40,000, he argued that the date for naturalisation should be put back, and that anyone who had entered France after 1 January 1936 could now be considered 'foreign'. On Himmler's orders, 90 per cent were to be fit, healthy men and women aged between 16 and 40; the other 10 per cent – the sick, children, the elderly – would be 'tolerated'. Laval was heard to refer to them as the '*déchets*', the dregs.

On 4 July, Vichy formally accepted that it would hand over 10,000 foreign Jews to the Germans for deportation. Bousquet told prefects to cancel all exit permits from the camps, as the plan was 'to rid your region totally of foreign Jews'. Henri Cado, a senior policeman, sent out instructions to say that the internees were to take with them nothing that belonged to the state – not even blankets. Orders went out to silence the newspapers; no one dared disobey. But not everyone in Vichy was totally discreet. It did not remain secret for long that Fourcade, acting chief of police, had been heard to say that trains bound for Auschwitz carrying foreign Jews had been arranged for 6, 8, 10 and 12 August. Deportation 'fever' had begun.

Rumours were spreading round Gurs and Rivesaltes. There was talk of being taken to a Jewish settlement in Galicia, of factory work in Germany, even mention of a programme of extermination in Poland, though it was generally agreed that this was far-fetched. 'This is like Germany,' the inmates told each other. 'This is how it started.'

The Nîmes Committee had somehow continued to cling to the hope that the Vichy south would remain safe from German demands. Just the same, the US chargé d'affaires, S. Pinkney Tuck, now called on Laval to warn that the US, and the civilised world as a whole, was 'shocked' by what appeared to be taking place. Tracy Strong, the general secretary of the YMCA, asked General Gampet, Pétain's secretary for military affairs, about the rumours. Gampet told him he had heard nothing. That same day, Strong called on Pétain but came away with the impression 'that the matter failed to register with the Marshal'. The Quakers, who by the summer of 1942 were providing on average three ounces of extra food daily to 84,000 children in France, felt that their contribution entitled them to some kind of hearing, but their delegate, Lindsey Noble, who spoke to Laval, was treated to a lecture on the troublesome foreign Jews and told that at least this new German initiative would give France 'an opportunity to get rid of them'.

On 3 August, Donald Lowrie, in his position as president of the Nîmes Committee, arrived in Vichy. He was made to wait. It was three days before he was told that he might see Pétain. Later, he described the meeting in some detail. He was shown, he said, into a crowded office in the Hôtel du Parc – Pétain's headquarters – where the tables were covered in bric-a-brac, though Pétain's own desk seemed 'orderly'. The Maréchal was not as tall as he appeared in photographs, but he was erect and physically well preserved, even though his skin seemed 'bloodless, almost waxen in colour'. It was soon clear to Lowrie that the men who surrounded Pétain – and particularly Laval and General Jardelle, Pétain's secretary, a man he described as a 'fortyish, alert, well fed, smooth' watchdog – were taking considerable pains to keep him in ignorance of their plans. General Jardelle was present at the meeting and did much of the talking.

Lowrie began by remarking that the foreign welfare organisations were having trouble believing that the Maréchal was aware that plans were going ahead to deport 10,000 foreign Jews – surely this was not something he would tolerate? Pétain reacted with 'a gesture of helplessness', and said: 'You know our situation with regard to the Germans.' When Lowrie asked that a period of grace be permitted during which the foreign organisations would try to expedite emigration and persuade the United States to accept child refugees, the Maréchal said that he would consult Laval and give an answer in 'a week or ten days'. Told that the matter was extremely urgent, he agreed to discuss it later that same day. Warned by Lowrie of the repercussions the deportations might have on deliveries of foreign food, Pétain simply waved his hand 'as though he deprecated this . . . and rose, terminating the interview'. Lowrie's conclusion was stark. Pétain, he thought, 'had not really grasped' what was going on, and Laval was acting independently.

In any case, it was all too late. A gigantic net was already descending over Vichy's internment camps. For the welfare organisations, it was a terrible moment of reckoning, their worst fears realised. They had done everything they could to make life inside the camps more bearable, and in so doing had fallen into a trap: the camps had become 'reservoirs' for deportation.

Before dawn, while it was still completely dark, police from the Garde Mobile surrounded the camps. In the preceding days, visits had been banned, including those from priests, and the women and the elderly who had been given permission to reside nearby had been brought back in. The camps had been sealed. Throughout the countryside, convents, boarding schools, presbyteries and hostels were searched and the forests patrolled for Jews; those found were arrested. Infirmaries were raided and elderly and sick men and women herded out in their pyjamas.

Frantic messages to the various homes and centres to which some 10,000 Jews had legally been moved were in time to save some, who now scattered into the countryside and hid. Police surrounded other places and took everyone inside away. In Nice, Jews were picked up on the beach. In Marseilles they were pulled off buses and trams. Visas to leave France were cancelled, even for those for whom all formalities had been completed and who were about to board ships to safety.

In the two and a half years of German occupation, HICEM had managed to get just 6,449 Jews out.

As it grew light in Gurs, the Jews with names beginning with the first 13 letters of the alphabet, A to M, were told to pack their cases. The others watched in silence as the frail, ragged inmates dragged their bags and their suitcases held together with string towards a designated hut. Informed about the list of possible exemptions – children, pregnant women, veterans, spouses of Jews, war widows, wives of prisoners of war – the young women from the OSE and Cimade bartered and begged, exploiting every loophole, obtaining the release of some, failing with others, always conscious that for every person whose name they removed from the list, another would have to be found to take their place. As with prisoners awaiting execution, those about to be deported were given a better meal. Jeanne Merle d'Aubigné noted that the selected became instantly unrecognisable, plunged in misery and apprehension. A Dr Bachrach, who had worked as a doctor inside the camp, was pulled back at the last moment, but 'in that space of time, he had become an old man'. None of the young social workers would ever forget the farewell notes they were given to post. Since there were no envelopes in the camp, they were obliged to read them to find the right names and addresses.

There were agonising scenes as people tried to kill themselves, swallowing anything they could get hold of. Others wept and struggled. Going from hut to hut to prepare the infirm and the elderly, Jeanne heard stories of cut wrists and poison. 'We lived somewhere outside life,' she wrote, 'In a bath of death.' When at last the first group was ready, it set off for the station, the infirm on crutches, the bedridden on stretchers.

At Rivesaltes, where the surrounding fields were golden with sunflowers in the strong summer sun, Friedel Reiter, the young Protestant nurse from Vienna, watched the deportees leave. 'I can see only a long file of people, going on for ever, expelled – hunted down – excluded. Where are they going? Can no one stop this slow motion slaughter?' Before leaving, each internee was given bread, mortadella, three tins of sardines, two kilos of fruit and a little jam. Able to parlay 10 children as 'simple-minded', and multiply that number to 20, Andrée Salomon was faced with the terrible question: which 20? How to choose them? The smallest? Those whose parents were most insistent? Those she had grown most fond of?

All over Vichy France, in the camps of Noé and Récébédou, Vernet and Les Milles, Argelès and Rieucros, similar scenes were taking place. The chaos was indescribable. At Récébédou, the departures were scheduled for the hours of darkness, so that the local villagers would not be aware of what was happening, and the deportees stumbled towards the station across the fields, under a full moon. At La Verdière in Marseilles, a young OSE worker called Alice refused to hand over any of the children; she was taken away with them and deported.

In the confusion of the moment, Vichy and the Germans continued to vacillate and disagree over their policy towards children; and in most places parents were still being given the option of leaving their children behind, providing there was someone to leave them with. The OSE and Cimade women moved quickly around the barracks, whispering to parents to leave the children, saying they would care for them.

As the Jews were led out of the camps, mothers clung to their children, giving them little personal objects: photographs, jewellery, letters. In Les Milles, only hours before the lorries left for the station, a team from the OSE led a group of 78 children out of the camp, having promised their parents that they would do everything in their power to get them to America. Some of them were babies. The children cried and clung to their mothers; the women, weeping, clung on to the lorries taking them away. In Rivesaltes, Andrée Salomon made last frantic efforts to get children out, hiding them in the boots of cars, or under the ample cloaks of her assistants. One small child was carried away in a shopping basket. When attempts were made to save the mother, by giving her a powerful sleeping pill and maintaining that she was very ill, the police took her away on a stretcher.

In the stations, the people were pushed on to goods wagons and packed in tight, and when the elderly had trouble climbing on to the high steps, they were shoved from behind. At Rivesaltes, Friedel Reiter watched as a young Protestant woman, come in search of her Jewish husband, was pulled on board a train to make up numbers, though she fought and shouted that it was all a mistake. As the train pulled away, her cries could be heard through the bars, 'terrible in the night silence'.

The first train from Rivesaltes took 900 people. Eighty-two of them were children, aged between 2 and 18. The OSE's frantic attempts had managed to reprieve just 20 in all. When the carriages pulled out of the station, the heads of some of the taller men could be seen through the upper slats, like those of animals. The train passed through Lyon-Perrache. Rabbi Jacob Kaplan was at the station. 'It was a heartbreaking sight,' he wrote later. 'People of all ages, even the very elderly, in a state of appalling feebleness. They seemed to be almost naked . . . broken by exhaustion. We were forbidden to speak to them.'

One of the 1,500 people in Gurs whose name fell into the first 13 letters of the alphabet was Hanne's mother Ella. Her visa had not come through, and it was later thought that the money had been stolen along the way. Not long before, she had written to Hanne, still under the OSE protection outside the camp, that she was not well. Hanne decided to return to Gurs to see her. She was instructed to make her way to Oloron and look for any of the young female assistants working for the OSE or Cimade, who had their base there. In Oloron, she learnt that none of them had been seen in days. It was 6 August; the deportations had begun. When Hanne reached Gurs, on foot, she saw that it was surrounded by armed police. She managed to find someone willing to get a message into the camp and was able to speak to her mother over the perimeter fence. Ella had already packed her suitcase. Hanne spent the night in a nearby field and returned to Gurs in the morning. She saw Ella again, and they talked across the barbed wire.

Next day, the Jewish prisoners were moved to the station at Oloron, where a line of cattle trucks awaited them. They were pushed on board. Hanne, who had walked the 15 kilometres from the camp, ran up and down the train, frantically calling her mother's name. A French policeman stopped her, gave her a drink of water and said to her: 'What is going on here breaks my heart.' He helped her to find Ella, and the two women had an hour and a half together talking, Hanne on the railway siding, her mother leaning out of the cattle truck. Ella was calm. Just before the doors were bolted, she said to her daughter: 'This is my last trip. I will never come back.' Years later, thinking of that day, Hanne remembered saying to herself: 'I will never see her again.'

She stood watching as the train pulled out.

All through August, the deportation trains crawled northwards through France, carrying foreign Jews from almost all the southern *départements*. As they passed through stations, police and soldiers kept people from getting too close. It was extremely hot, and there was never quite enough water on the trains. A new tally had suggested to Bousquet that there were 12,686 'eligible' foreign Jews in the south, but after the internment camps had been cleared of these eligible people, only 3,472 people had actually been put on trains between 6 and 13 August. For a brief moment, in order to ingratiate himself with the Germans, Bousquet tried to inflate the numbers. When the shortfall became too evident, he volunteered that he could soon find another 2,000. And then there was always the possibility of moving the year of naturalisation back still further, to 1931. People who believed themselves to have been French for 11 years would now suddenly discover themselves to be Polish or Russian after all. As for children, it was probably better, said Eichmann, to mix them in with adults, so that the French public, seeing them all together, would think that they had opted not to be parted from their families. The Germans for some time had not wanted to be bothered with children; under pressure from Vichy, they agreed to include some.

The trains were all bound for Drancy, the four-storey horseshoe of tenement-like buildings put up before the war, which had served as a barracks for a legion of *gardes mobiles*. Along with housing civilian detainees and prisoners of war on their way to Germany, Drancy had been acting since the end of March as the way station for the deportations to the extermination camps in Poland. It was a grim and ugly place, surrounded by a double row of barbed wire and watchtowers. The courtyard was made of clinker, which turned into dust in summer and mud when it rained. Inside was more barbed wire. By the time Ella's train reached Drancy, there were 120 people in dormitories designed for 30; the more fortunate slept three to a bunk, the rest on straw on the floor. There was not enough of anything – food, medicines, water, towels, clothes, bowls, spoons. The stench was overwhelming.

Among the new arrivals were many children, some of them orphans, others kept back when their parents were sent ahead but now dispatched ostensibly to join them. Many were clothed in little better than rags; several had no shoes and went barefoot. They arrived filthy, smelly, covered in sores and lice. The youngest, who could not yet speak, had labels tied to their clothes with their names on. But these were soon lost or torn off, as were the little bundles of personal items their parents had so lovingly given them, and they became numbers, with a question mark alongside. Impetigo was rife. Those who did not already have dysentery soon caught it. The very young ones, who could not negotiate the long walk to the communal latrines, used buckets on the stairs, which overflowed and dripped down from floor to floor. There was no room in the infirmary to take them all, and the few Red Cross nurses and social workers allowed in battled to keep them clean and fed. There were very few towels and very little soap. All night, you could hear the sound of constant crying.

By the time Ella was taken from Drancy and put on a train for Auschwitz, there were three *convois*, transports, leaving every week. No one could say for certain where the trains were going, but there was now growing talk of extermination. Several people chose to leap to their deaths from the fourth-floor windows. The first transport to take children on their own, without parents, left Drancy on 17 August. Five hundred and thirty of the children on board were under 13. Before they left, their bundles of belongings were searched by Gestapo officers and anything of any value was removed. Many of the children had had their heads shaved. One little boy, who had thick blond curls, kept begging to be allowed to keep his hair. His mother was so proud of it, and she would want to see it when they were reunited. Those who screamed and struggled as they were herded on to the buses that were taking them to the station were picked up by policemen and carried. Between 17 and 31 August, seven trains left for Auschwitz. Among those on board were 3,500 children. Most of them, commented a Quaker delegate grimly, 'may already be said to be orphans'.

It was against this background of terror and Vichy-led deportations that the remarkable story of Vénissieux took place. What happened in this small camp on the edge of Lyons says much about what could be done where there was the will, the imagination and the courage to do it. Vénissieux also marked the next step in France's war, one in which saving, not yielding, came to take on ever greater importance, and when safe, secluded places, full of courageous people, would come into their own. And it happened at the very last moment when it was still possible for such a public and bold act to be carried out on such a scale.

By the summer of 1942, Lyons, the second-largest city in France, former capital of Roman Gaul, was full of Jews, both those long resident in this city of manufacturers and industrialists, and the many thousands who had fled the occupied zone and the Germans in search of greater safety. When Bousquet announced plans for the deportation of 10,000 of Vichy's foreign Jews, the prefect of the Rhône, Pierre Angeli, and two of his more zealous subordinates set about preparing for the capture in his *département* of all those who had entered France after 1 January 1936. They opened a camp in a disused military barracks built around an arsenal and surrounded by high walls at Vénissieux, a suburb on the western edge of Lyons, hitherto home to a number of Indochinese workers. In the middle of August, Dr Jean Adam, the young medical student who had been detailed to care for these workers, was ordered to present himself to the camp.

Very early on the morning of 26 August, while it was still dark, police and *gardes mobiles*, in teams of three, set out with lists of names. Roadblocks were set up. Moving from district to district, they banged on doors, searched attics and basements, looked into cupboards and storerooms. One thousand and sixteen Jews were arrested and taken to Vénissieux by lorry. There would have been many more, but a marked lack of enthusiasm on the part of some of the policemen, along with the warnings of the impending round-up that had reached the welfare organisations, meant that a number of people had had time to escape. Enraged, Bousquet ordered manhunts. The police were instructed to shoot anyone who attempted to get away.

These same warnings had been received by the OSE, Cimade and the other groups working with the immigrant Jews, and so they had had time to make plans. Crucial to what happened next was the involvement of two Catholic priests, Père Chaillet and Abbé Glasberg.

Chaillet was a stocky, robust Jesuit in his early forties, with thin lips and shiny eyes behind heavy dark-framed glasses; he was a theologian, little known outside his group of students and colleagues. Glasberg, who was a little younger, had been born in the Ukraine to Jewish parents, but had converted to Catholicism at the age of 18, toyed with the idea of becoming a Trappist monk, and emigrated to France in 1930. He was a shabby, dishevelled-looking man, of great charm and energy, with an old soutane and shoes with flapping soles. He was often ill-shaven, and his prematurely grey hair and thick glasses made him look ten years older than he was. Some of his more conservative colleagues suspected him of being a communist; his friends said that he was both Western and Eastern in outlook, and that he brought together two faiths and two cultures.

Père Chaillet and Abbé Glasberg

Glasberg was a familiar figure around Lyons, pedalling on his bicycle between his parish of Saint-Alban and the city centre, and was regarded as being very skilful at charming officials into making concessions. He had long been a critic of the Nîmes Committee, of which he was a member, saying that he was maddened by its 'tone of universal goodwill and forgiveness' and that far more time should have been spent worrying about the very existence of the camps, rather than trying to improve conditions inside them. Chaillet and Glasberg had been founder members of an association of Protestants, Catholics and Jews, L'Amitié Chrétienne, which had been working with refugees since 1941. Cardinal Gerlier of Lyons, though earlier a supporter of Pétain, had accepted an invitation to become its honorary chairman.

It had been agreed that a *'commission de criblage'*, to monitor the suitability of candidates for deportation to the north, would review the arrested Jews. Eleven possible exemptions had been conceded, including the old, those married to non-Jews, and those with children under two. At this point, Vichy and the Germans were still dithering about whether or not all children would be obliged to accompany their parents.

Glasberg and Chaillet quickly got themselves into Vénissieux. In their wake, by one means or another, came Gilbert Lesage of the Service Social des Etrangers, Andrée Salomon and Madeleine Dreyfus from the OSE, Madeleine Barot from Cimade, and a Polish engineer from Vilnius called Georges Garel, who had no connections to anyone but whose anonymity might prove useful. For two days and three nights, working as a team, these people deployed their forces; they had helpers on the outside collecting documents and birth certificates, finding bits of evidence, consulting records in order to make the cases for exemption. One of these was Elisabeth Hirsch, known to all as Böszi, an extremely pretty young woman with very bright blue eyes, who had been working in Gurs; another was a young volunteer from the OSE's offices, Lily Tager, a girl with a mass of curly dark hair. From time to time, Glasberg was able to spirit away those who had been temporarily reprieved; his little black Citroën with yellow wheels conveniently looked identical to the one driven by the Prefect.

Inside Vénissieux, total chaos reigned. Orders arrived, were cancelled, then reinstated. The eleven exemptions were abruptly reduced to five. Glasberg, Chaillet, Dreyfus and Barot pleaded, bargained, prevaricated. There were far too many people for the bunks and most were now sleeping on straw on the ground. The few remaining Indochinese workers cooked. Guards, policemen, officious civil servants sent by Angeli milled around. Dr Adam, who had willingly been coopted by Glasberg, was given a rudimentary infirmary and was busy declaring as dangerously ill people who were not. Supposed cases of acute appendicitis were rushed to hospital, from where a few managed to escape. Some adolescent girls were dressed in scout uniforms and led out of the camp. Those of the internees who had experienced German brutality in their home countries were frantic. One night there were 26 suicide attempts. The noise was overwhelming. It was known that Angeli had decreed that the camp was to be emptied by 19 August. Lorries arrived to start taking people to the railway station. By now Glasberg and his colleagues were operating in increasing desperation, conscious that they were working against the clock.

It was Glasberg who by sheer chance intercepted a telegram from the Prefect to the police chief saying that it had been decided that there were to be no exemptions for children after all. He and Garel realised that something bold and dramatic had to be done, and that there was very little time in which to do it. Night had fallen and the final deportations were scheduled for the next day.

A storm had knocked out the electricity. Glasberg and the others moved through the barracks in the dark, going from family to family with their torches, asking parents to give them their children. They had hastily typed out and roneoed forms bearing the words 'Paternal responsibility and rights of guardianship abandoned by me' – a necessary formula under French law – and leaving room for names and signatures. The parents were told that they would be giving their children to L'Amitié Chrétienne and Cardinal Gerlier. Glasberg spoke both German and Yiddish. Some parents, as they signed, gave Madeleine Barot addresses of relations; others pressed bits of jewellery or small precious items into her hand. She put them into separate envelopes with the name of each child. The families were told that their children were simply being offered a better life until they were able to return to reclaim them. What Madeleine and her colleagues found so unbearably distressing was that it was clear that they understood perfectly well what was really meant. Lily Tager would be haunted all her life by the despair on the women's faces. When the moment came to part with the children, they clung to them and told them, in Yiddish, to be worthy of their Jewishness and not to forget. Several women fainted. As the night wore on, and the need for haste increased, so Glasberg and the others were forced to become more brutal. A few of the children had to be physically torn away. One father cut his wrists and covered his child in his blood.

By five o'clock in the morning there were 89 children in the refectory and the camp was full of crying people. The police chief asked Glasberg why everyone was so upset. 'Wouldn't you be upset, if they were taking away your children?' Glasberg replied. The children were of all ages; they came from Vienna, Brussels, Lodz, Graz, Berlin, Luxembourg, Warsaw, Breslau, Magdeburg and Liège. There were several brothers and sisters. Few spoke much French.

One of the children was six-year-old Rachel Kamienkar, a round-faced, bright little girl with short brown hair parted to one side. Rachel's father had run a grocery shop in Antwerp in Belgium after fleeing Poland in 1926. She had two older half-brothers and a full brother, Louis, who was three and had curly blond hair and blue eyes, and to whom she was greatly attached. After first her father and then her mother were arrested, Louis had been taken by the Germans while playing in the park with a neighbour's daughter. All three, her parents and her little brother, were deported. Rachel herself had fled with an aunt and her husband to France, from where they planned to cross into Switzerland. Rachel, to whom so many terrible things happened, has protected herself by remembering almost nothing. What she can remember is the day that she and her aunt and uncle walked many miles through the snow to the Swiss border, where they were turned back. At this point her uncle disappeared; where he went she did not know. She and her aunt made their way to Lyons, where they were living in a small flat on the day of the round-up. In Vénissieux, her aunt signed Glasberg's letter and handed her over to L'Amitié Chrétienne.

In the camp, it was beginning to grow light. By chance, the children happened to be in the brightly lit room that served as a canteen when their parents were herded out and on to the buses that were to take them to the station. Madeleine Barot and the others would long remember the expressions on the faces of the parents as, pressing their noses to the windows, they desperately looked back for a last glimpse of their children.

Even as the train taking them to Drancy pulled out, Glasberg was still trying to extract people. He managed to rescue an elderly Russian woman, passing her off as Greek Orthodox, but he was unable to take two little girls, whose mother kept trying to give them to him, her arms outstretched imploringly, and neither he nor Madeleine could do anything to save a woman who was eight months pregnant. When the train gathered speed, one man tried to escape by jumping out of the window, but the train was halted and he was caught.

That day, Saturday 29 August 1942, 545 Jews travelled from the local station of Saint-Priest to Drancy. Four hundred and seventy-five of them were put on the *convoi* to Auschwitz on 2 September; 58 followed on the 9th. There was only one known survivor. Rachel's aunt perished. Rachel, for the moment, was safe; but having lost her mother and father and her much-loved little brother, and then her uncle, she was now without the one person who had been left to her. She was six, and alone.

For the children in Vénissieux, a new drama was unfolding. Three buses had arrived, driven by volunteers, to take the children away. Those over 18 – technically the age at which the Germans considered them to be adults – were concealed under the seats. Rachel's only other memory of that time is of these hidden children. They were taken to the headquarters of the Jewish scouts, the EIF, in an abandoned Carmelite convent and handed over into the care of Madeleine Dreyfus and the OSE.

When the prefect Angeli learnt that his telegram had been intercepted by Glasberg, he immediately ordered that the children be returned; a train coming from Les Milles would pick them up and their coach would be joined on to their parents' train. However, a social worker in Angeli's office, overhearing the plans, hastened to the OSE offices to warn them. There was just time to scatter the children around Lyons, to convents, schools, hospitals and private houses. The older ones were put into scout uniforms and sent to join a pack leaving for a trip to the country. When the police arrived at the OSE office, the children had gone. Madeleine Dreyfus, pleading ignorance of their whereabouts, sent the officers to see Cardinal Gerlier.

Chaillet, Glasberg and Garel happened to be with the cardinal when Angeli's furious phone call ordering the children to be found was put through. For a moment, the cardinal seemed to hesitate. But then, pressed hard by his visitors, he told Angeli: 'These children, you're not going to get them.' There was an anxious moment when he asked the three men for the addresses of the places where the children had gone, saying that Pétain had assured him that they would not be handed over to the Germans. Garel and Chaillet produced false addresses, but not before Chaillet declared that, in all conscience, L'Amitié Chrétienne would never hand over children entrusted into its care by their parents. Word got out. A leaflet with the words *'Vous n'aurez pas les enfants'* was soon circulating around Lyons.

By now, the 89 children were disappearing, into schools and private families, into villages and isolated communities. Three of them – Rachel; a serious-looking 12-year-old boy called Manfred

Furst, whose little brother Oscar was saved with him, and Lea Wajsfelner, whose thirteenth birthday fell two days after the deportations from Vénissieux – were on their way into the mountains to join Simon, the two Jacques, Rudy and Hanne. L'Amitié Chrétienne, Angeli wrote angrily to his superiors, had 'thwarted the will of the government'.

As a punishment, Chaillet was put under house arrest and sent to spend two months in a psychiatric hospital at Privas, returning secretly from time to time to Lyons. Glasberg lay low until the arrival of the Germans a few months later, when, hearing that he was wanted by the Gestapo, he moved to Théas in the Tarn, where under the name of Elie Corvin he became the parish priest of Montauban, using his prefectory as a meeting place for the Resistance and bicyling around his parish delivering anti-German leaflets. As for the others, Madeleine Barot, and Madeleine Dreyfus and Georges Garel – who shared a birthday and joked that they were twins – they immediately started planning their next move. It was becoming perilous, as a Protestant or a Catholic, to help Jews; for the Jewish helpers it would soon be lethal. All were now conscious that the days of legitimacy, of working in accordance with Vichy rules, were finally over, and that what lay ahead was an increasingly dangerous time of clandestinity. In this, some of the churches, which had long slumbered amid the general sense of *attentisme* and acquiescence, were to play a critical part.

CHAPTER FOUR

A national disgrace

Between 8 October 1940 and 16 September 1941, Vichy's *Journal Officiel* published 26 laws, 24 decrees, 6 by-laws and one regulation on the Jews. By the spring of 1942, however, no religious authority in France, neither Catholic nor Protestant, had publicly condemned the anti-Semitic legislation nor spoken out against the inhuman treatment of the Jews. They had watched men, women and children rounded up and led away to internment camps, where they had fallen ill and starved, and they had said nothing. The speed of the defeat of France, so it is argued, had so stunned the higher clergy that they had somehow accepted that it was divine punishment for the godlessness and decadence of the Third Republic. Both Protestant and Catholic authorities took the same line; both, initially at least, supported Pétain.

The Catholic Church had been loudest in its praise for the Maréchal's New Order, seeing in its moral crusade a more pious France, in which God would be returned to the classroom and mothers to their babies. For over 150 years, ever since the separation of church and state, the Catholics had been dreaming of rechristianising France. Abortion, according to a widely circulated pamphlet, 'kills the child, kills the mother, kills France'. For the first two years of German occupation, Pétain, perceived as a republican in politics and a humanitarian in war, continued to attract almost universal adoration. Many of France's senior prelates were elderly, and longed to become once more important and influential in French life. Should I 'refuse to support this noble enterprise', asked 81-year-old Cardinal Baudrillart, 'in which Germany is taking the lead?'

In the upsurge of religious fervour that swept France with the German conquest, churches were again packed; crucifixes were hung on school walls. The memory of the impotence and incompetence of the Third Republic became fertile ground in which Vichy could take root. Its moral message, its acceptance of authority, its suppression of agitation and Napoleonic centralism, its rejection of laissez-faire capitalism, all found willing listeners.

This, however, was about to change. The French had been prepared to see non-French-speaking foreigners interned and even blamed for eating too much scarce food. But the spectacle of small children taken from their mothers, then put crying into cattle trucks, was too much. In their monthly bulletins to Vichy, prefects reported strong protests about this 'national disgrace'. Criticising the Jews was acceptable: this degree of bullying and brutality was not. Some of the churches – though not Vichy – paid heed.

Marc Boegner was a tall, balding, distinguished-looking man in his early sixties, with a pince-nez and a floppy, full white moustache. A pastor and the president of the Protestant Reformed Church, he is an interesting and remarkable figure in the history of French efforts to save the Jews, and has only recently received proper recognition. It was Boegner, it later turned out, who had proposed to Père Chaillet the plan to save the children in Vénissieux. He had been to Vichy early in July to remind Laval that the Germans had not as yet demanded the deportation of Jewish children under 16. Laval had told him that Vichy had been given quotas, which they could not meet unless they included children. Could some be saved? Boegner had asked. Not one, replied Laval, 'must remain in France'. Boegner had summoned Madeleine Barot and ordered her to leave at once for Lyons with her team of Cimade workers. His progress from Pétain admirer to outspoken critic of Vichy illustrates the mood of Protestantism in wartime France.

For the whole of the Ancien Régime, the Protestants had been an isolated minority within France. The decades of fighting that followed the Saint-Barthélemy massacres of August 1572 were halted by the Edict of Nantes in 1598, which allowed certain freedoms to 'reformed churches', while confirming Catholicism as the official religion of France. Its revocation in 1685 by Louis

XIV, 'this most Christian king', opened the way to fresh persecution, the destruction of temples – the name they gave to their
churches – and the flight of thousands of Protestants to Holland
and England. By the time they were allowed back, a century later,
with an edict of 'tolerance', fewer than half a million were thought
to have remained in France. The long years in the wilderness
became known as 'le Désert', after the story of the flight of the
Israelites from Egypt.

Dechristianisation during the French Revolution did not spare
the Protestants, who, like the Catholics, saw their priests
imprisoned and their temples destroyed. But with Napoleon's
Concordat of 1801, Catholicism lost its place as the state religion
and the 'reformed and Lutheran churches' were recognised and
granted legal status. From the 1820s, new temples, vast, severe,
their benches in dark wood, free of ornaments or statues, spread,
and with them came bible societies, charitable institutions, schools,
and campaigns against alcoholism, prostitution and pornography.
Austerity of spirit and of behaviour prevailed: no genuflections,
no sacred images, no confession; prayers and Bible readings every
morning and evening; no adultery, no theatres, dancing or luxury.
In their temples, men and women were separated, the sermons
were lengthy, and the psalms were sung. The Protestants played
little part in the revolution of 1830, mistrusting the conservative,
clerical, counter-revolutionary world of Charles X; but they
greeted Louis Philippe, who had spent many years among
Protestants, and married three of his children to Lutherans, with
relief.

By inclination, however, most Protestants were republicans.
They were also Dreyfusards, both because they understood about
persecution and because many of their religious traditions were
close to those of Judaism. By now, they regarded themselves as
a 'lay religion', having long since abolished the cult of the saints,
along with five of the seven sacraments, leaving only baptism and
communion. To be comprehensible to all, the services were held
not in Latin, but in French. The word of God, through the Gospels,
was to be received directly, with no mediation between God and
ordinary men.

The beginning of the twentieth century saw the 'Reveil', a
movement that came from England and Switzerland, and which

dwelt on the corruption of man and the expression of God's word through the scriptures. These revivalists were dynamic evangelists and promoters of good works. 'Orthodox' followers, sharing a more-or-less messianic belief in the coming of a redeemer, soon broke away from the 'liberals', who themselves splintered into various factions, some of whom declared that they did not even believe in the resurrection of Christ.

In 1827 came an attempt at harmony, with a first national synod and the adoption of a 'declaration of faith', and the acceptance of a number of agreed '*grands faits Chrétiens*', to be shared by all. Protestants of all persuasions remained committed philanthropists, promoters of schools and charitable establishments. Catholics complained that they were '*êtres tristes*', sad beings, as opposed to their own happy, light-hearted '*esprit Français*'. Nîmes, the capital of Protestantism, was sometimes referred to as '*la ville des bâillements perpetuels*', the city of perpetual yawns. When Protestants entered a room, said the Catholics, it was as if a block of ice came in with them; and who knew what hidden vices and sedition they harboured.

Socialism being regarded as close to the Gospels, the Christian Socialist movement of the 1880s brought with it ever closer commitment to a fairer society. Bible societies, youth movements, cooperatives and mutual banks were established, inspired by the Sermon on the Mount, St Paul's teachings and even Marx's *Das Kapital*. Though never numerically large, the Christian Socialists had a disproportionately strong influence. By the 1930s, most of them were pacifists, but there were splits here too, between those who saw themselves as conscientious objectors to all wars, and those who tolerated a small amount of violence to achieve a just society. Among the most prominent of these Christian Socialists was André Philip, elected a socialist deputy in the Front Populaire. Philip had been one of the 80 deputies and senators in the National Assembly and the Senate who had voted against Pétain.

By 1938, when Boegner was named president of the Reformed Church in France, bringing together the various reformed churches, the Methodists and the free thinkers, consensus of a kind had settled around a belief in the sovereign authority of the scriptures, and around good works. For all of them, the emphasis was on the individual, on his reading and interpretation of the Bible and his personal relationship with God – which would prove crucial in the last two years of German occupation.

From their pulpits up and down France, pastors proclaimed their personal messages of salvation and enjoined their parishioners to practise their own version of moral behaviour, without strict adherence to a hierarchical church. Some pastors were extremely liberal, others rigidly orthodox, with what was known as 'la haute bourgeoisie Protestante' inclined somewhat to the right. André Philip belonged to this high-minded, intellectual and prosperous group. Cimade, working first with the refugees from Alsace-Lorraine, and then in the internment camps, was a natural expression of the liberal branch of Protestantism, and it was very conscious, from the first, of the need to remain faithful to the duties and responsibilities of Christians. As Madeleine Barot and the other young Protestants saw it, the persecution of the Jews was not unlike the revocation of the Edict of Nantes in the seventeenth century, and racism was nothing other than a denial of the spiritual faith of France, to be fought by non-violent means.

Much of theological underpinning of this spirit lay in what became known as 'les thèses de Pomeyrol', so called after a gathering of Protestant intellectuals at Saint-Etienne-du-Gres in the Bouche-du-Rhône in September 1941. To it came Madeleine Barot and Suzanne de Dietrich from Cimade, and also Pastor Visser't Hooft, the Dutch general secretary of the new World Council of Churches in Geneva, who was closely in touch with the Protestant churches in other countries under German occupation. In Germany itself, 24 of the leaders of the Confessing Church, a movement of pastors who followed theologian Karl Barth – who had been expelled from his chair at the university in Bonn for refusing to swear allegiance to Hitler – were already in concentration camps. The thèses dealt with relations between church and state, with respect for civil liberties, and with anti-Semitism and collaboration. Christians, they concluded, owed obedience to the state, but such obedience was ordered by and subordinate to 'absolute obedience to God alone'.

For the group of Protestants and theologians gathered at Pomeyrol, Johan Maarten's book, The Village on the Hill, had become something of a cult since its publication in 1940. It told the story of a young pastor, Stefan Grund, a member of the

Confessing Church, who refused to proclaim that Hitler was the creator of an eternal and indestructible Reich. The day came when a Nazi was elected mayor of his village and succeeded in driving the pastor from his church. Grund took to holding his meetings outside, in the open air, telling his parishioners that the Nazi doctrines were anti-Christ and that true Christianity was disappearing from Germany. One morning, he was arrested by secret servicemen and led away; the villagers, singing psalms, tried, but failed, to save him. It was a message the Protestants of Pomeyrol took to heart.

Before the meeting ended, a resolution was passed: it had become a 'spiritual necessity', it said, to resist 'all idolatrous and totalitarian influence'. The resolution was taken to the Reformed Synod in May – not long before the round-ups of Jews in Paris in July. Though it was increasingly apparent that the time of 'attentisme', waiting and watching, was over, it was also very hard, in the France of Vichy and of occupation, to distinguish between refusal and endurance, saying nothing and saying no. It was only with hindsight that these moral thickets would become clear.

Though it had taken a while for Boegner – a man imbued with respect for the state and its institutions, to whom the moral discipline of the national revolution was appealing – to see his way clearly, his relatively recently published diaries show that he had been much concerned about the fate of the Jews from soon after the arrival of the Germans. His entries in 1940, on 28 and 30 October, 5 and 8 November and 9, 21 and 22 December, reveal that he was already in touch privately with influential contacts in Vichy. At this stage, the Jewish leaders themselves remained confused and largely silent and disbelieving, most of them hoping that by being more French than the French, they could somehow escape notice. Belief either that anti-Semitism was a mistake committed by bureaucrats or that it had been forced on Vichy by the Germans only helped to disguise the reality of what was taking place.

In March 1941, Boegner wrote a letter to the Chief Rabbi, Isaïe Schwartz, expressing solidarity between Protestants and Jews based on their shared reading of the 'Old Testament, in which Jesus of

Nazareth nourished his soul and his thinking'. He sent a second letter to Admiral Darlan, vice president of the Council at Vichy. To both he explained that while there had indeed been a problem in letting so many foreigners into France and granting them naturalisation so quickly, this should not be allowed to detract from 'respect for the individual' nor from justice, of which France had 'never ceased to be a champion'. In his letter to Darlan, Boegner went further. The Jews, he said, were facing 'cruel challenges and poignant injustices'. The internment camps were 'a disgrace'. Later, his colleagues likened his protest to that of Zola, in 'J'accuse', at the time of Dreyfus. It was not much, but it was something, even if it went largely unheard.

Shortly before the events of Vénissieux, Boegner wrote to Pétain to say that the way that the French were handing foreign Jews over to the Germans was disgusting the 'hardiest of people' and reducing witnesses to tears. In his diary he noted bleakly a recent exchange with Laval over the Jews. 'Will you embark on manhunts?' he had asked. To which Laval had replied: 'We will search for them everywhere that they are hidden.'

The Catholics, meanwhile, had pursued a separate path. Unlike the Protestants, their church was structured, hierarchical and authoritarian. Catholicism was regarded as a moral and natural order to which the Church held the key; good French Catholics were raised with the idea that the first virtue of a Christian was obedience, and that legitimate authority lay with the Pope and Rome. Since for many Catholics Jews were perceived as the killers of Christ, anti-Semitism often lay just below the surface, all the more so since the Pope had been at best ambivalent about the deportations, referring to the Statut des Juifs as only 'unfortunate'. National unity, not politics, Catholics were told, was the way to face the war; any suggestion of independence or criticism smacked of Protestantism. The Assembly of Cardinals and Archbishops in July 1941 had ended with a solemn declaration that France should display 'sincere and total loyalty towards the established power'. Monseigneur DuBois de la Villeravel, Archbishop of Aix-en-France, had gone so far as to criticise Radio Vatican for reminding listeners that the Pontiff had referred to fascism as 'barbarity'. All through 1940 and 1941, and well into the spring of 1942, the Catholic prelates, enjoying their new-found popularity at the heart of Pétain's national revolution, had kept quiet. Their silence did much to lend credence to Pétain's legitimacy.

Not all Catholics, however, remained silent. Individual priests, dotted in parishes around the country, were marshalling their forces. Foremost among them was Père Chaillet, the Jesuit from the rescue of the children at Vénissieux. At the very end of 1941, small grey booklets had begun to circulate clandestinely in Lyons aimed at Christians 'united by defeat'. Under the rubric 'Cahiers du Témoignage Chrétien', they reminded their readers of the moral dangers posed by Nazism. It was the first real spiritual call to resistance. In his short introduction to the first *cahier*, which had the title *France, prends garde de perdre ton âme* – France, take care not to lose your soul – Chaillet wrote that it was important to halt the slow 'asphyxiation of our consciences'. It was up to Christians, he continued, to be in the vanguard of the fight against racism, the cult of the Aryan superman and violence towards the '*Üntermenschen*'. Five thousand copies were printed and were quickly distributed. Further *cahiers* on anti-Semitism, human rights, collaboration and faith, profound, learned and deeply researched essays, written with a real understanding of the forces they were up against, appeared in 1942. Since it was dangerous to print them, stocks of paper were hidden in a belfry in Lyons. What made them so radical was their premise that, for a true Christian, conscience was ultimately more important than obedience.

Prefiguring much of Vatican II, 20 years later, the authors of the *cahiers* suggested that it was essential to include a sense of the spiritual in worldly affairs, rather than clinging to abstract theology, and to rediscover the Jewish roots of Christianity by returning to the words of the prophets. For Chaillet, Nazism was a 'perverse' ideology, and Hitler the negation of 'the spiritual heart of our civilisation'. The *cahiers* were much in demand. From now until the end of the war, Chaillet regarded his role as forcing the French to know and understand what was happening to their country.

And now, at last, in the wake of the round-ups in Paris, and the deportations of Jews from the internment camps of Gurs, Rivesaltes and Récédébou, the Catholic hierarchy stirred. In ones and twos, they spoke out. Not many of the senior prelates joined in, but the noise made by those who did was considerable.

The Archbishop of Toulouse, Mgr Jules-Géraud Saliège, who was elderly, aphasic and partly paralysed but who possessed great clarity of spirit, now decided that the moment had come to take a stand. 'Silences speak,' he declared. 'The silence of death. The silence of dignity . . . Silence which is itself an act.' He had trouble writing, so he dictated 23 lines of a pastoral letter to his secretary in his hoarse, rather shaky voice. His words were plain and simple, but his parishioners were accustomed to his haiku-like episcopal utterances. 'The Jews are men,' he declared, 'the Jews are women.' It should not be permitted to behave towards them as if they were different. 'They are members of the human race. They are our brothers like so many others. A Christian cannot forget this.' Saliège sent his priests and his secretary off on their bicycles to deliver the letter with instructions that his words be read aloud from the pulpit the following Sunday.

The local prefect got wind of the letter – apparently from a priest who deplored Saliège's radical tone – and protested strongly, telling the mayors of his *département* that they were to prevent it being read. With great reluctance, Saliège agreed to temper some of his more critical words. Several priests, hearing about the Prefect's ban, hurried to the archbishopric to ask what they should do. 'Read it out!' shouted Saliège from his bed. On Sunday 23 August, most of his priests obeyed. Those who did not were sharply rebuked. It was not for this that they had been ordained, Saliège told them, ordering them to read the letter out on the following Sunday. It was also published as a tract, causing Vichy to denounce its language as 'incontinent'. When Maurice Sarrault, the editor of the local *Dépêche du Midi*, was instructed by a Vichy official to print a rebuttal, he refused. 'I want to be able to look the Archbishop of Toulouse in the face,' he said.

In nearby Montauban, Mgr Pierre-Marie Théas also went on the attack. Describing 'dislocated' families, men and women treated as if they were an 'evil flock' and dispatched to an unknown destination 'with the likelihood of extreme danger', he announced that, for a Christian, 'all men, Aryan or non Aryan, are brothers, because created by the same God'. The current anti-Semitic legislation, he continued, was an 'insult to human dignity, a violation of the most sacred rights of the person and of the family'. This pastoral letter, too, was read from the pulpit during morning service. A social worker in Montauban, Marie Rose Gineste, typed up many copies, and, deciding that it was too chancy to trust to the post, delivered them herself, covering hundreds of kilometres every day on her bicycle. As she travelled around, she recruited other couriers, who got on to their own bicycles to spread the message.

Next it was the turn of Mgr Delay, Bishop of Marseilles; after him came a broadside from Mgr Gerlier, who had trained as a lawyer before finding his vocation and who declared that it was not with hatred and intolerance that Pétain's national revolution could be built; and then one from the Archbishop of Albi, Mgr Moussaron. By the end of the summer of 1942, 35 Catholic bishops and archbishops had spoken out. Even if not every prelate and priest joined in – and no senior figure at all in the occupied zone – what made these pastoral letters so important was that they were issued by men who had once been strong supporters of Pétain and Vichy. The Jews, long perceived as the problem, were now the victims. Chaillet printed in full in the *cahiers* the pastoral letters of Gerlier, Saliège, Delay and Théas, and Boegner's various contributions. 'We must proclaim to the ignorant and indifferent world,' he wrote, 'our disgust and our indignation.'

While French Catholics were absorbing this sudden change of direction, Boegner went public with a declaration of his own. On the first Sunday in September 1942, 4,000 Protestants gathered outside a farmhouse not far from Nîmes, shrine to the early Protestant martyrs, for the yearly Assemblée du Désert. It was here that not long before, André Chansom, the celebrated Protestant essayist and archivist, had spoken of the need always to resist, to remain 'faithful to oneself, even in defeat, even in chains'. Standing under the chestnut trees, they listened to Boegner take as the theme for his sermon 'Be faithful unto death and I will give you the crown of life' from Revelations; his words included many references to the duties of Christians and Good Samaritans to help the persecuted. There was no longer much point, Boegner declared, in continuing to press Vichy to behave differently. That moment had passed. The question now was quite simple: how could the Jews be saved? Afterwards, he gathered around him the 67 Protestant pastors who had come to hear him speak. He described to them in detail the deportation of the foreign Jews, the police with guns, children torn from their parents, the elderly dragging their cases, and urged them all to do everything they could to save those who remained in France. Later, the pastors would say that this was the moment at which biblical teachings became reality.

Boegner's next step was to return to Laval and Bousquet, to whom he protested strongly about the deportations; then he went on to Geneva and Berne. Here he tried to persuade the Swiss to accept Jews sent by charitable organisations like the OSE and Cimade. A deal, of sorts, was brokered.

For both Catholics and Protestants, the late summer of 1942 was a critical turning point. As Donald Lowrie wrote to his superiors in New York, on 17 September, 'Public resentment appears to be growing. The markets and the queues buzz with horror stories about the deportations and the disgrace thus brought upon France . . . For the first time since the Armistice, deep public feeling has united all the decent elements in France on a question of moral rather than political nature.' The challenge now was how to harness it.

Dr Joseph Weill, creator of the OSE's peripatetic team of doctors and social workers, had always known that there would come a moment when there would be no way to save the Jews from deportation other than by going underground. Even while he and his colleagues on the Nîmes Committee were negotiating with Vichy for improvements to the internment camps, he was preparing for the catastrophe he was certain would soon arrive.

In the wake of what became known as 'la nuit de Vénissieux', as trains with the words 'Colonies de Vacances de Rivesaltes' stencilled in chalk on their sides began bringing Jewish children – some of them babies – to Drancy on the pretext of family reunification; as terrified Jews scattered in panic across the countryside to evade capture, and as Bousquet called on prefects to 'pursue and intensify operations . . . using all police and gendarmes available', Weill acted. As a Jew who had grown up in a family of celebrated rabbis in tsarist Russia, he knew all about anti-Semitism and pogroms; and he had spent the last ten years watching the steady rise of the Nazis.

His first move was to make contact with Georges Garel, the electrical engineer who had helped the OSE at Vénissieux. Garel's real name was Grigori Garfinkel, and he had been born in Poland in 1909. The two men met in a hotel near the Perrache station in Lyons. Weill told Garel that he was looking for a new face, someone without political baggage, unknown to Vichy or to the Germans, to set up a clandestine network to save and hide Jewish children, whether orphans whose parents had already been deported, or those whose parents the OSE hoped to persuade to part with them, on the grounds that they were more likely to be safe. 'Let us save children by dispersing them,' he said. For this, he added, Garel would need a cover, helpers, money, families, false documents and safe houses. Garel, who had been thinking of joining the Resistance, agreed. He made two suggestions: that his new organisation would act as much as possible on its own, and that everyone involved in it would take on an Aryan identity.

For his cover, Garel became a travelling salesman in pottery, concealing documents and money under the cups and saucers in a false bottom to his bag of samples. He called on Mgr Saliège and explained that he needed Catholic families who were willing to take in Jewish children. Saliège gave him a letter of introduction to his most trusted priests, in which he referred to Garel as of 'good and certain faith'. This opened many doors. After this, Garel went to Montauban, to see Mgr Théas, who also promised help. Money would come from the JDC, brought into France from Switzerland and Portugal. Helpers were to be found among the many Jewish students, and the young social workers who had been gathered into Pétain's national revolution to help preach the message of a 'stable, faithful, fecund, united, educative' family. These young women, some no older than 19 or 20, remained in their official jobs while helping Garel on the side. It was one of the many anomalies of the occupation that, even as Jews were being rounded up and deported, others were continuing to work, and not all of them bothered to change their names.

The Circuit Garel was born. It would operate in the unoccupied zone, on the model of the Resistance, with small cells unknown to each other, and Andrée Salomon, chief inspector of the OSE's children's homes, would be in charge of recruitment and planning. Salomon immediately set about vetting helpers to screen out those who might be recognised as Jewish by their appearance or accent. Within the OSE, the Aryans were soon known as '*les purs*'; those who were Jewish but looked Aryan as '*les synthétiques*'. Garel, said Lily Tager, was a born organiser. She had worked at his side at Vénissieux and was soon to marry him.

For a while at least, until it all became too dangerous, Circuit A of the OSE – as distinct from Garel's Circuit B – remained above board, operating as one of the Jewish organisations formally affiliated to Vichy under the Third Directorate – health – of the Jewish umbrella union, the UGIF. This gave them the cover of legitimacy. The OSE had an office at 10 Rue Montée des Carmelites in Lyons and a total of some 280 workers, most of them doctors or social workers, scattered around the country. Madeleine Dreyfus, who had been drawing closer to her Jewish roots, was officially a psychologist with the organisation; unofficially, she would become the link with Garel and his circuit. Though her husband Raymond, who travelled around looking for leather for an American company, had taken a false name to disguise his Jewishness, she preferred to remain as Dreyfus. Raymond was constantly afraid that she might be arrested. Their eldest son, Michel, was now eight; the younger, Jacques, was five.

Madeleine now embarked on a double life: on the surface, she helped run the OSE's children's homes, still legitimate and full of Jewish children, in the peculiar and anomalous way in which the Germans allowed them to continue, but more and more of her time was spent clandestinely, making contact with convents, schools and orphanages, asking them whether, when the moment came, they would take in a false 'Dupont'.

But in the summer of 1942, the OSE was not the only organisation galvanised to act. Small acts of resistance were catching alight in every form and shape. Earlier paralysis over whether or not Vichy was indeed the legitimate government, and over fears of communism and the destruction of French morality, was giving place to a growing mistrust of the government. Péguy's celebrated line, '*Je désobéirai si la justice et la vérité l'exigent*' – I will disobey if justice and truth demand it – was much quoted. Both justice and truth seemed clearer now, with Catholics and Protestants turning their churches into places of asylum, monks becoming *passeurs* and helping people across the demarcation line, convents offering staging posts to safety. As Donald Lowrie rightly observed, this new feeling of moral outrage 'gives each one something he can do'.

Cimade, the Protestant group that had been working in the camps, was also turning to clandestine work, and setting up safe houses of its own. Madeleine Barot was already in touch with the Abbé Glasberg about places to put children. What was becoming known as '*la solidarité judéo-chrétienne*' was bringing together people newly angered by Vichy and the Germans, Catholics and Protestants working side by side as never before. Some of the most active were the Jewish scouts, the Eclaireurs Israélites de France, who had already been very helpful in spiriting the children out of Vénissieux. When the Jewish welfare organisations were forced either to close down or to merge under the UGIF, the Jewish scouts had found a home under the Sixth Directorate. Calling themselves the 'Sixième', they would become a crucial arm of Garel's enterprise. The Jewish scouts were sporty, altruistic and energetic, muscular rather than studious, and they were proving themselves skilful as rescuers of adolescents and producers of false documents.

Among the French Jewish authorities, however, there persisted an almost wilful blindness about what was taking place before their eyes. Obedience to Vichy seemed to remain their almost sacred duty. In September, long after Vénissieux and the *rafles* of the southern zone, and many weeks after they had themselves formally protested to Pétain that there was no longer any doubt about the 'fate that awaits the deportees', the Central Consistoire in Paris sent out a directive urging Jews 'not to conceal your Jewish identity . . . Keep informed about the laws and obey them . . . You will thereby be better Jews and better Frenchmen.'

They were making a terrible mistake. By late September 1942, most of the 38,206 Jews deported to Auschwitz on 41 trains since March were dead, among them the children, who, since they were not selected for work, were gassed on arrival. Few people now could still maintain that the 'unknown destinations' of the trains really meant mines, quarries or factories. Since early July, BBC

Radio Londres had been putting out bulletins saying that Jews were being massacred in Poland. Leaflets in Yiddish urged Jews, 'Do not wait passively . . . Hide, above all hide your children.' Flyers handed out on the streets of Paris spoke of the gassing of the weak and the elderly.

Meanwhile, negotiations were going on between Oberg and Laval for the dispatch of 15 trains from Drancy to Auschwitz between 15 and 30 September, at the rate of 1,000 Jews on each. The Germans were asking for 50,000 to be handed over, saying that they had requested 50 trains to be prepared; but Laval, pleading the sudden loud protests by the churches, begged for more time. Delivering Jews, he said, 'isn't quite like delivering identical items of merchandise from a single store'. He promised to 'settle the Jewish question' as soon as he could.

Heinz Rothke, the new head of Jewish Affairs in the Gestapo, remembering Eichmann's fury when one train from France had to be cancelled, and fearing his wrath when he discovered that most of the requested 50 were not going to be needed, proposed that Vichy immediately turn over all Jews naturalised since 1933, or, failing that, simply round up everyone wearing a star in the occupied zone, regardless of whether they were French or foreign born. A major cull of French Jewish families in Paris would net, he estimated, at least 15,000 people. His superiors decided otherwise. Plans for the deportation of French Jews were shelved – for the moment. Economic interests, keeping France quiescent and cooperative, its police vigilant against resisters, seemed a more prudent option, particularly as prefects all over France were reporting in their monthly bulletins that the French were expressing 'pity' for the Jews and 'hostility' towards Vichy. The hunt for Jews would proceed, but at a more measured pace. It gave the forces intent on saving them a small window of time. But it did not for a moment fool them.

On 5 September, Boegner had a meeting in Nîmes with Charles Guillon, a Protestant pastor who was working closely with the World Council of Churches in Geneva. Until very recently, Guillon had been mayor of a small village high in the mountains of central France. Its name was le Chambon-sur-Lignon. Guillon told Boegner that the consensus in Geneva was that although it was no longer possible to save adult Jews in France from deportation, something could still be done for the children, of whom some 5,000 to 8,000 were thought to remain in the unoccupied zone. They were scattered everywhere, from the OSE's children's homes to camps to special centres; some were even hiding in the forests. But there was very little time. Some of the OSE's centres had been emptied and Austrian, Czech, German and Polish adolescents arrested.

The scramble to save the children, and the remaining adults, desperately seeking hiding places among people whose sympathy for them was uncertain had begun.

Part Two
Arriving

CHAPTER FIVE

Walking near the Lord

Whether it was the Protestant Madeleine Barot or the Jewish Madeleine Dreyfus who first thought to bring the children rescued from Vénissieux and the internment camps of Gurs and Rivesaltes up to le Chambon-sur-Lignon and the Plateau Vivarais-Lignon is not clear. But what is certain is that by the time the race to save the hunted Jews began, this ancient stronghold of persecuted Huguenots was already home to many people from all over France wanted by Vichy and the Gestapo. Many but not all who had found refuge here were Jews. The high plateau was remote, inaccessible and defiantly independent; it thought of itself as an island, enclosed by mountains, protected by rivers and escarpments. And it was about to embark on an adventure remarkable for its boldness and intensity.

Le Chambon was only one of half a dozen villages and many hamlets scattered here, 1,000 metres up, across 500 square kilometres in the mountains of the northern Cévennes. Its name was said to come from the Gallic *cambo*, the source of a river. Lying between Le Puy-en-Velay to the west, Saint-Etienne to the north and Valence to the east, the plateau was a place of dense forests and open pastures, surrounded by high volcanic peaks falling away to the Rhône valley. It was renowned as one of the coldest areas of France; its famously long winters lasted from October to late April, when heavy snow, banking up in drifts across the road, would cut it off from the outside world for weeks at a time. Too cold, with sudden swings of temperature, for nearly all fruit trees apart from the occasional cherry, the area was thickly covered in Sylvester pines and fir trees, with a few oaks, larches, birches and chestnut trees, though many of these had been cut down to feed factories, to be replaced by broom, briars and juniper, which did well in the stony soil. It was said that a squirrel could travel all the way from Le Puy to the village of Fay leaping from branch to branch.

In the poor sandy soil grew cabbages, potatoes, turnips, rye, oats and swedes and not much else. However in the autumn, when the valleys and fields vanished under a silent white mist, the tall woods shone red under the rain, and the meadows were strewn with yellow leaves, mushrooms – boletus, chanterelles and cêpes – came up so plentifully in the forests that the villagers collected them in wheelbarrows, along with wild raspberries and blueberries.

Albert Camus, who arrived on the plateau from Algeria in the late summer of 1942, in search of mountain air for the tuberculosis that had infected both his lungs, called it a 'handsome country, a little sombre'. Sitting in the evenings on a stone bench in front of Le Panelier, a family hotel in which his wife Francine had spent the summers of her childhood, Camus listened to the 'flute-like' song of the toads. He thought of the fir trees massing on the crests of the hills as 'an army of savages', waiting as it grew light to rush down into the valley, 'the start of a brief and tragic struggle in which the barbarians of the day will drive off the fragile army of the thoughts of the night'.

Built of basalt and granite blocks to withstand the wind and freezing temperatures, the villages were grey and a little forbidding, the three-, four- and five-storey houses narrow and packed closely together under slate roofs. Only a single tarmac road, the Route Nationale 103, ran through le Chambon, connecting it to Tence and Saint-Agrève. All the way through the 1930s, there was very seldom a car to be seen. There were no tractors and very few harvesters. Everything was done by hand, with scythes, or by animal and horse cart, though only the richer farmers owned horses. The smaller holdings kept goats, chickens, cows and pigs, which they fed on chestnuts.

None of the isolated farmhouses, reached via rough tracks that wound in and out of the forest, had heating, and very few had electric light, though a turbine generator near Saulières lit le Chambon and some of the outlying houses. There were wood-burning stoves in the kitchens, and the warmth from the cows, stabled in adjoining barns. During the short summers, the people farmed; come the late autumn, they retreated indoors, the men to carve clogs and wooden tools, the women to make lace. Though never rich, the farmers of the plateau were well fed, with their own milk and butter and cheese, and enough produce to give to visitors and to sell to those who came up from the valleys in search of supplies.

In 1902, a small-gauge railway had been built to carry the Sylvester pines down from the plateau to the mining basin of Saint-Etienne to be made into supports for the pits. Its single train, known as Le Tortillard, a little toy train zigzagging slowly up the escarpment, snorting and creaking and constantly stopping, reached le Chambon and Saint-Agrève in 1903, opening the plateau to visitors.

Le Tortillard, climbing to the Plateau

The train became useful too in bringing up sickly and malnourished children, after a Protestant pastor called Louis Comte brought his own ailing two-year-old son up one summer and found him miraculously restored by the clean air and nourishing food. Having decided to start an organisation called

L'Œuvre des Enfants de la Montagne, he placed needy children and those abandoned by their parents in the villages and farms of the plateau for the summer months. With these young visitors – 2,398 in the summer of 1910 – came children's homes, hospitals and family *pensions,* in which hygiene, good behaviour and Christianity ran alongside healthy food and exercise.

Comte, an imperious figure with a large nose and a beard that flowed down over his collar, making him look a little like Tolstoy, had no time for sentimental piety, and was soon starting libraries and cooperative bakeries. The farmers received two sous a day for each child, who was expected to spend part of the day working in the fields. Other charitable organisations followed, and by the 1930s, children from all over the south of France, and even North Africa, were coming to spend the summer months in the fresh air and the forests. Daringly, there were even some 'delinquents', who were thought to benefit from the sturdy morality. Prosperity touched the farmers, who turned their barns and outhouses into guest rooms.

In the wake of these small visitors came not only doctors, medical students and social workers to oversee their progress, pedalling around the countryside on bicycles, but tourists. Long before Léon Blum's Front Populaire conceded paid holidays to French workers, causing them for the first time to explore the country's immense and empty landscape, families from Saint-Etienne, Lyons and Le Puy had discovered a taste for this solitary region, with its dry summers and cool winds. Taking the Tortillard, they rented rooms in le Chambon, Saint-Agrève and Fay, which was widely known as Fay-le-Froid on account of its exceptionally exposed and chilly position.

By 1939, le Chambon alone had 9 hotels, 38 *pensions* and 9 children's homes. In summer, the local population of fewer than a thousand people multiplied five and six times. There was much talk in the local Protestant paper, *L'Echo de la Montagne,* of some special spiritual link between religion and the mountain, described as a pure, morally uncontaminated outpost, and much quoting of Luke 6:12, 'Jesus went up into the mountains to pray', though André Gide, who passed through, took against the place, saying that the 'very pine trees seemed to introduce into nature itself a kind of moroseness and Calvinist rigidity'. The tourists took their picnics to the banks of the Lignon, which flowed through le Chambon, and bicycled over the flatter reaches of the plateau. Many came from Switzerland, and commented on how similar it all was to their own meadows and forests. At an international convention of Christian socialists held in a garage in le Chambon in May 1938, where the mayor, Charles Guillon, and the deputy for the 4th *département* of the Rhône, André Philip, warned against the perils of totalitarianism, the area was referred to as '*la petite Suisse*'.

Having picked the blueberries and gone mushrooming, the summer visitors and the children, fatter and rosier for their stay in the mountains, would return to the plains in time for the autumn school term. This had made the plateau, with its now empty rooms, a perfect place of refuge for the Spaniards fleeing Franco when they started arriving in 1937, though they were not always made welcome, the farmers being deeply suspicious of the 'reds', particularly after three small Spanish boys made a feeble attempt to derail a train. The Spaniards, they declared, were not only unhealthy, carriers of infections and venereal diseases, but also immoral, unruly and very likely agents of Moscow. It had taken all the persuasiveness of Guillon to make them accept at least women, children and the elderly, on the grounds that it was unthinkable to refuse hospitality to people seeking asylum.

Charles Guillon is a man often overlooked in the story of the plateau. The son of a Parisian concierge, he had studied architecture before finding his vocation and serving as a chaplain in the First World War. As a Dreyfusard, he voted with the left. Emerging as a driving force behind the Christian Socialist movement, he had been appointed pastor of le Chambon in 1921, at the age of 38, and soon turned what had been a sleepy community from which young people were drifting away to the cities into a centre for Protestant study. Churches in rural communities, as he saw it, should become 'reservoirs of men, of reflection and of spiritual life', and it was up to their pastors to be 'the best of their parishes'.

Travelling constantly to ecumenical conferences, Guillon encouraged everyone he met to visit the plateau, and though he stood down as pastor in 1927, he was seldom absent for long; he

Charles Guillon

became mayor in 1931. By the time the war broke out, he had visited 74 countries and set up Christian Unions on several continents. Profoundly devout, he was made the vice president of a new federation for 'moral action' in the Haute-Loire, and campaigned against alcoholism, brothels and pornographic films, and for more to be done on behalf of neglected children. On the plateau, he was known as 'l'Oncle Charles'. Returning from Munich, where he found himself at the time of Chamberlain's visit, he warned the villagers to prepare themselves. 'The worst,' he said, 'can become reality.' International promises, he added, seldom lasted longer than the 'brilliance of a firework'. Like Dr Weill at the OSE, he had no illusions about either Vichy or the Germans.

Nor, as it happened, did André Philip, another frequent visitor to the plateau. A political economist by training, former member of the Front Populaire, Philip spoke of the armistice as an act of 'dishonour'. Pacifist by inclination, he nonetheless felt that armed struggle against Vichy and the Nazis was preferable to submission, though this struggle had to be tempered by patience. Born into an old Cévenol family, Philip had often brought his wife Mireille and five children to spend summers in le Chambon, where he had joined in local life and given seminars on the

Gospels. Both Philips were ardent Protestants. André said of himself that his faith was 'Calvinist (of a Calvin warmed up by the sun of the Mediterranean)'. He had a neat beard, trimmed along his chin under a small moustache, and heavy dark eyebrows. He smoked a pipe.

The sturdy Protestant mood of the plateau was much promoted by a spirited Swiss evangelist called Marguerite de Felice, who as a child had come under the influence of Louis Comte, and who arrived in le Chambon with her only son, hoping to save him from the TB that had killed her husband. Mme de Felice, widowed at 30, had started a chapter of the Union Chrétienne des Jeunes Filles at Versailles, and was a fervent preacher against the perils of alcohol. On the plateau, she started a farm where the grapes never ripened and the tomatoes never turned red but where her particular strain of apples thrived, then stayed on to open La Pouponnière, to take in five Spanish mothers and their thirteen children. To feed them, she bought enormous vats of olive oil, having observed that her guests liked to dunk their bread in it.

Most of the Spaniards returned home before the outbreak of war in 1939; the villagers were deeply relieved, having feared the loss of their profitable summer visitors if their rooms were occupied. They proved considerably more welcoming towards the Austrians and Germans escaping the Nazis after the Anschluss, particularly as these first refugees from the coming war were people who were able to bring with them decent reserves of money. In the last summer before the war, there were said to be some 12,000 visitors in and around le Chambon.

When Madeleine Barot and Madeleine Dreyfus began their frantic search for homes in which they could hide the wanted children, it was only natural that they would turn to the plateau for help. Their earlier successes in sending up people released from the internment camps under police supervision in 'assigned residences' made them think that infiltrating newcomers among them might pass almost unnoticed. At Les Tavas, a hamlet some four kilometres from le Chambon, there was the Coteau Fleuri, a former hotel with 100 beds rented by Cimade and partly funded by the Swedes, where children released from Gurs, Rivesaltes and Récébédou had been taken in and sent to school, while adults had been given household chores and cut wood for the village. Those who had already spent months in the muddy, barren internment camps were overwhelmed by the carpets of gentians in the fields.

There was Beau Soleil, where Georgette Barraud and her 19-year-old daughter Gabrielle had taken in families sent up by Cimade, mixing up the newcomers with regular French summer visitors to the plateau. Georgette, who had known Charles Guillon from before the war, had been a missionary in Zambia. Both she and her husband, a carpenter and also a missionary in Africa, spoke good English. Somewhat to the anxiety of their neighbours, the Barrauds listened to the banned BBC French service bulletins, keeping their windows wide open and the volume at full blast as M Barraud was extremely deaf.

Georgette Barraud and her boarders

In the middle of le Chambon, not far from the main square, was Tante Soly, a tall, thin house giving directly on to the street, but with a lower level opening at the back on to a terrace and a side street, which enabled people to disappear if necessary. Tante Soly had been opened by Emile Sèches, who was Jewish, and his wife Solange – who gave her name to the *pension* – who was

Catholic. Emile had been working in Saint-Etienne for an insurance office before the war, but when he was demobilised in 1940, the newly introduced Statut des Juifs had prevented him as a Jew from returning to his job. Emile and Solange had a son and two daughters. The younger, Madeleine, had been a sickly baby and had spent some months in one of the healthy children's homes in le Chambon immediately before the war, so that it was to the plateau that Emile turned when he thought to open up a children's home himself. Caught in le Chambon during a heavy snowstorm, he had been directed by the mayor to a house for rent, at a time when renting to a Jew was already a brave thing to do.

Solange, like M Barraud, was very deaf; she did the cooking. Emile, strict, loving, conscientious and an excellent organiser, ran the home and acted as a kind of quartermaster for all the children's *pensions* in the immediate area, driving his little van to collect food from all over the plateau, which he would then scrupulously apportion according to numbers. In the early days at least, most of the homes were run by elderly spinsters, and Emile's firm hand with the adolescent boys was much in demand. What his daughter Madeleine, who was three when the family arrived in le Chambon, remembers is the boys fighting in their dormitory, and the fact that many of the children had no idea where their parents were.

In the spring of 1941, Secours Suisse had occupied its first house on the plateau, La Guespy, rented from Mme de Felice. It was presided over by a slightly glowering, very dark Catalan refugee doctor called Juliette Usach. Juliette had one leg shorter than the other and limped. She wore little round glasses and kept her hair parted in the middle and pulled tightly back into a bun. La Guespy took in adolescents between the ages of 14 and 18, most of them removed by Madeleine Dreyfus and the OSE from Gurs.

Among them were Hanne and Rudy, brought up to the plateau on the little train. At 17, Hanne was considered too old for school, particularly as she spoke very little French. Before she mastered enough to be allowed to finish her education, she worked for a nearby preventorium, where children in danger of TB were sent as a precautionary measure. Thinking obsessively about her mother, Hanne felt constantly picked on by Mlle Usach, who, the girls all agreed, was unnecessarily strict and definitely preferred the boys. By the spring of 1942, La Guespy had 22 resident adolescents from 8 nationalities and 4 different religions. Soon afterwards, a second home, L'Abric, was opened to take 30 children between the ages of 6 and 16. Auguste Bohny, the Swiss teacher who had worked in Rivesaltes for Secours Suisse, arrived in le Chambon to run the two houses. He was a pianist, who played both classical music and jazz, and he soon took over le Chambon's organ. The children loved him.

Collecting the milk from a farm in le Chambon

Hanne was not unhappy. Great pains were taken to isolate the children from the war. There was no radio, no telephone and seldom a newspaper. It gave her, she would say, a sense of peace, though at night she would listen anxiously to some of the other children crying for their mothers, and like them she was often hungry and spent much of her time thinking about food. Simply finding enough for the ever-growing numbers of teenaged children taxed even Emile's resourceful forays into the countryside. After school, the children foraged: for chestnuts, wild berries, mushrooms. They looked covetously at Mme de Felice's apple trees. At Beau

Soleil, Gabrielle was sometimes sent off to distant farmers in search of a pig or a sheep to buy. Hanne, before her mother was deported, kept back her bread, toasted it and sent it to Gurs, together with potatoes she stole from the larder. She had heard that her aunts had been able to leave for Cuba via North Africa. Max was now on a farm run by the Jewish boy scouts; he and Hanne wrote to each other.

At night, the children in La Guespy gathered at one long table for dinner. They took great care never to ask questions about each other's lives, knowing that the truth was likely to be both dangerous and painful. Even those who were not Jewish, like Jean Nallet, a 16-year-old orphan, had recent pasts too agonising to share with the others. Jean's father had died when he was three; his mother had recently succumbed to galloping TB, after which he had been made a ward of state and sent to La Guespy by Mme de Felice. He was, he would say, 'devastated', crushed by the loss of his mother, and the presence of similarly grieving and disorientated children was somehow soothing.

Morning exercises for the children of le Chambon

Until the summer of 1942, these refugee and children's homes on the Plateau Vivarais-Lignon occupied a perfectly legal, if somewhat shadowy, zone, their existence recognised by Vichy, which had found them useful in dealing with the overcrowding in the internment camps. When Jean-Marie Faure, inspector of the camps, visited the plateau and went to see the Coteau Fleuri, L'Abric and La Guespy, his report was admiring. So comforting was this 'peaceful retreat', he noted, that it would be good if similar houses could be arranged for the elderly and the sick, for whom camp life was inappropriate. He praised the exercise and the manual work carried out by the young and adult foreigners alike, saying that it 'eased' their suffering and gave them not only a renewed taste for life, but an altogether better view of France. 'A healthy and hard-working life,' he wrote in his report, 'is being provided for these youngsters.' The arrangement was 'excellent'. Of the fact that a large number of both children and adults were Jews, he surprisingly said nothing at all.

There was, however, something else that made the Plateau Vivarais-Lignon exceptional in France, and it would become crucial in saving the Jews in the months to come.

Among its inhabitants were not only a very high percentage of Protestants, steeped in the embattled faith of the Huguenots, but also a number of Darbyists, followers of a nineteenth-century English preacher, John Darby, sober, austere, very private people sometimes likened to Quakers and the Amish. By the outbreak of war, the plateau had 12 Protestant parishes, and some 9,000 of its 24,000 people were Protestant, in a country in which Protestants counted for less than 10 per cent of the total population. The Darbyists, and an even smaller and more obscure sect, the Ravenists, were said to number about 2,000, making these communities some of the largest in Europe.

The Protestants of the Ardèche and the Cévennes had a long and honourable tradition of defiance. The revocation of the Edict of Nantes in 1685 and Louis XIV's declaration that Protestants were to be considered heretics, schismatics and enemies of the state had driven tens of thousands into the mountains of central France, to join communities of earlier refugees from Catholic repression. Many had settled in the Haut-Vivarais and along the banks of the Lignon. They had brought with them a spirit of resistance, a code of strict morality and a number of underground churches they referred to as Les Eglises de la Montagne. Since if they were caught they were sent to prison and their children taken away, they met stealthily in secret cults, behind vast fortified doors and shuttered windows, where they read the Bible and told each other that the answer to their persecuted lives lay in the Old Testament. They knew the Bible intimately and were familiar with the history of the Jews; they likened themselves to the persecuted people of Israel, wandering in the wilderness, whom they recognised as the chosen people of God. They were willing to die for their faith.

Out of these independent-spirited Huguenots came the Camisards, the word probably taken from the Occitan *camisada* (surprise attack) or *camisa* (the shift that many of them wore). Although they were initially doctrinally identical to the Huguenots, worshipping in the vernacular and modelling every detail of their lives on the scriptures, their experience of persecution led them to develop a more ardent and apocalyptic form of worship, fuelled by ecstatic visions and relying on prophecy to inform their lives in the midst of chaos. In caves and 'rocks and dens in the earth', their children, some as young as three, spoke in tongues. Their symbol was the dove, which nested in the clefts in the rocks, to represent the persecuted church forced to worship in the desert; their heroine was Marie Durand, sister of the executed Camisard leader, Pierre Durand. Marie was locked up in the Tour de Constance at Aigues-Mortes for 38 years and carved '*résister*', resist, on a stone wall in her dungeon. 'Resist' was a word that would resonate down the years.

Through the late seventeenth and early eighteenth centuries, great assemblies of people gathered to hear prophecies, designed to console and to exhort, at secret nocturnal meetings, which could last as long as 12 hours, and in which the Catholics, the forces of the Antichrist, 'the devil and his followers', were branded as persecutors to be confronted in a holy war. Because many of the Camisards were illiterate, the teachings were distilled into images and utterances calling for militancy. Leaders inspired by prophetic trances led ill-clad and poorly armed guerrilla bands, who went into battle against the King's soldiers singing psalms. Lacking the money and contacts to join the Huguenots who had fled to England and Switzerland, they wandered around the villages carrying bibles bound to their backs with leather straps, which left their hands free for weapons. The Cévennes came to be seen as a 'sacred theatre' where these clandestine religions might survive.

After countless Camisards had been slaughtered, their farms torched and those who refused to repent tortured by the Abbé du Chayla and his inquisitorial troops in *dragonnades*, conversions enforced by dragoons of 'missionaries in boots', the few survivors surrendered. Once peace was restored, the Huguenot pastors built their reformed church, harking back to Calvin and not Luther, on a Geneva model, holding their first synod of the 'Désert' in 1715. The years without clergy had produced an independent style of prayer and extensive singing of psalms, such as the Puritans later developed in the New World. Adopting many of Calvin's teachings, the Huguenots took communion up to four times a week, and excluded from their meetings anyone they considered to be spiritually unready. Gambling, blasphemy and obscenity were punished. Social welfare and charity towards fellow believers was encouraged. From the days when the burial of Protestants was forbidden in Christian cemeteries came a tradition of planting a tree for every birth, and another after every death.

It was among this robust and persecuted people, the Huguenots and the Camisards, whose one source of authority and inspiration was the Bible, that the teachings of John Nelson Darby found fertile ground. Darby was the nephew of a soldier who had fought with Nelson at the Battle of the Nile; Nelson was his godfather. The Darbyists, as they would become known, were to play a crucial role in the battle against Vichy for the Jews.

In the early 1800s in Britain, a number of Church of England clergymen, unhappy with the formalities and rituals of the established Church and yearning to return to earlier and simpler times, broke away and flourished in Christian evangelical movements. There were, according to the theologian Thomas Edwards '176 distinct heresies'. Congregationalist, Baptist, Presbyterian and Methodist preachers travelled around the country on horseback, proclaiming a shared belief in a diligent study of the scriptures, a more direct form of worship and the possibility of doing without a pastor or priest to lead the church. When God promised salvation to Christians, they believed, this included the Jews; Palestine was regarded as their second homeland.

One of these preachers was John Darby, a fine-looking man with intense deep-set eyes and a full, wide mouth, the son of a family of Anglo-Irish aristocrats, who, having trained for the priesthood in the Irish Church, broke with it over matters of doctrine. The idea of an ordained clergy and an established Church, with links to the Crown, was, he said, contrary to the scriptures. Irascible and disputatious by nature, Darby joined the new Brethren assembled in Plymouth, who rejected all organisational structure beyond the level of the congregation. Before long these Brethren too fractured into small sects, and Darby emerged as leader of the stricter faction. He was an excellent speaker, fluent in Latin, Hebrew, Greek, French, German and Italian, a prolific writer of poems, hymns and interpretations of the Bible, and he also supervised new translations of the scriptures into English, German and French.

In 1837, Darby went to Switzerland, where the 'Reveil', the religious awakening from a lazy, unthinking faith to a more personal piety based on salvation and repentance, was winning many converts. He travelled on to France and visited the Ardèche and the Haute-Loire, where he preached to enthusiastic gatherings. God, he told them, was a covenant-keeping God, whose honour and integrity were linked to Israel, where Jews should be returned to their own land. In the Book of Revelation the Apocalypse, with its four horsemen, giant locusts and blood raining on the earth, was an unveiling of what was hidden. He found his listeners agreeably 'devoted and zealous' and remarked that the Brethren he encountered were 'well, and walking near the Lord in general'.

Essentially mystical rather than theological, Darby's often obscure and tortuous sermons included prophecies, an emphasis on the utter depravity of the human race, new birth through the word of God and the second coming of the Saviour. True believers, he told them, would be 'raptured' from the earth, rising to meet Christ in the air halfway to heaven, before the onset of the period of 'tribulation', the seven-year rule of the Antichrist. After the Battle of Armageddon would follow the second coming of Christ, when his elected would reign in happiness and prosperity for a thousand years. Much of what Darby preached was not new, but he wove the strands of earlier millenarianism and prophecy into a tightly spun system of his own, supported by Biblical texts, then communicated it to his followers in his endless writings and during his impassioned speaking tours. When he visited the Plateau Vivarais-Lignon in 1849, crowds gathered from all over the region to hear him speak. They took notes and later said that his words would feed their congregations for many months to come. Commenting on this foreign messianic preacher, the local prefect told his superiors that since his sermons were made of 'inoffensive dreams', he could see no threat in them.

The Brethren were, however, prone to schisms and jealousies, particularly in Britain. They disagreed over baptism, over the need for 'godly, elder Brethren', over prophetic events and over the relationship of the assemblies to one another. Protesting against what he called sectarianism and clericalism, Darby split away again. He remained a complex, enigmatic and authoritarian figure, thriving on ceaseless controversy, and he seems to have believed that he personally had been granted unique insight into the scriptures and appointed by God as an emissary to battle the forces of evil. His followers became known as the 'exclusive', as opposed to the 'open', Brethren, and as such, he told them, they would benefit from special blessings.

Of the many splits and schisms that followed, often over questions of discipline, both in Britain and on the plateau, the most important for the Haute-Loire and the Ardèche was that led by the son of a solicitor's clerk from Essex with a sweet and powerful singing voice, piercing eyes, and a large white beard and flowing moustaches. Frederick Edward Raven was 28 when he left the Church of England in 1865, meeting Darby at around this time. In Greenwich, where he took a job as secretary to the Royal Naval College to support his family of nine children – over whom he ruled with great strictness, much emphasis on fresh air and exercise, and a ban on the use of slang – Raven was in due course accused of blasphemy and heresy. He had preached that prayer and meditation, as well as the direct words of the Holy Spirit, were in fact as important as – or even more so than – Bible study, and that not all believers were the equal possessors of eternal life. Throughout the plateau, his followers in turn accused the Darbyists of being 'derogatory to the glory of our Lord Jesus Christ'. Calling themselves 'Ravenists', they set up their own assemblies.

Keeping to themselves and holding to their own interpretations of the word of God, these little communities of Ravenists and Darbyists, who preferred to be known as 'assemblies of Brethren', settled into parallel lives of quiet piety largely unaltered by the advent of war. Centuries of violence and persecution had lent them a mixture of wariness, pride and suffering, and a strong oral tradition as tellers of the stories of their heroic past. They met on Sunday mornings, after the cows had been milked, not to listen to sermons or prayers but to place their souls before God, unmediated by a priest, and again in the afternoon, for Bible studies or Sunday school. Their families were big, with eight or even ten children.

Darbyists in the woods outside le Chambon

Services were held in barns, or people's dining rooms, unadorned, bare of all religious symbol, without altar or cross. Men and women sat separately, the women in hats, with neat, rather severe black or white clothing, and the Eucharist was passed from hand to hand along the rows of chairs. It was the men, never the women, who spontaneously initiated the singing of the psalms or the commentaries on them, and no woman ever spoke. Newcomers, sent from other assemblies, would be carefully vetted before being invited to join in, and if found wanting, they would be excluded, the better to protect the assembly from sin. In the evenings, the silence that marked most Darbyist and Ravenist homes would be broken only by readings from the Bible, the *'parole de Dieu'*, the word of God, kept open always in a prominent place. What Darbyist children would remember as they grew up was the silence, the lack of laughter. These were, as one of them put it, people who were 'morally conscious'.

Since it was only possible to be a true Christian when living a life of faith, the solution was to have as little as possible to do with the ways of the world, which was seen as entirely evil. The heated political disputes of the 1930s had barely touched the plateau. People who drew their codes of behaviour not from the laws of the land but from the teachings of the Bible might welcome Pétain's return to a more moral France, but they would still not expect to associate themselves with its diversions. True Darbyist or Ravenist faith meant no cafés, cinemas, bars, alcohol, dancing, hotels, parties or even church festivals. It also meant being alive to the fate of the Jews, the chosen people, whose salvation was implicit for their own.

For the Catholics and Protestants on the plateau, whose generosity of spirit and courage was about to be tested in precisely the same way, the issue was rather simpler, more to do with conscience and obedience to ecclesiastical authority than inner faith. For all of them, however, whether Catholic, Protestant, Darbyist or Ravenist, their rural, highly literate community, with its economy revolving around the fields and the forests of pine and oak, was an island, marginal but protected by its isolation. It felt, at times, as if it were barely part of France at all. In such remoteness, there was little need to conform to others. Largely untouched either by the Enlightenment, or by the 1848 revolution, or by the Great War, they continued to hand down their religious observances from father to son and during their evening *veillées* kept alive the oral tradition of the Camisards. They all read the Old Testament, with its many references to the rescue of the oppressed, the sharing of bread with the hungry, the taking in of the homeless into one's house. As the war now swept through France, there was probably no single person on the plateau who had not heard the parable of the Good Samaritan a hundred times, or the words from Deuteronomy, 'I command you [to protect the refugee] lest innocent blood be shed.'

If the Protestants regarded themselves as rather more prosperous than the Catholics, their children more literate and their farms cleaner, there was very little animosity between them. The Catholics, it was said, voted more to the right, the Protestants more to the left, and the Darbyists seldom voted at all. None of them had much time for Pétain, Vichy or the Germans. The words of two local pastors, Jean Perret and Roger Casalis, in the late 1920s were applicable to them all. If any one of them were really tested, they had remarked, they would surely 'once again find, under other forms, the heroism of their fathers'.

CHAPTER SIX

A pure spirit

It was perhaps not all that surprising, given the defiant nature of the plateau, that when the incumbent Protestant pastor of le Chambon, Roger Casalis, decided to retire in 1934, his post should have been offered to a controversial pacifist, a man of uncompromising and outspoken views called André Trocmé. For the Protestant Church, pacifism and conscientious objection were not acceptable views. But the parish council of le Chambon had taken to this ardent preacher and his Italian wife Magda and bypassed the authorities by offering him a year's contract, providing he agreed not to proselytise. Of all the figures involved with the Plateau Vivarais-Lignon during the war, the Trocmés are among the most intriguing. That they later became legends, largely on account of Trocmé's own memoirs, thereby somehow losing their very defined personalities, should not obscure the fact that they were also complicated, overbearing and strong. They were both more and less important to the story than people would choose to believe; but they were not saints.

André Trocmé came from Saint-Quentin, near the Belgian border. His French Huguenot father owned a successful lace and textile business; 56 when André was born, he was vigorous, grey-haired and authoritarian and ruled over his household and 10 children, from his two marriages, with inflexibility and meticulous adherence to tradition. Family reunions were more like conventions than parties. 'If you always do your duty,' he told his children, 'then you will never make a mistake.' André's mother, a reserved German woman who wore a pince-nez and her hair in a tight chignon, was killed in a car accident when he was 10. His father, who was an irascible driver, had given chase to a smaller car; when the left wheel of their own car hit a pile of loose rocks, she was thrown out on to the road. All his life André would be haunted by the memory of his mother lying there covered in dust, blood pouring from her mouth. 'I understood then,' he wrote many years later, 'that there are some merciless things against which one cannot fight, decisive moments that no one, not even God, can undo.'

His father resumed his life as if the accident had never taken place. His elder sister, who took over the running of the house, was severe and cold; the atmosphere of piety and duty was so pervasive that it left little room for love or tenderness. As a boy, André thought of himself as timorous, impressionable and proud. He shared his bedroom with an older brother, a studious, humourless boy 'whom I never got to know'. The Trocmés read the Bible; they did not drink, smoke or dance. It was not, as André observed, 'a cheerful house'.

Saint-Quentin lay 20 kilometres from the battlefield of the Somme, and during the Great War the 13-year-old André saw wounded soldiers, heavily bandaged, struggling through the streets of the town. He watched the trains carrying corpses to the crematorium to the south. His father, briefly, was used as a human shield when French snipers began to shoot from the rooftops. André became intensely aware of the notions of identity and loyalty, his mother's German relations serving on one side, his French half-brothers on the other. His pacifism was born when a young soldier billeted on the family talked to him about non-violence; when the boy was subsequently killed, he took up his cause.

André's first break from the 'monotonous, disciplined, tamed and smothered life' of his family came when he attended a meeting of young Christian Socialists and heard people talking warmly and openly to each other about evangelism and poverty. More understanding came when Saint-Quentin was evacuated and he experienced for himself life as a refugee. It gave him a sense of what it meant to be poor, and he was struck by finding that the poorest were sometimes the most generous. Already what he most deplored was stupidity and 'boundless naivety', which were, as he saw it, far greater sins than wickedness.

Through a Christian youth movement, André became a theology

student in Paris, but in spite of his very public pacifism, he insisted on doing his military service, saying that he needed to experience what others went through. There was an incident when he might have been court-martialled for refusing to carry a gun on patrol, but nothing came of it. Not a particularly brilliant scholar, he was turned down on graduation for the best jobs, but accepted a one-year bursary offered to young French theologians by the Union Theological Seminary in New York. He was a tall, serious-looking, almost heavy young man, with bright blue eyes, and he wore a pince-nez. He was already thinking of his future in the Church as that of a friend and brother to his flock, and his temple as a communal, egalitarian place.

To pay his way in New York, André became tutor to John D. Rockefeller Jr's children. It was at the international student house that he met Magda Grilli, whose family was made up of Russian Decembrists and Italian aristocrats; both of her grandfathers had spent time in prison for their political views. Magda had lost her own mother at three weeks and grown up with a stepmother she did not get on with. A trained teacher, she had come to New York to attend a course on social work and to escape the confines of her unemancipated family. Like André, she spoke several languages fluently, though her French was coloured by a strong Italian accent. It made her deep, almost staccato voice somewhat raucous. By 1926, they were married.

Somewhat similar in temperament, both impatient, short-tempered, outspoken, highly educated and apparently sure of themselves, their approach to religion was strikingly different. Where André felt a deep religious commitment to orthodoxy, Protestantism and a faith rooted in reality, and agonised over questions of peace, poverty and social service, Magda's years at a convent school had left her imbued with a hotchpotch of Protestant and Catholic rituals and a profound scepticism. In Magda, André would say that he had found someone to shake him out of his 'somewhat sterile and egotistical meditations'. Both saw themselves as rebels. Both were marked by having lost their mothers young. Already they conducted their daily lives at frenetic speed, packing their days with worthy activities. Neither was ever quite what he or she seemed, but in each other they appeared to have found exactly what they needed.

André's first post as pastor was at Maubeuge in northern France, a town of steel mills largely destroyed by the Great War. Many of his parishioners drank heavily. Though conscientious objection remained forbidden to pastors, on the grounds that while Christians should not promote violence, neither should they shrink from resisting evil, if necessary by violent means, he came out strongly in support of those who refused conscription.

During their seven years in the north, Magda gave birth to four children, Nelly, Jean-Pierre, Jacques and Daniel, but by 1932, the smoggy, dust-laden air was taking its toll on them all and they began to look for a healthier parish. The first two that André applied for turned him down. The third, le Chambon, had a more robust attitude towards pacifists and, having listened to him preach and admired his 'overflowing faith', they offered him a one-year contract. A colleague writing about him to a friend observed that Trocmé possessed an openness and a courage 'unusual, alas, in our churches', and that he had rarely met a Christian 'so little frightened of the consequences of clarity'.

The Trocmé family, arriving in le Chambon

The Trocmés, bringing with them an au pair girl, arrived on the plateau at the end of September 1934. It was raining, and the first snows had already fallen. On the journey Jacques developed acute earache and he and his mother stopped in Saint-Etienne to see a doctor. The family's first glimpse of the fifteenth-century presbytery, once the winter home of the local counts of Fay, was profoundly depressing. A three-storey house built like a tower of three-foot-square blocks of dark grey granite, with a *porte-cochère* through which Louis Comte, bringing his sick son to le Chambon in the 1890s, had driven his horse and cart, it was filthy and full of junk deposited there by neighbours. One wall of the kitchen was carved directly out of the hill. It was damp and very cold, and little light was filtered by the narrow windows. Having asked that the rotting floorboards be mended, and a bath and central heating installed, the Trocmés lodged in one of the many village *pensions* while the work was carried out. They had always imagined themselves in a busy town; the sense of isolation and silence was alarming. Trocmé noted that his new parishioners were as grey as their granite farmhouses, and that they talked incessantly about death.

Determined to make the best of the unpromising house, Magda sewed white tulle curtains for the wood-panelled dining room, which doubled as a waiting room for André's parishioners, planted geraniums in boxes and bought a piano, a clock and a new dresser, which she covered in brightly coloured plates. André's study was gloomy and dark, but he papered it with reproductions of Michelangelo's *Creation*. Though rats scampered behind the wainscotting, Magda noted with pleasure that when the sun came out, the forbidding grey granite sparkled. Below the house were four layers of terraced garden, leading to the Lignon below, down which water rushed torrentially with the autumn rain. It was a measure of the remoteness and simplicity of the village that a town crier still beat his drum on the street corner and called out the news.

The Trocmés were a good-looking family. Magda took pains to see that the children were well dressed, embroidering their clothes herself. Seven-year-old Nelly wore her curly fair hair in tidy pigtails and learnt to ride her bicycle round and round the fountain in the square; the boys had belted pinafores, buttoned at the neck and shoulders, which made them look like Russian children. What Nelly would remember later was the drabness, the silence of le Chambon, after the noise and bustle of the north. When the snows came, and drifts banked up around the presbytery, the children left the house by climbing through the windows in their clogs and heavy wool Loden coats, which smelt strongly of dog once they got wet. The clogs had nails in the soles, to prevent them slipping. Jean-Pierre, blue-eyed and clever, was a gifted pianist and loved poetry; Jacques was delicate and easily frightened, but also lively and rumbustious; Daniel, with his mass of tangled straw-like hair and round face, was fearless. The Trocmés acquired a spaniel and called it Fido.

Appalled at first by the dinginess and cultural desolation of their new surroundings, the family slowly adapted. Both André and Magda threw themselves into parish life, paid visits to all the villagers, started classes and Bible groups. Nelly went to the village school and learnt to make lace and to crochet. Magda collected pine cones and devised a stove for the hall, fed by packed sawdust from a nearby mill, with metal pipes that snaked around the room and carried some heat to the arctic bedrooms. They were not unhappy; in fact, Magda would later say that this was the start of the happiest period of their lives.

Trocmé bought a small Citroën C4 and took the children on picnics; he built two ponds under a plane tree in the garden, calling the smaller the Mediterranean and the larger the ocean, on which they sailed paper boats. He played the accordion and had a gift for story-telling, illustrating his letters and messages to his children with charming little drawings. He carved small wooden toys. Though often serious and preoccupied, writing that 'those who seek their own happiness before all else risk to find themselves disappointed, discouraged and the unhappiest people on earth', he could be light-hearted and teasing. Magda made people laugh with her funny faces and caricatures. They had an extra table made for the dining room to accommodate the many visitors to the presbytery. And when the deep snows came, the children tobogganed, starting high above the village, crossing the railway line, winding through the streets – trying to avoid hurtling through the butcher's window – then round a corner, past the temple and over the bridge to the other side of the Lignon. The farmers who walked their cows through the village complained that the toboggans made the ice slippery.

Among his parishioners, who had started out 'lukewarm' in their attendance at the temple, there was growing admiration for André's forceful sermons, with his flights of mysticism and prophecy, his powerful voice carrying loudly from his raised pulpit across the large, austere wood-panelled temple, though some were in awe of his occasional outbursts of temper. As a preacher, he prepared his words with care and spoke in paragraphs. For his part, he was coming to regard his congregation with warmth, having discovered that behind their severe expressions and white lace caps lay considerable intelligence. The Chambonnais were even growing accustomed to Magda's exuberant and unconventional ways, though they had trouble adjusting to the fact that she refused to wear a hat in church and insisted, on warm days, on swimming in the Lignon, dressed only in an enormous enveloping towelling robe. No pastor's wife had ever done such a thing. She was quick to quarrel, they noted, but as quick to make friends again.

For all Magda's sewing and scrimping, the Trocmés were always short of money. They took in lodgers, who squashed into the little dining room and became part of the noisy, endlessly busy family. One day, a very good-looking young man appeared at the door of the presbytery, saying that he was a doctor, recently returned from missionary medical work in Cameroon, and that he was looking for a practice on the plateau. The elderly and loquacious local doctor, Dr Riou, sometimes overwhelmed by the numbers of people who came in the summer months, generously agreed to share the work, and Dr Le Forestier returned with his belongings to lodge with the Trocmés.

From the first, ever willing to visit his patients in their most distant farmhouses whatever the weather, he was much liked. He was high-spirited and somewhat wild, making up songs and rhymes, always laughing, charming the children with his practical jokes and stories. After studying at the prestigious Ecole des Roches in Normandy, where he became a keen scout just at the time that Baden-Powell visited France, he had gone through medical school, then his army medical service, before working with Albert Schweitzer in Cameroon. Having fallen out with Schweitzer after the leprosy doctor punished one of his patients for stealing a chicken by locking him up in a small bamboo hut, Le Forestier had set up on his own. He dreamed of curing leprosy, syphilis and malaria, and wrote that 'suffering, like love, cannot be understood by the brain. It is felt.' Invalided back to France with bilharzia, he had opened a practice in Grenoble. But he was a restless figure, in search of somewhere congenial to his Protestant faith, and his wanderings had brought him to the plateau, where he sensed the air would restore him to health.

In the evenings, Le Forestier made the Trocmé children laugh with his antics, pretending to be a monkey and clambering on to the dining room table, chattering loudly. He brought rabbits from his laboratory, having used them for pregnancy tests, and they went into the communal pot. Having offered to brighten up the gloomy rooms of the presbytery, he painted the main room yellow and cream, with a rust-coloured trim. His exuberance charmed the villagers too; he became president of a *comité des fêtes*, organised fancy dress parties and amateur theatricals. The Trocmés thought of him as another son.

Not very long after Le Forestier's arrival, the flow of summer visitors brought with it a strikingly pretty young woman. Danielle was 17, the granddaughter of a Darbyist who owned a grocery store in Cannes, and she had accompanied the two daughters of a corset-maker up to the plateau for their holidays. She and Le Forestier became engaged. Magda was a witness at the wedding in Cannes, after which the party was serenaded on the beach by a group of Dutch singers while they picnicked by a fire of driftwood. It was an occasion touched by sorrow. Shortly before the wedding, two of Le Forestier's three sisters, all of them doctors, had been killed in a car crash; his mother, who had been driving, survived. Danielle did not wear a wedding dress.

Dr Le Forestier with Danielle, at the time of their wedding

Le Forestier returned from his honeymoon in Cameroon bringing with him a young assistant, Tagny, who planned to attend a forthcoming reunion of Christians in Amsterdam, and a monkey called Fifi. Leaping around the Trocmés' house, swinging from curtain to curtain, Fifi became extremely jealous of the children. When the cold weather came, Magda made him a coat out of an old sock. But soon after Le Forestier and Danielle moved to a flat above the chemist's near the main square, Fifi died. Le Forestier always maintained that the chemist's wife, maddened by the monkey's cavortings and constant thefts, poisoned him. Later they moved into a rented house, the Côte de Molle, where he opened his surgery. Intensely gregarious, Le Forestier was soon on friendly terms with most of the village. But he was always on the move, thinking up outings on the spur of the moment. 'Pack,' he would say to Danielle, coming into the house. 'Pack, we're going.' Le Forestier burnt, observed a friend, 'with inner fire'.

At Christmas, there was a huge gathering at the presbytery. All the children played an instrument. Everyone sang. In the temple, an immense tree was carried inside and covered with decorations, candles were lit, and every child was given a bag with an orange, some dates, nuts, raisins and a small present. Pacing backwards and forwards, André told a story written specially for the occasion. Roger Darcissac, president of the parish council and leader of a male choir, showed slides with a magic lantern.

Just the same, by their third winter in le Chambon, life for the cosmopolitan Trocmés had threatened to become exceedingly dull. The Protestant faith of André's parishioners seemed somehow stuck in the rhythm of the seasons and a constant gloomy acceptance of the harshness of life and the approach of death. The few young people hung around the streets with little to do but drink. It was now that an idea that had long been brewing in the mind of Charles Guillon, the mayor, began to take shape. Guillon's plans for a secondary school, 'lay in spirit but Protestant and international in practice', had grown out of discussions with the Trocmés, the de Felices, Le Forestier and André Philip and his wife Mireille, on their regular visits to the plateau. Though there was an excellent primary school run by M and Mme Darcissac – for which the children wore little grey overalls and had wooden desks with inkpots, clustered around a stove – there was no secondary school in le Chambon, which meant that when the children moved up, they had little choice but to travel to Le Puy or Saint-Etienne, or to stay at home. Magda recalled a similar venture that had opened in the Vaudois in Italy.

Trocmé, who dreamt of making the new school pacifist, got in touch with friends and colleagues in international Christian circles. André Philip contacted Jean Zay, Minister for Education at the time. As a private institution, the school would have no need for French government accreditation. For headmaster, they turned to an old acquaintance of Trocmé's from theology college, Edouard Theis, who had also been a tutor for the Rockefeller family. Theis, who had been a missionary in Africa and was a committed pacifist, was a big, broad-shouldered, silent, enigmatic man, who spoke seldom and somewhat ponderously, and who had an American wife from Ohio and seven daughters. Money was raised surprisingly easily. The Eglise Reformée agreed to appoint Theis as a part-time pastor in le Chambon. He possessed, said his friends, 'elephantine determination', and without his obstinacy, his utter lack of all vanity and his total disregard for money, the college might never have come about.

As it was, the Ecole Nouvelle Cévenol opened its doors in September 1937 to some 40 pupils, though the numbers grew rapidly. Some were local children; others had been sent there in the summer for their health and now stayed on. Theis took Greek, Latin and French, Magda Italian. Her students found her handsome, imposing and somewhat regal, and her outbursts of sudden ill temper, followed by equally sudden laughter, could be disconcerting. Since the school was to be co-educational, a Mlle Pont was made joint director. From the first, it welcomed the broadest spectrum of views, but all committed to Christianity. Theis insisted that classes were to be free of nationalism.

The staff of Ecole Nouvelle Cévenol

There was another important and unexpected recruit to the school, a handsome, round-faced upper-class Englishwoman of the practical, self-reliant old school called Gladys Maber. She came from Portsmouth and believed that she, and everyone else, could do anything. An ardent Christian Socialist, she had been at university in France and Switzerland, and had taken an MA at Manchester

University, then a doctorate in Lyons, before doing social work in the Haute-Savoie. Having inherited a fortune at the age of 21, she had given most of it away. In the summer of 1939, Miss Maber took a party of children up to le Chambon. She decided to stay on, joined the staff and began to teach English; she was, by now, bilingual. She was soon joined by a friend, Jeanne Carillat, who had been widowed and was bringing up two small boys on her own, and the two women decided to open a *pension* for boys attending the school. They took over a tall, thin house on the edge of le Chambon and called it Les Sorbières.

Miss Maber (foreground) and Jeanne Carillat, on the Plateau

Miss Maber was humorous, imaginative and profoundly moral, and was soon friends with the Le Forestiers, offering to serve as nurse during operations. She was also an imaginatively terrible driver, infiltrating her small car between lorries on the bends of the mountain roads, but making her passengers laugh with songs and funny stories. She had been romantically attached to an aristocratic Frenchman who had been a planter in New Caledonia, but he had contracted leprosy and was not expected to live long.

In 1939, with war clearly approaching, Trocmé offered his resignation to the church council, saying that in the event of being called up, he would have to refuse to bear arms, and therefore did not want to embroil them in controversy. (Somewhat surprisingly, he also volunteered to go to Germany to kill Hitler.)

Boegner, who was known to regard Trocmé as potentially 'difficult and dangerous', agreed that he had done the right thing. Once again, however, the Protestants of le Chambon thought otherwise. They refused his offer. Personally, Trocmé worried ceaselessly about the German side of his family; his six aunts were all married to pastors in the Confessing Church. Throughout the first winter of the war, he and Theis and Darcissac, all three of them pacifists, all obdurate in their faith, fretted. They were upset when a Mme Bertrand, who had started a pack of cub scouts in the village, put it about that they were not 'patriotic'. One day, Trocmé found the words 'Go back to Italy with your Italian wife, Hun, and get the hell out of here' scrawled on his wall.

Theis, as the father of eight children – an eighth daughter had just been born – was exempt from military service, and in due course Trocmé was informed that he too, as the father of four, would not be called up. It left both men feeling relieved but confused. They offered their services to the American Red Cross, but were told that it was open only to volunteers from neutral countries. Trocmé had said he would be happy to serve as a 'chauffeur' in order to help civilians 'in the war zone and in a dangerous place, naturally at no salary'.

In May 1940, as the Germans were beginning their push into France, Trocmé wrote to Burners Chalmer of the American Friends Committee, who was also a member of the Nîmes group, to ask whether there was anything that he might do in the internment camps. The Quakers had been providing relief across Europe during the 1930s, and were as a result on good terms with the Germans. The two men met in Marseilles. Burners Chalmer was struck by Trocmé's 'imaginative, brilliant' talk, but thought that the pastor might be better suited to a more 'informal and non-institutionalised setting'. A report written after his visit noted that he was 'iron-willed, rock-like . . . tough and tender at the same time', dynamic rather than flexible, but also 'dogmatic and authoritarian'; in short, a 'pure spirit'. Out of their conversation came an idea that le Chambon might be a suitable place to take the children from the internment camps, for whom the battle was now under way. Burners Chalmer told Trocmé that money would not be a problem, and that the Quakers would fund them.

Soon after Trocmé's return to the plateau, the Germans occupied France and Pétain signed the armistice. Trocmé and Theis immediately decided to preach, together, a sermon on the war. The duty of Christians, they told a packed congregation on 23 June 1940, the day after Pétain's total capitulation, 'is to use the weapons of the Spirit to resist the violence that will be brought to bear . . . We will resist whenever our adversaries will demand of us obedience contrary to the orders of the Gospel. We will do so without fear, but also without pride and without hate.' Humiliation, they told their listeners, should never be confused with discouragement, nor should freedom ever be renounced. In a letter written at about this time, given to a friend for safe keeping and not found until many years later, hidden in an attic in le Chambon, Trocmé wrote a testament to his own pacifism. Speaking of Christ as a 'non-violent who allowed himself to be crucified by us', he said that his own vocation had been 'imperative'. 'I am not a fanatic,' he wrote. 'I have never had visions. I do not think of myself as better than other people.' He had, he said, no politics and no commitment 'other than to God'. It was God alone who commanded him, and it was because he was a believer that he did not believe in violence.

On the plateau, the winter of 1940–41 was again ferociously hard. Invigorated by his meeting with Burners Chalmer, Trocmé threw himself into his work, gathering his parishioners for fortnightly Bible studies, sometimes led now by the refugees arriving on the mountain. He divided his large parish into 13 *quartiers*, in which designated people conducted discussions, and introduced notions of asylum and refuge. The religious life of the plateau had never been so lively or so intense, with a programme of conferences on capitalism, the USSR and world affairs, André Philip and Le Forestier sharing the teaching. It was at this time, Trocmé would later write, that he thought through exactly what 'non-violent resistance' meant, and how it was an 'itinerary to be explored day by day in communal prayer and obedience to the directives of the Spirit'. Boldly, for many of his parishioners had sons in the army, he continued to preach on the need to love one's enemy.

Two new lodgers had arrived to live at the presbytery. They were both refugees, and both Jewish. One was Berthe Grunhut, a 50-year-old woman from Karlsruhe, who did not know where her children or her husband were. Madame Berthe, as she became known, took over the cooking, but she was an appalling cook and the presbytery soon smelt of burnt potatoes and turnips. The other was a M Cohen, who called himself Colin, a 25-year-old leatherworker from Berlin, whose experience of the Nazis had so aged him that he was almost totally bald, his skin yellow and parched. To give him 'dignity and something to do', Trocmé asked him to make furniture in the attic. Never blind to shortcomings either in himself or in others, he later noted that Cohen's incessant desire to please and sudden outbursts of ill temper made him both egotistical and irritating.

It was on one of these freezing, snowy days that there was a knock on the presbytery door. The story of what followed is one of the many that no one can agree on. Magda opened the door to find a bedraggled, desperate Jewish woman begging for help. She welcomed her in, sat her by the fire and gave her food before going to see the mayor. This is where the story falls apart. The mayor at the time was a man called Benjamin Grand, appointed to replace Charles Guillon, who had been fired for his clear hostility to Vichy; both men, however, were much loved locally, and Guillon, in particular, had long urged the plateau to be generous towards refugees. 'The mayor,' Magda later claimed, sometimes using Guillon's name and sometimes not, was horrified. 'Above all, no Jews,' he apparently told her. She was to turn the woman away, on the grounds that it would endanger the lives of French Jews already in le Chambon. Magda's story goes on: she returned to the presbytery, discovered that the woman's shoes had caught alight on the stove and gave her new ones, then helped her on her way, directing her towards Switzerland. Thus began, noted André Trocmé in the autobiography he wrote after the war, 'the first clandestine work'. And, as it happened, the first of the many variations of historical disagreement.

How true this story is, how correct the details of the mayor's intransigence, who the mayor in question was, has long been lost in conflicting views of history. What is true is that le Chambon, and the plateau generally, spent the first two years of the German occupation of France in relative tranquillity. Small acts of defiance – Amélie, the feisty little churchwarden, refused to ring the bells on a Pétain anniversary; a groups of boys in black tipped a mock coffin with Laval's name on it into the Lignon while chanting the

De Profundis – were carried out, but they were largely overlooked by the Vichy authorities. The boys who had carried the coffin were arrested, held for a few days in a cell in Tence police station, then released with a ticking-off. Jewish families, in ones and twos, arrived in the mountains, escaping the round-ups in the plains, and settled in rented farmhouses or in Mazet, Tence or Saint-Agrève. Jewish children like Hanne and Rudy found homes among accepting villagers. In the college, there was no saluting the flag, and no one sang 'Maréchal, nous voilà!'

The atmosphere on the plateau was bracing, energised by the classes organised by André Philip and Dr Le Forestier, at which everything from capitalism to the works of nineteenth-century French writers was discussed, with many references to the war, the Germans and Vichy, all disguised behind metaphor and classical allusion. The Ecole Nouvelle Cévenol, where the numbers of pupils had doubled and redoubled, now counted among its teachers many distinguished Jewish professors, sacked from their jobs in Paris and the French universities. Trocmé had never been busier, racing from meeting to meeting, holding surgeries for his parishioners in his house, where they would be certain always to find someone ready to advise. There was, as Miss Maber described it, a prevailing spirit of helpfulness. The Protestant temple, just down the road from the main square, had become the focus of village life, and the parishioners, in their black clothes and little white caps, had never attended the service in such numbers or with such enthusiasm, listening intently as Trocmé strode up and down, accusing, menacing, condemning, 'as terrible as an Old Testament prophet', heady stuff for people who had seldom strayed 15 kilometres from the plateau. In *L'Echo de la Montagne*, Trocmé repeated the words he had often used in his sermons: 'You will love the stranger, for you have been strangers in Egypt.' Theis, who had a slight stammer, was considerably less eloquent.

In her farmhouse up the road, the fiery Mme de Felice was busy typing out flyers. 'Do not despair! and above all, do not submit to the Maréchal's politics . . . Nothing is lost yet.' Already, rumours were circulating in Vichy about the presence of a 'nest of opponents' on the Plateau Vivarais-Lignon, and the names of Trocmé, Darcissac, André and Mireille Philip and Le Forestier were all being noted. The Philips had just sent their five children to the US, and André, aware that he was being watched, was preparing to escape to join de Gaulle in London.

Then came the summer of 1942, and on the plateau, as elsewhere all over France, everything changed. The question was whether and how the very nature of its inhabitants – dour, plucky, contemptuous of Vichy – and that of the wild mountain on which they lived could between them save the Jews now arriving by every train.

CHAPTER SEVEN

On Vichy's map

As the Vichy government saw it, their policies were to be both feared and obeyed; but they also wanted to be loved. From the very beginning, money and effort were poured into group activities, patriotic ceremonies and festivals reminiscent of the Jacobin extravaganzas of 1792, and above all into young people. Children were to return to a classical education, to the history of French imperialism and to religious instruction, taught by men and women who had shed their feeble secular republicanism and who, if they had not, or if they turned out to be communists or Freemasons or Jews, likely to prove 'an element of disorder, an inveterate politiciser or incompetent', could speedily be dismissed. To shape young French minds for the national revolution, there was to be no more cramming of arid facts and useless theory. In his classroom in Paris, Jacques Liwerant was only one of hundreds of thousands of schoolchildren all over France who had sung 'Maréchal, nous voilà!' and saluted the flag in weekly 'colour ceremonies'.

In their thousands, too, French children were enrolled as scouts and cubs of every type and hue: religious and lay, Protestant and Catholic, and even, until they were banned, Jewish. On the Plateau Vivarais-Lignon, as in every community in France, children joined packs, bought uniforms, played basketball and volleyball, went camping and celebrated the great outdoors. Miss Maber and Miss Williamson, a second English-speaking teacher at the Ecole Nouvelle Cévenol, were both called on to help. Miss Williamson, who had a snub nose, a high forehead and a long chin, her hair severely pulled back into a bun, was known as '*Castor*', beaver. The packs took the names of birds and animals; there were Wolves, Penguins, Storks.

Léon Blum had done much to encourage sport and fitness, but

Vichy wanted to do more. They wanted young men and women to walk, swim, run, jump, crawl, climb, balance, throw, lift and learn self-defence for at least six hours every week, in order to strengthen their bodies and train their wills. To this end, French teenagers were enrolled in youth movements with leaders, discipline and obedience, to acquire a new virility as opposed to the effeminate ways that had led to the collapse of France. The first of these movements to be formed under Vichy was the Compagnons de France, whose motto was 'Fight to be a Man', and who were organised into medieval units and put into military-style blue uniforms. They were to be the knights of a '*grande renaissance Française*', ready to lead a new France in a Europe essentially German. The emphasis was all on boys.

The second was the Chantiers de la Jeunesse, aimed at boys who would have been conscripted; after manly training in such things as forestry, strenuous sports and solemn ceremonies, there would be campfires and much singing. These activities would also serve to remove the young men from the influence of prostitutes, who, since they were unable to get rid of them altogether, Vichy had decided to keep out of sight in '*maisons closes*'. And there were the '*écoles des cadres*', the schools for leaders, where future priests, teachers and youth workers would learn to 'influence the structure of the French of tomorrow'.

At Uriage, a cavalry officer called Pierre Dunoyer de Segonzac, graduate of Saint-Cyr, took over a chateau that had belonged to Bayard, '*chevalier sans peur et sans reproche*', and combined a spartan diet of manual work and physical training with intensive courses on politics and economics, marching his students in military formation from one class to the next. Many evenings were spent reflecting on the spiritual crisis that had led to the military collapse. As the writer Jean Guéhenno remarked on a trip around France early in 1942, France had become a strange country, full of people in uniform, regimented into groups.

How seriously Vichy and the German occupiers took the behaviour of French students and their teachers, and how inventive these had become in defying them, is reflected in the list of crimes which were reported to be taking place: spitting at Germans, wearing British or American colours, reading *All Quiet on the Western Front*, ringing the doorbell of the German military police without a good reason, jostling German officers, carrying two fishing rods (*deux gaules* – de Gaulle), drawing caricatures of German soldiers, singing revolutionary songs. The list was interminable, the penalties sometimes draconian.

To oversee all these youth ventures, Pétain had appointed a General Secretary for Youth, a former engineer and director of the Renault works at Billancourt called Georges Lamirand. He was a fervent Catholic and a great believer in social paternalism, and for a while he dreamt of marshalling France's children under a 'charter for youth', a notion that soon foundered under general ridicule.

As part of his desire to be loved – though by the summer of 1942 the love was beginning to wear thin – Pétain made frequent trips around the unoccupied zone, processing regally through cheering throngs. In the spring of 1942, his official visit to the Haute-Loire was to have included the Plateau Vivarais-Lignon, but plans changed and he got no further than Le Puy, where he made a special pilgrimage to the shrine of the Black Virgin. As a consolation, the Prefect, Robert Bach, offered a visit by Lamirand instead, thinking it might also serve to win more recruits for the Compagnons de France. Theis and Trocmé were appalled. Their packs of enterprising young Penguins, Wolves and Storks were a far cry from the blue-uniformed Compagnons, with their bugle calls, march-pasts and cult of Pétain. They would have refused, had they not been warned that it would be unwise. Jean Beigbeder, head of the unionist scout movement, arrived from Paris to advise on procedure.

Lamirand visits the Plateau, 1942

The planned visit was fraught with danger. Who would sit next to Lamirand at the official banquet, given that Mme Theis was American, Mme Trocmé Italian, and most of the local dignitaries decidedly unenthusiastic about the Maréchal? Who would preach in the temple, since both pastors had already spoken out against Vichy's treatment of the Jews? How could the unruly cubs and scruffy scouts, let alone the independent-minded students from the Ecole Nouvelle Cévenol, be corralled into a welcoming party? It was decided to keep it all very simple. There would be no flags, no crowds lining the roads, no parade, no sumptuous banquet, no bouquets of flowers, only bunches brought in from the fields and put into jam jars. The lunch would be rustic and modest, and would take place in the YMCA's Camp Jouvet. The service would be taken not by Theis or Trocmé, but by Marcel Jeannet, who was the sober, uncontroversial Swiss pastor at Mazet-Saint-Voy and president of the Consistoire de la Montagne, the grouping of the Protestant parishes on the plateau.

The day was not a success. Lamirand arrived in a motorcade, as planned, on 10 August, just as the round-up of foreign Jews was gathering pace throughout the unoccupied zone. He wore a splendid sparkling blue uniform, with a military cut, and high leather boots. Bach was in his handsome prefectoral suit. If Lamirand was disconcerted by the lack of fanfare, he made little of it, praising the simplicity of the meal for its sensitivity to food shortages, and he behaved with dignity and restraint when Nelly Trocmé, carrying round a tureen of soup, spilt some down the back of his pristine uniform. In the temple, Jeannet reminded the congregation of the duties it owed the state, but observed that the Church should not be asked to disobey God's laws. When Lamirand made a speech ending with a rousing '*Vive le Maréchal!*', he expected loud cheers. There was complete silence.

And then, just as he was leaving, an incident took place. A group of students, led by one of the future theologians at the Ecole Nouvelle Cévenol, presented him with a document and demanded that he read it. In it, the students declared that they had heard all about the round-ups at the Velodrome d'Hiver in Paris, during which children had been wrenched from their mothers' arms. There were among them, the document continued, a number of Jewish students, but at the school no one made any distinction between

Jews and non-Jews, since that would be contrary to the teachings of the Gospel. And if any of the young Jews were threatened with deportation, 'they will disobey these orders, and we will do our best to hide them in our midst'. Whether it was in fact Trocmé who had written the letter, no one knows.

Caught unawares, Lamirand replied that Jewish matters had nothing to do with him, and that the students should take this up with the Prefect. Bach was furious. It was well known that Hitler was finding a new homeland for the Jews in Poland, he said, just as the British had done for the Jews in Palestine. For his part, he went on, he would very shortly be carrying out a census of the plateau's inhabitants and visitors, including the Jews he knew from 'seven informants' to be hiding in the villages. And then, according to an account of the day written later by Miss Maber, Bach added, addressing Trocmé, 'If you are not careful, it's you I will be obliged to deport.'

Robert Bach is an enigmatic figure in this story. Born in 1889, he was a military man, with a distinguished record in the Great War. A Catholic and a career prefect, he came from a family of Alsatian bankers. Legalistic, rigorous, a lover of calm, he was considered by some to be autocratic and arrogant, by others genial and impartial. Having been posted to the League of Nations in Geneva in the 1930s, he was appointed prefect of the Haute-Loire in June 1941, with his headquarters in Le Puy. Under Vichy, with the republican constitution abolished and the parliamentarians on permanent leave, the French prefects had again acquired the kind of power they enjoyed under Napoleon, little emperors in their own *départements*. Some, like Angelo Chiappe, under whom fell the internment camp at Gurs, were wholeheartedly on the side of the Germans. 'With every opportunity,' he had been heard to say, 'I repeat: let us collaborate, collaborate, collaborate.' Others, of whom Bach was one, seemed to admire the discipline of Vichy and enjoy the power, but felt increasingly wary as to where it was leading.

On being appointed, Bach had refused to sack 51 of the 80 mayors whose dismissal had been requested by Vichy on the grounds of their socialist and radical views, saying that they were too competent to remove. He spent his first months in the job listening and gathering reports. Though apparently more concerned about food shortages, crops, the black market and the health of those he had come to govern, he remarked on several occasions on the probity and intelligence of the Protestants in their 'Huguenot stronghold' in the mountains, observing of them that they were an 'elite from an intellectual and moral point of view', interested in liberal and international ideas, and that they clearly held 'very elevated ideals'. He visited the plateau several times, spending his holidays there in the spring of 1941, and, from records in the archives, clearly knew all about André Philip and his 'nest of socialist-Gaullist dissidents'. However, Bach not only gave Secours Suisse permission to open their children's home in le Chambon, but offered money for extra expenses.

Travelling around his *département*, Bach promoted lacework, increased salaries, and did what he could to boost rations and provide extra fuel. When, soon after his appointment, Pastor Marcel Jeannet said to him: 'If, even in France, Jews were to be persecuted, the Protestants would say: No!', Bach was said to have replied: 'M le Pasteur, I am Catholic, and I too would say: No!' Though a Pétainist in 1940, he was no lover of right-wing fanatics, and steered a prudent and calculating path.

What happened next, like so much else on the plateau, is contradictory. Prefects were required by Vichy to file regular reports on their area. As expected, Bach reported on Lamirand's visit to le Chambon. But instead of describing the cool reception of the minister, or the embarrassing final incident, he noted that the Protestant communes of le Chambon and Mazet-Saint-Voy had been particularly enthusiastic, and had proved beyond all doubt that any earlier misgivings about the loyalty of the plateau towards Vichy were misplaced. What was Bach doing? Was this a form of protection?

Fifteen days later, events took a different turn. On Saturday 26 August, some 50 to 60 police and gendarmes from Tence, Maufaucon, Fay and Saint-Agrève wound their way up the steep roads in police trucks and on motorcycles and stopped in front of the Mairie in le Chambon. Trocmé and the mayor were summoned and ordered to hand over the names of all Jews resident in the area, '*pour un contrôle*'. 'I am their pastor,' Trocmé is reported as saying. 'That is to say their shepherd.' He had no idea whether there were any Jews among his parishioners, and had he known he would not tell them. The policeman in charge informed him not politely but 'brutally' that he had just 24 hours in which to come up with the names, and that if he failed to obey, he personally would be arrested.

Furthermore, the police officer continued, it was absurd to say that these people belonged to his flock: they were foreigners, suspects and black marketeers. And if Trocmé refused to produce the list, the very least he must do was to advise all the Jews known to be in the area to come forward. As Trocmé wrote many years later in his unpublished autobiography, the police told him: 'All resistance is futile. You don't begin to know the means that we have at our disposal – motorcycles, cars, radios, and we *know* where your protégés are hidden.'

While Trocmé now dispatched scouts to warn the hidden Jews, the hapless acting mayor, Grand, a figure previously made the villain of Magda's story, apparently appeared and begged him, 'trembling', to capitulate, saying that he himself had been threatened with arrest. 'Me too,' replied Trocmé, according to his memoirs. 'But one must sometimes say no in public.' Next morning, the temple was packed to overflowing. Theis and Trocmé read out a prepared statement in which they invited their parishioners to 'obey God rather than man'. In the meantime, the hastily convened municipal council had held an emergency session in the presence of the policemen, who stood around holding their guns, after which an 'appeal' had been issued, 'firmly' urging the Jewish refugees to make their way to the Mairie to be counted. A 'sibylline and characteristic utterance', Trocmé noted sternly, many years later. But was this too just a smoke screen?

Once again, what actually took place is mysterious. In the departmental records at Le Puy are filed two reports written by the gendarmerie of Tence and Fay-le-Froid. Though orders for the visit to the plateau and the round-up of the Jews were only issued to the local police by the prefecture in Le Puy on 26 August, on the evening of the 24th – that is to say, 48 hours before the police descended on the plateau – moves were already afoot to conceal the Jews. Where the warnings had come from, whether, as would later be claimed, Bach had telephoned Trocmé, no one has ever quite discovered.

About what happened next there are no disagreements. When no list of Jews was forthcoming, the police, who had brought a list of their own with 72 names on it, began to search the village.

They checked documents, opened cupboards, combed through cellars and attics, banged on walls to see if they contained false panels. They found no one. Next morning at dawn, they set out to explore the surrounding villages and the countryside, and there was much mirth when a police lieutenant fell into a hidden cesspit.

One of their first visits was to the Coteau Fleuri, the house not far from le Chambon to which Madeleine Barot and Cimade had been sending Jews released under house arrest from the internment camps. Marc Donadille, a pastor who had arrived not long before to help the director, Hubert Meyer, was waiting for them. It was still dark when there were shouts and orders to open the door. Donadille went down, calmly greeted the assembled police, who seemed embarrassed by their task, looked at the list of names they had brought with them and led them to the bedrooms. They were empty. Donadille professed astonishment. 'They were here yesterday,' he told the police. 'I can't think where they have gone. But we aren't a concentration camp. Perhaps, hearing of the round-ups, they decided to escape?'

The preceding day, Donadille and Meyer had escorted those of the residents of the Coteau Fleuri who were Jewish into the forests. Some time before, Madeleine Barot had sketched out a plan showing precisely how, in case of sudden danger, people could leave the house through the cellars and out by a concealed back door that led directly into the woods behind. She had heard about the threatened raids and informed Boegner, who in turn had – so it was later said – spoken to Bach.

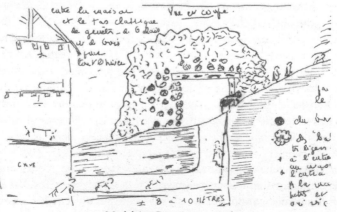

Madeleine Barot's escape plan

There were two bad moments. The first came when a Mme Bormann – who had insisted that, as a relative of prominent Nazis, her Jewishness would be overlooked, and who had therefore refused to join the others in the forest – was ordered out of bed and told to dress and accompany the police. Throwing herself on the floor, her eyes rolling, trembling all over, Mme Bormann apparently suffered an epileptic fit. A doctor was called and pronounced her too dangerously ill to move, but not before Donadille had caught her winking in his direction.

The second near-disaster came when one of the non-Jewish residents whispered to Donadille that a steady drip could be heard in one of the top rooms, coming through the floorboards from the attics, where three of the older Jewish women, paralysed by fear and refusing to leave the Coteau Fleuri, had been concealed in the rafters. They were urinating in terror. A bed was quickly pushed underneath the drips to muffle the sound.

The police remained at the Coteau Fleuri until late morning, then left empty-handed. They narrowly missed bumping into one of the Jewish residents, an elderly and absent-minded professor who had somehow got lost in the woods and bumbled his way back towards the village, where he had encountered a local policeman who kindly directed him home. They now moved on to the homes run by Secours Suisse. Mlle Usach was away, and had left 17-year-old Hanne in charge of La Guespy. Alerted the night before, she took her group of young Jews down to sleep at L'Abric, where Auguste Bohny supervised the younger children. Bohny opened the door to the police, but refused to let them in. His children, he told them, were under the protection of the Swiss government, and there would be a nasty international incident unless the gendarmes were able to produce clear written orders from their superiors. By the time they returned with signed documents from Le Puy, the children had vanished. Hanne, helped by the older teenagers, had taken them off into the forests, where they spent the day picking blueberries and wild raspberries.

As darkness fell, the children were collected by the scouts and moved to more remote farmhouses, where they were hidden in attics or behind wood piles, only emerging after nightfall while the police remained on the plateau. Though the farm dogs, trained to bark at strangers, usually gave ample warning, there was a day when Hanne and another girl only had time to get into a cupboard when the police arrived. Hidden behind clothes, they were terrified that their feet would be seen if the cupboard doors were opened. They listened as the gendarmes asked the farmer if he was absolutely certain that there were no Jews hidden on his property. 'Jews?' replied the farmer. 'What do Jews look like? I hear they have big noses.' After drinking glasses of red wine, the police left.

Day after day, for three weeks, the villagers listened to the police firing up their cars and motorcycles in the early morning before leaving to scour the countryside for hidden Jews. Donadille and the other pastors, aware that they were being watched, lay low. Threats of imprisonment for two to five years had been issued for anyone harbouring a Jew. By now, someone had mysteriously pinned up a list of names and addresses on a wall in le Chambon, indicating the places that the police intended to visit. There were, the villagers were told, still 51 or 52 'Israélites à ramasser', Jews to be collected. The policemen themselves spent much of their time helpfully in the cafés, talking loudly about where they planned to go next. Encountering a small boy sitting under a tree one day, they called over: 'You there, we haven't seen you.' The boy, bemused, fled; he was not Jewish and did not realise what it was about.

It was only when the police had been roaming the plateau ineffectually for some time that Miss Maber understood the full extent of their reluctance to take part in these round-ups at all. One day she received a visit from a young police lieutenant. He asked her whether she knew if there were any Jews left on the plateau. She asked him why he wished to know. He replied that if she would be willing to sign a piece of paper declaring that there were none, then he thought that the police would be recalled to Le Puy. She signed. Before leaving, the young lieutenant sat down at her piano and played 'God Save the King'. He would come back, he told her, bringing a bottle of champagne, when the British won the war.

After three weeks, only one Jew had been discovered, an Austrian called Paul Steckler. Sitting waiting in the truck that was to take him to Le Puy, Steckler, in tears, was given little presents by the villagers; Jean-Pierre Trocmé came with a precious piece of rationed chocolate. However, he was soon back, his degree of Jewishness deemed too small to merit deportation. Of the Jews on Bach's list, the 26 adults from the Coteau Fleuri (21 German, 3 Polish, 1 Czech and 1 Russian) had all, according to the records in the archives of the Haute-Loire, 'disappeared', as had 16 boys aged between 17 and 23 (10 German, 2 Austrian, 2 Polish, 1 Russian, 1 Lithuanian). These young men should have been found in La Maison des Roches, a home run by another Protestant-backed organisation for students, the Fonds Européen de Secours aux Etudiants, but when the police got there, the house was empty, though there was plenty of evidence that the rooms had recently been occupied. Before leaving, the men made an inventory of what the bedrooms contained: shirts, shoes, ration books, passports, shorts.

After the brigade of police from Yssingeaux picked up traces of the missing Jews from the Coteau Fleuri in a barn in Les Tavas, and the farmer admitted to having given some food to strangers, a number of the Jewish refugees decided to seek safety elsewhere. Though the fate of all of them is not known, there are records for a few.

Kalman Scheizer, who was not apparently on any of the police lists, was picked up some way from the plateau and transferred to the camp at Rivesaltes. From there he was sent to Drancy and joined Convoi 33 for Auschwitz on 12 September. Remarkably, he survived. Another Jew from the area did not. This was 24-year-old Ida Besag, arrested when she opened the door of the presbytery where she was hiding. The policeman outside, evidently wanting to give her a chance to escape, told her that she should pack and that he would return later to collect her. When he went back, she was still there. Ida had come from Gurs, where she had been with her mother and twin sisters. She managed to climb out of the truck taking her to Rivesaltes and escape, but was caught and later sent to Drancy. She too was on Convoi 33, but she did not survive.

Most poignant of all was the story of 32-year-old Selma Schneider and her Russian husband, who in 1933 had fled from the Rhineland to Brussels, where they ran a grocery business. When war broke out, they fled again, this time to Paris. Arrested in November 1939, probably as an enemy alien, Selma spent the next two and a half years in various internment camps, until released under Cimade's negotiations with Vichy and sent to the Coteau Fleuri, where she became the cook for the refugees. Fearing for her life after the *rafle* in August, she and her husband eventually managed to cross the border into Switzerland, where she believed herself to be safe. Despite her name being on a Cimade list of protected people, she was picked up by the police in Geneva, returned to France, and deported to Auschwitz on Convoi 75 in May 1944, one of the last transports for the death camps. In 1946, searches revealed that nothing was known of her fate, nor that of her husband Hermann, nor of her mother, last heard of in the camp at Noé.

Six other Jews lost their nerve after the police visit and tried to get away. They were picked up by the French border guards as they were attempting to cross into Switzerland. Since their names do not appear on any of the deportation lists, nothing is known about what became of them.

Of the 160 Jews sought by Bach throughout his whole *département* of the Haute-Loire in the *rafles* of August 1942, 73 were eventually caught and turned over to the Germans before being deported. However, as the records show, nothing that took place on the plateau was ever straightforward. Soon after this, Bach, his behaviour once again surprising and ambiguous, informed Auguste Bohny that the '8 foreign Jewish children' in his care, including Hanne, 'could return home, without fear of being disturbed again'. He then wrote to the Minister of the Interior in Vichy to say that his police had failed to find any missing Jews, that the whole area, including isolated farmhouses, had been searched, and that the Jews had probably long since fled, since it was far too cold for them to survive for long in the forests. Sergeant Jean Dubrueil from Tence reported that he and his men had paid 625 home visits on the plateau and inspected the papers of 1,350 people. Together with his colleague Silvani, head of the gendarmerie for the Haute-Loire, he suggested that it would be absurd to spend any more money on petrol searching for the Jews. Bach agreed. Dubreuil's zeal in rounding up Jews was described as being '*nul*'. Silvani's name appears in the records of the Commissariat Général aux Questions Juives as 'official protector of the Jews of Le Puy'. All, it seems, were playing a double game.

On the Plateau Vivarais-Lignon, however, the war had come a step closer. For all the complicity of Bach and his men, for all the bravery of the area's inhabitants, as a place of refuge it was now on Vichy's map. It was a map no one would wish to be a part of.

With the police gone, calm of a kind returned to the plateau. The Jewish children left the forests and the isolated farm buildings and came back to their homes and *pensions*; the pastors resumed their parish visits and Bible classes; the farmers once again took up the slow rhythm of their agricultural lives. It was just possible to believe that the sudden eruption of Vichy's police might be a single event, not to be repeated.

More Jews, both French and foreign, began to arrive, having managed to escape the round-ups and terrified of being tracked down in the precarious hiding places they had found. Some of the first were a small group who had been infiltrated among the Protestants on the day of Boegner's address at the Musée du Désert and who, instead of boarding the buses returning the faithful to their towns, travelled on up to the plateau at the end of the day. Their escorts, a band of Jewish scouts from the EIF, had sent word ahead, using one of the many codes adopted by the saving organisations. 'We are sending you *marmites* [pots]. Will you be ready to receive them?'

A pattern had now been established, especially when dealing with children. Several times each month, either Madeleine Dreyfus or Madeleine Barot would collect a group of children of assorted ages from some central point in the unoccupied zone, take them by train to Saint-Etienne, then catch the Tortillard to le Chambon. There they would walk down the hill to the main square, enter the Hôtel May on the corner and sit down in the café. The hotel was owned by Jean and Eugenie May; Jean was a renowned chef from Saint-Etienne; Eugenie ran the hotel and the café, with the help of their adult children. The word would go out that homes were needed for a new batch of refugees. Within minutes, the café door would open, and a farmer would appear. 'I can take two girls,' he would say, or a small boy, or a brother and sister. The children would gather together their few belongings, follow the farmer to the horse and cart tethered in the square, and disappear.

Many arrived very thin, with almost no hair, their skin 'as dry as a snake'.

Sometimes it was hard to find homes for boys over the age of 12; the farmers told Madeleine Dreyfus that they 'talked back'. One day, she was trying to place two teenaged boys. Going from farm to farm, she told her usual story: that these were sickly children from the mining communities who needed feeding up, this being the agreed policy at the OSE, who thought it safer that no one should know they were taking in Jews. No one volunteered to take the two boys. In growing desperation, Madeleine decided to play her last card. Throwing herself on the mercy of an elderly man and his wife, she confessed that the boys were in fact Jewish, that they were brothers whose parents had been deported, and that they themselves were being sought by the Vichy police. 'Of course we'll take them,' the previously reluctant farmer replied irritably. 'Why didn't you say so immediately?' There is another, similar story, much told. A desperate woman appeared at a remote farmhouse asking for help. She explained that she was Jewish. The farmer immediately called out: 'Family! Father! Mother! Come quickly: we have amongst us a representative of the chosen people.'

Two of the children who reached the plateau with Madeleine Dreyfus in the late summer of 1942 were Simon Liwerant and his brother Jacques. Jacques was now two years and four months old; Simon thirteen and a half. He found Madeleine's serenity, her air of calm and composure, infinitely reassuring. The boys were taken in first by Léonie Déléage in the hamlet of Les Tavas, four kilometres from le Chambon. Mme Déléage, who acted as Madeleine's main contact in the area, was an affectionate, large, smiling woman, dressed in black down to her ankles. That first night, she fed the boys well and tucked them warmly into bed. From here, they were taken to a farmer at Digon, eight kilometres away, who was willing to offer them a home as long as Simon took charge of his goats. The farmer and his wife were reserved and remote in their manner, firm but not unfriendly. Jacques cried all the time and wet his bed. When the farmer's wife got angry, Simon took to getting up before dawn to wash the sheets. He begged Jacques to stop.

One day, when the two boys were in the high pastures with the goats, Simon spotted two gendarmes climbing up in their direction. Realising that they had probably been seen, he made no effort to hide. One of the men asked him who he was, and what he and his brother were doing on the plateau. Simon, as arranged, told him that they came from Saint-Etienne, that they had both been ill, and that they had been sent up to benefit from the good air and better food. When the men left, clearly suspicious, he went to see Mme Déléage, who decided to split the two boys up, sending Jacques to her niece Mme Gilbert and Simon to Mme Barraud at the Beau Soleil. The arrangement pleased Simon greatly. He had been longing to go back to school, and was now sent to join Darcissac's classes. He was the youngest in the *pension* and was put to share with another Jewish boy. There were three Barraud daughters, and Gabrielle, the eldest, looked after him, took him tobogganing and mended his trousers when they got torn. Simon had heard nothing more from his mother, and knew only that she had been put on a train to Drancy. He had news of his father, still on the work placement for foreign Jews, and of his sister, safe in Lyons.

But this arrangement did not last either. Mme Barraud's husband began to complain that there were too many children in the house, and that the money they brought in – small sums from the OSE – was not enough to cover their keep. Simon was moved again, this time to a family of Darbyists, M and Mme Bard, whose only daughter had recently died. In exchange for his keep, he was expected to help on the farm and look after the cows and goats. An elderly grandmother lived with them, and on Sundays Simon accompanied the family to the Darbyist meetings. He slept in an alcove off the stables. At five in the morning, before it grew light, he was woken by the farmer and worked with him until 7.30, when he had breakfast and left to walk the four kilometres to school in le Chambon. After dinner at night, the three adults knelt and prayed. They were kind, and always fair, but Simon never saw them make any gesture of affection or tenderness towards each other, or to him. Neither did they mention the war, or the Jews.

Jacques, meanwhile, was not doing well. He continued to cry through the nights and wet his bed. Mme Gilbert, at first sympathetic and understanding, grew irritated, particularly after Jacques started soiling the bed every night as well. After school,

Simon walked to the Gilberts' farm to see his brother. He reasoned with him, begged him, told him again and again that he had to stop. The little boy listened, cried, nodded. The bed-wetting continued. The day came when Mme Gilbert informed Simon that she was not prepared to put up with it any more. Jacques would have to go. What happened next is a scene that would haunt Simon all his life. He told Jacques that he would punish him, hit him hard until he stopped wetting the bed. He did what he had threatened, and Jacques, finally, stopped. But now, when Simon came to visit him, Jacques avoided him. Nothing that Simon did made any difference. Jacques refused to speak to him.

When the autumn term started, the Jewish children hiding on the plateau were mixed in with the villagers and went to school. Rachel Kamienkar, the little Polish girl saved from Vénissieux, had been put into a family in nearby Silhac; closing her mind determinedly to the past, she set about making friends in the local school.

Hanne was being given French lessons with an Austrian girl by one of the teachers at the Ecole Nouvelle Cévenol. She and Rudy continued to live and work at La Guespy, into which more new Jewish children were being crammed, often arriving with nothing but what they stood up in. There was a constant problem with shoes, since leather was scarce and rationed, and most of the children wore clogs.

Two of the new arrivals at La Guespy were Joseph Atlas, come from Gurs with his twin brother. The boys were 16; Joseph was bookish, his twin sporty. They were Polish, and their family, who owned a business selling *objets d'art*, had been driven from Warsaw in the late 1930s by anti-Semitism, only for the boys to encounter it again in a boarding school in Fontainebleau, where Jewish teachers and pupils were regularly mocked with gestures about long noses. At Gurs, where Joseph had watched his mother turn from being tall, blonde and strong to frail and piteous, he had been constantly hungry and wretched; in le Chambon he felt 'fed, protected, safe'. At night over dinner in La Guespy the children talked. Not all were Jewish, which, Rudy felt, seemed to make the place safer, particularly as here no one knew or cared who was Jewish and who was not.

Food was on everyone's mind, and particularly on the minds of the growing boys. By the autumn of 1942, many parts of France were down to 1,100 calories per person per day, with the cities suffering the most. The British blockade had become so stringent that at one point Pétain contemplated appealing to the Pope in an attempt to bring food into France under the Vatican flag. Transport by road was almost at a standstill; due to the dearth of fertilisers and fodder, crops were meagre and more cows were being slaughtered, which meant less milk. Sugar, coffee, rice, soap, meat, milk and potatoes were all rationed. Though the inhabitants of the plateau were somewhat insulated from the general hunger, their diet was monotonous and much reduced, especially since farmers were supposed to deliver punishing quotas of their produce to the Germans.

What made food even scarcer locally was the presence of the weekend '*touristes alimentaires*', the families from the surrounding mining areas who came up to the plateau on their bicycles or by the Tortillard to barter for eggs and chickens and butter, or anything else that the farmers might be prepared to sell. A black market flourished, with local people complaining that the richer refugees, who had managed to escape with money, were pushing prices up. Writing to his brother Robert, Trocmé observed that although they were certainly far better off than people in the cities, his salary no longer covered the food and wood for heating that the family needed. 'Our farmers,' he wrote, 'overwhelmed by these offers [of money] have quite literally lost their heads, which means that we are having to dip heavily into our small capital.' Miss Maber, longing for a more varied diet, gave her fur coat to a farmer's wife, to be paid off in butter.

In the presbytery, Magda dried mushrooms by hanging them on a line across the kitchen, and made blueberries into tarts and jam. During her midday break from teaching Italian, she bicycled around the countryside to see what else she could find. Though Trocmé continued to refuse to allow her to offer the farmers wine coupons in exchange for food, saying that it only promoted alcoholism, she took with her their cigarette coupons and occasionally came back with supplies of butter and cheese. At Tante Soly, Emile Sèches was struggling to find enough provisions for the ever-growing number of children, while at L'Abric, August

Bohny was constantly conscious of the hunger of his 75 small charges. Foraging had become part of daily life. Frogs, caught in the fields, were a necessary delicacy.

Nor was it only food that was lacking. Few of the children arrived with clothes to grow into. As they became taller, clothes were handed down from child to child, trousers and shirts and sweaters increasingly bleached and threadbare as time passed. Hanne, who could sew, spent hours patching and mending. In Faïdoli, a third house opened by Secours Suisse, Bohny divided the children into four teams – lions, tigers, eagles and squirrels – and each took turns at cooking, washing and taking the handcart several kilometres down to the village to collect supplies. To keep warm, the children wore many layers of ill-assorted clothes, which gave them a ragged, unkempt look. A signal had been devised: when all was safe, the Swiss flag flew over Faïdoli, L'Abric and La Guespy. If the flags were lowered, it meant the children had to hide.

On Sundays, many of the Jewish children went to hear Theis and Trocmé preach, knowing that their feigned Protestantism gave them a certain protection. For Hanne, isolated in La Guespy, it became the day she saw other people and heard news of the plateau and of the war. Trocmé's brother Francis, who came to hear him preach one day, reported to Robert, another brother, that he had never in his whole life encountered such original and profound oratory. 'He starts in a familiar, simple tone,' he wrote, 'then his voice grows stronger, he analyses what he has said, he becomes almost confessional, sincere, with a clarity that is almost troubling . . . His voice rises, becomes grave, the sentences flow in larger and larger circles, and then, in a great spiral of words, he seems to rise and rise, higher and higher, with great sweeping gestures, magnificently confident, rising further still, leading you to the very summit of religious thought, to the very limits of the ineffable, and having reached that peak, he keeps you in a veritable state of ecstasy; then, slowly, his voice becomes gentler, his tone more intimate, and he brings you gently back to earth and to a sense of peace.'

To listen to him, said Francis, was to feel yourself in a dream, and it was hard to stop your eyes filling with tears. What was most impressive, he thought, was Trocmé's unmistakable sincerity, his lack of all artifice, as well as a richness of language and expression that appeared to be completely spontaneous. Francis was not alone in his admiration for his brother's sermons. Few of the adults who heard Trocmé preach ever forgot it. Among the refugee children he sometimes inspired awe, and when he lost his temper, he could be truly terrifying. Theis, gentler in manner, was more loved. Magda, for all her raucous voice and sometimes overwrought manner, was liked for the way that she was always looking around her to make certain that no one was being left out.

At the very heart of le Chambon life stood the Ecole Nouvelle Cévenol. Long after the war was over, people who had spent their childhood on the plateau hiding from the Germans would think about the school and marvel at its warmth and intellectual brilliance. As an educational experiment, it was new and original; for the children in mourning for their families, constantly afraid of the future, their thoughts filled with memories of violence and loss, it provided both an anchor and a distraction. Conceived by Guillon, Trocmé, Theis and Mlle Pont as a bastion of international, pacifist Protestantism, it was also liberal and unstuffy. Long before such things became fashionable, it encouraged friendly, informal relations between staff and students, pupil assemblies and a measure of self-governance, as well as a focus on individual interests. There was no rote learning. None of its students forgot what they had lived through.

Edouard and Mildred Theis

In large part, the school's excellence came from its unusual teachers: foreigners such as Miss Maber; outstanding professors who had lost their university jobs in Paris; Jews who had fled

Austria, Poland and Germany and had found refuge on the plateau. Between them, they created a sense of enormous intellectual excitement, so that children who had never read Ronsard or Racine and barely spoke French were soon visiting M Barbezat, the bookseller in the village, to find the French classical writers.

The school librarian was M Schmidt, who had worked for the Bibliothèque Nationale in Paris. There was Mlle Hoefert, a small, talkative Austrian woman, who smiled so much that her eyes remained permanently crinkled, and who 'trotted along like a busy little mouse'; she taught her pupils German and introduced them to Rilke in a 'soft, melodious' voice. There was the very tall, very thin Mme Dreyer, who had a 'majestic nose' and a pale, grave face. She taught mathematics and had two sons as tall and thin as herself. She reminded her pupils of a Greek tragic heroine. There was Mme Lavandes, professor of French and Latin, who looked like a black ant, with her black hair and eyes and black clothing from head to toe, but who for all her apparent severity had a generous heart. Miss Maber, determined that everyone in the school would speak the King's English, made the students recite, again and again, 'Timothy Tim has ten pink toes, ten pink toes has Timothy Tim'. She forbade them to call her anything but Miss Maber, saying that 'miss' alone was common. At weekends, there were long, laughing hikes across the plateau and up the Mézenc.

The teachers did not simply teach. They entered the children's lives. Acutely conscious of the need to fill their minds with the present, they found things for them to do after school, arranged outings and fancy dress parties, debates and a great deal of sport. Mlle Hoefert dressed up as an American newspaper reporter, in plus fours and a green eyeshade. On Sundays, after church, the children were dispatched on bicycles to nearby farms to collect the *picaudons*, small, round local cheeses, and they competed as to who could come back with the most.

The students, too, came from an extraordinary collection of nationalities and backgrounds. One of Hanne and Rudy's companions was Alexander Grothendieck, the future mathematician, who arrived from the internment camps one day with Madeleine Barot.

When not confounding his professors with his brilliance, he taught himself to play the piano. For many of these children, the Trocmés' presbytery offered comfort and home life; there was the confident and beautiful Nelly playing the piano, the somewhat mysterious Jean-Pierre seemingly always writing something, the angelic curly-haired Jacot, and little Daniel who looked a bit like the actor Jean Gabin.

What they all had to battle with, teachers and children alike, was the sheer geographical impracticality of the school, which meant that as numbers grew, so classes were farmed out to out-buildings, hotel rooms, empty *pensions* and huts. The teachers sped between them, the younger and fitter by toboggan or skis once the deep snows came and the drifts made many of the paths impassable. For the four months of snow, tobogganing became an essential part of le Chambon life, the children casting off from the highest corner of the hilly village, each clinging on to the ankles of the child in front, so that a train of tobog-gans would come hurtling down the perilously icy tracks. The children were sometimes sad, and often a bit hungry, but they were never bored. At a time of mayhem and uncertainty, when all of France was consumed by its uneasy relations with the Germans and its struggles to make ends meet, they were soothed by le Chambon's implicit moral message, that of compassion and charity. Most would remember all their lives singing the psalm so beloved of Theis and Trocmé: '*A toi la gloire / La foi renverse les montagnes / Restes avec nous Seigneur*'.

And yet, as everyone knew but did not dwell on, behind the seemingly cheerful faces and intellectual curiosity lay much grief and sadness. Many of the Jewish children had lost contact with their parents or their brothers and sisters, having heard nothing more after a final frantic note as a train was leaving for Drancy. At post delivery time, they hovered in the hall. A boy called Peter Feigl started a diary, addressed '*à mes chers parents*'. Photographs of his mother and father were stuck into the small black notebook, and he surrounded them with borders patterned in coloured ink. Day after day he wrote: 'I am anxious . . . I am worried . . . I fear for you, my dear parents . . . Still nothing from you . . .' On 13 September, he heard that they had been taken to Drancy. After that, nothing. Now, every day, he wrote: 'no news of you . . . no news of you' again and again. He also wrote about trying to contact the Red Cross, the Quakers, about getting himself to Marseilles, to America.

And then the entries stopped. When they resumed, in 1944, there was no more mention of his parents.

CHAPTER EIGHT

Rats in a trap

On 8 November 1942, the British and American forces landed in North Africa. Three days later, at seven o'clock in the morning, the Wehrmacht crossed the demarcation line and occupied the French south. In Vichy, Bousquet ordered the police and army to offer no resistance. Following the Wehrmacht soldiers came the Gestapo and the Abwehr, to set up their offices in Lyons, Marseilles, Montpellier, Vichy, Toulouse and Limoges, bringing with them auxiliaries and calling in collaborators and informers. Some of the ground had already been prepared: since the end of September, naming their operation Donar, after the God of Thunder, plain-clothed Gestapo officers with false French documents had been operating in the south, successfully infiltrating the Allied secret service networks set up by SOE to gather information and supply the French Resistance.

In the south-east, the Italians moved beyond the French *départements* they had occupied in 1940 and took control of Toulon and all of Provence up to the Rhône, previously under Vichy; Italian irredentists claimed Corsica.

By the end of the month, Vichy no longer had a free zone, nor an army, nor an empire, nor a fleet. What remained of its navy was scuttled in Toulon. Tunisia was in the hands of the Axis powers, Indochina in those of the Japanese. Out of some dim and mocking consideration for Pétain and Laval, what had been known as the 'unoccupied' zone was now to be not a zone of 'occupation', but of 'operation', for though nothing was left of France as a sovereign state, the Germans still needed French civil servants and policemen to administer the country. Swastikas went up;

the clocks were put on to German time. German military forces were moved around and a commander-in-chief of France-Sud, General Rolf Muller, was installed in Lyons. The ornate and imposing Hôtel Terminus by the Perrache station was made into Gestapo headquarters, and Klaus Barbie, veteran of countless murders of Jews, communists and Gypsies across Holland and the Ukraine, arrived as one of its senior officers. Strict censorship was imposed; letters and phone calls were monitored; anyone circulating unauthorised material was threatened with savage punishments. In le Chambon, where he had settled for the winter, Camus was hard at work on *La Peste*, whose story echoes the position in which the French now found themselves. In his diary, he wrote: 'Like Rats in a Trap!' In the novel, in which the city of Oran is sealed off after a plague of rats spreads bubonic plague, Raymond Rambert, the journalist stuck in Oran after the gates are closed, says that until that moment, he had felt like a stranger, but now 'This story concerns us all.'

Throughout what had been Vichy France, the Germans began to move their men in, commandeer hotels and offices, reserve the cinemas and restaurants, hang their enormous flags and take stock of the gendarmes and policemen on whose help they would have to rely. Julius Schmähling, a small, round man with spectacles, a balding egg-shaped head, a rolling gait and the look of a benign hamster was made commander of the Haute-Loire. His headquarters were at Le Puy, on the Boulevard Maréchal Fayolle, named after the much-decorated hero of the Somme and the Marne. He brought with him a garrison of some 200 auxiliaries, more or less unwilling Croats, Russians, Georgians and Tartars, and a small number of elderly and not always reliable German officers, whose idea it was not to find themselves suddenly transferred to the eastern front. The Tartars, under an ambitious officer called Coelle, were regarded as brutal but uncertain in battle. How all these blunt and violent men would get along with Bach's hesitant policemen and his 36 brigades of gendarmes, under their noticeably anti-German commander, Sébastien Silvani, who were the effective police of the countryside – the regular police operated in the towns – was still to be seen. All were enjoined to keep a keen eye on the

'Protestant circles' on the plateau, whose 'memory of the wars of religion' had left them attached to notions of 'liberty and internationalism'.

The *Kommandantur* in Le Puy

Schmähling is another of the plateau's enigmatic figures. Called up as a reserve officer in 1939, he was 50 when he arrived in Le Puy. Somewhat lazy, amiable and intent on surviving the war without mishap, he was a professor of history from Nüremberg, more interested in his food and drink and discussing the Thirty Years War than in hunting down wrongdoers in the Haute-Loire. In his memoirs, written after the war, he spoke of his desire to keep his area neutral and peaceful. This, it became clear from their fortnightly meetings, was also exactly what Prefect Bach wanted, as he explained when he was later accused of 'having courteous, even cordial' relations with the Germans, and of having permitted his wife to accept a box of chocolates from Schmähling. In this story, neither of the two men, the equivocating Bach and the calculating Schmähling, is ever quite what he seems. They wait, watch, adapt.

What both had to contend with, however, was the growing zealousness of the Service d'Ordre Légionnaire, the 'shock troops of the Revolution Nationale', flag-waving, thuggish young patriots in their blue uniforms and berets, who had sworn allegiance to Pétain and vowed to oppose 'bolshevism, Gaullism, Jewry, pagan Masonry, anarchy, egalitarianism, false liberty, apathy, scepticism' and much else besides. The SOL had been forbidden to operate in the occupied zone, but they had been gaining unpleasant strength throughout the south.

Schmähling's reasonableness, he would say, stemmed from an incident that had taken place when he was a young teacher in Bavaria. One day, having started to give a lesson on lions, and looking forward to all the dramatic tales he had prepared on the king of the beasts, he noticed a hitherto totally silent boy at the back of the class imperiously waving his hand. Schmähling ignored him and kept talking. Suddenly the small boy jumped up and called out – without permission, a heinous crime in a Bavarian classroom – 'Yesterday, Herr Professor, I saw a rabbit! Yes, I saw a rabbit!' Schmähling was enraged: 'Shut up, you idiot! Sit down!' The small boy sat. For the rest of the year, he never spoke again. Schmähling took note. His hot temper had been wrong: in destroying that 'moment of sunlight' in the little boy's life, he had destroyed something in himself. He had vowed, he would tell his listeners, never to exercise such cruelty again and to make room always for people to speak; and as he saw it, he kept that vow.

As an officer of the Wehrmacht, Schmähling had no authority over the Gestapo, who in principle chased political refugees and Jews, while the Feldgendarmerie tracked down German deserters. But Le Puy had no Gestapo office – the nearest was at Saint-Etienne, 75 kilometres away – and, along with matters of resistance, the black market and requisitions of every kind, all denunciations of Jews, hidden or otherwise, came to his office. The portly middle-aged Schmähling now had total power over the Jews of the Plateau Vivarais-Lignon. What was crucial was how he would use it.

Pétain made one stand, which he won, over the Jews, both French and foreign, who now found themselves in the new 'zone of operation', insisting that they should not have to wear a yellow star. But the reality was that no Jew was now safe, anywhere in France. By the middle of November 1942, Vichy had allowed 17 *convois*, deportation trains, to carry 11,012 foreign Jews from independent French territory to German-occupied France, from there to be deported to the Polish death camps. How many were left, in the internment camps, in hiding, in the cities, in the Italian zone – desperate, terrified people, spilling out all over the countryside in search of better hiding places, protectors, documents to get out of France – no one knew.

What exactly awaited them in Poland was still a matter of conjecture; many found it impossible to believe that it was mass murder. But what was clear was that with the German occupation of the whole of France, another step had been taken in the delivery of Jews for deportation. The little optimism that had remained among Vichy's Jews now died. Orders went out to mayors and police to report every incident, 'however anodyne', even those taking place at night and on holidays. Posters, propaganda, suspicious people, sounds of aeroplanes, suggestions of discontent: all and everything was to be noted and reported. Along with, of course, the name and identity of every Jew. Under a new edict, law number 979, Jews were no longer allowed to leave their residences without special papers. They were to be numbered, considered possible chips for bargaining with the Germans; or simply kept in readiness for Vichy's next step in helping Hitler towards his Final Solution.

The arrival of the Germans in the unoccupied zone had a further, bitter, result. For over two years, the Jewish organisations had been battling to secure visas for children to emigrate. Several hundred, after interminable wrangling, had done so, often after precarious and fearsome adventures. One young Austrian girl who had been hiding in le Chambon had finally heard that her visa for the US had come through before the snows melted in the spring of 1942. During a last heavy snowstorm, when the little train had been halted by impassable drifts, she had walked 15 kilometres down into the valley, got herself to Marseilles, negotiated with the authorities and caught one of the last boats out to the US. She was 16.

Before the occupation of the Vichy zone, Marseilles had been the centre of diplomatic life for those still desperately hoping to emigrate, and foreign consuls had been able to issue visas for anyone possessed of all the necessary documents. The Czech consul, Vladmir Vochoc, was a committed anti-Nazi, and when his stock of passports ran out, he had false ones printed and issued, until he was put under house arrest. All through 1941, Varian Fry, the young American working for the Emergency Rescue Committee in New York, had continued to organise departures, both legal and illegal, from his office in the city, most often across the border into Spain, then to Lisbon and from there by sea to Shanghai, the Belgian Congo or Mexico. One of his *passeurs* was Dina Vierny, a Trotskyite, and former model for the sculptor Maillol. Of the 20,000 people who had approached Fry for help, he had managed to arrange departure for about 2,000. But for some of the people on the list drawn up in the US he had been unable to do anything. The Czech writer Ernst Weiss had taken poison in Paris; the art critic Karl Einstein had hanged himself near the Spanish border. Hannah Arendt, André Breton, Max Ernst, Golo and Heinrich Mann and Max Ophuls had all got out.

On 28 September 1942, six weeks before the arrival of the Germans, under heavy pressure from the Quakers, the OSE, the YMCA and the JDC, the American State Department had finally granted 1,000 visas for Jewish children coming from France, to be accompanied by 75 escorts from Marseilles to Lisbon. On 15 October, it increased the number to 5,000. Laval prevaricated. On the 16th, he and Bousquet, piously declaring that they were interested only in 'bona fide orphans', said that Vichy would never let children cross the Atlantic while 'their parents are left in Poland'. At last, after more wrangling, Vichy gave permission for a first shipment of 500 children, saying that this was a dry run for the others, in exchange for an undertaking that there would be no adverse publicity about the French treatment of Jews. The children were collected from camps and children's centres by the OSE and the Quakers, and assembled to wait in Marseilles.

Meanwhile, a separate rescue operation, led by Böszi – Elisabeth Hirsch – from the OSE's team in Gurs, set out across the Pyrenees with another group of 12 children, aged between 8 and 14, to cross into Spain and then Portugal, where the *Guinea* was waiting to take them to Palestine. It weighed anchor on 26 October.

At last, it seemed, in little groups, Jewish children were escaping the Nazis. But it was an illusion.

Early in November, the children in Marseilles had been issued with both their visas and their tickets for the US from Portugal to New York. Their escorts had been chosen. A boat, chartered in Lisbon, was waiting. There were more delays, more last-minute caveats. They were told that only 100 of them were to be allowed to go, and that they needed to be vetted. Then Vichy announced that only women could act as escorts. After this came disagreements over definitions: who was an 'orphan'? Who was an 'abandoned' child?

On 4 November, Vichy vetted a first group of 37 and abruptly rejected eight of them. The children waited. Then five of the escorts were detained as 'deportable'. Some more children were held back on account of having impetigo. They were still waiting when, on the 8th, the Allies landed in North Africa and relations between Vichy and the US broke down, and they were still there when, on 11 November, the Germans arrived in Marseilles, effectively putting an end to all further hopes of emigration.

Chaos and confusion spread around the voluntary organisations, many of whom were now forced to leave France. On 16 November, as they packed up their offices in Marseilles, handing their work over to Secours Suisse – which still had diplomatic relations with Germany – the American Friends Service Committee informed the State Department that they were 'placing all applications for United States visas on behalf of applicants in Southern France into a suspense file'.

What every Jew in France needed now was a false identity. Under a law introduced soon after the total German occupation, Jews, whether French or foreign, were obliged to carry ID with a 'J' stamped on it, without which they could neither travel nor collect ration cards. For French Jews, vulnerable to denunciations from covetous neighbours or spiteful employees, it was still sometimes enough to move house, change district or *département*, and declare themselves not Jewish. For foreign Jews, many with strong accents and little French, concealment became almost impossible. They needed wholly new identities, new stories, new pasts.

Children, more confused and forgetful, had to be coached to remember who they were supposed to be. At the OSE, the young social workers would make their charges rehearse their new identities again and again, until there was no hesitation:

'What's your name?'

'Philippe Crochet.'

'Repeat it.'

'Philippe Crochet.'

'Where is your father?'

'He died.'

'How did he die?'

'He was killed in a bombardment.'

'Where?'

'In Lille.'

'Now start again. What is your name?'

By the end of 1942, France was awash with false documents. The simplest were those obtained by using an authentic certificate; a school diploma, say, with a different photograph, obtained from someone who was prepared to say that they had lost it. This could be taken to the Mairie, and used as the basis with which to acquire all the other missing papers. Birth places could then be chosen from areas where it was known that the local government offices had been destroyed, and with them all the archives. What was important was having not only enough corroborating documents of every kind – student card, marriage certificate, ration book – but the confidence to proffer them nonchalantly when stopped by the police.

Friendly mayors, printers, civil servants willing to stamp documents, falsify papers or turn a blind eye were crucial cogs in the scramble for papers. But now, as the war entered its most lethal phase for Jews, master forgers emerged from the most unlikely backgrounds to work for the underground Jewish organisations, for nascent resistance networks, for the churches, and for themselves and their friends. One of these was an 18-year-old medical student called Oscar Rosowsky, a curly-haired Russian Jew who was trilingual in Russian, German and French.

Oscar's grandfather had been a successful exporter of oak in Riga before moving his family and three sons to Berlin in the 1920s. It was here, in 1923, that Oscar was born; he was an only child and the family lived in considerable luxury, first in an apartment appropriated from a German officer, later in six magnificent rooms in Charlottenburg. But Oscar's father was a gambler, not a businessman, and soon the family drifted to Nice, where he lost in the casinos what little money he had left from his own father's fortune.

When, occasionally, his father's luck turned, Oscar would be treated to a Pêche Melba. His mother Mirra, meanwhile, had learnt the fashion business and in one of the two small rooms to which they had been reduced set up a millinery studio, finding customers for her elegant little hats, copied from the pages of *Vogue*, among the rich Russian émigrés on the Côte d'Azur. Oscar's father sat in a café, read the papers and tried to think up schemes to make money; Oscar played chess. In the summer months, when there was less call for hats, the family went hungry. Oscar's expensive fountain pen was hocked. He was sent to the prestigious Lycée Parc Imperial and joined the Jewish boy scouts. It was 1940. Nice under the Italians was peaceful. That summer he passed his first baccalaureate; the following year, he passed the second. The Rosowskys were not observant Jews; the war was never discussed; there was no radio in the house. If Oscar was conscious of the Statut des Juifs, it was only through fights in the playground between anti-Semitic Pétainists and the Jewish boys.

The first signs of trouble came when Oscar was refused entrance to the next stage in medical school on the grounds of the exclusion of Jews. Instead, he was apprenticed to a mechanic who mended typewriters, and who had a contract to service the machines in the Prefect's office. Oscar accompanied him on his rounds. He spent his spare time with the scouts; he loved the camaraderie of the life, the talk, doing things together.

One day, at the end of September, when he returned from camp, his mother told him that his father had been arrested and had disappeared; and that a letter was waiting for him, ordering him to a work camp set up for foreign Jewish men. Oscar put on his scout uniform and reported. The man in charge was sympathetic and sent him to an Italian enterprise, where they cooked him snails in tomato sauce.

Three weeks later, he went back to Nice and for the first time realised what danger his Jewish mother was in. They decided to try to reach Switzerland together, but since her false papers

– obtained through contacts in the Russian community – were not ready, Oscar went on ahead. He reached the border and crossed, but was picked up by the Swiss police and returned to France. When he got back to Nice, he discovered that his mother had been arrested; on the train taking her to the Swiss border, a beady-eyed inspector had spotted that her papers were false. She was sent to Rivesaltes.

Oscar understood that he had very little time to act. He had gone back to work cleaning typewriters and knew that he would be able to get hold of blank ID forms in the prefecture. He stole what he needed, filled in false details for his mother's name and background, and sent the papers to Rivesaltes. Miraculously, they worked. Walking in the streets of Nice soon afterwards, he bumped into his mother, just released from the camp. She had lost 25 kilos. It was November, and the Germans had occupied the whole of France, and though Nice was still theoretically safe for Jews – for the moment occupied and protected by the Italians – Oscar knew that they had to find somewhere else to hide. Too many people knew that they were Jewish.

Through friends, he had heard about the Plateau Vivarais-Lignon. He decided to go on ahead and explore. He caught a series of trains, and met a contact who was living in one of the students'

pensions in le Chambon, who sent him to Fay-le-Froid, where the new pastor, Daniel Curtet, agreed to help. His mother arrived in Fay under the name of Mlle Grabowska, a Russian émigré widow. She stayed a few nights in the Hôtel Abel, then moved into a small apartment, where she cooked stews of offal and potatoes. Oscar, taking the name Jean-Claude Plumme, went to live in the Barrauds' *pension*, Beau Soleil, in le Chambon. It was like being a scout all over again, a collection of some twenty young people from all over Europe, some Jewish, some not, all talking. Oscar was able to fill them in with news of the round-ups and describe what he had heard about the black hole into which the deported Jews appeared to sink. Every ten days or so, on the pretext of taking Russian lessons, he visited his mother in Fay. Only Pastor Curtet knew that they were mother and son.

At Beau Soleil, he was introduced to a young man called Louis de Juge, who was a student at the Ecole Nouvelle Cévenol, though he was spending more and more time involved in plans to oppose the Germans, and through him to Roger Klimoviski, another Jewish scout, who under the name Roger Climaud was helping to find hiding places for the Jews on the plateau. From them, Oscar learnt that teachers in the college were using a primitive form of photo-copying to manufacture false documents, buying supplies of paper and ink from the stationery office in Tence. One of these was Jacqueline Decourdemanche, the school secretary, whose former husband, Daniel,* had just been arrested as a resister in Paris and shot by the Germans. Jacqueline had a beautiful copperplate hand and was much in demand when the flowery signatures so beloved of French bureaucracy were needed. Oscar, who had little with which to fill his time, volunteered to help. He soon discovered that he had a natural aptitude for the work. He was deft, quick, diligent, imaginative. The *rafles* in the south, the tracking down of Jews in the north, the closure of borders and emigration were driving more and more people up the mountain and on to the plateau. They all needed documents.

Using drawing pens, inks, stamps, stencils, tracing paper and a special kind of gelatine, Oscar was soon turning out

---

* Daniel was the lover of Maï Politzer, one of the 230 women who appeared in *A Train in Winter* and who died in Auschwitz.

ration books, demobilisation papers, birth certificates, school diplomas, marriage licences, hunting permits and college diplomas. An intricate form took him an hour to forge; the simpler ones 15 minutes. If you heated the gelatine for the transfer too much, it dripped; too little and the transfer did not take. Twenty-year-old Gabrielle Barraud helped with the stencilling and printing; she was watchful, she would say later, and wary, but she never really thought that anyone would catch them. The ration books, which came in various shapes and colours, took the longest. What made the job easier was the state of bureaucratic confusion into which the war had plunged the French civil service, which helpfully meant that it was impossible for the police to check documents against their supposed sources; and the fact that, apart from a couple of forms that were standard throughout France, all the others came in different shapes, colours and sizes, according to the *département* in which they had apparently been issued. Whenever he required a flowery flourish, Oscar turned to Jacqueline. Often, he and Gabrielle worked through the night.

After Convoi 45 left Drancy for Auschwitz on 11 November 1942, with 33 elderly residents of the Rothschild Foundation Hospice on board to make up the numbers, there was a mysterious lull in deportations. But on the plateau, almost every week the little train brought more Jewish families, more children gathered up by Madeleine Barot and Madeleine Dreyfus, to be met by Mme Déléage, taken to the Hôtel May and dispersed among the farmers.

In the children's homes run by Cimade and Secours Suisse, and in Emile Sèches' Tante Soly, where Jewish and French children continued to be mixed in together the better to conceal them, the French ones who now arrived from the plains and the cities were hungrier, less healthy than before the war, long, thin, children with the first signs of rickets, who had trouble concentrating at school. The Jewish children went about the streets openly, because they were obscured by other children. The Jewish adults stayed indoors, fearing to draw attention to themselves and feeling protected by the habitual silence of their Huguenot and Darbyist hosts. Everyone was conscious of the need not to know too much: who the Jews were, where they were hidden. Later Gladys Maber would say that in the Ecole Nouvelle Cévenol, she went to great lengths to avoid learning the religion or backgrounds of her pupils, and that it was only after the war that she discovered that one of her close fellow teachers had been a rabbi.

More important for this sense of isolation and safety on the plateau than its remoteness and lack of transport – only Dr Le Forestier, for his rounds, and Emile Sèches, for his food-gathering, had cars – was the fact that none of the local people had ever strayed far, and that they had no tradition of talking. When the international and sophisticated Trocmé and Theis preached their worldly sermons about international affairs, they were addressing people who had seldom moved many kilometres from the place in which they had been born. Robert Ebart, whose family owned a farm six kilometres from the village, would later say that during the entire course of the war he very seldom went as far as le Chambon, and that he never once saw a German. As a small boy, he observed the *touristes alimentaires* who came up from the plains over the weekends in search of butter and eggs, and he knew of the existence of a cave in the woods in which people hid, just as he knew there was something strange about some of the children in his class, but what all this was about, he had no idea. He did not ask, and he was not told. His parents, he would say, were '*pas bavards*', not talkative.

Refugees arriving on the plateau remarked on the '*esprit de frondeur*', the spirit of rebellion, that seemed to unite the inhabitants – the doctors, the teachers, the pastors and the farmers – even when nothing was said and though many knew of each other only by name. The Darbyist families who from the first had so willingly concealed Jews on their isolated farms, hiding them among their many relations and children, continued to go about their lives in their orderly, separate, silent way. In the cub and scout meetings, much encouraged by the schoolmaster Darcissac, children re-enacted the heroic legends of the Camisards and sang ballads celebrating the Huguenots holding out against the King's dragoons. When Trocmé sent out messages to let people in the Bible groups know what text to discuss that week, they were written on postcards of Marie Durand imprisoned in the Tour de Constance. To make his point plainer, he often wrote '*résister*' on the bottom. Watching the snows arrive, bringing with them an even greater sense of isolation and safety, the refugees felt that they had arrived on a little island, not part of occupied France.

L'Echo de la Montagne, the Protestant paper assiduously read by every household, had spent the first two years of the Vichy government piously praising Pétain's pronouncements and lamenting France's moral collapse, while filling its columns with attacks on alcoholism and calls for sacrifice and duty. Nothing had been said about the persecution of the Jews. Now, under a new editor, the pastor of Tence, Roland Leenhardt, triumphant '*maréchalisme*' was replaced by exhortations to give asylum to strangers. The word '*résistance*' made its first appearance in an issue in December 1942: the 500 Biblical circles of Jerusalem were likened to the 12 Bible groups in and around le Chambon as '*noyaux*', kernels of resistance.

What form, precisely, this resistance might take, however, was becoming a slightly awkward undercurrent among those divided over questions of pacifism. While Theis and Trocmé continued to preach absolute non-violence, there were beginning to be stirrings of something more assertive among the younger people, who resented the way that Trocmé imposed his views on the parish and did not seem to mind hurting feelings. They found it irksome that he saw himself not only as a pastor but as the leader of the community, so that inevitably, when something needed to be done, someone would ask: 'What would Pastor Trocmé say?' Yet this endlessly self-doubting man, longing to do good, whose notebooks are filled with angst and uncertainty, and whose manner veered between the stern and the homely, also found compromise very hard. The whole village would remember his wrath when a woman in the congregation who had left young children at home tried to slip away from the temple just as Trocmé was preparing Communion. And relations were not always easy between Trocmé and the former mayor

Guillon, who continued to travel back and forth between the plateau and Geneva, carrying false documents, letters and funds for the children's homes. Beneath the apparent harmony, tensions and disagreements simmered.

From the archives of the Commissariat Général aux Questions Juives, opened after the war, it is clear that Guillon, still known to everyone as 'l'Oncle Charles', was already marked out as a helper of Jews and fabricator of false documents. For the transport of money from the JDC in Switzerland into France, he had taken to using a secretary and old friend, a woman who dressed herself up as a little old lady and pretended to visit relations over the border. She was soon a familiar figure with the border police at Annemasse. One day, when her bag was particularly full of money, a jocular guard asked her: 'And how much money do you have today, mademoiselle?' 'Millions,' she replied, and they laughed merrily.

Dr Le Forestier, who took few pains to conceal what he felt about the Germans, was also conscious of being on a list of suspects, but paid very little heed to anyone. 'The medical apostolate is a ministry without words,' he wrote in his diary, 'a silent activity which can be an expression of faith.' A first son, Jean-Philippe, had been born to the Le Forestiers in 1940; a second, Bernard, in November 1942, just as the Germans swept south.

The autumn brought Max Liebmann to the plateau to join Hanne. In November, Max had learned that his mother had been deported from Gurs. He had been living on a farm run by orthodox Jewish boy scouts but felt increasingly isolated by his lack of religious commitment, and, knowing that Hanne was hiding on the plateau, he decided to go in search of her. Not sure precisely where or how to find her, he was standing in the road near le Chambon when six young girls ran past, laughing. Max whistled; they stopped; one was Hanne.

They had very little time together. Max was now in great danger of being caught and deported. She took him to see Mireille Philip, who, now that her husband André, the former socialist deputy, had got to London – his safe arrival was broadcast in code over the BBC – was becoming increasingly involved in the hiding of the Jews. Mireille asked Hanne: 'Can we trust him?' By nightfall, Max was in the hayloft of a Darbyist farm an hour's walk from le Chambon. There were said to be police in the forests looking for him. The farmer cut a hole in the floorboards above the stable, to act as a lavatory. Max emerged from his hiding place only after dark; the only book the house possessed was the Bible. After four weeks, by which time he felt himself to have been entirely forgotten, he received a note from Hanne. Plans had been made for him to join three other teenage boys who were leaving for Switzerland. They agreed that she would follow him as soon as she could; they made a pact that whatever happened, they would survive, not become victims. Max knew that his father had just been arrested in Nice. Both their mothers had been deported to Auschwitz. Having each other was the only thing that made sense of their lives.

The winter of 1942 also brought, for the first time, the Germans. Until now, it had been the French police and gendarmes alone who had patrolled the area. One day the Service Français des Relations Franco-Allemands, one of the many collaborationist bodies, arrived in le Chambon to announce that 80 beds for German officers and 90 for enlisted men, all convalescents from injuries received on the eastern front, were to be commandeered. To the dismay and initial terror of the Chambonnais, they took over the Hôtel du Lignon on the main street, less than a hundred yards from the square, and next door to Emile Sèches' Tante Soly, now home to some dozen Jewish children, mixed in with the same number of French ones. From her bedroom window, five-year-old Madeleine Sèches looked straight out on the terrace where the Germans did their exercises. She could hear them talking.

Soon the roads leading in and out of le Chambon rang with the sounds of marching and singing. When the Chambonnais seemed to avoid them and disappeared as soon as they emerged, the Germans observed that it was obvious that the French had never cared for music. Dr Le Forestier, already someone who refused to act with caution, took to blowing his car horn loudly whenever the soldiers gave a concert in the square. For a while,

Emile and Solange Sèches at Tante Soly. Madeleine is the little girl at the front on the left hand side

the villagers with radios were terrified that they would be over-heard listening to the French BBC service and reported. But as the Germans seemed intent on being friendly, behaving correctly and doing what they could to avoid being returned to the eastern front, and as they expressed no interest of any kind in the foreigners and the refugees, the Chambonnais began to feel reas-sured. They went back to listening to their radios, crouched round their sets, waiting for the familiar opening bars of Beethoven. When one day a German soldier overheard a boy mutter 'sale Boche', he yanked him by the arm, saying no, not 'sale Boche', but 'bon Allemand', and ordered him to repeat it over and over again.

Not least the oddest aspect of the plateau's war was the pres-ence of all these German soldiers living in the very heart of the village, apparently unaware that they were surrounded on all sides by Jewish children.

Relations between Bach and many of his men in the prefecture in Le Puy remained ambiguous. What was Bach thinking when, in December, he asked André Haussard, a policeman in Fay, whether some kind of home could be found on the plateau for ten adult Jews? Who these people were, and why they had not already been interned, is not clear, and nor are Bach's motives. What is revealing is Haussard's reply. As far as he knew, he told Bach, there were no Jews on the plateau, and since the local hotels were not heated, and food was scarce, it would not be a good idea to send any. From the archives, it is plain that Haussard, who after the war was put up for a medal for his work on behalf of the Jews, knew perfectly well the extent of the hiding operation already in place. Were he and Bach in league with each other?

There were heavy snowfalls on the plateau in the days leading up to Christmas. The children tobogganed at terrifying speed down the icy tracks. Madeleine Sèches dreaded these snowy times, when, carrying 15 litres of milk on her back for the household, she would sink deep into the drifts, her feet freezing and ill protected by the wooden clogs she wore. In the mornings, when she woke, the panes of glass on the inside of her bedroom window were thickly cased in ice.

At the presbytery, Alice Reynier, who took the nickname Jispa – from 'joie de servir dans la paix avec amour' – a nursery school teacher whose lay community of Protestant women in Pomeyrol had closed for lack of food and heating, arrived to help Magda, who was overwhelmed by the tasks that filled her day. Jispa was very small, gentle and competent; she had a round, unlined face, beady eyes and a haircut like a boy's. Magda, at first apprehensive at taking in someone so pious, learnt to love her. To the family, she soon became 'petite maman', mother to Trocmé and Magda, who had both lost theirs as children, grandmother to Nelly and her brothers. She helped with the accounts, the homework, the parishioners and the refugees, who sometimes gathered in great numbers in the dining room to see Trocmé. Jispa, Nelly would later say, injected a note of calm and orderliness into their 'intemperate' household. The villagers referred to her as the 'Martha of the presbytery'.

Never had Trocmé been so busy. The Ecole Nouvelle Cévenol had 300 students and 30 teachers and was being forced to turn applicants away; among them were 20 future pastors, the *'futhéos'*, who acted as monitors, leaders of Bible classes. 'We have had <u>too much</u> success,' André Trocmé wrote to his brother Robert. There were Bible meetings, choirs, sermons to write, visits to sick parishioners. The parish was an exceptionally large one. Both he and Magda were exhausted; he was also suffering from the acute backache that often plagued him at times of overwork, while Magda had lost weight and looked grey. But the children were thriving and 'learning very young the lessons of life', both from the dramas that seemed to crop up every day, and from the remarkable men and women who were now living on the plateau.

Nelly, though not pretty, might become so, Trocmé told Robert, and she was a keen cub leader. Her character was 'rugged' and conscientious. Jean-Pierre, growing up fast, was a philosopher, a musician, a reader and a great charmer. Jacques was a dreamer, a boy made in Andre's own image (though thinner), with 'something of a Russian aristocrat' about him; while Daniel, at five still the baby of the house, was practical, steady, the 'stockman' of the establishment, who knew where everything was. And another kind of 'grave peril' had just been averted. An enterprising newcomer had proposed opening a cinema. Trocmé managed to sabotage what he feared would be immoral and corrupting entertainment by persuading the parish council to buy a projector of their own, and to install it in an annexe of the temple, where it could show improving films. The newcomer's application for a licence was turned down.

On Christmas Day 1942, Magda decorated the house with candles stuck into potatoes cut in half and covered in red paper. The children each played an instrument, as they did every year, and sang songs and psalms; Trocmé played the accordion. In the temple, under the enormous Christmas tree hung with small presents for the children, he recounted one of his fables, adapted from a Bible story to suit modern times. The packed congregation included many of the hidden Jews, some of whom struggled to reconcile Trocmé's message – that what was taking place was a test of man by God – with their own view of the persecution of the Jews. For them, it made no sense at all.

*   *   *

Camus, at work at Le Panelier on *La Peste*, feeling lonely, seeing in his trapped occupants of Oran a metaphor for the exile and isolation of the plateau, was longing for the arrival of spring. Was it possible, he wondered, to be both 'happy and solitary'? 'In this country,' he wrote in his journal, 'where winter has abolished every colour since everything in it is white, the slightest sound since the snow stifles it, all fragrance since it is overladen with cold, the first whiff of spring grass must be like a call to joy, the bursting trumpet of sensation.'

CHAPTER NINE

An open pen of chickens

Hardly was Christmas over when the fortunes of the Jews on the plateau began to change. The Prefect, Bach, sent a police inspector to le Chambon to keep an eye on the Coteau Fleuri and La Maison des Roches, and to spy on the 'movements of Jewish refugees'. Léopold Praly was a Protestant, a pleasant-looking, eager, apparently amiable young man of 23. He took an office on the main square and rooms in a small hotel nearby, the Pension des Acacias, but spent much of his time sitting in a café and flirting with girls. Behind the bonhomie lay considerable shrewdness. In the café, Praly overheard much useful information.

It was not long before he was reporting back to Bach that Darcissac was known as an ardent socialist and a 'very doubtful' character, as indeed were many of the Protestants on the mountain. Meeting Trocmé one day in the street, he remarked to him that he was perfectly well aware that the Maison des Roches was a 'dangerous den of Jews and anti-patriots'. When Trocmé reprimanded him for being a spy, Praly replied: 'We each of us earn our living as best we can.' Soon he was ordering all Jews to come forward and register themselves, and it was not all that long before he learnt the name of a young Jew, Serge Vollweiler, hiding in the Secours Suisse house Faïdoli, and arrived to arrest him. The quick-witted cook of the house offered Praly a cup of coffee while Serge went to pack his bags before climbing out of a window and disappearing into the woods.

Praly had not been in le Chambon many weeks before he acquired a girlfriend; he appeared anxious to make friends on the plateau. This very young police inspector is another of the story's

Praly (far left) and a group of friends, in the fields outside le Chambon

ambiguous characters. Although he is generally regarded as a villain, some later claimed that he too had entered into the prevailing spirit of resistance. Miss Maber, ever a canny observer of local affairs, who got to know Praly well through his girlfriend, always believed that his intentions, at least, were good.

Before Praly had a chance to show his true colours, the German assault on the Jews in the newly occupied zone took a sudden turn for the increasingly lethal.

Marseilles had long been a problem in the minds of both Vichy and the Germans. With the fall of France, thousands of refugees, fleeing Paris and the north, had come to settle in and around the charming old port, with its ancient hidden underground passageways and its narrow streets and alleyways, the washing hung out between the houses. It reminded visitors of Naples. The exodus brought Germans and Austrians belonging to the pre-war intelligentsia of Vienna, Munich and Berlin to join the many Italians, Spaniards, Armenians and North Africans who over the years had made the city their home. By 1942, there were some 35,000 Jews living and sheltering in its parishes, making Marseilles, along with Lyons, the southern city with the highest population of Jews; slightly over half of them were French Sephardic, descended from families expelled by Spain and Portugal in the fifteenth century, or drawn by trade and the links between North Africa and mainland France.

Right up until 12 November 1942, when the Germans entered the city and drove their tanks with swastikas flying along the wide and magnificent La Canebière, past the Bourse and the grand hotels, Marseilles had been a lively cultural centre, a place of theatres, concert halls and learned societies, where Golo Mann, Walter Benjamin and Max Ernst all spent time hoping to find visas and ships to take them away. The city was also a centre for the many welfare organisations, their offices crammed into hotel rooms and rented apartments. For a long time, despite the presence not far away of Les Milles, one of Vichy's largest internment camps, opened in an old tile factory and used as a transit area for those awaiting permission and visas to leave, the Jews of Marseilles had felt safe. They were not required to wear yellow stars, France was their home, and most considered themselves more French than Jewish. This sense of invulnerability had somehow stretched to many of the newcomers, though it was not a sentiment shared by everyone. As Donald Lowrie, still in France and working hard to support the scattered Jews, observed, Marseilles was 'like an open pen of chickens with a hawk in the sky, circling ever lower'.

Lowrie was right to feel apprehensive. From the summer of 1941, the Germans had been running a secret information service in the city, which they well knew to be full of German deserters, 'negroes . . . and above all Jews', its narrow streets concealing precisely the people they wanted to be rid of. Marseilles, they said, was the 'capital of anti-France', 'openly hostile' to Vichy and the Reich. Much of the right-wing press agreed. In an article published in October 1942, Louis Gillet, an academician, spoke of 'this empire of sin and death' and asked: 'What means are there to rid these districts full of riffraff of their pus, and to regenerate the city?'

His answer was not long in coming. On 3 January 1943, a bomb exploded in a brothel, injuring several German soldiers, then another in the Hôtel Splendide, which had been commandeered by the army, killing a maître d'hôtel and wounding the wife of a German consular official. A curfew was imposed. Posters appeared announcing reprisals. Germans took over various primary schools as barracks.

Early on the morning of 22 January, some 12,000 French police from various forces, together with about 5,000 Germans, all under the command of SS Karl Oberg, who had come down from Paris to direct operations, set out to comb through the city. They stopped people in the streets, in bars, in restaurants, on trams and buses, and they banged on people's doors. Forty thousand IDs were checked; 5,956 people – 'irregulars', those with no papers – were arrested; 800 bars were closed. Operation Tiger took 786 Jews – of whom 570 were French nationals, many of whom, against all evidence, continued to believe themselves inviolate – put them on a train marked with a yellow Star of David, and sent them directly to Paris, to await deportation. A further 1,642 people picked up during the *rafle* were sent to Fréjus, to sit in the freezing cold in a vast bare field to await their fate. Of those deported to Sobibor on Convois 52 and 53, none returned.

But this was only the beginning. Fearing an Allied landing along the Mediterranean coast, the Germans wanted no potential hiding places for resisters. On 1 February, having cleared the Old Port, house by house, street by street, they moved in with tanks and explosives. Over the next 17 days, they blew up the entire area, demolishing some 2,000 buildings and reducing 14 hectares to a desolate waste of dust and rubble.

One of the Jews who witnessed the destruction of old Marseilles was a 13-year-old boy called Gilbert Nizard, who climbed every day to the top of the Basilica of Notre-Dame and watched the buildings crumble.

Gilbert and his parents thought of themselves not just as French, but as Pétainist. They liked the speeches of the heroic Maréchal and did not blame him for the disasters visited on the Jews, choosing to believe that the Germans and the men Pétain surrounded himself with, such as Laval, were alone responsible. As good Frenchmen, totally assimilated into every aspect of French life, they felt safe. Whatever happened to the hapless foreign Jews could never happen to them. Armand, Gilbert's father, had arrived in Marseilles in 1907 from Tunisia, bringing with him his two brothers, Albert and Simon, and his mother; his father had died not long before. The three young men were enterprising and hard-working and were soon running a profitable import business, bringing sugar, coffee, cocoa and spices from the French colonies.

In Marseilles, Armand met Bella Veill, who had come to France from Strasbourg. They married in 1913 and had nine children, all of them born in their large family house at 46 Boulevard Notre-Dame. Gilbert was the seventh; two younger boys followed. André, the eldest, worked with his father, as did Marthonne and Suzanne, until she married in 1939 and moved to Avignon. Apart from Blanchette, who had also married and emigrated to Portugal, the entire family lived at home, in considerable comfort. There were four maids. Even if the economic crisis of the early 1930s had made a dent in the Nizard fortunes, they continued to entertain lavishly, and once the German Jews escaping from the Reich began to reach Marseilles, they kept open house for them too.

Armand and Bella Nizard, with seven of their nine children

The first two years of Vichy rule were uneventful. The name Nizard did not sound Jewish. The younger children went to various lycées, where they sang 'Maréchal, nous voilà!'. Armand continued to shower Bella with costly pieces of jewellery. As the mother of nine French children, she was awarded the Médaille de la Famille. André, who had been called up on the outbreak of war, had been decorated with a Croix de Guerre with palm before being demobilised. They all felt, the parents as well as the children, secure in their Frenchness; as Gilbert would later say, fearing nothing, protected by Pétain, even after Armand's business had to be put in the name of an Aryan – he had a trusted colleague who volunteered to act as a front – and after 20-year-old Maurice was banned from sitting his final medical exams. It did not occur to any of them to leave France. Were they not French? Was André not a decorated war hero? Rationing had made inroads on their lavish lives, but what could not be found in the shops could usually be bought on the black market.

The round-ups and the clearances of the old town of Marseilles stopped just a few hundred yards from the Boulevard Notre-Dame. But after they had destroyed the port, the Germans kept going. They did more spot checks; they arrested new groups of people. Marseilles was suddenly full of alarming rumours. Day by day, it became harder to cling on to the carefully nurtured illusion about assimilation, about the legacy of the French Revolution, about liberty and fraternity.

Armand's brother Simon was married to Marthe, the niece of an antiquarian, who, being childless, was studying to be a doctor. One day, with no prior warning, the couple were denounced as Jews, arrested, taken to the prison of Saint-Pierre, put on a train for Drancy and deported to Auschwitz. It was all so sudden, so unexpected, that the strongest reaction throughout the rest of the family was one of shock. When they were able to consider their position, take stock more calmly, they realised that they all had to leave Marseilles. Suzanne and her two small children, briefly detained in Avignon but then released, decided to make their way to the Plateau Vivarais-Lignon, whose reputation as a place of safety they had already discussed. Mireille, who was 16, was called in to see her philosophy teacher, who, having heard talk of further arrests, begged her not to come to school. As she left the lycée that evening, Mireille was stopped by the police and her ID was checked; she was allowed to go, but her friend Jacqueline, stopped with her, was not. Jacqueline was deported.

One night very soon afterwards, at around seven o'clock, a German interpreter called Muller rang on the Nizards' bell. He came, he said, 'in friendship', to warn the family that they were in danger. Muller had a revolver, and when he left, he took away with him 110,000 francs that Bella had hidden in the linen cupboard. When he returned two days later, bringing with him two German soldiers, he was considerably less friendly. This time he carried off Bella's magnificent collection of jewellery, which had been kept in a desk in her bedroom. The Nizards agreed that they could wait no longer. They packed, Gilbert remembers, a mountain of luggage, and hid their valuable paintings in the coal cellar, but in their haste abandoned an important collection of Saxe porcelain. Armand, Bella and André went to Nice, to see whether they could raise some money. The four younger children, in the care of Maurice, left to join Suzanne and her family in the mountains.

When the Nizards arrived on the plateau, having wound their way up on the Tortillard through the forests of pine and fir trees heavy with snow – they reminded Camus of almond trees in flower – they went to join Suzanne in Fay-le-Froid. The village, which jutted out on a hill, had wisely renamed itself Fay-sur-Lignon in an attempt to dispel its entirely accurate renown as a place of exceptional cold, glacial winds driving straight down from the peak at Mézenc and snowdrifts that could reach eight metres for weeks at a time. For the next two years, Fay and its outlying farms and hamlets would become a haven for those seeking refuge.

Fay was the commercial heart of the plateau. If le Chambon had cornered the market in guest houses and children's *pensions*, Fay, with its grey granite houses and slate tiles, its dour architecture broken only by occasional surprisingly decorative fretwork metal balconies, was where people shopped and gathered. It had 6 butchers, 3 bakeries, 11 grocers and an astonishing 33 cafés, and on the many market days that filled the agricultural calendar, people from all over the Haute-Loire and the Ardèche came in search of tools, produce and livestock. At Easter, the large sloping square in the middle of the village was full of lambs and sheep; in October it was given over to a widely celebrated horse fair, farmers buying and selling the elegant, hardy beige animals with their distinctive white manes, which they used to plough the fields. Even the Germans coveted Fay's horses and came in search of them.

On the surrounding farms, people kept cows, pigs, ducks and chickens; they made their own butter and cheese, and smoked, salted and cured hams, for use in soups and patés during the long winter months. Few had indoor bathrooms; even fewer had electricity. Fay, like le Chambon, Tence and Le Mazet, had a large Protestant community, and among the villagers were many Darbyists. As long as the children married within the Protestant faith, mixed marriages were accepted. The local patois, which owed something to ancient Occitan and something to Italian, was widely spoken. Although in Fay's three schools the children were taught in French, most of the small children reached the age of six without a word of the language.

In the 1930s, Fay had become a popular tourist resort, visitors coming up from the surrounding plains to spend a month in the Abels' hotel, to walk over the fields and up on to the Mézenc, and to eat in the excellent restaurant, which was famous for its trout, caught in the local rivers. Once war was declared, they came in fewer numbers and stayed for shorter periods, but the hotel stayed open, run now by Mme Abel, who was in her seventies, and her daughter Lydie. And as the cities grew short of food, and rationing left many people hungry, so parties of *touristes alimentaires* could be seen every weekend, going from farm to farm in search of eggs, butter and meat. What the farmers did not sell on the black market, or deliver in forced requisitions, they used as barter. One enterprising man, whose family had run out of shoes, wrapped a string of sausages round and round his body, covered them with a coat, whose pockets he packed with meat, then set off on the Tortillard to Saint-Etienne, where he made a deal with a local shoemaker, meat for shoes, to be taken a pair at a time, to avoid detection.

When Gilbert and his brothers and sisters arrived in Fay, they found Suzanne and her family staying with Albert Exbrayat, who owned a garage on the edge of the village. Albert's mother Marie ran the ironmonger's on the main square, where she sold the vast cauldrons used by the famers' wives for their soups, along with every kind of tool, cartridge, implement and plough, her wares displayed outside on the street on balmy days. Marie was a formidable woman, strong, canny, small and thickset, who spoke little but patois and had introduced a glass-cutting machine to the village for her customers to order and measure their windows.

Nothing happened in Fay of which she was not a part. Above her shop was a large flat, in which she and her family lived. The Exbrayats were Protestants, believers, and with that belief had come a certitude that hiding people sought by Vichy and the Germans was the right thing to do.

The Nizards stayed for a while with Chazot, the mayor, who ran another small hotel; Chazot was also steeped in village affairs. From the hotel, with the help of Marie Exbrayat, they moved into two floors of a house on the square belonging to the Girand family, which felt safe as it had a second door at the back, giving on to a side street. They were soon joined by Bella, André and Armand, who had narrowly avoided arrest in Valence. Maurice began to offer his medical skills to the neighbouring families; Bella, Marthonne and Mireille kept house, and the boys went to school. Mireille continued her studies by correspondence and Maurice coached her in physics and chemistry.

Though impoverished, the Nizards were busy and cheerful, except for Armand, who found his enforced idleness unbearable and – foolishly – filled his time writing letters to his associate now running the business in Marseilles. Although the Jews hiding in various houses in and around Fay found it more prudent to mix little with each other, everyone knew that a constant stream of people seeking refuge passed through the Abels' hotel, and that Esther Furet, who was related to the Exbrayats, had taken in a family of strangers, some of them into her farmhouse outside the village, where a trapdoor above the manger led to a hidden space in the rafters. A haystack concealed another unseen safe place. M Robert, the baker, whose son had just escaped from a German prisoner-of-war camp, was also an active organiser of safe houses.

The Jews arriving in Fay could not have known that its new young pastor was a great admirer of Boegner and a man absolutely dedicated to saving as many people as he could. Daniel Curtet was just 25, the son of a pastor from the Vaudois, when, hearing of the work being done on the plateau and finding Switzerland's isolation and neutrality irksome, he applied for the post at Fay, which he had known from holidays as a boy. He was a slight, nice-looking man, with very round, rather large spectacles and wavy dark brown hair, cut short and combed straight back, gentle and humorous in manner, with none of the severity of some of his more austere colleagues. He spoke slowly, listened carefully. Curtet is a figure about whom there is no ambivalence.

He reached the plateau in late October 1942 and immediately wrote to his parents describing the appalling cold in his presbytery, his parish of 400 Protestants scattered over 16 square kilometres, and his first impressions of his flock, who seemed to suffer from a 'total lack of culture', their lives given over to their cows and their conversations to the weather, crops, food, rationing and the war. Naturally bookish and very well educated, Curtet worried about how to preach sermons that were sufficiently simple and direct, but said that it would do him good having to think things out more clearly. Over the next 13 months, he wrote 45 letters and postcards to his parents; 15 of them bear traces of a censor's blue pen.

Soon after settling in, Curtet attended the monthly gathering of the plateau's Protestant pastors, six of whom were Swiss, five French and one Italian. Along with Trocmé and Theis in le Chambon, there was Leenhardt in Tence, Besson in Montbuzat, Morel in Devesset, Bettex in Riou, all men he would soon know well. Together with the refugee pastors, there were now 24 on the plateau. From them, he discovered that an active system was already in place to hide the refugees, with a password, changed every month, as well as a code to be used on the telephone or in letters. Curtet became a master of the coded reference, mining the Bible for suitable phrases, and his letters to his parents are full of elegant and humorous allusions. As a pastor himself, his father, he knew, would have no trouble deciphering them.

One of Curtet's first encounters was with Oscar Rosowsky and his mother, still very desolate from the loss of her husband; they told him their true identity and the fact that they were mother and son. He realised that Mme Abel and her daughter Lydie, as well as M Robert the baker, were allies, and that help could reliably be found among his parishioners, and particularly in the homes of the Darbyists, whose habit of discretion and silence he soon came to admire and rely on. The Darbyists, he said, were the most faithful and the most secure of them all. M Robert, who was also the vice president of the parish council, was the only person in whom he decided to confide everything, so that were he to be suddenly arrested, there would be someone to take over.

It took a few false starts, however, to perfect the code, and his first experience was confusing. He was paying a visit to Les Vastres, a hamlet that lay within his parish, when a telephone call came for him. There was no telephone in his presbytery. Pastor Besson, whom he had yet to get to know, barked down the phone: 'Can you hear me clearly?' 'Yes, very,' replied Curtet, having no idea that this meant that the call was important. 'I need to send you a book.' This was baffling. 'What book?' Besson sighed with exasperation. 'An Old Testament, you idiot!' *Livres*, books, which had to be moved, delivered, put into libraries, were the newly arrived Jews in need of homes.

Soon Curtet was writing to his parents: 'I am continuing my studies of Christian names (Mark 13/14b) and I can find no trace of the name of Hans; on the other hand, my collection grows with those of the 12 sons of the patriarch, who, as I have discovered with pleasure, my parishioners and the Darbyists cherish and love dearly. I have also found some "*Ignaces-en-ski*", and even some "*chiens-au-tri*".' Mark 13/14b referred to 'let him that readeth, understand'; 'Hans' to the Germans; the 12 sons of the patriarch to the Jews, descendants of Abraham; '*Ignaces-en-ski*' to Polish refugees and '*chiens-au-tri*' to '*Autrichiens*', Austrians, inverted. In subsequent letters, 'the lost sheep of the house of Israel' (Matthew 15/24) meant the hidden Jews; the '*syndic des Vastres*' the friendly mayor of Les Vastres, Jean Bouix, 'who is passionate about this kind of book' and very 'skilled at raising lambs'; '*ceux du Weisshorn*', the name of a peak in Switzerland often referred to by its nickname of '*gendarme*', the local French police. Curtet's father was a mountaineer.

In January 1943, noting the arrival of the Nizards, Curtet wrote: 'Today I must hasten to find a place for my many copies of the Old Testament: five are to be delivered tomorrow, and I am especially proud of my parishioners, who have shown themselves to be fascinated by this kind of literature. This particular edition was published by a press in Marseilles. It seems that they have printed a great number.'

How necessary Curtet's elaborate code really was even he never quite knew; but it clearly gave him great pleasure and he felt a constant need to recount to his parents what was happening on the plateau. Modest and uncritical, he was a devoted and assiduous pastor, skiing from his presbytery to his distant parishioners when the snows came, battling with the sudden flurries that steamed up his glasses and froze his eyelashes, walking and cycling through the mud when the snows melted. A keen hiker and sportsman, he loved the rugged plateau. To feed his growing number of hidden Jews, Curtet made an arrangement with Mayor Bouix in Les Vastres to take his forged ration books, obtained from Rosowsky, which the mayor exchanged for real ones without complaint, saying that his superiors were also on their side. As both a teacher and a farmer, Bouix was a well-known figure on the plateau, and he saw it as his mission to supply all the Jews arriving in his area with false IDs. A 13-year-old shepherd boy acted as his courier, ferrying documents backwards and forwards to Rosowsky, doing the journey at night, whatever the weather. His name was Paul Majola.

When Curtet had people hidden in the presbytery, Mme Abel sent over vats of soup. Later, when the events of the war came to be discussed, Mme Abel and Lydie would be described as 'reserved, discreet and agreeable'. Soon, Curtet had a network of helpers taking in, moving around, hiding, feeding the Jews. Another unexpected ally turned out to be the Catholic curé of Fay, Bernard, one of the many Catholics on the plateau whose helpful actions were later overlooked. Curtet began his first visit to him by talking very generally about the refugees. Sensing the curé's warmth, he pressed on to discuss the hiding of Jews in his presbytery. What did the curé think he should do? Bernard replied that it was an excellent idea, and that since he assumed that Curtet was incurring considerable expenses, could he give him 100 francs to help cover them?

What Curtet's parishioners were soon remarking on, with approval, was the way that their young pastor never laid down the law, very seldom started any sentence 'Je pense', I think, and entered into their culture of silence and discretion as if by instinct.

He never saw himself, his son Alin would later say, as 'an actor in history'. Curtet regarded the Trocmés, with their loud voices and strong, didactic manners, with some wariness.

When the deep drifts of snow came, Curtet kept on paying visits to his distant parishioners, but complained that every outing took him at least two hours, and that when he wanted to visit le Chambon, some 15 kilometres away, the snow lay too thick for him to use his skis. In the evenings, by the fire in his cold presbytery, he read books on philosophy with 'a Daniel who is my neighbour'. He had decided, he told his father, to spend some years in Fay, because the local Protestants had seen too many pastors come and go, and they were people who were 'slow to open up'. He noted with pleasure that in his regular congregation there were now as many Darbyists as Protestants. Although he was somewhat lonely at first, his life changed when he met a young woman from Tours, Suzanne, whose father owned a shoe shop in Tournus and who had come to Fay on holiday; they talked after the morning service and met in the library. Before long, they were engaged; Curtet told his parents that she was 'a pearl among fiancées'.

Through the snow one day appeared two new 'goats from the breed of the Otrichtal' (*Autrichiens*), as he reported to his father, both seemingly very happy to have found a new owner – himself – who had transformed a corner of his house into a stable. These were two Austrian Jews, a painter called Schmidt and a history professor, Lipschutz, who had seen both his parents and his fiancée executed after the Anschluss. Writing to his father at this time, Curtet described them as '*tchekas*', this time using a word from the patois of his childhood village in Switzerland to mean someone hidden secretly in your home. The two men spent three weeks in the attic of the presbytery, reading the books from Curtet's library, and in the evenings, when the shutters were closed, they came down and sat in his study. One night, the bell rang. When Curtet went to the door, he realised that the young girl who had brought him a message could not have failed to have caught sight of his visitors. That same night, he led them on a two-hour walk up into the mountains, to the house of a farmer called Bonnet, who took the men in and asked no questions. Next morning, Bonnet drove his horse and cart into Fay and appeared at the presbytery in search of mattresses for his guests.

Since silence and discretion were the essence of the inhabitants of the plateau, it is not always easy to know either how many Jews there were in hiding, nor where precisely they were being concealed. It did not take very long, however, for Curtet's deeds and network of helpers to become known; once one family had found its way to Fay, others followed. During the snowy months of early 1943, when heavy downfalls cut off the village for days at a time, and Curtet struggled through the drifts to pay his pastoral visits, the knitting families of Roanne began to make their way up the mountain.

At the end of the Great War, there had been three French Jewish families living in the little textile town of Roanne, not far from Vichy. All through the twenties and thirties, knitters and weavers arrived from Poland and Germany, driven abroad by poverty and pogroms, drawn to Roanne by the promise of work in this bustling, thriving area. Most were related; others were friends. As a community, they were not particularly observant, but they were attracted by Zionism and believed passionately in the traditions and culture of Judaism. They worked as a cooperative, spoke Yiddish, and celebrated the Jewish holidays with much singing. Kristallnacht brought new families and with them a greater consciousness of danger, but the outbreak of war and then the months of the phoney war passed uneventfully, even though they knew that their relations still in Poland were being herded into ghettos.

The 92 knitting families settled in Roanne had between them a great many children, who spoke French by day in the local schools, and Yiddish at home and in the many scouting and cultural activities arranged by their parents. Much was made of their education, schooling being regarded as crucial to their future, wherever it took them. Many of these children would later say that the winter of 1940–1 was the last happy winter of their lives.

Genie and Liliane Schloss were sisters. Their father Max had grown up in Lodz, come to France at the age of 19 to escape the Polish draft, tried to reach Israel but been turned back by the British at Jaffa, and had then settled in Vienna, where he became a knitter, learning to operate one of the first knitting machines. Chancing one day to meet a French Jew working in Roanne's textile business, and hearing of its possibilities, he took his wife and small daughter, Genie, and both his and his wife's families, and emigrated to France. It was 1930, and the French needed Polish labour. Liliane was born in 1933. Both Max and his wife worked on the knitting machines, making pullovers. The little girls were happy, feeling themselves part of a large communal family; they joined the Jewish scouts, went camping, learnt to play musical instruments and sang. What both would remember later was the music of their childhood. When Pétain visited Roanne early in 1942, they called out 'Maréchal, nous voilà!' with great enthusiasm.

Genie and Liliane Schloss

But then the Germans crossed the demarcation line and occupied the Grand Hôtel in Roanne, and no one felt safe any more.
Rumours of round-ups and arrests spread rapidly through the
little community. At school, French children hissed '*sale Juives*' in
the playground. One of the knitters heard from his dentist, who
was a Protestant, about the plateau in the Cévennes where Jews
were being hidden. Having been given an introduction to Trocmé,
Max decided to send his daughters up the mountain on the little
train to live in one of the children's homes, Clair de Lune, run
by a childless Spanish republican couple in a hamlet not far from
le Chambon. At 14, Genie took seriously the task of looking after
9-year-old Liliane. They kept their surname of Schloss, which
sounded German and not Jewish, and passed themselves off as
Alsatian refugees who had been living in Tulle.

Clair de Lune had ten boarders, half of them Jewish. The kindly
Spanish director taught the girls how to ski, and how to sing the
psalms popular on the plateau; but his wife struck the sisters as
avaricious and unsympathetic, rationing their already small
portions of food, and quarrelling with her husband when he lit
a fire to make them feel warmer. They ate a great many watery
carrots, and when they walked into le Chambon, they would stop
and gaze at the rows of blueberry tarts in the bakery. From their
bedroom window they watched the convalescent German soldiers
run past during their daily exercise.

Genie was sent to Theis and the Ecole Nouvelle Cévenol,
Liliane to Darcissac and the primary school. Having been
instructed to say that they were Protestant, they decided, on
their first Sunday, to go to the temple in le Chambon to hear
Trocmé preach. It was unlike anything they had ever known.
They were impressed and intrigued by the service, by the long
silences, by the pastor's forceful and commanding presence. Very
occasionally, Max found ways to visit the plateau to see them.
One day, a group of French and German police arrived at the
pension in search of refugees. The sisters were terrified. Genie
hid in the cupboard in their room, in which happened to be
hanging an old coat of their father's, which, she knew, had a
Jewish calendar in its pocket. The police left the house without
checking their room, but that night, Genie and Liliane cried
with fear.

Early in 1943, Max decided that it was no longer safe for him and his wife to stay in Roanne. Most of their Jewish neighbours had left and were already hiding in various parts of the plateau. Taking a stock of sweaters with them, which they hoped to sell bit by bit to pay their way, they reached Grenoble, from where they sent word to the girls to help find them a refuge on the plateau. Genie, though still only 14, set off on her bicycle to visit the farms around Fay, knocking on doors and asking for a room for her parents. She was cold and wet and very tired when a farmer's wife, Mme Ruel, invited her in to sit by the fire, gave her a bowl of soup and said that she would arrange with Mme Exbrayat for Max and his wife to have rooms underneath another family of knitters, Hélène Grundman and her husband, and Mireille, their eldest daughter. The Grundmans' two boys, aged six and seven, had been sent to a farm belonging to Esther Furet, while their five-year-old daughter had gone to an orphanage in Draguignan.

For the rest of the war, Mme Ruel looked after the Schlosses, providing them with ham, eggs and butter and acting as a postbox when they needed to leave messages for each other. Through Oscar Rosowsky, they obtained forged IDs as Alsatians; they met and made friends with Mme Rosowsky and the Nizards. Since German soldiers occasionally brought their cars to Albert Exbrayat's garage, and wandered through the village while they were mended, they seldom left the house by day, but on Sundays they attended the temple and Max, who had a powerful voice, was taught by Curtet to sing the psalms. On Yom Kippur, Curtet held a special service for the Jews. The Schlosses lived frugally, eking out their stock of sweaters. Whenever they could, Liliane and Genie, still living at the Clair de Lune, bicycled over to see them.

The plateau was now full of Roanne's exiled knitters. Ruth Golan and Rita Goldmayer, whose German fathers had been friends in Berlin, lived together with their families in a small house deep in the forest owned by a woman who had moved out and gone to live with her daughter-in-law. The two men worked on a farm, looked after the cows and dug potatoes; when a pig was killed, they received a share of the meat. Eggs and cheese were regularly delivered to their door. After the two families became too nervous to send the girls to school, teachers came out from the Ecole Nouvelle Cévenol every few days to give them lessons.

Because Ruth and Rita loved singing, they practised the psalms and sang them in the temple on Sundays. They were told to sing, very loudly, 'Alouette, gentille Alouette' if they saw strangers in the street, to seem like little French girls.

The house had electricity, but none of the roads were lit, and though they knew the forest to be full of other families from Roanne, hidden away in similar farmhouses, the blackness that separated them felt dense and dangerous. One day, collecting bread on her bicycle from the village, Ruth was stopped by two German soldiers who asked for her papers. They waved her on, but for a long time, she could not stop herself trembling. As Miss Maber said, however safe the surface of life seemed, everyone was always afraid.

Those of the Roanne children who found themselves alone, for greater safety, separated from their parents and brothers and sisters, and from the colour and love and noise of their communal lives, suffered from the isolation and harshness of their new surroundings. They were intimidated by their dour hosts. What they would think about later, long after the war was over, was not the cold or the hunger, though both had filled their days, nor the lack of electricity or running water, but how long it had taken them to get used to the silences, and the fact that when someone spoke, it was only ever to give instructions. There was no touching, no warmth. What one girl, just 12 when she found herself alone in a Darbyist household in the forests, remembered was that she had had to force herself to learn to live apart, detach herself from other people, and that once she had learnt that lesson, she found it impossible to feel close to her parents again. She had changed, become another person; she was no longer a child. In a school essay, long after the war, another wrote of the day she had lost her mother, her home and the loving centre of her life, and how the grief she felt then she was never quite able to lose.

Many of the Jews hidden on the plateau were afraid, particularly the men, reduced to idleness and mindful of the stories reaching France of the fate of the Jews in Poland. They knew that many of their relations had disappeared, though just where they had gone was still not clear to them. Max, who worried constantly about their future, was made still more anxious when his 19-year-old sister-in-law went to meet her fiancé in Lyons, and was picked up by the police and sent to Drancy.

Soon afterwards, a German soldier convalescing in le Chambon got into difficulties swimming in the Lignon, and was saved by a Spanish boy from the Ecole Nouvelle Cévenol. On being pulled out, the German asked whether there was anything that he could do in return. That night, lying in bed in their *pension*, Genie said to Liliane: 'Do you think he could save our aunt?' It was already too late. She had been put on Convoi 57, bound for Auschwitz.

CHAPTER TEN

A lethal year

Nineteen forty-three was a lethal year on the plateau.

Towards the end of January, the Clermont-Ferrand office of the Commissariat Général aux Questions Juives uncovered what they decided was an 'escape network for Jews' among the Protestant villages on the mountain. They began to put together a list of those involved, helped by Inspector Praly, who was seen every evening at the post office handing in large envelopes to send to his superiors in Le Puy. The name that came up most often was that of Charles Guillon, but he was known to be living in Switzerland. Also high on the list, however, were the names of Trocmé, Darcissac and Theis. Darcissac, claimed Praly, was the moving force behind a 'Judeo-Gaullist circle' that was peddling 'pro-Jewish propaganda' on the plateau. Several times every week, he had observed the schoolteacher meeting secretly with men such as Le Forestier and Barbezat, the bookseller, to listen to the BBC, plot how to hide the Jews, and help forge false IDs.

Magda was knitting in the kitchen of the presbytery when, at seven o'clock on the evening of 13 February, two uniformed gendarmes banged on the door asking for the pastor. Trocmé was at a village meeting, so she showed them into his study. She had expected this moment ever since Lamirand's unfortunate and threatening summer visit. Trocmé returned, and was informed that he was under arrest. He suggested that they eat dinner before leaving. Magda and Jispa repacked the suitcase of clothes that they had prepared in anticipation of such an event long before but had recently unpacked when the pastor ran out of clean shirts. Cohen and Mme Berthe, one hiding in the attic, the other in the cellar, were warned to keep quiet and not show themselves.

The gendarmes, apparently very ill at ease, declined to eat. Anxious that there should be no fuss about the arrest, they insisted that no one be told. As it happened, the young daughter of a church councillor unexpectedly arrived to remind the Trocmés of her father's birthday celebrations, realised what was happening and hastened off to spread the news.

February 1943 was exceptionally cold, even for the plateau. It was minus 10 degrees when Trocmé emerged from the presbytery between the two gendarmes to find a double row of villagers lining the path to the square, clattering their clogs as they tried to keep warm. They had brought with them small presents of things hoarded up for special occasions: a box of sardines, a bar of soap, a piece of sausage, some eau de cologne and a surprising roll of lavatory paper, on which Trocmé later discovered his parishioners had copied out verses from the Bible. There were also a few candles and when it was realised that matches were missing, the two policemen furtively produced their own. They seemed much relieved by the peaceful behaviour of the crowd, which had started to sing Luther's hymn: 'A safe stronghold our God is still / A trusty shield and weapon'. Trocmé felt, he would later write, 'almost elated'. 'This was the moment I had long been waiting for, the moment when I would have to bear witness to my deepest convictions.' He had always believed that there were two powers, good and evil, fighting over the Kingdom of the World; it was now that he decided that 'there is a third: stupidity'.

From the presbytery, the police went on to arrest Theis, who came quietly, and Darcissac, who escaped through his cellar and into the woods, until Mme Darcissac was persuaded to urge him to turn himself in, since it would be much worse for them all if the Germans came to get him. Darcissac, noted Trocmé somewhat smugly, was 'frozen with fear', 'overwhelmed' by terror that he might be sacked from his job and 'dishonoured'. The police, anticipating trouble, had cut the telephone and telegraph lines to the village.

The prisoners were driven off to the police station at Tence, then taken in a cortège of six police cars down the mountain to the barracks in Le Puy, where they were locked into cells but given sheets for their bunks and treated with embarrassed civility.

Next morning, all signs of politeness gone, they were put on a train for Lyons, then on another for Limoges, to be interned at the camp of Saint-Paul-d'Eyjeaux, where they were received with great 'uncouthness' by the captain of gendarmerie. The camp, a series of low grey wooden barracks surrounded by barbed wire, was home to 500 men, most of them prominent communists from south-west France, interned at the time of the Soviet–German pact, along with a number of Catholic and socialist opponents to Vichy. The inmates were thin, from many months eating little but Jerusalem artichokes, salsify and turnips, and extremely bored. Saint-Paul-d'Eyjeaux had been designed as a 're-education' camp, not a work camp, but had long since abandoned all attempts at persuading the men to look on Vichy more favourably, leaving them with nothing to fill their days. They spent the time surreptitiously listening to radio receivers made of lamps and bits of wire hidden inside tins, and were currently celebrating the fall of Stalingrad. They were not unfriendly to the newcomers, joking that the camp was already full of Catholics and they had a rabbi, 'but pastors! That's all we need!'

The camp commandant appeared dubious when Theis proposed holding Protestant services, saying that he could not imagine that anyone would wish to attend, but he had not reckoned with Trocmé's powers of oratory, nor with the acute boredom of the men. A first service drew a congregation of nine. Trocmé preached, Theis took the liturgy, Darcissac, whose voice and skills as choirmaster were legendary, led the singing. The nine became twenty; the twenty, forty. Soon the barrack hut was too small for the meetings that followed and the overflow of prisoners had to listen from outside, leaning on the open windows. Deftly, Trocmé and Theis used codes, substituting the name of Pétain for that of Marx, and a lively debate started up among the prisoners; pastors and Marxists alike agreed that after Stalingrad, anything was possible, even the overthrow of capitalism and the crumbling of evil through non-violent means. Walking around the camp, the pastors heard some of the inmates humming the psalms.

The commandant, sitting in the front row to make certain that nothing seditious was taking place, was delighted to see such eagerness for re-education, and felt so lenient towards his new prisoners that he allowed them unlimited visits and parcels. Darcissac's son Marco smuggled in a camera and took pictures; Trocmé, who had a real talent for drawing, did sketches of the prisoners and their surroundings. The shelves above their bunks began to look like a grocery shop. On the night when one of the prisoners managed to escape through a tunnel, there was widespread rejoicing, in which the three men shared. They had come to like and admire their companions, and would later say that their talks on communism had been a revelation to them; they were surprised, then pleased, to find themselves so popular.

From left to right: Theis, Darcissac and Trocmé

In le Chambon, Magda had been visited by the captain of police from Tence, who apologised for her husband's arrest, and said what a fine man he considered Trocmé to be. The village was calm, Curtet wrote to his father, 'as after a storm'. In Nîmes, Boegner, as head of the Protestant Church, was alerted to the arrests. The Bible circle at Mollé expressed their great sympathy; the Catholic curé sent his warm support. In the Ecole Nouvelle Cévenol, the students had never been so hard-working, nor the farmers in the surrounding countryside so generous with supplies; Noël Poivre, one of the plateau's fieriest pastors, preached a sermon on Herod and John the Baptist, only thinly disguising Laval, Pétain and the Jews. This would be the start of a far more robust and outspoken attitude towards the 'unhappy, the prisoners, the persecuted', in which Bible texts and commentaries would henceforth deal implicitly with resistance.

Writing to reassure him, Le Forestier told Trocmé: 'The Church of le Chambon may not be the dove of the Holy Spirit, but it is like a duck: even when you chop off its head, it keeps on walking automatically.' Characteristically light-hearted, he added that he recommended that the pastor stay on in the camp, where there were grown men to convert and bring to God, while in le Chambon 'there are nothing but women who have already been saved and many children whom we will look after with tenderness and perseverance'.

Taking with him the pastor's nephew, Daniel Trocmé, recently arrived on the plateau, Dr Le Forestier went to Vichy, where he was given an audience with the *chef de cabinet* of the police minister. The captives, Le Forestier reminded him, pastors and teachers, the fathers of eight, five and three children respectively, were neither spies nor traitors. On the contrary, they were men of God, preaching the Gospels, and Vichy would be making a grave mistake if it turned them into martyrs. They were quite wrong in imagining 'charity towards enemies, political plots and Gaullism'; what they should have seen was that it was all about 'love, faith in God, the church of Jesus Christ'. What Le Forestier proposed was a proper inquiry, not one based on 'anonymous informers'. Bach, it soon transpired, had already put in place an inquiry of his own, warning Vichy that these arrests might well undo all the previous goodwill he had brought about on the plateau.

It was while Trocmé, Theis and Darcissac were at Saint-Paul-d'Eyjeaux that change, of a radical and lasting kind, drawing in farmers and pastors, Jews and communists, students and Darbyists, came to the plateau. It represented everything that these three pacifist, reasonable, believing men most mistrusted.

In 1942, Laval had agreed, under pressure from the Germans, to set up recruitment offices throughout the unoccupied zone for workers to go to Germany. Fritz Sauckel, the officer in charge of coordinating foreign labour, arrived in Vichy to instruct the French that they would have to supply a quarter of a million workers, over half of them skilled metallurgists. The scheme was given the name 'Relève'. The terms settled on were designed to appeal to the families of the million or so prisoners of war still held in

German camps: one to be released for every three Relève volunteers. Anxious to retain French control, Vichy set about implementing Sauckel's demands – with a notable lack of success. Only 12,000 volunteers could be persuaded to take up the offer in June; 23,000 men left for Germany in July, 18,000 in August. It was far short of Sauckel's demands, which were increasing all the time.

Seeking not to lose the initiative, Vichy tried coercion. In September, a law was passed making national service working for the Germans obligatory for men aged 18 to 50 and single women between the ages of 21 and 35. On 16 February 1943, the Service du Travail Obligatoire, known as STO, came into force. The first to be called up were young men born in 1920, 1921 and 1922.

If by the winter of 1942 the brutal round-ups and deportations of the foreign Jews, and the unfeeling behaviour of the French police, had cooled not only the attitude of the churches but that of a large swathe of the French population towards Vichy and Pétain, the STO sparked off a far more serious rupture. It was no longer foreigners and strangers who were at risk, but the French themselves. Outrage and anger spread. There was a scramble to find reasons to avoid call-up: women hastened to marry, young men to join the police, the railways or mining companies, all of which carried deferment. Employers were enraged at being left without skilled workers. Women lay down on the rail tracks. When the trains left for Germany with the first men on board, singing the 'Internationale', there were shouts of 'Laval au poteau!' – Laval to the stake. From London, André Philip was only one of the many Free French exhorting young Frenchmen to take to the countryside, 'prendre le maquis', rather than allow themselves to be sent to Germany.

The Protestant Church had come out clearly and rapidly against STO, saying that there was an 'insurmountable' contradiction between the Gospels and forced labour. It was imperative, declared Pastor Boisset in Montpellier, to remain faithful 'to God in the face of authoritarianism . . . total war and deportations'. Among the Catholics, many of the lower clergy were also loud in their criticisms of the STO. The hierarchy, once again, remained silent. But then Cardinal Liénart of Lille spoke out, saying that the occupiers had asked for more than they were entitled to, and after the spring conference of bishops and archbishops came a declaration that to evade the STO was not a sin. There was much talk about the justness of disobeying unjust orders. On the plateau, where the STO was compared to Napoleon's unpopular '*levée en masse*', the young men refusing to leave were spoken of as heroic descendants of the Camisards.

There was a tradition among the villagers, when young men left for the army, to gather them together and give them advice. In the absence of the pastors and Darcissac, it was Dr Le Forestier who took it upon himself to summon a meeting in the annexe of the temple for all those ordered to present themselves to the authorities. Thirty young men, due to leave the following day, turned up. This meeting marked another crucial moment in the plateau's war.

Le Forestier's message was unambiguous. No one should serve the Germans. Furthermore, if anyone did accept, he would do well to take with him a little bag of earth, for that way he could be sure that when he was killed – as he surely would be – he would at least lie under the soil of his native land. The glamorous young doctor was persuasive. He would help, he said, anyone who chose to refuse the summons. After a heated hour of talk, only four volunteers went ahead and presented themselves to the authorities. Before long, there were 41 '*réfractaires*', refusers, reported missing, hiding out in the isolated farmhouses, where there were farmers prepared to say that they had seen no one, heard nothing.

Reports began to circulate that the Plateau Vivarais-Lignon was a good place to hide, and that there was a doctor called Le Forestier who was waiting to help. 'That day was a turning point for the Resistance in the whole area,' one of the young men, Victor May, son of the owners of the Hôtel May, would say later. 'Le Forestier was the spur, and his words acted as a spark.' Police sent from Yssingeaux to report on what was going on noted a general lack of cooperation on the part of the inhabitants; even the '*notables*', they said, claimed to know nothing. Bach, possibly to cover his back, asked his superiors for reinforcements. By now, only one in ten of all those called up across France was actually on a train to Germany. The rest had wrangled deferments or disappeared.

Among the young men appearing on the plateau was a boy scout called Pierre Piton. He was 17, a wily, resourceful, generous-spirited boy with a round face and bright blue eyes, who had been working in the shipyards on the Normandy coast and sending back messages to the Allies about German troop movements. His father was a naval officer, his mother a teacher. Somewhat austere by nature, Piton had for a while thought of becoming a missionary. On the plateau, he found another kind of vocation.

He took a room at the Pension des Genêts, where in return for his keep he agreed to supervise the evening homework of the young theologians studying at the Ecole Nouvelle Cévenol. He soon met Mireille Philip, who recruited him to help find more hiding places for Jews as well as for the new STO evaders. Passionate about his scouting, he was welcomed into the ranks of Penguins, Wolves and Storks, and was soon made second to the leader of the unionist troop, Pierre Brès, who preferred to call his packs by the names of Camisard heroes.

Brès, another important local figure, was a devout Protestant, a keen sportsman and a print designer; he had arrived on the plateau with his wife and son after being demobilised from a tank unit. As scout leader, he brought together local children, tourists, Catholics and Protestants and schooled them vigorously in basket-ball, as well as taking them camping, where they sang hymns and acted out valiant Camisard deeds. His wife became professor of gymnastics at the college, and they were soon friends with Le Forestier and his family. But Brès had ideas beyond simple scouting on his mind, and the young men escaping the STO were perfect recruits. The early resistance in France had been essentially urban, concerned with writing and distributing literature hostile to the Germans and organising a number of specific attacks on the occupying forces; it had not given much thought to guerrilla warfare in the countryside. With the STO came the beginnings of a Maquis.

Nor was Brès alone in envisaging another step towards the liberation of France. In Yssingeaux, there was a teacher called Jean Bonnissol, whose brother-in-law, M Valdener, ran a café that acted as a letter drop for people on the run, and who was already in contact with the Franc-Tireur resistance movement active in Lyons and along the Rhône. There was Pierre Fayol, an engineer and former army officer, newly arrived with his family in le

Chambon, having helped the Jews in Marseilles before the German assault. And there was Léon Eyraud, a former miner who now ran the Pension Les Ombrages, within sight of the station in le Chambon, from where he would watch out for the train bringing new Jewish families and hasten up the hill to gather them into his *pension*. Eyraud was musical, a humorous, sly, astute man who possessed a great deal of authority; his wife treated their 14 guests as '*mes gosses*', my own children. Between them, these five men, Piton, Brès, Bonnissol, Fayol and Eyraud, brought with them stirrings of a militancy far from the pacifist dreams of Theis and Trocmé.

What the draft evaders needed was precisely what the plateau was already providing for the Jews: safe hiding places, food, sympathy and false IDs. Galvanised by Le Forestier, Emile Sèches was soon adding concealed STO young men to his list of people for whom he needed to scrounge food, while Mme Barraud and her daughter Gabrielle were finding them beds at the Beau Soleil.

Early in March, while the imprisoned pastors were still absent from the plateau, Rosowsky decided that he needed more privacy for his ever-expanding forgery business. Eyraud had already asked him to increase his output to take in the new STO evaders, for whom he now had to produce a whole range of IDs, making them younger than their real ages and therefore not subject to call-up. He borrowed a bicycle and cycled off on the road towards Mazet. After four kilometres, at a hamlet called La Fayolle, he saw a young woman knitting outside her house. She directed him to the tenants of a farm owned by Henri and Emma Héritier, who had five young children and four cows, stabled in outbuildings. Rosowsky told them he was a student. They asked no questions, offered him a room in the barn and provided him with meals. M Héritier registered him as a necessary farm worker, to protect him from being called up for the STO.

In desperate need of extra forgers, Rosowsky recruited a local boy, Samy Charles, who had good contacts throughout the Ardèche and the Haute-Loire. A local farmer offered to include false documents along with his deliveries of bread to distant farmhouses. Rosowsky had never worked harder. One day a consignment of blank ration books, organised by André Philip, who was now with de Gaulle in Algiers, was dropped by parachute from an

Allied plane. Piton, going to collect them from Mireille, was overwhelmed by the rich and delicious smell of jam and would forever associate it with his days on the plateau. Mireille told him that she had used her entire sugar ration for many weeks to make the jam.

Whenever he went to see his mother in Fay, Rosowsky took with him batches of newly forged IDs for Curtet's own ever-growing number of hidden Jews. He had been delighted at the proof of his skills as a forger when one night, on his way back from delivering a consignment of false documents to Fay, he was stopped by a policeman for riding his bicycle without a light. He produced his own false ID; the policeman professed himself content.

Writing of his new protégés, the STO boys, Curtet told his father that he was busy collecting a number of 'specialist books', particularly on metallurgy, about which he felt very warmly, since most of them had been edited in the nearby towns of Saint-Etienne and Firminy, 'where this kind of work is very popular'. This *exercise de math, 15/24*' (Jews) was taking a lot of his time, while 'Daniel 1:3–4 continues at an ever-accelerating pace'. (In Daniel 1:3–4, the King orders Asphenaz to 'bring him certain of the children . . . in whom there was no blame'.) What Curtet's father made of it all is not known.

The very mood of the plateau was changing, becoming angrier, more militant. With the arrival of young men from the plains and the mining communities, and the threat of capture of their own sons, more local families came forward to offer sanctuary. Some of the most active rescuers were women, and two of the most important ran cafés.

Together with Tence and le Chambon, Mazet was the heart of the Protestant and Darbyist enclave; though the village itself was small – not much more than a collection of the grey-stone houses typical of the area, a Protestant temple, a Catholic church and a Mairie – its commune stretched across 50 square kilometres and comprised some 2,000 people, nearly all of them farmers. Thursday was market day, when they came on horseback, by foot and driving carts to exchange news and buy and sell their produce; on Sundays, they returned to attend the Protestant service in the temple. Perfectly placed on the central square, which was also the crossroads for the village, opposite the Mairie and just below the temple, was a café, built by Benjamin Argaud at the end of the nineteenth century and run now by his niece, Lucie Ruel, known as Lulu, with the help of her 20-year-old daughter Lucienne. Lulu's husband, Paul, had died not long before the war; Lucienne was married, with a small baby.

Lucie Ruel (centre), 1945

The Café Argaud, which doubled as a restaurant and a wine shop, was the centre of Mazet life. Several members of the family were butter-makers, and Lulu was friends with the mayor, Pierre Salque. Better still, the café, reached by climbing the stairs above a former coach house and stables, where the casks of wine were stored, had a barn and outbuildings, a back entrance originally used as a gate through which straw could be moved in and out, and a little window from which could be seen everything that happened in the square. On Thursdays and Sundays, the crowds and the bustle were ideal for every manner of deception.

During the exodus of Spanish republicans at the end of the civil war, Lulu had taken in a mother and her two small children. When they were moved to a prison in Yssingeaux, she had continued to visit them every week, taking food. After the great *rafles* of the summer of 1942, she took in Jewish families, some of them sent by the Trocmés via a young Protestant widow called Simone Mairesse, who had settled in Mazet with her small daughter, Nicole. Simone had learnt of the death of her husband through reading a list of casualties of prisoners of war in the *Paris-Soir*; instead of grieving, she threw herself into saving Jews. She found hiding places with farmers nearby for those for whom Lulu had no room, and they came to eat at Lulu's table, paying her what they could. If they had no money, they ate for free. The more resourceful spent their days foraging for food for the pot. A Darbyist farmer's wife sent extra butter and vegetables; Lulu's son-in-law, who worked for the local cooperative, provided milk and cheese.

One of Lulu's hidden Jewish lodgers, André Weil, who went by the name of Colombo, was a chemist from Paris. One day on his scourings of the countryside he met a young Jewish girl stumbling through the melting snow in very thin shoes; he brought her back to Lulu's café, and fell in love with her. Lulu found room for her too, as well as for her parents. In the evenings, they listened to the BBC, and one of the visitors, René Nordmann, who owned a large textile business not far from Paris, marked the progress of the Allies with little flags stuck on to a map, though to have such a map at all was dangerous. Lulu kept a lamp burning all night during bad weather, to act as a beacon for anyone out on the roads.

When the STO began to bring scared, defiant young men to her café, she took them in as well, beginning with a worker from Saint-Etienne, more a boy than a man, though he had a wife and two small children with him. The ever-expanding group of hidden people began to fill the barns and the outlying buildings. Whenever a raid was threatened, they hid in the attics of the temple, or in a hole Lulu had cleverly had dug in the garden, with a roof made of stones and earth, large enough to fit six grown men.

It was the schoolteacher Bonnissol who first approached another café owner, Dorcas Robert, for help in hiding STO evaders. Dorcas, like Lulu, was a widow, a small, sturdy, energetic woman with grey-green eyes; she was the mother of an eight-year-old daughter and two younger sons, and she ran a grocery shop and café in the middle of Yssingeaux, to the north-west of the plateau. Her mother was a Darbyiste. Bonnissol asked whether he might use her sitting room as a meeting place, and when she agreed, he arranged for the buses from Le Puy, which stopped outside her door, to deliver communiqués and orders from the Resistance leaders in the plains. These she took in and hid under the counter until he could come to collect them.

As in Mazet, Thursday was market day in Yssingeaux, and the confusion produced by the farmers and the *touristes alimentaires* provided an excellent cover for the comings and goings of Bonnissol and the STO boys. Some now spent their nights in the café, along with a priest on the run from the Gestapo and an escaped prisoner of war. Helping in the grocery was a young woman called Rose Bérard, a farmer's daughter who had been brought up to 'know the value of good causes' and whose brother had been taken prisoner at Dunkirk. From time to time, a local policeman called Gauthier, who knew exactly what they were doing and supported them, dropped by to see them.

Gauthier and his colleagues were no longer the unswerving supporters of Pétain that they had once been. The events of the summer of 1942 and the arrival of the Germans in the south had between them eroded much of the loyalty and obedience to Vichy, and nowhere more so than on the plateau, where the local policemen, who had grown up in the area and felt close to its inhabitants, were increasingly turning a blind eye to the presence of hidden Jews and STO evaders. There was, however, a new force, a new alliance of pro-German, pro-Vichy men; and this one would prove altogether more threatening.

In January 1943, the Service d'Ordre Légionnaire, the 'cavalry of modern times', flag-waving, beret-wearing saviours of Pétain's moral values and *la France éternelle*, freed themselves from the old Légion Française des Combattants – Vichy's fusion of all previous veteran associations – and became a *'milice française'*. Joseph Darnant, the crude, thuggish supporter of the extreme right-wing movements of the 1930s and of the secret terrorists, the Cagoulards, became their secretary general; Laval took the role of president. Their mission was to maintain order and, if need be, to defend France; their symbol was the *bélier*, Aries the ram, with its message of strength and renewal.

This new militia, profoundly anti-communist, anti-Semitic and nationalistic, was tightly organised and hierarchical. Members wore badges and lived ordinary lives, except when called on. But there was soon also a military wing, the Franc-Garde, made up of professional soldiers, and a youth section, l'Avant-Garde, composed of fit, strong, sporty gun-carrying youths, some no older than 16 or 17, and a number of girls. Pétain urged them all to be disciplined, level-headed, moderate and blameless in their conduct. But as recruiting proved slow, so the outcasts of French society – petty gangsters, ex-prisoners, fanatical anti-terrorists – were drawn into their ranks, lured by a sense of adventure and the opportunity to loot, requisition and play the black market at will. On the plateau, in ones and twos, there were young men who began to find the whole idea very attractive.

On the evening of 24 February, in Le Puy, the commander of the gendarmerie for the Haute-Loire, Silvani, was handed a list of 82 foreign Jews, with orders to arrest them. The 'ramassage', a simultaneous action to take them into custody, was set for seven o'clock the following morning. This sudden call for Jews was the result of the assassination of two German officers in Paris, for which 2,000 Jewish men aged between 16 and 65 were demanded in reprisal. There were no warnings. If Schmähling and Bach were of a mind to protect the Jews, on this occasion they chose not to.

On the plateau, Hubert Meyer, the young director of the Coteau Fleuri, had no time to evacuate his resident Jews, nor to hide them. A special detachment of police, including the gendarmerie, arrived at daybreak and took away a young man called Wolfradt; among the eight Jews seized that day were Schniebel, from a Quaker childrens home, Les Grillons, and Winitzer, from La Maison des Roches. There was, noted Silvani somewhat drily in his report, 'a certain emotion among the onlookers'. It took the form of anger and protests, but did not prevent the captives from being driven off to Le Puy. What is known, from the records held in Le Puy, is that of the 82 names on Bach's list, 58 people were found and arrested, and 24 of those were sent to Gurs.

Hanne's friend Jakob Lewin, who had been with her in La Guespy since their transfer from Gurs, had a very narrow escape. He had recently been joined by his older brother Martin, and on the morning of 25 February they were in the new carpentry workshop set up by Cimade. Inspector Praly appeared at the door, saying: 'At last, I've caught you.' The two boys were taken to the Mairie, then put on a police bus for Le Puy. A group of villagers gathered, trying to prevent the bus from leaving by lying on the ground in front of it; then, as had become the pattern when people were arrested, they began to sing. As they waited, a young pupil at the Ecole Nouvelle Cévenol, Christian de Montbrison, arrived with a piece of chocolate and pressed it into Jakob's hand. When the bus left, Le Forestier followed it down the mountain in his car. He managed to get Jakob released, on the grounds that he was still only 17, and therefore under age; but he could do nothing for the slightly older Martin, who joined those sent to Gurs.*

Three days later, with no reason given, Miss Maber and Miss Williamson were ordered to present themselves to police head-quarters in Le Puy, and to bring with them blankets and warm clothes. They left weighed down by little gifts from the villagers. Later, Miss Maber, who was reticent about this as about all things that touched on herself, would say that they had probably been denounced as 'enemies of the people' by Praly. After an uncomfort-able and unnerving four days, they were released, apparently on Bach's orders. It seems that he had discovered that not long before the war, Miss Maber had adopted two French children abandoned by their prostitute mother, and was paying for their upbringing. The order for the women's release arrived only after they were already on a train taking them north towards Drancy and depor-tation. The train was stopped, and Miss Maber and Miss Williamson were taken off. No one else on board that particular train survived.

On 15 March came other releases. Five weeks after their arrest, Trocmé, Theis and Darcissac were summoned to the commandant's office in Saint-Paul-d'Eyjeaux and told that Laval had ordered that they be freed; they were to pack their bags immediately and leave to catch a ten o'clock train home. First, however, they needed to sign some papers containing an undertaking to pledge support to Pétain. Theis and Trocmé, without hesitation, refused. As Trocmé would later recount in his unpublished autobiography, the commandant, furious, told them that they were 'insane', and 'dangerous anarchists'. Darcissac signed; as a teacher, to do other-wise would have cost him his job. He had been, wrote Trocmé not entirely without malice, 'so afraid'; he was now both 'sheepish and very happy'. While the teacher left for the station, the two

---

* In due course, having hidden and escaped one deportation train, Martin was also returned to le Chambon.

pastors, to the incredulity of their fellow prisoners, returned to their barracks.

Next morning brought a new summons. Laval had sent orders that they were to be released anyway, providing they would at least agree to 'respect the person of the Maréchal of France'; this they could do. Their return to le Chambon was greeted with subdued warmth, Pastor Jeannet having warned against too much public rejoicing. Praly reported to his superiors that the five weeks in detention seemed to have done the men good: their attitude towards the government was definitely more respectful. He would continue, he added, to keep a very close watch on all three. The following Sunday, the packed temple heard the story of the men's adventures.

To what or to whom exactly they owed their release has never been discovered. It may have been due to the fact that Laval had an eye to the future, and that in the aftermath of Stalingrad, the war was swinging in the direction of the Allies; or it may have been, as Trocmé believed, that the commandant feared the men's disruptive popularity in the camp. More simply, it may have been brought about by the intervention of people like Bach and Bohny. Certainly Boegner used his connections at Vichy to argue for the men's release with René Bousquet, Secretary General of Police. Whatever the reason, it came not a moment too soon. A few days later, the camp was closed and the 500 prisoners were deported to Poland and Silesia. Few are thought to have returned.

The first stirrings of spring were appearing on the plateau. There were days of pale sun, when the women would come outside and sit on their doorsteps to make their lace. The ice on the Lignon began to break up, bringing surges of water coursing down the river bed. A young Jewish boy called Lecomte caught a trout with his hands. Underneath the snow could be heard sounds of melting water and the croak of frogs long dormant below the ice. On 9 March, Camus noted that the first periwinkles had come up through the last patches of snow.

The pastors were delighted to be home. But the village was not quite the one they had left behind. It was an edgier, less tranquil and pacifist place, one in which new cross-currents of thought were moving events forward at a faster, more brutal pace. The plateau did not seem quite so inviolate, and the Jews, the resisters, the STO young men felt anxious. Saving people had moved into a grey area, and grey areas were not what Trocmé liked.

La Maison des Roches, home to a number of young Jewish men, struck Rosowsky as particularly vulnerable, and he urged its director, Daniel Trocmé, to disperse the students. And it was not long before Curtet received a visit from his Viennese former lodger, Lipschutz, who had returned for a while to live at La Maison des Roches, and who told him that he was shocked by the insouciant optimism of the *pension*. 'They can't see the danger,' he said. 'They make light of everything. They are convinced that there is always a way out of everything.'

CHAPTER ELEVEN

An unknown and unknowable oblivion

It was not only on the plateau, but across the whole of France, that the mood was changing. The early spring of 1943 was relatively mild. Even so, people were cold and hungry. The number of cases of TB was rising all the time, along with diabetes, typhus and scurvy. Lack of vitamin B and sugar was resulting in sudden deaths from malnutrition. Hospitals and chemists were running out of codeine, quinine, insulin, gauze, iodine and disinfectants of every kind. The welfare organisations, unable to meet the ever-greater demands on their resources, reported feeling 'menaced by starvation'. There were now, said the Quakers, at least two million 'seriously malnourished' people in the cities, not so much because of a shortage of food, but because so much of it was going to the Germans and to the black market. Across the country, the French, angry with Vichy about the privations, were angry too about the pervasive repressions, the all-too-visible ill treatment of the Jews, the round-ups of their own young men, and the predatory militia recruits, swaggering around with newly acquired weapons. It gave strength to those bent on saving people.

Despite the savage reprisals, the attacks on the occupying forces by the Resistance were becoming bolder and better organised. In January 1943, the three principal resistance movements in the south – Combat, Franc-Tireur and Libération-Sud – had merged into Les Mouvements Unis de la Résistance. Henri Frenay, head of Combat, was often to be seen in le Chambon, staying at Les Ombrages with his sister, Mme Eyraud, just across the street from the convalescent Germans, all part of the curious inviolability of the plateau.

Since the execution of hostages seemed only to alienate the population, Eichmann ordered that the trains carrying people to the concentration and extermination camps, a more effective measure of control, be resumed. After a lapse of five months, during which the trains had been needed to carry men and supplies to the eastern front, the deportation of the Jews from France began once more.

February was a murderous month. A first round-up of Jews in Paris took away children – whose names had been found through lists held by the Jewish umbrella organisation the UGIF – the sick and the very elderly. Four 90-year-olds and 54 men and women in their eighties, taken from the Rothschild Hospital in Paris, as well as seven three-year-olds, were on the 49th *convoi* of the war to leave Drancy for Auschwitz. On arrival, a little girl called Sylvia Menkes was gassed; it was her first birthday. All but a very few of these new deportees were foreign Jews, but the net around the French Jews was drawing tighter all the time. By mid March, 49,000 people had been sent to the death camps; almost none were still alive. Plans were afoot to increase the number of new deportees to between 8,000 and 10,000 every week. Deportation, it was announced over the radio, was a question of 'public hygiene'. That many would be French was no longer in doubt: like foreign Jews, they were obliged to have *'Juif'* or *'Juive'* on all their IDs. To make their arrest more palatable, those now rounded up were carefully branded as 'criminals'. The Germans had played their cards with Laval with skill and cynicism; but France was running out of foreigners.

There were fewer people in Gurs, Rivesaltes and the other internment camps, so many having already been deported, but they continued to be places of extreme hardship and constant fear. Rivesaltes, noted a visitor, had become a 'sorting station for people who pass into an unknown and unknowable oblivion'.

Except that this oblivion was not any longer unknown. It was over six months since Gerhart Riegner, the outspoken and sober young secretary of the World Jewish Congress in Geneva, had begun supplying reliable information about the Final Solution, obtained from dozens of different sources throughout Europe, to the Allies, to the Vatican, to the International Committee of the Red Cross and to Jewish leaders all over the world. He had sent eye-witness accounts of the gassings, the mass shootings, the round-ups, the deportation trains. He had even reported precise details of the gas used by the Germans, Zyklon B, and of the numbers of Jews they planned to murder, where, when and how. An account of an order issued by Hitler regarding the 'extermination' of all Jews by the end of 1942 had been received by Carl Burckhardt of the International Committee of the Red Cross and passed on to the US Secretary of State. All of which had resulted, on 17 December 1942, in a joint Allied denunciation of the 'bestial policy of cold-blooded extermination directed mainly against the Jews' being carried out by Germany.

The statement, read out in the House of Commons in London by Anthony Eden, and in Washington by Roosevelt, concealed none of the facts: the 'infirm . . . left to die of exposure and star-vation' or 'deliberately massacred in mass executions', the hundreds of thousands of victims, 'entirely innocent men, women and chil-dren'. But the world was not much minded to listen. Earlier in the year, at the ICRC in Geneva, an extraordinary plenary session called on 14 October to decide whether or not to go public with the information had resulted in a virtually unanimous vote against – ostensibly in order not to jeopardise the work being carried out with prisoners of war. The piecemeal, often uncoordinated, requests by the Jewish leaders – for safe havens for escaping Jews, for evacuations from Bulgaria and Romania, for the bombing of the gas chambers at Auschwitz – were ignored, denied, or conveniently put aside. No Western Allied power wished to put the saving of the Jews high among its war aims; their liberation would have to come about only as a by-product of military victory.

When, on 18 January 1943, the French ambassador to the Vatican was called in to see Pope Pius XII, he was warmly congratulated on the excellent work being done by Pétain 'for the renewal of religious life in France'. About the Jews, not a word was said.

In Lyons, Amitié Chrétienne, though knowing itself to be closely watched by Vichy and the Germans, had continued, behind its pious, respectable front, to provide new papers and hiding places for Jews, and to put out its *cahiers*, to an ever-spreading number of readers. Early in 1943 it brought out a *cahier* on the STO, with a clear message that it was to be resisted. The widely respected

Catholic and monarchist author Georges Bernanos wrote a *cahier* called *Où allons nous?* – where are we going? – which went out to 85,000 people.

But the Gestapo had long since opened a dossier on the 'great conspiracy' of which the Abbé Glasberg and Père Chaillet were the principal suspects. Very early on the morning of 27 January 1943, they rang the bell of the offices of L'Amitié Chrétienne on the Rue de Constantine. By ill fortune, Chaillet was in the office, and it was he who answered the door. Together with his fellow editor of the *cahiers*, Jean-Marie Soutou, he was taken to the Gestapo headquarters in the Hôtel Terminus. Left standing with his face to the wall, the stocky, bespectacled Jesuit was able to extract some incriminating documents from the ample sleeves of his greatcoat. He proceeded to chew and swallow the papers. When they had all been destroyed, he began to complain loudly about his arrest.

Before long, Cardinal Gerlier intervened and Chaillet was released, but Gerlier could do nothing for Soutou, who spent the next three weeks in a Gestapo prison. In the office, meanwhile, Germaine Rivière, who worked with Glasberg and Chaillet, passing herself off as the cleaning lady, had managed to station herself just outside the front door, where she was able to warn and turn away any Jews arriving in search of help. On his release, Chaillet, more determined than ever to reach a larger audience for his messages about spiritual duty and resistance, started work on a new series, more popular and easier to read, less weighed down by theological arguments, to be called 'Le Courrier Français du Témoignage Chrétien'. For what he imagined would be greater safety, he moved for a while to the Italian zone in the south-east. It was thought more prudent for Soutou to go to Switzerland.

Though officially no order had been made public about the fate of the French Jews, in practice, no Jew, neither French nor foreign, was any longer safe in France, and no organisation working on their behalf either. On 9 February, apparently acting without formal authorisation from either Berlin or the German headquarters in Paris, Klaus Barbie, the SS officer stationed in Lyons, decided to raid the offices of the UGIF in the Rue Sainte-Catherine. Here he found 86 people, some of them staff and social workers, others clients unlucky enough to be there that day. Two men escaped. The rest were sent to Drancy, from where 78 were put on the next *convoi* to Auschwitz. The spring of 1943 saw the appearance of flying squads of Gestapo, making up for their small numbers in France by carrying out sudden raids in Nîmes, Avignon, Carpentras and Aix. Trains were checked and people taken off. In April, Bousquet renewed his police accords with Oberg and committed his men to the 'struggle against terrorists, communists, Jews, Gaullists and foreign agents'. Orders were issued that no Jewish child should henceforth be removed from his assigned place of residence.

These arrests only served to convince both the Jewish scout movement and its underground wing, the Sixième, as well as the OSE, of the urgency of finding more false papers and, above all, better hiding places for the children in their care. The Sixième was reorganised into regions and *départements*, working closely with the OSE, and the young social workers were given false papers of their own. Liliane Klein-Liebert, who had taken part in the rescue of the children at Vénissieux, became a Protestant scout leader. There were no more reunions now, no more of the great scouting gatherings of the early years of the war; the scouts, Protestants as well as Jews, were too busy. In Paris, a spectacular escape was organised for 63 children aged between 3 and 18 in a home on the Rue Lamarck. A group of women, some Jewish and some not, claiming to be relations and friends of the children, arrived one Monday to take them, in ones and twos, on an outing. Once out of sight, they spirited them to the Protestant presbytery of L'Oratoire du Louvre, where the pastor, Paul Vergara, had helped arrange for families to take them in. By nightfall all had disappeared; a list of their names, new identities and addresses was buried in the garden.

But these bold escapes were very hard to pull off. Now that it was known that the Gestapo either already had lists of children from the offices of the UGIF, or knew how to get hold of them, it was a question of stealthy and steady planning, with every appearance of calm so as not to alert the authorities. As Dr Weill had long argued, there was very little time left in which to close down all the homes set up in the unoccupied zone during 1942; the children had to be moved, rapidly, preferably to Aryan homes, under new Aryan identities.

By early 1943, the OSE had 1,025 children in its care, 50 of them under the age of 3, and all but a few of them orphans or those whose parents had disappeared. There were also more children to be extracted from the internment camps. Many of these were ill, severely malnourished, covered in sores. They were suffering, noted one social worker, from 'a psychosis of anxiety, even terror', always watchful, waiting for something to happen, crying for their mothers, unable to take in what was happening to them. For all these children too, the OSE needed to find homes. To make certain that their true identities were not lost, that they could be identified and returned to their families after the war, a central register, with real names and fingerprints, was started in Switzerland, and a copy lodged with the International Committee of the Red Cross.

Ever since the rescue of the children from Vénissieux, Georges Garel had been at work setting up his clandestine Circuit B for the OSE. His headquarters were in Lyons, but he was very seldom there, spending his days and nights on trains or moving from place to place on his bicycle to find new havens and to have meetings with the young social workers whose job it was to scout out hiding places and then monitor the children they placed there, as well as delivering money and food coupons to their hosts. Garel preferred to hold his meetings on trains, saying they were safer. He kept up his cover as a salesman in pottery, using the false bottom to his case of samples to store money and forged papers. One of his helpers was Lily Tager, one of the young women who had taken part in the escapes from Vénissieux; the pair were now engaged. Garel's circuit extended across 30 French *départements*. Like Pastor Curtet in Fay, he used codes for everything, referring to his Jewish protégés as 'books' or 'stationery', to be delivered on specific days. Twenty-four 'Aryanised' children from Vénissieux had been lodged with a Catholic organisation for poor children, Sainte-Germaine. By 1943, some 350 others were hidden all over the south and centre of France. The Plateau Vivarais-Lignon was not alone in hiding children; but it was perceived by all as exceptional for the safety it offered.

For many of the children, who had already been separated once from parents and no longer knew what had become of them, this fresh upheaval was often extremely upsetting. From the archives of the OSE, collected after the war, emerges a picture of children overwhelmed by confusion, loneliness and loss, sent on sudden long and terrifying journeys, sometimes on foot, to isolated farmhouses. The memories exude sadness and fear. Long after the war was over, many of the children remembered being schooled never to speak Yiddish, and never to mention their real names; listening out all the time for the sound of lorries, which might spell a Gestapo visit; trying always to appear 'normal', that is to say, not Jewish. They retained a fear of uniforms. Many spoke of having grown up overnight; many said that they would never feel themselves to be a child again. Not least of the remarkable aspects of the plateau's story is that so many of the children hidden there by the OSE felt safe, protected.

To clothe this growing collection of children, most of whom had arrived with nothing beyond what they were wearing, and in any case at an age when they were growing fast, Garel employed a number of knitters and seamstresses in Grenoble and Limoges, where he set up a clothing depot. Garel had an air of authority; he was a methodical and rational organiser, who seldom lost his temper or mislaid anything. His nature was warm, but, said one friend, 'he had a secret garden'.

His link with the Plateau Vivarais-Lignon was Madeleine Dreyfus, who was now pregnant with her third child. At least twice each month she took the little train up the mountain to le Chambon, where she met Mme Déléage and her daughter Eva, visited the Mays in their hotel on the square, and set out on her rounds of the farms in which the children were hidden. In a small red notebook she recorded their names and wrote down a list of their requests for future visits. Sometimes she brought new children up with her, a dozen at a time; as before, the word would go out and farmers would arrive with their horses and carts to collect their new charges. Though the monthly payments of 500 francs allocated for each child barely covered their keep, there were no demands for more money. From time to time, having run out of possible homes, Madeleine placed an advertisement in the local paper: 'Social worker seeks to place children from a broken marriage in the countryside, with remuneration.' Nothing was said about them being Jewish. When a child had a living parent, every effort was made to keep the hiding place a secret, the OSE acting as go-between for letters and parcels, to avoid unannounced visits from mothers and fathers who often spoke very little French.

The notebook in which Madeleine Dreyfus wrote the names of
the hidden children

Just occasionally, when they realised that the child in their care was circumcised, a family would ask for him to be removed. But this happened very seldom. For the most part, the natural silence and discretion of the Huguenots and the Darbyists ensured that nothing was mentioned, nothing repeated. One day, returning to Lyons from le Chambon on the train, Madeleine found herself sitting next to two policemen. They were talking over their visit to the village. 'Well,' said one to the other, 'we didn't find any Jews, but we were certainly well fed.'

It is now that a new figure enters the story. His name was Joseph Bass, known to his friends as 'l'Hippopotame', on account of his immense girth and his loud, genial personality, and to his contacts as Gart, Georges, Bourgeois, Roure or Rocca. Born in Byelorussia in 1908, he had lived in St Petersburg until he was eight, when he was sent to an aunt in Paris who housed him in a maid's room in the attic. He was a quick-witted, ambitious boy. While studying for his baccalaureate, he kept himself financially afloat by working in a factory and as a porter in Les Halles. He then took two degrees, one in engineering, the other in law, and set up in business on his own, looking after industrial patents. Interned in the camp for 'undesirables' at Vernet as an enemy alien, he escaped, made his way to Marseilles and met two men who would shape the rest of his war. The first was Léon Poliakov, a Russian Jewish historian already active in the underground, whose friends, the Bardones, ran a café restaurant in Saint-Etienne called L'Auberge des Musiciens; the second was Maurice Brener, associate director of the JDC, who had sources of money from the US. When the Germans flattened the Old Port of Marseilles, and sent the Jews they rounded up to Drancy, Bass set up a network similar to Garel's Circuit B. It became known as 'le Service André'.

Joseph Bass (centre), surrounded by le Service André

His first move was to recruit a number of young assistants, many of them members of the Sixième, the clandestine wing of the Jewish scouts, to act as couriers, forgers and finders of safe houses. His two closest collaborators, whom he regarded as his lieutenants, were a big, dark haired, voluble Corsican nurse in her forties called Anne-Marie Quilici, and a 19-year-old EIF scout leader, Denise Caraco, who had been working for the OSE office in Marseilles. Anne-Marie became Bonnet; Denise, Colibri. The two women forged papers, using bleached oxygenated water and ironing them dry, mindful of the friable nature of the cardboard used for ration books, which quickly turned into blotting paper. They fashioned a code – 'musician' for Jew, 'pianist' for communist, 'saxophonist' for a member of the Resistance, 'saxophone' for a weapon, and '*labo*', laboratory, for a safe house.

With Bass, they identified 30 possible safe houses along the coast, some of them in Catholic convents. Money came from the JDC, via Lisbon and Geneva, and from Bass's own generous pockets, taken from his earlier successful schemes. When they travelled, they went first class and ate in the restaurant car, Bass maintaining that it was far safer to mingle with the Gestapo officers and Vichy officials. He was not a man to miss in a crowd. Along with his great size, he had a loving nature and a terrible temper, and he ate, and read, voraciously. He seemed to need almost no sleep. With Denise, he behaved like a close, affectionate, demanding uncle.

Soon after Trocmé and Theis returned from their internment camp, Bass was taken up to the plateau by Poliakov. Their first stop was Lulu's café in Mazet, where the two men, looking like plain-clothed Gestapo in their dark clothes and leather jackets, asked for Magda Trocmé. Appalled, Lulu hastily sent word to le Chambon to warn of an impending raid. Once the confusion was sorted out, Trocmé agreed to help Bass make contact with local families who might be willing to house some of his most desperate cases. Bass was instantly impressed by the spirit on the mountain, saying that what struck him was the evident sense of community, the feeling that morality was of greater importance than obedience to dishonest laws. Not long afterwards, he was denounced to the Gestapo in Marseilles; there was just time for him to hide and for Denise to leave for Grenoble, but his friend and colleague Pastor Lemaire, who refused to leave the city, was picked up, tortured and deported to Mauthausen. The Service André continued to run just the same.

Bass's contact on the plateau was Simone Mairesse, the pretty young widow from Mazet. They met in the Auberge des Musiciens in Saint-Etienne, where the proprietor's wife, Lea, was an excellent cook and where they spent many merry evenings dancing and drinking. Behind the bonhomie, Bass was shrewd and intensely practical. He was scrupulous about secrecy and discretion, telling his assistants that he wanted to know as little as possible about what they were doing, and certainly neither the names of the people they were hiding nor their whereabouts. Papers were hidden in packets of butter; stamps for the forged IDs in the heels of shoes. Later, Bass would say that in the course of 1943, he sent a thousand people up to the plateau, ranging from babies to orthodox rabbis, and that no one was ever betrayed. It may have been an exaggeration, but there were certainly many of them.

It was, however, becoming increasingly obvious that hiding people from Vichy and the Germans was no longer enough. There were too many of them and too few hiding places, particularly for those who looked most foreign and spoke little French. Every farmhouse on the plateau seemed to have someone hiding, and no one any longer quite trusted Bach's ambiguous messages. Somewhere safer was needed, where they could sit out the war and wait for Allied victory. The question was where.

One possibility was Spain, more or less neutral and apparently accepting of refugees. But when the Germans occupied southern France in November 1942, they assumed direct control of the 435-kilometre border with Spain, established a frontier zone, suspended the French police presence and sent in military police of their own, Feldgendarmerie and the Gestapo. Furthermore, crossing the Pyrenees was an arduous affair, taking from two to five days on foot, and involving climbs of up to 3,000 metres, some of the way under snow for most of the year. Though after November 1942 increasing numbers of people did attempt to cross, in practice those most likely to succeed were the strong young scouts, and Zionists hoping to reach Palestine. For those from the Plateau Vivarais-Lignon, the Spanish border was simply too long and difficult a journey: over 500 kilometres away, with no easy roads or connections.

The Italian zone was, for a while, another possibility. After unification in 1861, Italy's small numbers of Jews had been assimilated into Italian life; anti-Semitism had found little purchase. Though Mussolini's personal attitude towards the Jews was one of suspicion and intolerance, racial laws played a relatively small part within Fascist policy. When Italy took control of eight *départements* to the east of the Rhône, the assumption by the Germans was that the Italians would implement anti-Semitic measures similar to the French and send their Jews, along with Vichy's, to Drancy. But it did not quite work out that way.

To the intense irritation of Berlin, the Italians simply ignored orders to arrest Jews. Diplomatic missions to Rome concluded with Mussolini agreeing that he 'fully intended to march with Germany to the end of the road', but when they returned to Berlin, nothing happened. Ciano, at the Ministry for Foreign Affairs, stalled. The 'Jewish topic' was quietly dropped. Faced with cables, memoranda, pressure of one kind or another, the Italians dug their toes in. In theory, policy was decided in Rome. In practice, much of it was shaped in Nice, where a rich, well-connected, profoundly anti-Fascist businessman and banker from Modena called Angelo Donati, together with the Italian consul general, Alberto Calisse, joined forces with a number of priests and the welfare organisations that had moved to the Italian zone to foil the occupier's plans, and to protect, shelter and if possible facilitate the emigration of the Jews. On Calisse's orders, the 11 December law requiring Jews to have all their papers stamped was shelved; the Jews in the Italian zone, he announced, would be treated as they were in Italy, that is to say, 'humanely'. Röthke, the German chief of police in France, declared that the Italian attitude was 'particularly revolting'.

Though some 3,000 Jews were moved inland, away from the coast, and interned in places such as Mégève, they were neither arrested nor deported, and when in January 1943, the Germans carried out a raid on Savoie and the Drôme, and took away a number of Jews, the Italian prefects not only ordered the arrests to cease, but arranged for the release of those who had been taken. Grenoble became a centre for forgery of false papers. The Germans, faced with such mulish obstinacy, apparent incompetence and wilful misunderstandings, grew increasingly annoyed. Italian sanctuary was not to last. But for the ten months between November 1942 and September 1943 that Italy remained in control, Jews reaching their zone found a cultural and political haven in Nice, where carabinieri could be seen standing guard in front of synagogues.

And then there was Switzerland, neutral, historically a land of refuge, its 200-kilometre border with France accessible, with many easy crossing places. But Switzerland was not minded to save the Jews.

Not long after the end of the Great War, a movement of Catholics, farmers and white-collar workers had come together in Switzerland to form a coalition that opposed not only communism but many aspects of social democracy. By 1938, a fear of being 'overrun by foreigners', particularly those deemed 'unassimilatable' – that is to say, Jews from Eastern Europe – permeated much of Swiss life. The Anschluss brought some 6,000 refugees and served to harden attitudes still further, particularly as most had been impoverished by the plunder of their property and money by the Nazis. On 4 October 1938, a mandatory visa for German 'non-Aryans' was imposed; and under Swiss – not German – pressure, passports had henceforth to be stamped with a 'J' for Jew.

During the time that emigration to other countries – the US, South America, China – remained possible, Switzerland was prepared to act as a transit country, against many guarantees that people would rapidly move on. But as these possibilities closed, and particularly after the entry of the US into the war, so the Swiss federal government, which had assumed emergency powers in October 1939, instructed the cantons to expel all refugees who had entered Switzerland illegally and to intern those they could not send back. People with no papers, and no guarantee that they were merely en route to somewhere else, or could soon return home, now lost all chance of entering legally: to do so, they needed to apply for a visa, and by admitting that they were refugees, they forfeited virtually all hope of obtaining one. The Swiss did accept escaped French soldiers, whom they knew would eventually go home and whom they interned. They also agreed to take a small number of 'needy' children from France, as long as they did not include 'undesirable' Jewish ones, judged 'dangerously unstable' and with no guarantee that they would ever leave.

Determined to guard the country against unemployment, Bolshevism, excessive *'enjuivement'* and general disorder, and with strong banking and economic ties to Germany firmly in place, the federal government restricted all rail traffic with France to a single line, Bellegarde to Geneva. The army was sent to reinforce the cantonal police and border guards on the frontier; barbed wire, lights, mines and dog patrols were increased. A 'military zone', some 600 metres wide was established across which no one without valid documents to enter Switzerland could pass.

Until the summer of 1942, however, loopholes could be exploited, and penalties for those aiding refugees remained vague.

But on 4 August, with news of the round-ups of Jews throughout France – along with incontrovertible evidence of the fate that awaited them at Auschwitz – Switzerland moved to seal its borders hermetically. There were few dissenting voices, few to point out that Switzerland had once been a country of asylum; very little debate at all, in fact, either on the radio or in the newspapers. Heinrich Rothmund, director of the police division in the Federal Department of Justice, drafted a new decree: all illegal refugees, whatever their story, were to be repelled and expelled, 'even if this could have serious consequences for the foreigners in question (danger of life and limb)'.

Thousands of frantic people, whether Jews, resisters or, soon, STO evaders, would be given one chance to turn back voluntarily into France, in which case they would not be handed over to the Germans; but they would not be given a second chance. The Swiss boat, Rothmund famously declared, 'was full'. It was not prepared to allow any other boarders. Article 2 of the regulations published on 13 August specified that 'those who have fled on account of their race, for example the Jews, cannot be considered political refugees'. '*Refoulement*', the sending back, could be '*sauvage*', immediate, with no documentary trace; it could be straight into the hands of the occupying power; or it could be 'disciplinary', as punishment for anyone escaping an internment camp. For all those for whom remaining in France spelt certain death, the question now was what else might be possible.

Contacts between the Protestant and Swiss churches had long been excellent, and there were 33 Swiss Protestant pastors serving in France. With the border sealed, Pastor Boegner travelled to Berne and to Geneva, where Charles Guillon was already exploring all conceivable loopholes and continuing to act as a conduit for money into France. After many negotiations, Boegner was able to make a deal with the federal government for a number of '*Israélites chrétiens*', almost all of them Jews who had ostensibly in some way converted to Christianity, to be given safe passage into Switzerland. Together with Abbé Glasberg, and another determined Catholic priest working in the internment camps called Abbé Gross, and working closely with Madeleine Barot at Cimade as well as the other organisations with offices in Geneva, Boegner began to draw up a list of candidates, for whom he had to provide 'guarantees of morality'. It was a slow and fraught process, involving many negotiations to get the names of the *'non-réfutables'* accepted by the Swiss and transmitted to the police on the borders, but by and large, it worked, even if there were moments of anguish and confusion. The list, however, was, inevitably, extremely short. And some 200,000 Jews remained in France.

There was only illegality left. The organisations rallied, joined forces, and set up bold, imaginative, highly perilous *'filières'*, escape routes, and in ones and twos and small groups, the Jews in greatest danger began to be guided over the mountains and into safety in Switzerland. One of the main *filières* went from le Chambon and the Plateau Vivarais-Lignon through Lyons to the border, a journey of some 250 kilometres. From now until the end of the war, adults and children particularly in danger would be taken to safety in a daunting game of cat and mouse in which the determination of the Swiss to allow no one on board their boat was matched only by the cunning, courage and resolve of the rescuers.

CHAPTER TWELVE

Crossing the border

One of the first people to leave the plateau for Switzerland was Hanne's companion Max Liebmann. He and Hanne had agreed that, in order to survive, which they had firmly resolved to do, they would need to escape from France. Though neither had had any further news of their mothers, they firmly believed that both were dead. Max still hoped that his father was alive, somewhere in the Italian zone, but he had had no news of him either. All they had now was each other.

Max left le Chambon late one night just before Christmas 1942 with false papers in the name of Charles Lang, obtained for him by Mireille Philip. He walked across the fields to a hamlet near Mazet, where he hid in a barn for 18 days, waiting for instructions, before joining three other German Jewish boys to take a series of cross-country trains to Chamonix. His aunt had been a fashionable dressmaker in Mannheim and he would always remember that Mireille Philip, who was an ample woman with a large bust, wore tight angora sweaters of which he knew his stylish aunt would not have approved.

The four young men were met in Chamonix by a small boy, no older than 10 or 11, who took them to his parents' house, where a pastor was waiting to make the journey with them, in order to learn the route for future crossings. That evening, once again guided by the small boy, they joined a group of some 40 others hoping to enter Switzerland. It was raining hard and they spent the night under an overhanging rock. The food ran out and they were very hungry; Max's thin shoes split. Next day, they continued to climb. When they reached the top, the boy pointed to a track leading down into the valley and told them that it was Switzerland, and that they were now safe. The Swiss border guards, however, were waiting. The boys were taken into custody, told that they were to be returned to France, and urged to go voluntarily.

Disconsolate, the party started back up the mountain, but the moment they were out of sight of the soldiers, Max broke away, saying that he had nothing to lose and would try to find another path into Switzerland. One other boy followed him; the others, dispirited, returned obediently to France. Max and his companion crossed the border without being spotted. They were given something to eat by a kindly farmer, and money for tickets by a Catholic priest, and were warned not to take the express train to Geneva, for it was routinely inspected. They reached the city without being stopped, and Max made his way to a Jewish community organisation, who advised him to turn himself in and assured him that he would not be deported. He followed their advice, and the authorities sent him to an empty school in St Gallen, but allowed him out for Christmas Day to visit a cousin. In the New Year, he was put to shovelling snow. Naturally efficient and diligent, he soon found work in the offices of an organisation dealing with refugees. Still technically interned, he spent every day thinking of Hanne and how she would make the journey. Later he remembered feeling intense relief: there was no barbed wire anywhere, and there was always enough to eat.

Hanne was now 19. She did not set out until the end of February 1943, having obtained false papers with Bohny's help. She had an aunt in Switzerland, who could do little to help her escape beyond arrange for and pay a *passeur*, a guide across the border, but she could make matters easier once Hanne got across. Taking with her some bread and cheese, for she had no ration cards in her false name, she dressed in two skirts, two blouses, a sweater, a cardigan and a coat, and started by walking the eight kilometres from La Guespy to Tence, where she spent the night in Pastor Leenhardt's presbytery. Bohny was on her train to Lyons, which was full of German soldiers; she suspected that he had come on purpose, to watch over her. On the next train, to Annecy, she sat in a corner seat and pretended to be asleep. No one bothered her. She had been given the address of a convent, but felt very nervous because a strange man followed her to the door. When there was no answer to her repeated knocking, she resourcefully found a room for the night, in what she later discovered was a brothel. Next day she returned to the convent and the nuns put her on the road to Annemasse. Walking along the highway, she was stopped by a German patrol. 'Are you Jewish?' they asked her. 'Certainly not,' she replied. 'I have nothing to do with that dirty race.' They let her pass.

A priest in Tournon was waiting to introduce her to the *passeur* paid for by her aunt. Due to cross with her were five other people, and they whiled away the time by playing bridge. As night fell, they set out; when they reached a stream, the *passeur* kindly carried Hanne across. Though it was pitch dark, confusing, full of menace, they made it into Switzerland and caught, as instructed, a tram. In Geneva, Hanne rang her aunt. She was safe. Despite the fact that she was unhappy with her dictatorial aunt, who refused to believe that Hanne's mother was dead, for Max and Hanne the war was effectively over. They met when they could, and they planned for their future. Later, when they married and Hanne found herself pregnant, Max was asked what he wanted to put as his nationality on the baby's birth certificate. The Germans had made him '*apatride*', stateless, he said, and stateless was how he chose to remain.

When Joseph Weill, who at every stage feared what Vichy and the Germans were preparing next, was forced to leave for Switzerland early in 1943, he gathered together a group of people to discuss the setting up of *filières*, escape networks, to rescue those Jews for whom simple hiding places were no longer enough, and for whom Boegner would be able to arrange Swiss entry visas. In this group were the Trocmés, Theis and Mireille Philip, and it was around these last two that an elaborate chain was formed, involving Cimade and Madeleine Barot, the scouts and the Sixième, the OSE and Madeleine Dreyfus, Dora Rivière, a doctor and Christian Socialist in Saint-Etienne, Charles Guillon in Geneva, and several courageous priests, pastors and nuns. Over the next 18 months, they combined to take a great many people – there are no exact figures – to safety.

It was a perilous activity, made worse when, in February 1943, the French increased their border brigades from 8 to 12, and the Swiss sent an extra 800 soldiers to reinforce their border guards.

On the plateau, a meticulous procedure was devised. If until now the operation had largely been a matter of silence, people working on their own, saying nothing to anyone, the journeys to Switzerland would need perfect timing and coordination. Mireille and Theis, already busy hiding people, made certain, with the help of Darcissac and Rosowsky, that everyone had convincing forged papers, with their true ones, which they would need on arrival, sewn into their clothes, usually in the lining under their armpits. They also kept closely in touch with Boegner and Geneva, ensuring that the names of the people who left were on the approved Swiss list, something that Olivier, Mireille's son, would later say was made very much easier by his mother's friendship with Switzerland's commander-in-chief, General Guisan. Though Guisan was better known for his robust attitude towards keeping the Swiss army up to the mark, capable of defending itself against a German invasion, and was later criticised for his open mistrust of refugees, he also, Olivier maintained, opened important doors for Mireille.

By now there were few farmhouses in and around le Chambon, Mazet, Fay and Tence where no Jew or STO resister was hidden, and the farmers had taken to leaving lights burning to indicate when all was safe. After the Germans occupied the south, and Boegner could no longer travel freely backwards and forwards between Nîmes and Geneva, Guillon, able to go anywhere as secretary general of the world YMCA, took over most of the transporting of money; though he too was now in danger of arrest, having been identified by Vichy as a ringleader in 'the clandestine emigration of foreign Jews'. To Mireille's network, which she called 'le réseau des presbytères', Guillon was known as 'le visiteur de Genève'.

Mireille Philip is one of the quietest, most modest and most efficient players in the story of the plateau. After the war, she said and wrote nothing, and when offered the Yad Vashem medal for the Righteous, she turned it down, saying that she had not acted the way she did in order to receive a medal. As her husband André rose to become a minister in the French government, she retreated back into domesticity and good works.

In 1942, Mireille was 41. Her five children were all in the US, the eldest, Olivier, having been born there in the 1920s while André was doing a thesis on methods of production and the working classes. Like André, she was a practising Christian, a believer in social equality and extremely well connected throughout the '*haute bourgeoisie protestante*'. Before the war she had worked at Cimade with Madeleine Barot. After her husband's departure for London to join de Gaulle in the spring of 1942, she stayed on in the third-floor flat of La Bergerie, above Pastor Theis and his eight daughters.

Until the end of 1942, a man called Pierre Gallant was her principal guide to the frontier, but after his cover was blown, his place was taken by the 17-year-old scout Pierre Piton, who, with his chubby face and very blue eyes, and wearing his scout uniform, looked very much younger. After the theology students Piton was supervising in the Pension des Genêts went to bed, he would take his sledge and collect the hidden people next on the list for departure, escort them to Mireille for a final briefing and prepare to leave with them on the 250-kilometre journey to the border. Sometimes, when time was pressing and the travellers were frail, he borrowed a lorry, pretended that he was helping to move furniture, and drove in broad daylight through le Chambon, the Jews hidden in a cupboard at the back.

Using a Polish or German speaker as interpreter when one was needed, Mireille and Piton would explain to the travellers that they were to follow Piton at a certain distance, that they were to appear to be asleep on the trains and in the station waiting rooms, and that they should never speak, make eye contact with anyone, or mention anyone's name. Piton, in his scouting beret and shorts, positioned himself nearby, but not with them, travelling in the corridor of trains to keep an eye out for Gestapo inspections.

The first leg of the journey took them to Saint-Etienne, either in the little train or concealed in the Rivière lorries belonging to the family haulage business, which regularly made the journey up the mountain. They spent a night in Dora's house before catching a train to Lyons, then another to Annecy, where, close to the station, there was a Protestant temple and a pastor, Paul Chapal, who took them in and gave them food. Mireille had made contact with the chaplain of the Jeunesse Ouvrière Chrétienne, the JOC, Abbé Camille Folliet, whose parish was also in Annecy, and with the Abbé Rosay, curé of Douvaine. Both priests had good relations with nearby monasteries and convents, and the men waiting to cross were put with the Trappists in Tarnié, the women with the nuns at Chavanod.

One possible crossing was to take a boat across Lake Leman, but Mireille and Theis preferred two other routes: one across the plain, entering Switzerland between Collonges-sous-Salève and Douvaine, where the frontier ran along the side of roads, past people's gardens and across streams; the other over the high mountain passes of Balme, Buet and Barberine, safer, because less patrolled, but hazardous and steep, and impossible for small children or elderly people. When taking the Collonges-sous-Salève route, another priest, the Abbé Jolivet would receive the party of travellers in his presbytery and hide them in the attics, from where they could see the fields and peaks of Switzerland behind forbidding rows of barbed wire, until a safe moment came to cross. Everything had to be left behind, and the presbytery was piled high with abandoned bags and cases, to be collected, they told each other, after the war. Patrols passed every 20 minutes, the sound of their metal-tipped boots usefully audible on the roads before they came in sight.

Immediately after one had passed, Piton would lead his group – never more than three people – over the road and into a ditch just by the barbed wire. There they would wait for a second patrol, and when that had passed, they would negotiate the wire. Piton told them that the moment they were through, they were to run as fast as they could across no-man's-land towards the waiting Swiss guards. Usually he waited, crouched in the ditch, until he was certain that the Swiss had accepted the group, having checked that their names were on the list. After this, he returned to the presbytery, slept, then set off back for le Chambon. Lyons, always full of Gestapo and the Milice, was particularly dangerous.

After 20 successful crossings, Piton felt confident. One day, he left the plateau with a husband and wife, both magistrates, and a nurse, all three of them German Jews. All went well until the barbed-wire fence. As they were pushing through, the whole area was suddenly floodlit and shots were fired. Piton shouted to the two magistrates, who were already across, to keep running, while he and the nurse were arrested and taken to a police post, and from there, to his great relief, not to the Gestapo but to the Italian authorities in Grenoble. Both of them had false papers relating to places in the north where the archives were known to have been destroyed by bombing. Piton was roughed up, but not badly hurt. Three weeks later, the two of them were released.

Piton decided to try again, wanting to get the nurse across as soon as he could, fearing that her name might be passed to the Germans. On the train taking them to Annecy, he was arrested by the French police, handcuffed and taken into custody. The nurse was not spotted. Chapal, who was waiting for them at Annecy station, saw what had happened and notified Folliet. The abbé had good relations with the local French police captain, and he agreed to let Piton go. As the young scout left, the captain said to him: 'I don't know exactly what you do, but I congratulate you. But do not let me see you again.' The German nurse, helped by Folliet, made it to Switzerland. When Piton recounted his adventures to Mireille, she decided that someone else should take over his role. He had taken 60 people to safety. Now he turned to helping STO evaders instead. Mireille, Piton wrote later, was 'our sole chief of staff, our unique commander . . . For her, I would have done anything.'

Mireille herself was often on the move, checking on the routes, collecting money, meeting contacts, taking lists of new people screened by Boegner for submission to the Swiss. The original number agreed was 80 people, but the list kept growing. Later it became known that one of Mireille's disguises was a bulky, oil-stained boiler suit and cap, in which she travelled in the cabs of trains crossing the border with engine drivers friendly to the Resistance. Unable always to find enough safe places on the plateau, she also put people into remote farmhouses in the

Haute-Savoie, much nearer the border and with shorter journeys involved. And when eventually her cover too was blown, she went to the Vercors, to help with the nascent Maquis, returning to the plateau with money and information, and keeping in touch with London and the French provisional government in Algiers. Her place was taken by a young lawyer with Cimade, Suzanne Loiseau-Chevalier. 'Be frightened,' Mireille told her, 'but keep going.' Suzanne had been working in the internment camp of Brens in the Tarn, but had been sacked by Vichy for helping people to escape.

Another man to whom Weill turned when he needed someone to negotiate the perils of the closed Swiss border was a sports master named Georges Loinger. Born in 1910 in Alsace, to a Jewish father who served in the Great War before becoming an antiquarian, Loinger was a tall, good-looking, sporty boy who loved to trek in the mountains with his Zionist scout troop and swim in the wild waters of the Rhine. The family was observant and patriotic, keen admirers of Bismarck. Studying engineering in Strasbourg, Georges met Weill, then working as a specialist in digestive disorders on both sides of the Rhine, and already very anxious about Hitler's growing power. He gave the young man *Mein Kampf* to read, and told him that, as a Jew, he must prepare himself for terrible things to come. Now, when Loinger listened to Hitler's frenzied speeches relayed over the radio, he feared for his family's future.

On Weill's advice, and to the displeasure of his father, who wished to see his eldest son practise as an engineer, Loinger moved to Paris to train as a sports teacher. That way, Weill told him, he would be able to spread the word among the young. While studying, he lived in a rabbinical college; to keep fit, he ran backwards and forwards across Paris to his classes. On the outbreak of war, he served in a French infantry regiment on the Rhine, and was taken prisoner and sent to a stalag in Bavaria. He escaped, and made his way back to Paris, where his wife was working for the Rothschilds in a home for Jewish children. For a while, he helped at the home, and worked with a group of resisters to get Allied soldiers and agents out of France.

Unexpectedly encountering Weill one day in Montpellier, Loinger learnt about the OSE's 12 homes and the need to distract the children from the loss of their parents and the uncertainty of their futures. He became the OSE's director of sport, teaching the children how to trek and swim and play games; he arranged competitions and matches and trained other teachers to do the same. And when Weill decided that the moment had come when the homes were no longer safe and the children were going to have to be moved, he sent Loinger to take a diploma in gymnastics at a training centre for Pétain's Compagnons de France in Mégève.

Angular and patrician-looking, Loinger did not appear Jewish, and his Alsatian name posed no problems. As a trained Compagnon, a transparently good Pétainist, the holder of an impressive official Vichy card, he was entitled to go anywhere on the Maréchal's business: he visited schools, factories, colleges and student groups all over southern and central France. It provided the perfect cover. His wife had just given birth to their second son. The OSE sent a nurse to live with her, and Loinger became a *passeur*, working with Garel in Circuit B. They specialised in getting children to Switzerland, starting with those most traumatised by events and those most observant and hardest to conceal. In the OSE homes, Andrée Salomon and another veteran of the internment camps, Jenny Masour, prepared the children for the journey, coaching them in their new identities. At this stage, Garel estimated that they needed to get between 200 and 300 children across the border, some of them those rescued at Vénissieux, others from Gurs and Rivesaltes, others again from Mireille and Theis in le Chambon.

One of Loinger's first and luckiest breaks was an introduction to the mayor of Annemasse, a known centre for children's homes before the war. Jean Deffaugt was a tailor, with a shop selling men's clothes. Uncertain as to his reliability, Loinger approached him warily. But the mayor had already heard about Circuit B. Standing beneath a large, fine portrait of Pétain, he told Loinger: 'I don't agree with these manhunts. I will certainly help you.' The border was full of smugglers, dealing in cigarettes, silk stockings and other luxuries, who now doubled as *passeurs* of people for the final journey across the wire and through no-man's-land. Their services were not cheap – between 1,500 and 3,000 francs per child – but Deffaugt introduced him to the most trustworthy. The most venal were already making small fortunes out of people they agreed to guide into Switzerland, demanding more money from them at the last moment, and then turning them over to the Gestapo just the same.

Annemasse was always full of children, and the Germans had become accustomed to seeing parties of them arrive for holidays at the various *colonies de vacances*. Those who came with Loinger were Jewish orphans. A new train stop, ostensibly in order to lessen the overcrowding at the main station, was arranged with the help of *résistant* train drivers; as a Vichy sports professor, Loinger met the children and took them to a centre for the night. Many arrived exhausted, anxious and excitable; they needed to be calm and strong to make the crossing.

It was Deffaugt who showed Loinger a sports ground that skirted the frontier. When they were ready to cross, he took a large group, Jewish children mixed in with locals, and they played football, vanishing in ones and twos over the wire during the game. The number going home at the end of the day seldom tallied with that of the original teams. There was also a cemetery nearby. Parties of mourners, wearing veils and evidently distressed, arrived to kneel and weep around the graves. When the *passeur* decided that the road was clear, they gave back their veils and crossed into no-man's-land and then into Switzerland. The veils were used for the next group. And not far away, at Ville-la-Grande, there was an order of Salesian monks and a college, whose gardens lay along the border. One of the brothers, Raymond Boccard, positioned himself at a high window, and when a patrol had passed, flapped his hat; the fugitives, who had been waiting in a ditch, used a carefully concealed ladder to clamber across.

Between February and May 1943, Loinger, with the help of various *passeurs,* got 81 children, aged between 4 and 17, in 9 groups, into Switzerland. The total figure for those months, for he was not alone in helping children across, was 123. Once in no-man's-land, they were told to cry, appear pitiable, but give nothing away until they were taken to Geneva, where Weill was waiting for them.

Among the adults who made the journey from the plateau, guided by Piton, Mireille and Suzanne, during the winter of 1942 and spring of 1943, were 20 of the Jews who had been rescued when the Coteau Fleuri was raided and who had been hiding in the woods and the mountains ever since. They were Poles, Germans and Austrians. For some, and for their *passeurs*, the journeys were terrifying. Soon after taking over from Mireille, Suzanne, who had become known as '*la jeune fille au turban*', on account of the funny round hat she always wore, set off on the little train from le Chambon with four young women, all travelling on forged Alsatian papers. The tickets somehow got lost as the train drew into Annemasse, and only immense good fortune got the party past the barrier unchallenged. When the Abbé Rosay met them at Douvaine, he seemed acutely anxious, saying that there was no *passeur* available. Suzanne decided to act as *passeur* herself. The party set out, the abbé carrying their few belongings on his bicycle, but were spotted by frontier guards and arrested. In the police station, while Suzanne swore that not one of the women was Jewish, the four lost their nerve, and despite all instructions to stay silent began to argue and plead. There was only a single policeman on duty. He listened, but said nothing. Then, very quietly, he told them to proceed. Just before 11 p.m., they crossed into Switzerland at Chevrens. They had been extremely lucky. By the spring of 1943, more and more policemen were shifting away from Vichy.

Luck, as Suzanne soon discovered, played an enormous part. She would never forget the night she took four children across the border, the oldest a staunch, uncomplaining little Polish boy of eight whose parents had been deported. The three others were sisters, aged four and three, and a baby of one. They too were Polish, and their parents had vanished. The journey from Annecy to Douvaine passed without problems, but the baby was feverish and kept crying. At Douvaine, Suzanne found a cloth and made it into a clean nappy. By now, both the little girls were clinging to her, desperate not to be abandoned.

Towards dusk, she set off for the border, carrying the baby; soon, the three-year-old could walk no further, so Suzanne was forced to carry her as well. The four-year-old clutched her skirt. A French border guard suddenly appeared, but instead of arresting them, he took one of the little girls on to the handlebars of his bicycle and helped them to the border. Suzanne had been told to wait by the side of a church until the *passeur* arrived. Night fell. The baby kept crying. No one came. Eventually a French policeman arrived and looked them over, then said to Suzanne, 'We know who you are, you're the girl with the turban,' and showed her where to cross. Out of the shadows a young *passeur* appeared and they set off over a stream and across the fields. By now all the children were in tears, even the brave and stoical eight-year-old. They reached the border and crossed it. On the other side, Suzanne placed the children by a large rock, putting the baby on the knees of the four-year-old. Then she left them and went back into France, where she hid behind a tree and watched. 'And then,' she wrote later, 'through the dark, I saw the Swiss border guards approach, their torches glowing. And I knew the children were saved.'

All of the guides had stories of near disasters. One day, while taking across a group of small children, Madeleine Barot heard the sounds of a patrol approaching. She pushed the children through, but in her haste knocked over one of the wooden staves to which the barbed wire was attached, injuring both herself and a Swiss guard on the other side. Since she was technically in Switzerland, the Germans on the French side did nothing. Madeleine was taken to an improvised prison in a school and told to stay put. She got hold of a bit of paper and wrote a note to Visser't Hooft at the World Council of Churches, then wrapped it around a stone and threw it out of the window. Miraculously, it was seen and delivered; she was rescued and her wounds were treated by Dr Cramer, the ICRC delegate who had done the inspections of Gurs and Rivesaltes in 1941. Madeleine recovered and was able to return to France.

Not all *passeurs* were so lucky. Before the war was over, many had been arrested, and some deported or executed, though very few of those whose lives they were saving were ever caught. What all the *passeurs* would remember for the rest of their lives was the terror of the crossing, the crying babies packed into rucksacks, the exhausted small children able to walk no further, the men and women frozen into immobility by fear. The survivors too would be haunted by memories of these journeys, stumbling through the dark, tripping over roots and stones, listening out for the tramp of boots, convinced that every bush hid a guard and every sound heralded the arrival of the Gestapo.

CHAPTER THIRTEEN

Living on a volcano

Spring came late to the plateau in 1943. The snows did not melt until early April; all through December, January, February and March the people in hiding felt safe, cocooned, the roads up to the plateau blocked for days on end by drifts and ice. Long after the plains below showed new shoots of grass and buds, the forests and meadows around le Chambon, Tence, Mazet and Fay remained sombre and wintry. Up here, noted Camus, 'the eyes are perpetually confused between spring and winter'. But when spring did finally arrive, it brought narcissi and daffodils in profusion, scented yellow fields that filled the air with their distinctive sweet smell.

The spring also brought a new family to le Chambon, one of the many French Jewish families finally conscious of the trap into which, unawares, they had been led by Laval with his promises that, as Frenchmen, they would be safe from the Gestapo raids. The story of the Blochs is a Catholic story, not a Protestant one, rare on the plateau, but not unique. The 24 Protestant pastors, though appreciative of the Catholics' help, tended to remain wary of their intentions. As Pastor Lhermet put it to Madeleine Barot, when he was offered assistance by a Catholic priest in Le Puy, there was much goodwill towards the Jews, but the Catholics 'will not commit themselves to the bitter end'. How fair he was being is hard to tell.

Pierre and Robert were 12 and 13, the sons of a salesman, liberal and non-practising Jews on both sides of the family, when their father decided that the city of Lyons was no longer safe. Familiar with the plateau from holidays before the war, he rented the top floor of a remote farmhouse at Devesset, just inside the

Ardèche; the elderly farmer lived below. Fifty metres away lived another farming family, the Bruyères, who had two daughters. The four children attended the local school together, a kilometre's walk away. Mme Bloch spent the long, dark days of winter knitting with another neighbour, Mme Duny, while M Bloch continued to spend part of each week in Lyons. One day when the boys were at the Bruyères' farm, two policemen arrived on bicycles. Mme Bruyère hastily hid Pierre and Robert, but when the men seemed well meaning, she called the boys out of their hiding place. The policemen asked them whether they were circumcised; the boys told them that they were.

The Blochs, 1942

Whether it was this incident, or the fact that M Bloch's elderly father, still living in Lyons, was suddenly arrested, put on a train to Drancy and deported to Auschwitz, or that his sister Paulette saw her husband picked up by the Gestapo when he was out buying cigarettes, that caused M Bloch to move the boys to greater safety is not known. But early in 1943, he found a four-roomed house in the middle of le Chambon, cold and uncomfortable, but somehow making them reassuringly anonymous among the many other visitors to the plateau, and installed his family there. It belonged to M and Mme Roussel, whose coal and timber business was opposite, and who lived above their shop. The Roussels were Catholics, two of the hundred or so Catholics in le Chambon. M Bloch gave up his visits to Lyons, pinned a map of Europe on the kitchen wall, and began to chart the military advances of the Allied forces; in the evenings, along with most of their neighbours, they listened to the BBC. Mme Bloch was an anxious woman, her fears made more acute by the arrests of both her father-and-law and her brother-in-law; every untoward event alarmed her, and she was always watchful of the convalescent soldiers stationed in the Hôtel du Lignon, less than a hundred yards away.

For the boys, it was all an adventure. They loved the deep snow, and tobogganing down the icy run from the top of the village. Pierre became very friendly with Jean-Pierre Trocmé, and was drawn into the chaotic, affectionate life of the presbytery. When the spring came, they fished for frogs and went in search of butterflies and grass snakes. Jean-Pierre, who was a bit older, was an imaginative companion. They joined the Eclaireurs Unionistes, Darcissac's pack of Protestant scouts, and became a Penguin and a Wolf.

Pierre was not exactly frightened, but he was always conscious of danger. M Bloch insisted on keeping the shutters of the windows that gave on to the railway line closed, so that it would appear as if there were no one living there. One day, walking past the Hôtel du Lignon, the boys were hailed by one of the German soldiers. 'We know there are a lot of Jews here! Are you Jewish?' No, no, replied the boys, we're Protestants, like everyone else.

Asked how it was that as a Catholic, Mme Roussel chose to hide Jews, she would say: 'Yes, we're Catholics – but is Hitler not a Protestant?' When Magda Trocmé's Russian aunt Olga, come to visit her niece, decided to pay a pilgrimage to Lourdes, Mme Roussel's grandmother agreed to accompany her. The Catholics and the Protestants, said Mme Roussel, were close and friendly in le Chambon. As a *commerçant*, a shopkeeper, she knew everyone's business, even that of the Ecole Nouvelle Cévenol, and she also shared a *femme de ménage* with Miss Maber. She knew about the Jews in hiding all over the plateau and in many of the houses in the village; about the STO boys making their way into the Maquis; about the fact that one of the leaders of the Resistance, Henri Frenay, had an aunt who lived opposite the Germans in the Hôtel du Lignon; and about the way that Emile Sèches was feeding all the Jews in the village schools. But it would never have occurred to her to say anything to anyone. The famous Darbyist silence was shared by them all, Catholics and Protestants alike; none of them, as she said, were talkative people.

But spring brought danger, too. The Gestapo and the Milice, with their orders to keep supplying Jews for the quotas demanded by Himmler and Eichmann, could once again visit the plateau with ease, and Praly's reports would no longer be filed away unread. In the anomalous way in which everything to do with the Jews was still somehow arbitrary and unclear, there were a number of '*Juifs en règle*' on the plateau, registered and known to the authorities but as yet untouched. In February 1943, the Bureau of Jewish Affairs reported the existence of 244 French Jews *en règle* in the Haute-Loire; as well as over 100 foreign ones, 23 of them in Tence and 35 in le Chambon, most of them Polish, German, Russian and Romanian. What was less well known, however, was that the prefecture had other, secret lists with names and addresses for a great many other people, suspected of being Jewish and in hiding. How long these, or those *en règle*, could now remain safe was the question. For them, the plateau was entering its most perilous phase.

On Friday 11 June, sitting in his presbytery at Fay, Daniel Curtet finished one of his coded letters to his father, begun a few days earlier. 'On Tuesday,' he wrote, 'two high peaks of the Weisshorn in plain clothes paid a visit here to a family of Mt 15/24. Total: two lambs were requisitioned, an old and a young one, both male. Nothing to be done of course . . . sad affair!'

The two male lambs were Gilbert Nizard's father, Armand, and his eldest brother, 28-year-old André. Tuesday 8 June was a clear, fine, hot day. At 11 o'clock in the morning, a taxi, an old Citroën C4 running on *gazogène*, drew up in front of Chazot's hotel in the main square of Fay, and a man giving his name as Decarpentier and producing a card complete with swastikas and German signatures, stating that he worked for the Gestapo, demanded the whereabouts of the Nizard family. He had with him a second man, who appeared to be German; both wore the leather jackets favoured by the Gestapo when out of uniform. The chief of the gendarmerie, Louis Glaizon, was summoned, looked over their papers and announced that there was nothing that he could do to interfere with Gestapo orders.

While Bella looked on appalled, the two men ransacked the Nizards' apartment at the top of the Exbrayat house, demanding money. Fifteen-year-old Gilbert was mesmerised by the sight of a Luger with its long barrel, which he associated with gangster movies, Robert and Henri, the two youngest boys, had been spirited away by neighbours and hidden in an attic. Armand handed over all the money he had, which came to about 100,000 francs. The leather-coated men then forced Armand and André into the Citroën and they drove off, leaving behind them a shocked and silent crowd of onlookers. They had wanted to take 22-year-old Maurice as well, but there was no room for him.

Next morning, Bella and Maurice went to Le Puy. At the prefecture, M Romeuf, the secretary, who happened to be a member of the Resistance, tried to comfort them, then took them to see the Procureur de la Republique, M Bernard. Bernard was brusque and unhelpful.*

They returned to Fay, where Marie Exbrayat, who had become a devoted friend to the family, urged them to go into hiding. She found an empty farmhouse, isolated well away from the road, and the next day, a group of men from the village helped Bella and the children, still in a state of confusion and disbelief, to make the house habitable. It had neither water nor electricity. Whenever there was a threat of danger, Mme Exbrayat sent someone to the farmhouse, so that they could take to the forests. 'We kept asking ourselves,' Gilbert would say, many years later, 'why was she doing this for us. What sort of mysterious inspiration moved her?' The Exbrayats were Protestants, faithful attenders of Curtet's temple. Their ironmonger's shop thrived, and Mme Exbrayat ran a successful food business on the side, providing butter and cheese to people coming from Saint-Etienne. The Nizards lacked for nothing. What Gilbert would later remember were the rich meat soups, full of lard and potatoes and vegetables of every kind. There were Catholics who helped them too, he would say, but their kindness seemed sometimes to be a little too much like charity. 'The Protestants just opened their arms.'

Curtet, meanwhile, having discovered that the man driving the taxi had himself been very suspicious of the two armed men, went

* When France was liberated, Bernard was shot as a collaborator.

to Le Puy, where he soon learnt that they had most likely been impostors, since Bach had secured an agreement with the Germans that no arrests would be carried out in the Haute-Loire without the presence of the French police. Curtet was taken to see Bach, who, interestingly, began to shout at him for not having acted more quickly to alert the prefecture to the incident, for then he might have been able to save the Nizards. It turned out that the Citroën had made several stops on its journey to Lyons, even spending a night at Lemastre, and there would have been many opportunities to rescue them. Later, the family would find it hard not to feel a sense of blame towards the pastor.

By the time Bach was alerted, André and Armand were in Drancy. The two men had indeed been impostors. Having pocketed the money, they proceeded to sell their captives to the Gestapo. The Nizards had been tracked down, it transpired, through Armand's letters to his business associate, intercepted in Marseilles.

In Drancy, Armand soon got hold of some paper and wrote to Bella, entrusting the letters to the unfortunate men and women released for a few hours at a time from Drancy so that they could go to their homes and collect the members of their families still in hiding. Their return was guaranteed by the children they were forced to leave as hostages in the camp. Armand's letters were calm, without self-pity. It was a great comfort to him, he wrote, that the rest of the family were not with them, and particularly not Bella and the girls, for what he saw happening to women in Drancy was sickening. He described sleeping in a bunk below André, with a blanket but happily no fleas; of having three cold showers and one hot every week; and of having met several old friends from Marseilles, among them Mireille's friend Jacqueline, taken by the Gestapo the day that the two girls were stopped as they left their lycée. He counselled the children to remain 'dignified and brave and above all of exemplary behaviour'. Maurice was to carry out the duties of head of the household.

Since the two prisoners lacked everything, and their daily rations consisted of just two bowls of thin vegetable soup, Armand asked that the family send them parcels, of soap and clean clothes and above all food: hard-boiled eggs, sugar, bread, sausage, jam and biscuits. Even the tins they sent would be useful as plates and cooking pots. 'We are learning to be perfect *clochards*' – tramps – wrote

André on 23 June, 'but we are dirty among friends, which is a consolation.' Apart from the filth of the toilets, Armand reported that their sleep was 'untroubled', and that, having nothing else to do, they spent most of the day lying on their bunks. This shared misfortune, he said, had made equals of them all, and in Drancy there were no class distinctions. Two kind women were washing their few clothes, in exchange for sugar and bread, 'far more valuable here than money'. Albert Exbrayat, who as a garage owner had a car, drove the 500 kilometres from Fay to Drancy with his brother to take them money and provisions; they were not allowed to see the prisoners, but they handed in their parcels and later learnt that Armand and André had received them.

On 3 July, the Germans dismissed the French who had been running Drancy, and a fanatical anti-Semite called Aloïs Brunner, aide to the chief of the Gestapo in France, Heinz Röthke, and fresh from the deportation of 43,000 Greek Jews from Salonika to Auschwitz, took over the management of the camp. Conditions worsened dramatically. Two men caught trying to smuggle out letters were whipped before the assembled 2,000 inmates; the sight, wrote Armand, was 'painful and revolting'. Trains were departing regularly, some, he thought, destined for Cherbourg, where men were needed to help build the Atlantic defences, others probably towards the east, to 'Upper Silesia, to a salt mine where death comes in slow stages . . .' He found these departures 'heart-rending'.

On 4 July, by which time the Nizards had been in Drancy 15 days, Armand wrote to tell Bella that they had been placed into category 6, among those held back from deportation until their families could be tracked down and brought to join them. 'Whatever you do,' he wrote, 'you must move and hide, so that you won't be found'; that way, perhaps, they would all remain safe until the end of the war. He had learnt that his brother Simon and sister-in-law Marthe had been sent to Metz, where they were possibly working in a big food factory. On 21 July, he wrote that there were fresh deportations all the time, and that he had been ordered to send Bella a letter telling her and the children to come to Drancy. She was to 'pay no attention' at all, and he underlined the words.

Mussolini's fall, on 25 July, brought excitement and optimism to the camp, and Armand reported the prisoners' faces as 'shining with hope . . . that this might herald the End'. On the 26th he wrote on a scrap of torn paper, saying that he had run out of everything else except lavatory paper. 'I am persuaded that, within ten, or fifteen days at most, we will be free . . .' But then, three days later, came a sudden order for Armand and André to join the next *convoi*, 'probably, let us not fool ourselves, to the east, destination unknown'. Whatever happened, they would 'obey our destiny, as it is ordained; our morale, despite everything, remains strong'. For a moment it looked as if André, a much-decorated war hero, might be spared; but it was not to be. Since they were likely to stop at Metz, they hoped to find Simon and Marthe. 'Every night,' Armand wrote on the 30th, 'I recite each of the children's names to place them under divine protection . . . I worry about you all, and if I felt reassured that you would be safe, I would leave with a lighter heart . . . Do not expect a letter any time soon. I embrace you all very tightly.'

This was the last letter to reach Bella. On 31 July, Armand and André were among 541 men, 486 women and 95 children deported to Auschwitz. Armand was gassed on 5 August. André was sent to a work battalion. Simon and Marthe were already dead, gassed in Sobibor.

Bella and the children knew nothing of this. At the end of the summer, Gilbert, Robert and Henri moved to le Chambon, to attend the Ecole Nouvelle Cévenol and live with Georgette and Gabrielle Barraud, sharing the house with all the other hidden Jews, living under false names provided for them by Curtet and Simone Mairesse, and coming home at weekends. Bella, Mireille and Marthonne remained in hiding in Fay, waiting for news of Armand and André, which never came. The Exbrayats, Curtet, the baker M Robert and the Chazot family did everything they could to help them, and the policeman Glaizon, asked by his superiors to report on them, sent a glowing testimonial saying that their 'morality' was impeccable, their behaviour 'excellent' and their attitude towards France and Vichy unfailingly good.

Precisely why the Germans decided to raid the Maison des Roches on the morning of 29 June 1943 is a mystery. It may have been because its new young director, Daniel Trocmé, had been making a nuisance of himself with Vichy over his students; or that responsibility for the hostel had just passed from the Ministry for Labour to that of the Interior and it was therefore under closer scrutiny by the Gestapo; or that there had been complaints from the convalescent soldiers in le Chambon about the disrespectful attitude towards them of some of the villagers; or that two young men had been caught painting a Croix de Lorraine on the walls; or, quite simply, that the constant failure to catch Jews or dissidents on the plateau, either by Vichy or by the occupiers, had not gone unnoticed. Whatever its cause, the raid became one of the defining events of the plateau's war.

The house itself, an old farmhouse on the outskirts of the village, with the dense forest behind and a terrace in front with views over the valley of the Lignon, had opened its 30 rooms to summer guests at the turn of the century. In 1941, a retired local pastor, Noël Poivre, had a meeting with the Fonds Européen de Secours aux Etudiants and put to them the idea of renting the place as a *pension* for some of the anti-Nazi, Spanish republican and Jewish students being held in the internment camps. Its first directors, both refugees themselves, M and Mme Pantel, were elderly and found the task of caring for 30 troubled, penniless and often agitated young men too strenuous. In March 1943, they were replaced by Daniel Trocmé, cousin to André, a thoughtful, philanthropic young man of 31, with thick glossy brown hair, a full mouth and little round spectacles. Daniel had grown up confident and willing, someone who fought doggedly in defence of his friends. He was a man with a mission.

His father, Henri, Pastor Trocmé's first cousin, was the head-master of L'Ecole des Roches, an affluent and intellectually rigorous boarding school run on the English system in Normandy – the similarity in names was coincidental – and the father of eight children; a ninth was adopted after he returned from the Great War, in gratitude for not having been killed. Daniel, who was clever, adventurous and a good linguist, taught mathematics, chemistry and physics in lycées in Beirut and Rome, from where, in the late spring of 1940, he wrote to his parents that he was sure that they had joined the underground Resistance, and that he felt proud of them. 'I believe,' he wrote, 'that you have brought up children who will know how to be worthy of you.' Like Daniel, both Henri and his wife Eve felt strongly about loyalty.

After the Ecole des Roches migrated south during the exodus, Daniel briefly joined the staff, but found the comfort and exclu-sivity irksome. Knowing something of the work being done in le Chambon, he wrote to André to ask whether there was something useful he could do. His letter came just as a new influx of children was reaching the plateau, and Trocmé invited him to become head of the Quaker-supported Les Grillons, home to 25 children between the ages of 10 and 18, most of them with parents in the camps. Daniel was a loving and considerate house father, boiling up great vats of soup and lugging them down into the village so that his pupils attending Darcissac's classes could have a hot lunch, and working late into the night trying to repair their shoes with bits of rubber. He worried constantly about where he might get hold of gloves and galoshes, and was anxious when the temperature dropped to many degrees below zero and he had trouble finding extra clothes. He reported a disastrous evening when, having put them to dry too close to the fire, he was obliged to watch two brand-new cloaks, a coat, a pair of trousers, two berets, two mufflers and a chair go up in flames.

To his parents, he wrote that he saw his job as a 'contribution to the reconstruction of our world . . . Perhaps also as an affir-mation, a vocation, an inner conviction, of an almost religious nature . . . I chose it, not because it is an adventure, but because this way I will not have any reason to feel ashamed of myself.' When Christmas came, he decided to stay with his charges, rather than join his family. He was, he said, very happy, regarding himself not only as their father, but as their 'advocate and protector', though only the future would say whether he had been 'equal to the task'. His health was, he told his mother, '<u>excellent</u>'. Jean-Pierre, André and Magda's 13-year-old son, had come to stay with him, and there was much joking and laughter.

Then, in March 1943, the Pantets left, and Trocmé asked him to take over the directorship of La Maison des Roches; Daniel accepted and said that he would combine it with his work at Les Grillons, spending his nights with his younger charges. He had become very fond of his group of little orphans.

The Maison des Roches was a very different proposition. Its 30 inhabitants, aged between 20 and 30, with a few teenagers and a couple of older people, all unmarried men, came from across the whole of occupied Europe. At least half were Jewish, three of them orthodox Jews, but there were also Catholic Spanish republicans and a few Protestants. Most had already been in exile and on the run for several years and nearly all had been through the French internment camps. Though no formal classes had actually been planned for them – Poivre's idea had simply been to get them out of the camps – the fact that so many among them were students in law, medicine and engineering, or talented musicians and painters, meant that there was a considerable thirst for knowledge.

La Maison des Roches

Soon, classes were being set up with the distinguished refugee professors sitting out the war in le Chambon. Miss Maber took English, Jacqueline Decourdemanche typing and shorthand, a Sorbonne professor philosophy, a leading pre-war Viennese artist art history. In the evenings, the students congregated on the terrace to talk and play musical instruments. There were heated debates. The Fonds Européen de Secours sent chess sets, collections of books in various languages, boxing gloves and inner tubes for bicycles.

Even had Inspector Praly not been ordered by Bach to keep a close eye on the young men, their identities and origins were no secret: Daniel was a meticulous keeper of records, and his ledgers listed all their particulars, including their religions. The more security-minded Pastor Poivre concealed their ration books behind the books in his library and the accounts for the Maison des Roches inside the pages of the complete works of Calvin.

Many of the young men had reached the farmhouse severely malnourished, and Madeleine Barot and Cimade, brought in to help, scrounged, begged and borrowed blankets, coats and shoes to make them more comfortable, though there was never quite enough to eat.

It is possible that Daniel should have taken more heed when, in May 1943, two men from the Feldgendarmerie suddenly arrived to arrest a 45-year-old German called Martin Ferber. Ferber was considered 'uncommunicative and somewhat Prussian looking', and no one was very close to him; he was not Jewish, but had let it be known that he had been an anti-Nazi before the war. He went off with them unprotesting and was not seen again. Daniel did not evidently pay much attention either when, at different times, both Miss Maber and Mme Decourdemanche noted that the Maison des Roches was 'in the sights of the authorities and becoming dangerous' – though this warning, according to Miss Maber, had been transmitted by Praly. Certainly, some of the young residents were fearful of capture, and chose to spend their nights in the forests. But there was something stubborn about Daniel. He not only apologised to the Prefect about the seemingly random comings and goings of the young men, but forbade them to leave the premises for any length of time without written permission.

Daniel clearly felt safe. The warnings, such as they were, were ignored.

At 6.40 on the morning of 29 June, the household woke to shouts, bangs and German commands. Fourteen Germans, in civilian clothes, armed with revolvers and machine guns, surrounded the building. There was no time for anyone to hide. In their pyjamas, with blankets around their shoulders, the students were hustled into the dining room, then taken away, one by one, to be interrogated against a list of 'wanted terrorists'. When they emerged, many had bruised faces.

At 7.30, having discovered that Daniel Trocmé slept at Les Grillons, someone sent a car to collect him. At this point, he could still have escaped, gone to hide in the woods; but he insisted on hugging each child before being led away. Poivre and Le Forestier, alerted by the villagers, arrived but were denied entry; Magda, still in her apron, inveigled herself into the kitchen by pretending to be one of the cooks. As the boys filed past her on their way back from being interrogated, they whispered requests to her to contact their parents, and instructions about what do with their belongings.

Daniel managed to remind her that one of the students, Luis Gausachs, had saved the life of one of the German convalescents when he fell into the river, and she hastened away to the Hôtel du Lignon in search of someone who could provide a testimonial. She bullied and cajoled her way past the guards, found some of the older patients and managed to persuade two officers to accompany her back to La Maison des Roches. On the way, she commandeered bicycles from two passing girls so that they could get there quicker. Luis Gausachs was duly hauled out of the line and sent upstairs to join a very ill boy, who could not be moved, and a couple of others who were clearly not Jewish. One 19-year-old Dutch orthodox Jew was severely beaten with his own phylacteries, the small leather boxes containing Hebrew texts worn by Jews, while the Germans shouted, 'Schwein Jude! Schwein Jude!' – Jewish pig.

When, at midday, the three lorries and two black cars drove off, they took with them 18 students and Daniel. From the doorway opposite the Maison des Roches in which she was sheltering, 14-year-old Genie Schloss from Roanne watched in horror as the boys were led out, one by one, in silence, carrying suitcases. Jean-Pierre Trocmé was there with his mother, and Daniel said

247

to them: 'Tell my parents that I was very happy here. It was the best time of my life. Tell them that. And that I'm going with my friends.' From the windows on the first floor, the boys who had been freed looked on in silence.

The prisoners were taken to the top floor of a chateau at Moulins, which had once belonged to the dukes of Bourbon. They were given very little to eat, and, since there was nothing to do, Daniel got hold of a German newspaper and read it aloud, translating as he went. Five of the young men were eventually released; the rest were sent to Drancy, from where a couple more managed to get freed. On 18 July five are known to have been put on Convoi 58 for Auschwitz, where they were gassed. The youngest was a 16-year-old Belgian student called Alexandre Stern. Another was Lipschutz, one of the young men who had gone to Curtet in Fay to say that he felt that Daniel was being too careless, but who had returned to spend that night at La Maison des Roches. Six others vanished from the records, but it is highly likely that they died too.

As for Daniel, he was held in Moulins until the end of August. His parents went everywhere, visited Vichy, called in favours. Though not allowed to see their son, they stood outside the chateau hoping to hear his voice. Daniel was given their letters, and wrote to say that his morale was good and that he was hoping to see them very soon. He wished his mother and his sister Suzie happy birthday. He was transferred to Compiègne, the main station from which the trains left for Poland, where he met several old pupils from his father's school. He also wrote a touching and tender letter to his charges at Les Grillons, promising them that he would never abandon them; and he told his family how moved he was to hear that his brother's new baby was to be called Danielle. Being neither Jewish nor a wanted resister, he managed to resist deportation for several months. Then came a formal, typed card. 'I am being transferred to another camp,' it said. 'Do not send any more parcels. Wait for my new address.' After which there was silence.

In Le Puy, Bach, who claimed to have known nothing about the planned raid, sent a formal telegram of protest to Vichy, but received no answer and no explanation. What made the whole episode peculiar was that it appeared to have been not about rounding up Jews, but about the 'Germanophobic' spirit of the Maison des Roches and its 'detestable inhabitants'. This theory gained credence when it became clear that the captives had been held not by Barbie, in charge of anti-Jewish operations in Lyons, but by the Wehrmacht, who in theory dealt with deserters and anti-Nazis. Finding the Jews had simply been a bonus.

People now were very frightened. 'We are living,' noted André Trocmé, 'on a volcano, whose muffled rumbles we can hear, some far off, some close to.'

One night early in August, three men came to dine at the Pension des Acacias in le Chambon. Having eaten, they paid their bill, then went out to sit on the terrace. At nine, Inspector Praly came out of the dining room. One of the men got up and shot him. A little girl standing nearby narrowly avoided the bullet. The men fled on bicycles, but when the chain on one of them snapped, they ran off into the forest.

Dr Le Forestier was called, but there was nothing he could do, because the dumdum bullet had exploded in Praly's stomach. In considerable agony, the young inspector was put into a car and driven to a hospital in Le Puy. He died soon afterwards. Later, there would be claims that Praly had in fact often acted to save Jews, but for the plateau, he became the symbol of collaboration.

At first there were thoughts that Praly's assassination might have had something to do with the raid on La Maison des Roches. But quickly it became clear that it had been ordered by the Maquis, now assembling in ever greater number on the plateau and afraid that Praly might have been discovering too much. The killer was identified as a 19-year-old butcher's assistant, Jean Brugière. Four brigades of police arrived on the plateau and scoured the villages and the forests, but in vain.

On 9 August, Praly was buried in le Chambon. Trocmé offici-ated at the funeral, which displeased some of his congregation. But Praly had been one of his parishioners and it was his duty as a pastor, he said, to bury him. Bach, whose stance remained as ambiguous as ever, gave the address. The killing had been, he declared, an act of terrorism.

For a while, local people felt angry, lest there might be reprisals, or that a larger police presence might be sent up from the plains. Nothing happened, however; no one came to replace Praly.

But the sense of inviolability that had hovered over the villages for the past three years, the feeling that they were somehow different, a *terre d'asile*, a place of sanctuary, had gone; and it would not return. As the summer continued, as the fields were covered in scarlet pimpernels, buttercups and blue campanula, and André and Magda Trocmé took their children to picnic in the forest, while seven-year-old Madeleine Sèches, who watched the Germans taking the sun on the terrace outside her bedroom window every day, went swimming in the Lignon, so a stronger sense of secrecy, a need for ever-greater vigilance, settled over the inhabitants of the plateau. To reach the end of the war unharmed, there would have to be silence, of the most total kind.

CHAPTER FOURTEEN

Whatever else we do, we must
save the children

It was now the fifth autumn of the war, and the second of the German occupation of the south and of the Plateau Vivarais-Lignon. The French were exhausted, resentful, demoralised. In July, the Allies had landed in Sicily and were preparing to liberate Corsica; the Soviets, after their victory at Stalingrad, were advancing. An Allied landing on the coast of the Midi was perceived as imminent. In Vichy's pastel-coloured palaces of neo baroque splendour, grown a little shabby, Pétain's army of civil servants continued to carry out his bidding, but the Germans had grown wary of the French police, many of whom had become plainly hostile, and the Gestapo had set up a special section to keep them under observation. Darnand's Milice, on the other hand, were proving far more biddable in the hunt for 'all Jews, either hidden or not', whether French or foreign, adult or child. And they were not averse to doing a little hunting of their own, as the Nizards' capture had shown.

In a country that had lost its rights, everything had become suspect. Posters listing rewards for denunciations – of 'hidden or *camouflé*' Jews, of caches of weapons, of Gaullists and resisters – were everywhere, but even without them, the denunciations poured in, most often signed '*un bon Français*'. In the case of a Jew, the informer was to be paid on the spot, with money taken from his victim.

By the late summer of 1943, there were still some 10,000 Jews in the internment camps. Gurs and Rivesaltes had become holding pens for families awaiting deportation; since most doctors had long since been deported, and very few medicines reached the camps, the number of deaths was rising. After Helmut Knochen, chief of the German police in France, realised how many Jews were managing to escape from the trains taking them to Drancy, he ordered that they be tied together with long ropes, like convicts. The trains leaving for Auschwitz now carried as many French as foreign Jews. There were no more pauses between departures, which were scheduled for two every month, and no more dispensations for anyone. An association of 'Aryanised' organisations had been set up to make sure that after the war, no one would be legally obliged to return their stolen enterprises to a returning Jewish owner.

The French were also hungry. France had become a country of black marketeers and of inventive cooks, supplementing their endless diet of macaroni and swedes with grasses, weeds and roots, and there was much debate about the best way to cook black salsify, rampion and kohlrabi, and whether such food could really be made edible. For the inhabitants of the cities, meat, eggs, butter and cheese had all but vanished.

On the plateau, however, there was still food to be had, even if Emile Sèches had to go ever further afield in search of supplies for the hidden children. With meat severely rationed, animals were slaughtered secretly and distributed between families under cover of darkness. When Magda was offered part of a pig, she was not told where it came from; it arrived on the night of a full moon with a young man, one of ten who had volunteered to carry 10 kilos each to various households, with Pastor Jeannet lending two of his sons to take portions to the hidden Jews, who had agreed to a dispensation on eating forbidden pork.

After the events of the summer, André Trocmé thought that he detected a new religious fervour on the plateau, as if his parishioners, crushed by the never-ending war, the demands of the hidden refugees and the threat posed to their sons by forcible conscription, were turning back to the Church for help. A recent publishing venture in le Chambon, Les Messageries Evangeliques, was doing good business with religious books, the sale of bibles had gone up and the readership of the protestant *Echo de la Montagne* was rising all the time. When Daniel Curtet decided to hold a study meeting in his temple at Fay, taking as his theme Jesus's words to the Pharisees about rendering to Caesar and to God what was due to them, over a hundred young people turned up to debate when, and under what circumstances, it was right to disobey an idolatrous and oppressive state.

Camus, still on his first draft of *La Peste*, had his hero and narrator Dr Rieux say: 'We are working together for something that unites us beyond blasphemies and prayers. That is the only thing.' But Camus was tiring of his solitary life. 'The will, the mind gain from it. But the heart?' He had made friends with André Chouraqui, the Algerian Bible scholar and Madeleine Dreyfus's link on the plateau, who cooked him North African food and instructed him on the significance of the plague in the Bible, and its appearance in 49 separate places. At last, repeating that 'the only cowardice is to get down on one's knees', and escaping a second long winter of snowy loneliness, Camus left for Paris, where he was in contact with Resistance groups for whom he began to write and edit clandestine material, while working by day as a reader for the publishing house Gallimard.

What Madeleine Sèches would later remember was not hunger, but the monotony of the food her father was able to find, and the fact that the only fruit she ever saw was an apple. That, and the cold. Only the ground and first floors of Tante Soly were heated, and in their attic dormitories the children shivered. By the autumn of 1943, most of the boarders were Jewish, but the household remained curiously untroubled by the authorities. The German convalescent soldiers next door, certainly aware of what was happening, were apparently choosing to pay no attention. Though the names of the children had not been disguised, Emile Sèches was careful not to mention their religion in the neat, brief notes he kept on every child, just as he was careful to say nothing to his own children, reasoning that ignorance would keep them safer; so that it was only after the war that Madeleine discovered that the house had been full of Jewish orphans.

There was 10-year-old Jean-Pierre Brunswick, a nervous, clever boy, 'mature but spoiled by his parents', and his brother Michel, who wet his bed every night; 15-year-old Jacques Goldschmidt from Lyons, 'brought up to be somewhat girlish, with a viper's tongue, oversensitive and easily frightened at games'; 14-year-old Nicole Meyer from Saint-Etienne, 'sensitive and rude, perhaps because her parents are so far away'. Henri Fesser lied and stole, and had 'no moral sense'; Huguette Spitz was quiet and good at washing up, but so pliant as to have almost no defined character. These were not easy children. Few knew where their parents were, and most had witnessed and experienced terrible scenes and painful departures. Emile ran the house with a strict hand, trying to lend, with order and discipline, some counterbalance to the fears that filled their minds. But on their behalf he was ferocious. When Dr Le Forestier, whose easy manner and teasing ways could be insensitive, mocked one of the young boarders for being circumcised, and the boy was extremely upset, Emile went round to the doctor's surgery and protested to him.

Madeleine's father had other preoccupations. Her mother's deafness had become more severe and she now took very little part in the running of Tante Soly. His 15-year-old niece, Danielle, who had spent some time with the family in le Chambon before going with her mother into hiding in the Vendée, was reported to have been arrested and sent to Drancy, and he kept a photograph of her in his bedroom, hoping for news. In the photograph of all the children together, taken not long before she left, Danielle, with her short hair held back by bows, looks out boldly, seemingly untroubled. And one of the boarders, 17-year-old Joseph Emir, who thought that because he had a Turkish passport he would be safe, suddenly left for Lyons to look for his family, and news came that he had been picked up by the Gestapo and shot.

All over the plateau, in remote farmhouses, in village attics, in schools and *pensions*, Jewish children were struggling, missing their families, trying to make sense of the secrecy and silence that surrounded them; and, simply, waiting.

Though later most would recall these months with gratitude and appreciation, there were some who were very unhappy indeed. One of these was Jacques Stulmacher, the boy from the Passage Alexandrine in the 11th arrondissement in Paris.

Jacques was now 13. He and his 7-year-old brother Marcel had been living in hiding in Lyons with their Lithuanian father and Polish mother. With the help of the OSE and Madeleine Dreyfus, the two boys reached the plateau on the little train in the early autumn of 1943. Arrangements had been made for them to join five other refugee children on adjoining farms at Pont du Cholet, three kilometres from le Chambon, owned by the Franc family. Jacques' first sight of his new home was of a smoky, dirty farmhouse, built around a muddy courtyard, with goats, chicken, pigs and five cows in one wing, the family in the other. There was no heating. Jacques and Marcel, together with 10-year-old Pierre Cohen, and 11-year-old René, who was not Jewish but who had lost his mother, were given a mattress of dried leaves to share in a small, windowless room in which potatoes were stored. It was damp and extremely cold. In a nearby farmhouse, with the other side of the Franc family, were three other Jewish children, Nicole, Rapha and Max.

The Francs, with Pierre Cohen directly in front of Madame Franc

Though M Franc was being paid by the OSE to take the children in, he was reluctant to allow Jacques to attend school, saying that he was of an age to do full-time farm labour. Jacques, a clever boy, accustomed to being top of his class and desperate to continue his education, pleaded and fought and was eventually permitted to accompany the other children on their two-kilometre walk to the small local school at Les Tavas. Before and after school, he worked on the farm. His schooling having been so much interrupted, he was forced to repeat his last year, but he did well, liked his teacher, and soon rose to join his peers.

The seven children were consumed by hunger. It was not just that they were forced to watch as eggs, cheese, butter, chickens and meat were sold on the black market, or directly to people coming up from the plains in search of food, and that nothing was ever left over for them, but at night, at supper, any lump of meat or lard that made its way into their bowls was immediately transferred to M Franc's plate. If the children worked in the fields with the men, they were never invited to share their elevenses of sausage and ham. Soon, they could think of nothing but food. When Jacques was foolish enough to tell Mme Franc that at school the other children had been amazed to see how little food she sent with them for their lunches, hoping to provoke more generous rations, she stopped giving them any at all, and told them that if they wanted lunch, they had to walk the two kilometres back to Pont du Cholet. Jacques tried to get the others to run away with him, but Mme Franc got wind of the plan and threatened to report them to the police. He stayed. It only occurred to him later that she could never have denounced him, for her position harbouring Jews was no safer than their own. He took to stealing whatever he could lay his hands on: raw eggs, onions, crusts of bread.

For all his cleverness and determination, Jacques was a timid boy. But something snapped the day that Nicole was caught stealing another child's lunch, and the teacher called her to the front of the class, yanked her hair and scolded her sharply. As Nicole wept, Jacques leapt to his feet and shouted out that she was starving, that she never got enough to eat, and that stealing food was not like stealing money or jewellery. The teacher listened, clearly appalled. He sent Nicole back to her place and told the class that they were to arrange a rota, and each in turn was to bring in an extra lunch for Nicole. Unhappily, the same good fortune did not stretch to Jacques and the other children living with the Francs, but it gave him a first taste of what it was to plead a case; and it was this that led him, he later said, into a career in the law.

The Jewish children, for everyone's safety, had no contact with their parents. On this, the OSE was strict. During the entire year that Jacques and Marcel lived with the Francs, they received just one visit from their mother. They told her how hungry they were and she remonstrated with Mme Franc, agreeing to leave extra money so that the boys might each be given an egg every day. This happened for a few days, then stopped. The weeks passed, cold, full of thoughts of food, loveless. The Francs showed no signs of affection or tenderness towards the seven young children in their care, no human contact of any kind. Jacques thought of himself and his brother as cows, for when a police inspection of the farm was threatened, they were sent into the forests with the unregistered cattle, 'all of us, clandestine creatures'. When the Francs wanted to punish them for various misdemeanours, they sometimes slapped them, but more often they simply deprived them of food.

To get more to eat, Jacques took to staying back after school and helping the other children with their homework, in return for the bread and jam or sausage they had brought in with them. However little it was, it was still more than the soup he was forced to forgo when he arrived back at the farm late for supper. The Francs' form of dour neglect extended to health. The boys were given only clogs to wear, without socks; they got chilblains and blisters. When a sore on Marcel's head spread and would not heal, the Francs refused to let him see Dr Le Forestier until Jacques made a scene, by which time it was too late to prevent a bald patch, on which the hair never grew back. The farm dog, kicked by one of the cows, developed an infected eye; it died, slowly and in agony, without being taken to a vet.

Later, recounting his year on the plateau, Jacques would agree that he had been unlucky. On other farms, children were loved and well cared for, though some would later say that they had lived in a sort of 'bubble of unreality', as if play-acting in their own lives. Of the farmer's wife who took her in, Carole Zalberg, one of the girls from Roanne, would later write: 'No, she was not unkind. It was just that in the arc of her emotions there was only severity.' In her own family, Carole had been loved and spoilt; the more bewildered and lonely she felt, the more she clung to her Jewishness. 'We became different,' she wrote. 'We learnt to live apart.'

Jacques later held to his tale precisely because it countered the often overly self-righteous taste of all-pervading goodness with which the war years came to be associated. It was a reminder, he said, that it was not all gentle and untroubled, and that even those who were physically well looked after were most often lonely, frightened, haunted by what had happened to them and terrified of what lay ahead. When, in addition to their unhappy thoughts, they were mistreated and starved, it pushed them to the very edge of what was bearable. They survived, Jacques would say, and without the Francs he might easily have died; but the scars that were left were not the kind that healed.

Simon Liwerant, whose little brother Jacques, still with the Gilberts, was now almost totally withdrawn from him, was having troubles of his own. Simon remained with the Darbyist couple, M and Mme Bard, who, though often silent and somewhat severe, treated him kindly and fed him well. When the circus came to le Chambon one day, Simon got tickets and took Jacques. A German soldier came and sat next to them, an older man, with grey hair. He offered to take Jacques on his lap, but Simon got up and moved away. The soldier followed them, again attempting to take Jacques into his arms. Later, Simon would realise that he was probably the father of a small boy himself, and longed for the warmth of the child. But at the time, he could feel only hatred. He picked Jacques up and left the tent.

The boys received a visit from their father Aaron, allowed out from his work camp for a few days' leave. The Bards offered to find him work, and he could easily have stayed on the plateau, with false papers, in hiding. But he told Simon that he knew that he would soon be leaving for Germany, and this was exactly what he wanted to do, in order to look for Sara, who, he was certain, was alive and in a camp somewhere. Nothing that Simon or the Bards could say would persuade him otherwise. Not long after leaving le Chambon, Aaron wrote to his daughter Berthe, now 16 and still working as an apprentice in Lyons, and she sent the letter on to Simon. He was, Aaron told them, writing from a train not far from Lourdes, taking him and 30 other Jewish men north. 'Naturally, we don't know where we're going . . . I am certain that we're going somewhere to work, but where? . . . I am leaving full of hope in my heart, and I will go on hoping until I find your mother, my Sara. My heart grows warm knowing that I will see her . . . I am setting out full of courage and my morale is excellent.' He was sending them some money, he said, as well as his ration books, and he wanted Berthe to buy something for 'my adorable Jacquot, and you must tell him that it was sent by his father and mother from Lyons'.

Aaron wrote again, this time from a second train taking him and 700 Jews in 23 carriages towards Paris. 'If you can, keep these letters and hide them, for memory's sake . . . Never forget that you are Jews and also free human beings, and you must say this to Simon too, remain free beings and look at everything with your eyes wide open.' People, he wrote, were fickle, not easy to read, and however honest their faces, they were often full of bad thoughts. 'Never forget this advice, remember it always.' He told Berthe that she should never have cold drinks when she went swimming, and that she should tell Simon to work very hard, because he was capable of doing important things. 'I kiss you again and again. I leave with the certitude that you will grow up a good, beautiful and intelligent child.' He signed the letter 'your papa, who hopes very much to see you very soon'.

After this, Berthe and Simon heard nothing more.

One morning, Simon woke very early, to a strange noise. It was still dark, and when he went outside, he saw lights climbing up towards the farm from the valley below. From the sound of the motor, he knew that it was petrol, rather than *gazogène*, which meant that it could only be the Milice or the Germans. He woke the Bards, who hastily hid him under bales of hay in the manger among the cows. A group of men arrived and told M Bard that they had information that he was hiding Jews. They searched the farmhouse, the dairy, the outbuildings, but were driven back from the stables by the stench of the manure. When they left, they took with them all the Bards' store of pork, cheese and butter.

It was no longer safe for Simon to stay. He went to see André Chouraqui, who made arrangements for him to be taken in by a school in Figeac, in the Dordogne, where one of the teachers was already hiding 11 young Jews. On his way, Simon stopped in Lyons to see Berthe. Jacques stayed behind with the Gilberts, who, now that he no longer wet his bed, treated him like their son. A spell apart, Simon reasoned, might make the little boy forget that he had hit him, and he might come to love him again.

Armand Nizard, imprisoned in Drancy, would not have celebrated Mussolini's downfall with such enthusiasm had he realised what it spelt for the Jews sheltering in France's Italian zone. As the dictator was deposed by the Fascist Grand Council, and General Badoglio began what would be his 45-day rule, the Germans moved troops into Savoy, claiming that they were merely using it as a route for transit to the south. The 3,000 or so Jews who had been living in 'assigned residence' in Mégève, Saint-Gervais and Barcelonnette, were brought down to the coast, many of them in Italian military lorries, guarded by carabinieri, where they joined the 30,000 others already crammed into Nice and its surrounding 30 kilometres of coastline. For a very short while, it seemed that they might be safe. Angelo Donati, the ebullient businessman from Modena who had led the campaign to find sanctuary for the Jews, and whom everyone desperately wanted to believe, still maintained that his negotiations with Badoglio and with the Allies would result in their transfer either across the sea to liberated North Africa, or over the border into Italy itself.

It was not to be. On 3 September, Badoglio signed a secret armistice with the Allies. The day set for the Allied landings in Italy was 12 September. However, on the 8th, without warning, Eisenhower landed his forces in Salerno, just south of Naples. Whether those few extra days could have changed the fortunes of the trapped Jews is not clear: Donati's optimism was boundless, but the chaos into which Italy had been plunged suggests that an orderly evacuation of Jewish refugees would have been highly unlikely. As it was, the Germans, who had been waiting and planning for this moment, acted at great speed. Within 24 hours, much helped by the men they already had in place, Wehrmacht troops had occupied Nice and disarmed the unresisting Italian forces. Nice was now a *souricière*, a mousetrap, with 30,000 Jews caught in its spring.

The next day, 10 September, Aloïs Brunner, former commandant of Drancy, arrived to purge the city of its Jews. He brought with him an equally vicious anti-Semite called Brückler, a 25-man squad of interrogators, willing volunteers from the Milice and Jacques Doriot's Parti Populaire Français, founded by former communists turned Fascist, and a group of '*physionomistes*', men ostensibly trained to recognise Jews by their appearance, who were dispatched into the streets like truffle hounds. Soon, the elegant bedrooms of the Hôtel Excelsior, commandeered by

Brunner as his headquarters, resounded to the cries of people under interrogation. For the Niçois, the Excelsior became a metaphor for horror. 'The city of Nice,' reported the representative of the Commissariat Général aux Questions Juives to his superiors, with smug satisfaction, 'has lost its appearance of a ghetto . . . there are now seats on the Promenade des Anglais for Aryan walkers, which until now have been occupied by the Jews.'

From his informants, Brunner knew that there were at least 25,000 Jews in and around Nice; he planned to catch them all. His men stopped the trains in and out of the city, and began to comb the streets, house by house, alleyway by alleyway, emptying the hotels and the hospitals, shouting, dealing out blows, bullying, forcing the men to drop their trousers to see whether they were circumcised. The French police, mistrusted by Brunner, were given the job of manning the roadblocks. Brunner's first setback came when he ordered the recently elected Prefect, Jean Chaigneau, to turn over all his files on the Jews, only to be told that Chaigneau had taken the precaution of burning them. His next was when it became apparent that, far from denouncing the Jews, many local inhabitants were choosing to hide them instead. Rewards of 5,000 francs – the equivalent of two months' average salary – for every Jew failed to yield the number of victims he had hoped for, and even the informers, of whom there were many, produced disappointingly meagre results.

It was not long, however, before trains began to leave Nice station for Drancy. Over the next three months, 1,819 Jews would be deported, far fewer than Brunner's goal, but still enough to send many trains north. The low number proved what could be done when neither the local population nor the French police were prepared to help. But it made the Germans all the more determined; and those who escaped the round-ups in Nice were now in great danger. Never had the rescue organisations – the OSE, Cimade, the Jewish scouts, Garel's Circuit B – worked harder, or, as it turned out, at greater cost to themselves. New groups of Jews began to leave for the plateau, both orphans and families.

When the Germans had taken over the south, in November 1942, the rescue operations had been driven ever deeper into hiding, or had transferred their offices to Grenoble, Chambery and Nice, at that point still safely within the Italian zone. From here, they had continued to forge documents, find hiding places and conduct parties of Jews across the border and into Switzerland. In Lyons, where she had remained, Lily Garel worried constantly about her husband, ceaselessly circulating around the south to check up on his team of helpers. By the early autumn of 1943, Garel's circuit had 1,600 children on its books, scattered around central and southern France, several dozen of them on the plateau, with 29 full-time workers, organised into four sectors. When Nice fell, he sent two of his best helpers, Huguette Wahl and Nicole Weil, to the coast. Joseph Bass, 'l'Hippopotame', and his assistant Denise, 'Colibri', were also in Nice, and had been joined by a young Italian anarchist called Ermine Orsi, who had been working as a cook at Les Grillons in le Chambon until Daniel Trocmé's arrest, after which she hid the 45 children on neighbouring farms before leaving for Nice. Ermine became Bass's main conveyer of children from the coast up to the plateau.

With Nice occupied, and no safe zone left anywhere in France, the need for hiding places and for getting people across the border intensified dramatically. The Jewish scouts, the EIF, quickly closed their children's homes and dispersed the 400 children there, taking them in groups of 10 to Loinger in Annemasse, though the former sports instructor was finding the task of negotiating the border ever more hazardous. 'The entire Jewish community,' wrote one woman later, 'gradually built itself deeper and deeper into an underground existence.' It had become, the rescuers told each other, a race against time, for the war was at last turning in the Allies' favour; but how many people, and in particular how many children, could they keep safe until France was liberated? A sort of frenzy enveloped them all. They hardly slept, filling their days and nights with audacious plans, the forging of ever more documents, scouring the countryside for people still willing to help. 'Whatever else we do,' they repeated to each other, 'we must save the children.'

The night of the bold rescue of children from the camp at Vénissieux had thrown up one hero, Georges Garel; the events in Nice created another, a man just as resourceful and unconventional. His name was Moussa Abadi, and he was a scholarly Syrian Jew who had come to Nice to write a thesis on medieval literature; he was also a successful actor, having worked with

Louis Jouvet in Paris. Walking along the Promenade des Anglais one day, Abadi had seen a *milicien* hit a Jewish woman over the head. She had a small child with her. He asked a bystander what was going on. 'It's nothing,' the woman told him. 'They are just disciplining a Jew.' In the summer of 1943, Abadi and his 29-year-old Parisian girlfriend, Odette Rosenstock, who had been forced to give up her practice as a doctor on account of the Statut des Juifs, had met an Italian chaplain, Don Giulio Penitenti, recently returned from the eastern front. Penitenti described to them the atrocities carried out against the Jews by the Einsatzgruppen. 'When the Germans get here,' he told them, 'your children will really suffer. I am warning you.'

Abadi took heed. When the Germans arrived, he acted. And in the same way that Garel had found a bishop, Mgr Saliège, to protect him, so Abadi sought out the Bishop of Nice, Mgr Paul Rédmont. Later, the conversation between the two men would be reported in several different versions, but at the end of it, Abadi emerged from the episcopal palace with an office in which to forge documents, the rank of inspector of schools, a letter of recommendation to everyone working for the diocese, a pile of blank birth certificates and a soutane to wear as a disguise, in case of need. Odette was made a 'social worker, to take care of the children under the charitable arm of the church'. She took the name of Sylvie Delatre.

Working independently from, but in close cooperation with, Garel, the Jewish scouts and Bass, and like them using money sent in by the JDC, Abadi and Odette set up a network of their own, the Réseau Marcel, taking charge of the Jewish children along the coast, providing them with false documents and getting them into convents, hospitals, orphanages, children's homes and presbyteries. They set up sub-offices in Grasse, Antibes, Cannes and Juan-les-Pins. The hardest part, Abadi would later say, was having to 'depersonalise' the children. 'We had to steal their identities. We became identity thieves.' As with all the rescuers, they quickly discovered that the children hardest to conceal were the youngest, who could not understand what they were told to do, or those who, like Jacques Liwerant, wet their beds, or those whose looks might give them away. Having spent many hours coaching them in their new names and altered pasts, Abadi kept a file of their true names, which, like Garel, he hid for after the war. Constantly moving the children about, trying always to keep one step ahead of the Germans, Abadi and Odette asked a local pastor, Edmond Errar, to visit le Chambon and the plateau, and soon more of Nice's Jewish children were making the journey up into the mountains on the little train.

Just how dangerous it had become, for children and rescuers alike, was brought home when the Germans, having got hold of the lists of Jews from UGIF and announced that henceforth no one might be moved from a children's home without permission, descended on a house at La Verdière, near Marseilles, and took away 40 children. Deportations from Drancy of children whose parents had already been sent to Auschwitz had become common; but Convoi 77 long haunted those who watched it leave. This train carried 299 children, of whom two were a year old, and a third a baby. Over half the children were aged between 4 and 12. 'The little ones went first,' wrote a witness later. 'They trotted along, whimpering, clutching some little toy in their hands. They kept falling out of line, stopping, turning back . . .'

The OSE, at the time of the German occupation of Nice, had 840 children in homes throughout the south. Fearful that their names would now be seized by the Gestapo – the OSE, like all the other Jewish welfare bodies, remained formally under the auspices of the UGIF – the organisation decided to close all the homes and hide the children elsewhere. The Jewish scouts, to pre-empt further Gestapo raids, carried out a number of bold kidnaps of children remaining in UGIF homes. Interestingly, the OSE made no move to close La Guespy, L'Abric or Faïdoli, clearly believing that the plateau remained one of the last places of true safety. Madeleine Dreyfus continued to go up and down the mountain once or twice a week, checking on the welfare of the children in hiding, and bringing new ones to Mme Déléage to find homes for. 'I have to deliver four "Old Testaments",' she would say, getting off the train. The children whose features might give them away, she bundled up in hats and scarves for the journey.

Remarkably, until this moment, most of the rescuers had escaped capture. It could not last. Very quickly, one after the other, Claude Guttmann of the Jewish scouts, Jacob Weintrob of Loinger's network, and Huguette Wahl, Garel's assistant in Nice, were arrested, tortured and deported. The Haute-Savoie had become particularly dangerous since the Prefect, Edouard Darliac, had ordered the gendarmerie to check every train and every station for suspicious travellers. When the number of arrested Jews reached 500, he spoke of 'edifying results'. Nicole Weil, who with her new husband Jacques Salon had been frantically closing the OSE's homes and taking parties of 15 to 30 children at a time to Loinger in Annemasse, was arrested in Nice on 24 October. Nicole had been indefatigable, rushing from task to task, place to place. She was a slender, short young woman, little more than a girl herself.

From Drancy, she was able to send her husband a coded message, warning him of a possible informer in their midst. She told him that in the camps she had met up with Huguette Wahl and several other young rescuers. 'Our morale is superb,' she wrote. 'Tell everyone not to worry about us – we'll hold on.' In Drancy, Nicole had taken charge of three small orphans. On 23 November, they were all deported together to Auschwitz. It would later be known that though selected as a worker – and therefore for a while at least safe from extermination – Nicole had refused to be parted from the children, and went with them to the gas ovens.

On the plateau, while the hidden Jews now seemed to exist in a curious limbo, continuing to be ignored by the convalescent German soldiers, the predatory Milice and Bach's inspectors, the same was not true of the rescuers. On the evening of 5 October, Dora Rivière, the Christian Socialist reforming doctor from Saint-Etienne, who had been at the heart of a network placing Jews on the plateau, using the lorries and horse-drawn drays of the family haulage business, was arrested by the Gestapo. She was at dinner with her family when a group of French policemen, accompanied by three plain-clothed men in trilby hats and raincoats, forced their way into the house, demanding to see everyone's papers. Dora was taken to Montluc, already infamous as Barbie's head-quarters. Her elderly mother was held briefly as a hostage, but then released. A few days later, Dora was put on to a train for Paris. Not being Jewish, she was held for a while in the resisters' prison, Fresnes, before being sent to Ravensbrück, where she worked in the infirmary as a doctor. It soon became known that she and her family had been denounced by a disgruntled young man, angry at having been turned down by their network as too unreliable.

The next to go was Dorcas Robert, the robust, no-nonsense café and grocery owner from Yssingeaux. She had taken the *nom de guerre* of Tabitta and was much loved by the young men she hid, whose feet she massaged when they returned from long journeys. 'Dorcas became a mother for all of us,' one later wrote. She was arrested on a Sunday morning, along with her sister and her sister's baby, and her assistant Rose Bérard, the young girl who had grown up to know 'the value of good causes'. The women were in the shop shelling peas when three armed men came in and demanded to see their papers.

One of Dorcas's hidden Jews, always known as 'Le Parisien', managed to get away through the attics, and the local policeman, Gauthier, who had helped Dorcas before, was able surreptitiously to retrieve a gun hidden in a sack of dried beans, while Dorcas's 10-year-old daughter Berthe concealed some papers in a cupboard. But the women were taken off, along with eight young men. They made a lot of noise as they went, to warn others to keep away. That night, in their police cells, the young men asked for a drink of water. The guard brought it in a heavy pitcher, and they used it to knock him out, after which they fled into the darkness, but they could do nothing to rescue Dorcas. Next day, her sister and baby were released but Dorcas and Rose, having been interrogated and beaten about, followed Dora Rivière to Montluc and into Barbie's hands. Flyers were pasted up all over Yssingeaux's walls: 'Yssingelais! Protest against Mme Robert's arrest! Force them to return this mother to her 3 children!' In the prison, Dorcas sang psalms to comfort the other detainees. Berthe and her two little brothers were taken in by relatives.

Most upsetting of all, because she had played such a crucial role in the plateau's crusade to save the Jews, was the arrest of Madeleine Dreyfus. Her sons Michel and Jacques were now nine and six, and at the end of August she had given birth to a daughter, Annette. All through September and October, as one rescuer after another fell into Gestapo hands, Raymond had begged his wife to hand her work over to someone else. But Madeleine seemed possessed, saying that no one minded about the children the way she did, no one knew where they all were, nor had such good contacts all over the plateau. In the little notebook in which she kept the true and false names of those in her care, there were now dozens of addresses of families and farmhouses where children were hiding. Who, she would ask, can possibly take my place?

At last, worn down by Raymond's entreaties, and mindful of the fact that she was still breastfeeding Annette, she agreed to find a replacement. The danger that they were in was brought home to her when Raymond's sister and her two children, aged 11 and 2, were suddenly picked up and deported. But then, on 27 November, Madeleine received a phone call from the father of a child she had hidden in the school for deaf and dumb children in Villeneuve, just outside Lyons. Madeleine frequently used the school for children preparing to depart for Switzerland. He had heard, the frantic father told her, that the place was to be raided by the Gestapo.

Madeleine rang the school, which was run by a M Pellet and his wife, to be told, in a curious, formal tone, that she was urgently wanted and should come as quickly as she could. Though suspicious, she decided to investigate. Taking the precaution of locking away incriminating papers in a trunk and putting it in a storeroom, she caught a bus to Villeneuve. The door of the school was opened by the Gestapo. René and Marguerite Pellet had, it turned out, been running the Marco Polo Resistance network in the area, collecting information on the Germans and the Milice and transmitting it to London. It had been one of the biggest and most effective networks, with contacts all over the south, René using the school as cover for his comings and goings, Marguerite in charge of encoding and transmitting. The Gestapo had been watching them for months. Having arrested everyone on the premises, they had sat tight for 17 days, picking off the Pellets' associates when they came to call, eating their way through the supplies of condensed milk, jam and chocolate intended for the children.

Madeleine found a way of hiding her little book with the names of the children in it. She asked to be allowed to go home to breastfeed her baby. When that was refused, she begged to be allowed to make a phone call, so that someone would give Annette a bottle. Her real fear was that, discovering that she was Jewish – though not the nature of her clandestine work, of which she professed complete innocence – they would raid her home in search of her Jewish relations. She used her one permitted call not to ring home, but to speak to the offices of the UGIF; when she got through, she just had time to say that she had been arrested by the Gestapo, knowing that they would then warn everyone, before the phone was seized from her hand and she was slapped. René Pellet had managed to escape, but Marguerite was deported to Ravensbrück.

When Raymond got home later in the day, he found Madeleine gone and the baby unfed. He went for news to the Garels' house, where he found Lily and another the OSE helper called Raia, and the two young women, who knew of Madeleine's connections to the Pellets' school, offered to go there to see if they knew anything of her movements. They too fell into the Gestapo's hands, but not before Lily caught Madeleine's eye and saw in it a mixture of horror and disbelief that anyone could have been so stupid as to follow her there. Taken into custody and interrogated, Lily, who was pregnant, told them that she was Catholic and that her horrible Jewish husband had abandoned her and she knew nothing of his whereabouts. On Raia was found a list of Jewish names. She denied knowing anything about it. Neither woman was physically assaulted, but the Gestapo took pleasure in spelling out to them, in great detail, the sorts of torture they reserved for Jewish women, and from nearby cells they could hear screams and shots. Two months later, in the odd and random way in which these things sometimes happened, Raia and Lily were released.

Madeleine was finally allowed home late on the day of her arrest, but only briefly, in order to feed Annette. To her immense relief, she found the place deserted, Raymond, the baby and the two boys gone, the UGIF having clearly sounded the alert. The phone rang while she was there. It was her mother, frantic for news. 'Go away . . . Leave . . . All of you,' Madeleine told her.

Raymond had taken Jacques and Michel up to le Chambon, and Mme Déléage found a safe hiding place for them under the name of Drevet, with the Lebrat family. Madeleine's mother and her sister took charge of Annette, finding a wet nurse and a hiding place for the four of them in Ain.

Madeleine was transferred to Montluc prison, where she was interrogated and asked whether she was Jewish. When she said that she was, her German interrogator, with an expression of disgust, threw a carafe of water over her. Looking back on it later, she concluded that the German had been Barbie, and that she was lucky that he had not tortured her, as he had so many others. She was held in Montluc for two months; from the window of her dormitory, she could see people being led out to the courtyard below and shot. She had no news of her family, and worried ceaselessly about the safety of the children. When at last transferred to Drancy, she had the good fortune to meet an old friend, who had been put in charge of registrations; he agreed to pass her off as the wife of a prisoner of war, which meant that, for a while at least, she was not deported. Receiving news that the boys were in le Chambon, and fearing that the plateau might be subjected to raids, she wrote a coded letter to Raymond. 'You must stop the boys eating too much *jambon* [ham], as our Alsatian friends pronounce it.' Through the OSE, arrangements were made to get Michel and Jacques to Switzerland.

Between the end of August and the end of October, some 413 Jewish children were taken safely across the Swiss border. But then a group was stopped and arrested, and the crossings were halted. There would be no more until March 1944.

As with so much that touches on le Chambon and the plateau during the war years, there are several versions of why André Trocmé decided, in the late autumn of 1943, to go into hiding.

After Inspector Praly's assassination, there were real fears that reprisals might follow. Trocmé, as the very visible pastor, already known for his views on the Jews, appeared to be the perfect target; were he arrested and tortured, what might he not be forced to say, what names might he give away, what hiding places reveal?

More importantly, he had never abandoned his absolute belief in non-violence. If anything, it had grown stronger, and with it his opposition to the band of armed young *maquisards* forming across the plateau. It was perfectly possible, he kept repeating, to deal with the Germans, most of whom were decent men and could be reasoned with; it was through faith, obedience, patience under persecution and by acting as witness that this war would be won.

If you were a Christian there was, he insisted, no other way. Why couldn't le Chambon be a citadel of non-violent resistance? When one day the aunt of a young STO resister hiding in the mountains asked Trocmé if he would send a message of support and comfort to the boy, Trocmé replied no, never, not to a fighter. Among the *maquisards*, there was growing nervousness about where this intransigence might lead. Oscar Rosowsky, turning out as many false documents for the hidden resisters as for the Jews, felt that Trocmé had become a 'loose cannon. He posed a danger for us all.'

Later it would be said that Trocmé was ultimately persuaded to go by the Resistance, in the form of either Léon Eyraud in le Chambon or a cousin of Daniel Trocmé's father, Maurice Rohr, who happened also to be vice president of the Reformed Church. It was Rohr who pointed out that there had been enough martyrs already, and that by staying, Trocmé would not only endanger his own family, but also, if killed, turn the whole village over to violent reprisals. What is certainly true is that Trocmé himself agonised over the decision, telling Magda that he felt it to be cowardly, that it would send out the wrong message, and that the least he could do was to preach his pacifist credo until the bitter end. However, after a visit from a young *maquisard*, posing, it was later said, as a double agent, who told him that he had overheard orders being given for the Gestapo to assassinate him, Trocmé finally agreed to leave. Theis, whose pacifism was no less heartfelt, was persuaded to go as well; he went off to Switzerland, and spent the next few months acting as a guide across the mountains and a conveyer of funds from Geneva.

There was a thought of encouraging Dr Le Forestier to leave too, as his behaviour towards the Germans was constantly provocative, and as he continued to blow his horn loudly whenever the Germans put on a musical performance in the village square. But Le Forestier was judged too useful on the plateau. 'The two shepherds have had to become hirelings,' wrote Curtet to his father, referring to the hireling in John 10:2 who, seeing a wolf arrive, flees; a somewhat ambiguous choice of verse, given that the wolf then caught the sheep.

Borrowing bicycles from their neighbours, the entire Trocmé family accompanied the pastor on the first leg of his journey, across the flat middle of the plateau in the direction of Saint-Agrève. Trocmé had taken the precaution of shaving off his moustache, putting on a beret and dark glasses and getting false papers in the name of Béguet. Just outside the town, he was met by the ironmonger from Lamastre, M Lespet, who drove him to the presbytery, where an old friend was acting as temporary pastor. A few weeks later, the incumbent returned, not best pleased to discover a hidden guest, and Trocmé moved to a remote farmhouse high on the mountain; it was just as well, for the Gestapo soon came looking for him.

His new home was an attic above a barn. The farmer was a prisoner of war in Germany, and Trocmé spent his evenings helping the young wife and her son peel chestnuts, the staple local wartime diet. During the day, he walked in the pine forests, reflecting on the nature of his faith. The months of exile reveal a gentler, less judgemental, more doubting side to Trocmé's nature. He had decided that it was too dangerous to correspond directly with Magda, so letters had to wait for travellers to le Chambon. Trocmé was lonely. Scrawled across the top of a letter dated 26 November are the words 'total solitude'. Addressing Magda as 'My dearest', he wrote after receiving a letter: 'At last some news of you! I feel myself come alive again! I exist once more! I am no longer a pale little retired *monsieur* who is sitting around waiting for death!' When no letters came, he fretted.

But the farm was soon judged too dangerous and Trocmé moved again, this time to an isolated property owned by a businessman who was hedging his bets by selling cement to the Germans for their Atlantic wall, while hiding resisters and their weapons in his house. '*Drôle d'atmosphère!*' noted Trocmé, adding that it was a very far cry from the elevated ideological debates of le Chambon. 'I suffocated morally.' He also felt suffocated by the behaviour of his hostess, the businessman's surly 40-year-old daughter, who treated him like a servant and sent him out to mind the goats, which drove him mad by straying and, when he finally found a way of tying them together with a piece of string, by refusing to eat. She had also put him in a room without heating. Magda, receiving his plaintive letters, arranged for him to move again, this time to far greater comfort in a chateau in the valley of the Drôme. Here the food was excellent and he had the company of a hidden Jew, with whom he was able to debate the issues of the day, though he found him annoyingly contrary.

When Christmas came, Magda sent over Jean-Pierre, with whom Trocmé had snow fights, and after him came Jaques, now 12, who had been doing badly at school and whom Trocmé planned to coach, while sending him for a term to the local school. Their meeting at Lyons station almost ended in disaster. Having left Jaques to watch the suitcases while he went off to collect a bag deposited by Magda in the left luggage, Trocmé found himself in the middle of a Gestapo round-up. He was seized, jostled and thrown into a lorry. Since he spoke excellent German, he was able to persuade first the guard, then his superior officer, to let him collect Jaques and tell him what was happening.

Later, waiting in a long line of suspects with Jaques to be interrogated, Trocmé was riven by doubts. Would it not be best to tell the truth, for otherwise would he not be tempting God? If he lied, would this not be yet one more step along a downhill path 'for which God did not call me'? On the other hand, what was he to do about Jaques if he told the truth? Paternal responsibility won the day. While the German soldiers had their backs turned, Trocmé and Jaques slipped behind a pillar and disappeared into a throng of passengers waiting for a train. God, Trocmé told himself, had not, at that moment, wished him to die. Many years after the war, he learnt that the Gestapo had in fact discovered who he was, but only after he and Jaques had got away. The officer responsible was demoted and sent to the eastern front.

In their vast vaulted and wood-beamed room in the chateau, Trocmé and Jaques settled down to work, to make up stories and jokes and to raise an orphaned family of field mice in a metal tub. Trocmé started writing a book he intended to call '*Oser Croire*' – daring to believe – which he conceived as a theological treatise for lay teachers, to help them navigate their way through questions about rationality and empiricism, Marxism and the teaching of the Gospels. His pacifism unshaken, he wrote: 'I believe in the final triumph of good over evil.' Reflecting on his own nature, he concluded that his patterns of thought were disorderly and his memory was poor, but that, wherever he was, whatever he was doing, he was always thinking, and that he was rarely at peace, but rather incessantly juggling with hypotheses and problems. If he sometimes appeared strong and sure of himself, he noted, it was because he chose to voice only positive things, never his doubts and fears of failure. The snowy, companionable weeks passed.

But on the plateau, events had moved on. It would be neither the pastors and their pacifism, nor the Darbyists and their silent sense of morality, who would determine the last months of the war in the Haute-Loire, but something more martial. Describing his time in hiding, Trocmé noted later, with some complacency, that it had coincided with a magnificent period of piety on the plateau, when 'belief in non-violence spread around the area, perfectly expressing the hopes and desires of nearly everyone'. He was deluding himself.

CHAPTER FIFTEEN

Perfect Maquis country

The Plateau Vivarais-Lignon was perfect Maquis country. The isolated farms, with their barns and outhouses, and the dense pine forests and rocky hillsides, which had provided such excellent hiding places for those escaping the Gestapo, were ideal for sheltering the young men gathering to form units for the Resistance. It snowed hard all through December and into January and February 1944, with metre-deep drifts along the roads and tracks. Secure in this still white world, people waited for the spring.

Throughout France, repression was if anything intensifying. Vichy, once apparently eager to distance itself from the more unpleasant aspects of occupation, was busy conferring legitimacy upon the most collaborationist period of the war. In December, Bousquet, head of the police, judged insufficiently aggressive by the Germans, was ousted and Joseph Darnand, chief of the Milice, was made secretary general for the maintenance of order. He was now in control of both the police and the 25–30,000 young *miliciens*, who, regarding themselves as above the law, looted, robbed and menaced at will. The Germans had originally been reluctant to arm the Milice, but, bit by bit, the *miliciens* had acquired weapons, often stolen from Allied parachute drops. Some moved into the administration; others into prison service and the legal system. Darnand set up court martials for those they arrested for resistance activities, often held inside prisons, three *miliciens* acting as judges. There was no representation. The judges arrived and left in secret, unidentified, having handed down death sentences, against which there was no appeal.

Ordered to flush out 'suspects' of every kind, wherever they could be found, the Milice recruited informers, rounded up communists and organised manhunts, assisted by Laval's decision finally to turn over all prefectural lists of French Jews to the Gestapo. Vichy's pretence of sheltering French Jewry, long a mockery, was officially abandoned. Almost unimaginable brutality – persecution, violence, murder – was now being carried out by the French against the French. Wherever they could, the Resistance fought back. 'Your duty is clear,' read one of the many clandestine flyers circulating around the country. 'Kill the *miliciens* . . . exterminate them like rabid dogs.' For their part, the *miliciens* were becoming ever more efficient torturers.

Simon Liwerant was one of the people who very nearly fell into their hands. After reaching Figeac, he had been sleeping in an old monastery with ten other Jewish boys, several of them members of the Jewish scouts, who went by the names of animals and birds. His two particular friends were Souris (mouse) and Giraffe. One morning, before it was light, a party of *miliciens* and SS men arrived, forced their way in and ordered everyone to assemble in the courtyard. In the confusion, and urging the others to do the same, Simon, Souris and Giraffe slipped away and hid. The others were taken away in lorries. When the Jewish scouts heard what had happened they took Simon to join 30 other young Jews preparing to cross into Switzerland. Twenty-year-old Marianne Cohn, who called herself Colin, had volunteered to be their *passeur*. Marianne was a gregarious, laughing young woman, a little overweight, with a mass of curly black hair and round spectacles. Her parents were German Jewish academics; after their arrest and internment in Gurs, Marianne had been taken in by the Jewish scouts and became one of their first couriers. Arrested in 1942 and held for three months in a prison in Nice, she had unexpectedly been released, upon which she had returned to her job as *passeur*.

Wearing scout uniforms and loudly singing Protestant hymns, the group marched boldly towards the frontier, passing themselves off as a scouting expedition. Here, too, Simon was almost lost. Having run up a grassy slope and through some trees, the young people reached the double row of barbed wire and began to clamber through, each pair holding the wires for those that followed. Two of the last were Simon and a girl with very long hair. As she scrambled across, her hair caught in the wire. Simon stayed with her to unpick it. At first he assumed that the guards who ran up shouting were Germans, but they turned out to be Swiss, and he was allowed to cross. Simon, like Max and Hanne, was safe. Jacques, his little brother, was with the Gilberts in le Chambon, safe too. Later, he heard that Souris and Giraffe, who had joined the Maquis, had been shot. Later, too, Simon married the young girl with the long hair.

It was just as well that Trocmé and Theis had left the plateau. The mood had altered. There was little taste any longer for gentle acceptance, the belief that powers of persuasion were enough to make people behave better. In their own ways, Dr Le Forestier, Miss Maber, Daniel Curtet and Oscar Rosowsky, who had earlier tacitly accepted the pastors' pacifism, had all shifted in the direction of armed struggle, and how they could best help the final push towards liberation. That it could only be violent, no one doubted. In this story, the hidden Jews and their godly protectors now move backstage. For the moment, they are safe.

In December, the Combined Allied Chiefs of Staff had committed themselves to Overlord, the invasion of France across the Channel. General Eisenhower had been appointed Commander of the Supreme Headquarters Allied Expeditionary Force. In March 1944, de Gaulle, in Algiers and head of the Committee of National Liberation, announced the setting up of the Forces Françaises de l'Intérieur. Plans were being finalised for the invasion and liberation of France, in which the Resistance, and the Maquis, intended to take a major role.

By the spring of 1944, there were some 14 different groups of *maquisards* in the eastern Haute-Loire, about 350 to 400 men gathered under the umbrella of the Gaullist Armée Secrète, under that of the Mouvements Unis de la Résistance or under the fighting arm of the communist Francs-Tireurs et Partisans Francais. Some of them were local boys, evading the STO draft. Others came from further afield, drawn by the area's reputation as an inaccessible wilderness and for its rebelliousness towards Vichy France. From Bolbéc in Normandy, sent by a pastor who knew Piton – who had become a saboteur near Nîmes – came 20 young men escaping a summons to work on the Germans' Atlantic wall, and more were arriving all the time, in ones and twos, to be taken in and fed in Mme Jouve's farm or Louis Manon's Hôtel des Lilas, before being sent on up into the mountains with a password.

Pierre Brès, the local chief scout, had left his job as sports instructor at the Ecole Nouvelle Cévenol to join the Maquis, adopting the name Naho and taking with him a number of his students. Brès worked closely in parallel with the *pension* owner Léon Eyraud, and Pierre Fayol, the engineer in overall charge of much of the Resistance on the plateau, to train and occupy the new recruits, who found the snowy months of enforced idleness irksome, and who clamoured for action. To keep them busy a new '*école des cadres maquis*' laid on classes in navigation and map-reading, in weapons and sabotage, and much physical training. Eyraud, who had a fine collection of ancient weapons, lent them for practice, since equipment, arms and ammunition were severely lacking. Brès, idealistic and sporty, kept his *maquisards* in their shorts and scouting uniforms and made them sing psalms and read the Bible. When not otherwise occupied, the boys were urged to offer their services to the local farmers.

Constantly fearful that their inactivity might lead to foolish pranks against the convalescent German soldiers in le Chambon, who continued to jog heedlessly around the village every morning, the older men stressed the need for patience and caution. Eyraud, a short but exceptionally strong man, with a quiet voice and great affection for the recruits, had natural authority, which came with a strict sense of the plateau's spirit of Huguenot morality. He did much to curb their turbulence and impatience, but there were still times when the endless waiting threatened to explode into violence. When he learnt that they were planning to ambush the German soldiers as they swam in the Lignon, he patrolled the banks to ensure their safety.

Also recruited to instil discipline was a much respected teacher at the Ecole Nouvelle Cévenol, Olivier Hatzfeld. Under the name of Pingouin, he led his patrol of birds on missions to identify good spots from which the convoys taking food to the military garrison in Le Puy might later be ambushed.

Daniel Curtet had developed close links with the Maquis groups around Fay. He wrote to his father: 'Our Daniels are a bit overexcited, our Matthews pleasant and calm.' Curtet had agreed to take Communion to clearings in the mountains for the *maquis-ards*. He was also instructing a young man who was soon to marry a local girl from a devout Protestant family, who spent his days up in the mountains and came down at night to study in the presbytery.

Fayol had set up a medical service, with several local doctors, a Jewish chemist called Weill and Dr Le Forestier as surgeon; Maurice Nizard offered to act as a nurse, since he had not been allowed, as a Jew, to qualify as a doctor. Since Trocmé's departure, Le Forestier seemed to have taken on the role of spiritual guide to the parish, and increasingly people turned to him for guidance. Mme Fayol and M Girard of the Salvation Army helped with food, while a number of *'pères tranquilles'*, older, married men in the villages who worked at their ordinary jobs by day and for the Resistance at night, agreed to take charge of the distribution of ration books and supplies.

All the strategies for saving the Jews perfected over the 18 months of occupation now played neatly into the plateau's new role. Oscar Rosowsky and Samy Charles, in their farmhouse annexe, worked day and night turning out false papers. A postman, M Arnand, listened in on the central telephone lines for any troop movements; Mme Roux, who ran the grocery in Chaumargeais, kept an eye on the Tence police, M Manon on those in le Chambon. Jules Valdener, in Yssingeaux, kept a list with all the Maquis camps. In Mazet, Lulu and her daughter Lucienne continued to be a centre for hidden Jews and *maquisards* alike, and when warning came of a possible raid, Lulu took all her protégés to hide in the rafters of Pastor Jeannet's temple, to which villagers brought blankets, hot-water bottles and tea and coffee. The Armée Secrète, to which Fayol belonged, provided 25 francs a day towards each *maquisard*'s keep, but even so there never seemed to be quite enough to eat.

Early in October 1943, 79 prisoners, many of them communists but among them 25 young STO evaders, had escaped from the Maison d'Arrêt at Le Puy, and most of these had made their way up the mountain. Though vigorously hunted down by the combined forces of the police and the Milice, all but seven managed to vanish into the forests, to regroup and establish a base, Camp

Wodli, in a farmhouse near the hamlet of Chièze. The escape cost the equivocating Prefect Bach his job; the man who replaced him, André Bousquet, was said to be made of sterner stuff. But even he could do little against the growing reluctance of the French police to track down the young resisters. Increasingly they were now choosing to leave the chasing of suspects to the more willing and eager *miliciens*. There was not much eagerness for finding the *maquisards* that they had turned into either, despite rechristening them 'terrorists' and talking of mopping up 'disreputable elements'.

So disaffected did the police and gendarmerie seem to have become across the Haute-Loire that Jean Bonnissol, the teacher in Yssingeaux, who went by the name of Soumy or Dubois and led a group of resisters called Zinnia, had no hesitation in trying to recruit his old friend Alfred Morel, a senior local policeman, into the Resistance. Morel refused, but undertook to send warnings of any Gestapo raids. This obvious and growing connivance on the part of the police did much to bolster the Maquis' sense of moral rightness and legitimacy, and that of those who sheltered them on the plateau. Even among people so schooled in independence of thought and morality, the sharing of rebellion with the forces of order and authority was reassuring.

The young *maquisards* were not, however, always popular. Lawlessness and banditry was spreading throughout rural France, and though many of the raids on shops and businesses were in fact being carried out by the 'faux Maquis', small groups of criminals or *miliciens* disguising themselves as resisters, the real *maquisards* were not always totally blameless. Curtet, for his part, was extremely critical whenever a theft was known to have been committed by the men he called 'our good Maquis', or the 'men from the forests', branding their actions burglaries and vandalism. As spring approached, and the snows melted, opening the roads to the outside world again, Brès and Eyraud needed all their tact and firmness to keep the peace. Bonnissol decided to set up a Maquis police force on the plateau, declaring that anyone caught looting or 'requisitioning' would be handed over to the authorities.

Something of the extreme tension in the area, and the pressures exerted by the arrival of ever more young men seeking a role in the Maquis, exploded one day in a sudden verbal attack on Brès, who had continued to insist on the need to wait until the Allied forces had landed before resorting to sabotage. Driven frantic by his caution, longing to make forays against the Germans in the plains, a group of the young men under him accused him of authoritarianism and '*attentisme*', endless procrastination. Reluctantly, Brès stepped down, telling Fayol sadly that once 'something is broken, it's broken' and that it would be very hard for him to work again with the young boys he had trained. His place was taken by a more aggressive leader, known as Bob, who soon sanctioned the 'requisitioning' of cigarettes from tobacconists, and a raid on a dairy said to be owned by a collaborator.

Skirmishes between *maquisards* and the Milice intensified. A *milicien* called Lambert, working for the Gestapo, was shot dead in a café in Yssingeaux, and several young men were caught. One of these was Jean Bonnissol himself, whom Morel had not been able to warn in time, and with him 14 others. Bonnissol had apparently been denounced by nine local people, suggesting that even an area as apparently harmonious and watertight as the plateau was not without its active collaborators; though exactly who these were has never been established. Some of the young *maquisards* who escaped capture decided to leave the area, to join the better-provisioned FTPF in the Ardèche and the Loire, where they were promised stouter shoes, the prospect of immediate guerrilla warfare and more to eat.

In Mazet, Lulu's grocery and café had become a depot for arms, hidden under the hay and in the deep hole in her garden. One night, an entire lorryload of clothes stolen from a depot was concealed in her barn. On 22 April, a joint operation of Milice and French and German policemen, fanning out across the plateau, encircled a group of isolated farms, set fire to them and murdered farmers and FTPF fighters, including the two young sons of a farmer called Charles Valla, Marc and André, aged 19 and 21. Eleven more people were arrested. On Monday the 24th, Pastor Jeannet, Pastor Besson and a Darbyist preacher together officiated at the funeral of the dead men in the temple in Mazet; the congregation overflowed into the square outside.

The next day, the Germans returned to conduct a house-to-house search of Mazet. They found nothing. When they questioned

Lulu about the various bags and cases she seemed to have lying about, she explained that these were all part of the regular post service that she ran with the local bus company.

Over the following days, word got out that the *maquisards* and the Valla brothers had been given away by a tinker who lived with a family of sedentary Gypsies between Tence and Mazet. Marcel Bachon was 19 and always seemed to have money in his pockets. The rumours reached the police in Tence, and Sergeant Tavernier, who had never made any secret of his sympathy for the hidden Jews and the young *maquisards*, went to arrest him. The Armée Secrète was informed. They arrived, took charge of the boy, made him repeat his confession, then told him to dig his own grave. In 2012, Mme Tavernier, at the age of 100, remembered the terrified young man asking to be allowed to go home to get his shoes, saying that he did not want to be shot in the clogs that he was wearing. His request was refused.

All through May, skirmishes between the Maquis and the Milice continued. The Yssingeaux sector, the most militarised, now had three battalions of men, Y1, Y2 and Y3, and their numbers were growing all the time. In le Chambon, the proprietor of the farm where Oscar Rosowsky carried out his forgeries asked his tenant, M Héritier, to get the young man to leave, fearing raids and counter-raids. M Héritier merely told Rosowsky to move his equipment to some empty beehives at the bottom of the garden.

The wait for liberation, on the plateau as all over France, was taking too long and proving costly.

During his rescue operations in Marseilles and Nice, Joseph Bass, the buccaneering, quick-tempered, bossy Byelorussian businessman, had become increasingly concerned with the need for young Jews to take their part in the battle against Vichy. Why, he would ask, when Protestants and Catholics are losing their lives to save us, are we not doing more? There had been, since the end of 1941, a clandestine Armée Juive, intent on protecting France's threatened Jews and planning later to take their fighting skills to Israel, to defend the creation of the Jewish state. By late 1943 it was said to have some 1,500 members, scattered in various parts of France.

But Bass wanted a Maquis of his own, a Jewish Maquis, and when he was forced to leave the coast and fall back on his safe house in the Bardones' restaurant in Saint-Etienne, he remembered his dealings with Trocmé and the isolated farmhouses in which he had been able to place some of the children he had rescued. He came up to the plateau, rented rooms near the station in le Chambon, bought revolvers on the black market, and contacted Léon Eyraud to discuss what he might do. And then he began recruiting. Driving his distinctive motorcycle with its sidecar, on which his huge bulk could barely perch, Bass went around the countryside looking for Jewish families who might donate funds towards the keep of his young fighters; when they proved reluctant, he was not above a little blackmailing. In the evenings, sitting at his kitchen table, he wrote flyers and pamphlets in German and Russian as part of the campaign to win over disaffected Tartar, Georgian and Armenian soldiers serving with the Wehrmacht in Le Puy. Bass, as Rosowsky would say, had the temperament of a poker player.

Recruits were not hard to find, hidden in their isolated farmhouses and restlessly awaiting liberation, but the young Jews needed somewhere to train. Through the OSE, Bass had met André Chouraqui and his wife Colette, who lived in a house with a courtyard at Chaumargeais, a hamlet outside Tence, which acted as the OSE's headquarters for the hidden Jewish children, now that Madeleine Dreyfus had been caught. Tence, like Mazet, Fay and le Chambon, had from the very beginning taken in and hidden Jews – the knitters from Roanne, people rescued from Gurs and Rivesaltes, refugees from Baden and Wurtenburg, but above all French Jewish families. It had no children's homes; most of those the villagers rescued were adults, and by the winter of 1943, some 163 Jews were in hiding in its village houses and on the many scattered farms that made up the community.

Unlike the other three villages, however, Tence was largely Catholic, and it was among the Catholics here that the Jews had found sanctuary. Just the same, the mastermind behind much of the rescue operation was the Protestant pastor, Roland Leenhardt, who maintained that protecting the Jews was a political as well as a spiritual obligation and who willingly lent his presbytery for

Jewish occasions. Leenhardt hid the people sent to him in a concealed room under the rafters, reached by a ladder and trap-door, and from which they could escape over the roofs. He had rigged up a long piece of string with a bell, by which warnings could be sounded. The mayor, Franchet, was generally regarded as a staunch Pétainist, but the local police were clearly sympathetic to the refugees, and the Jews of Tence had enjoyed a remarkably untroubled war. In Chouraqui's courtyard, Bass's small army began to learn to shoot and handle weapons, trained by a Spanish republican fighter called José Vera Martinez. In the evenings, they were joined by younger boys and girls, who came to learn Hebrew and sing Jewish songs.

It was not surprising, then, that it was in Chaumargeais that a small yeshiva had started under a Lithuanian philosopher and Hebrew scholar called Jacob Gordin, who had helped to write the Jewish Encyclopedia in Paris before the war. Gordin was in his late twenties. The six or seven young men who came to join him were all younger, some little more than boys. Most had lost their families. What they wanted to do was to survive, study, sit out the war. The local people called the yeshiva 'l'Ecole des Prophètes', the Prophets' School. Before he left for Paris, Camus was an occasional visitor.

One of the youngest of the prophets was Itzhak Mikhaëli. His grandfather, who had owned a button factory in Lodz, had raised the boy after his mother fell ill, and sent him to study in Paris. There Mikhaëli had been drawn into the world of left-wing Zionists, preparing to go to Palestine. The outbreak of war found him working on a fruit farm near Valence, and his wartime adventures had included teaching sport to children taken in by the Jewish scouts, helping Loinger with his crossings of the Swiss border, and a spell in the internment camp of Rivesaltes, from which he was the only one of a group of friends to be spared deportation. On one occasion, taking a party of 8–12-year-olds to the frontier by train, and finding no seat for them anywhere, he knocked on the door of a first-class compartment full of German soldiers and asked whether they might find room for his party of 'Catholic schoolchildren on their way from one school to another'. The Germans obliged. Mikhaëli was a bold young man.

Shunted from contact to contact, he had eventually received instructions to make his way to Tence, and had been told that there he would find somewhere to hide. Alighting from the little train that took him up the mountain, he found the snow waist deep. He struggled along the road, following the directions he had been given, but was stopped by a group of *maquisards*, who, taking him for a *milicien*, threatened to shoot him on the spot, until prevented from doing so by an older man.

In the Prophets' School, Mikhaëli spent his days studying, analysing texts, discussing, and pooling his reading and his knowledge of Jewish culture with the other young scholars. There was no Talmud, but Gordin knew many of its passages by heart. Mikhaëli lived in a room above a cowshed; the farmer provided the yeshiva with eggs, milk, cheese and butter. One day, when it was his turn to collect supplies from Tence, he was stopped in the café by two policemen, who asked to see his papers. He handed over his false documents. 'What was your mother's maiden name?' one of the men asked. Mikhaëli had failed to memorise the details: the name he produced was wrong. 'Next time,' said the policeman, 'learn your mother's name.' Many years later, telling this story at a conference, he heard a young woman shout out: 'That policeman was my grandfather.'

Ever since the arrival of the Germans in France, Mikhaëli had imagined that his fate would be to join the Jews on their journey to the death camps. As the weeks passed, safe and intellectually occupied, as spring came and liberation began to seem a real possibility, the young prophets started to talk about the future, of how they would help build a new intellectual Jewish life once the fighting was over. As Passover approached, and with it the seven days of celebrating the story of the Exodus, when the ancient Israelites were freed from slavery in Egypt, Mikhaëli took a candle and went out on to the plateau. There he sat and by its light read the Book of Ruth.

The groups of *maquisards* on the plateau were short of everything; but above all they lacked weapons and ammunition. All this was suddenly changed by the arrival of one of the most improbable and exotic figures to enter the story.

Her name was Virginia Hall. The daughter of a Baltimore banker who had married his secretary and made a fortune in movie theatres, Virginia had studied at Radcliffe and Barnard. Sporty, a keen basketball and hockey player, and wilful, she persuaded her father to let her do a year at the Ecoles Libre des Sciences Politiques in Paris, following it up with courses in Vienna, Strasbourg, Grenoble and Toulouse. She returned to the US with good Spanish, German and Russian to study further French at George Washington University. Her appearance was as striking as her abilities: she was tall, with reddish-blonde hair, high cheekbones, a determined chin and grey-green eyes, spaced far apart. She had a fiery temper and could be imperious; of herself she would say that she was difficult and capricious. But she was a born organiser.

In 1931, soon after her twenty-fifth birthday, Virginia joined the American Foreign Service as a secretary in the embassy in Warsaw. By 1933 she had been moved to Izmir. Out hunting one day, she slipped; her gun went off, and a bullet lodged in her left foot. When the wound became infected and gangrene set in, a surgeon rushed down from Istanbul and decided that her leg would have to be amputated just below the knee. She was given a wooden leg, with a brass foot she referred to as her 'aluminium puppy'. She insisted on a new posting; this time it was Venice. But when she applied to the State Department for a full diplomatic position, she was turned down: women, and particularly one-legged women, were not considered suitable candidates. No amount of high-level intervention helped.

Virginia was not a woman given to retreating. After a short spell as a secretary in Tallinn, she resigned. She reached Paris in January 1940, during the phoney war, joined the French ambulance service as a private second class and was sent to the Maginot line, to serve with an artillery regiment stationed near Metz. Demobilised soon after the fall of France, she crossed to London, via Spain, where she soon found a job as a code clerk with the American military attaché.

After the evacuation of Dunkirk, a Special Operations Executive, SOE, had been set up to coordinate subversion and sabotage against the Germans and, if necessary, to initiate it. Major Maurice Buckmaster, former manager for Ford in France, was put in charge of the French, or F, section. At odds with de Gaulle and the Free French, subject to endless internecine rivalries, SOE operated much like a club, to which membership was by invitation only. In 1941, it was looking for recruits, strong, cool-headed French speakers, with a bent for improvisation and organisation. Though women were not their preferred choice, there were not many candidates who knew as much about France as Virginia did, nor who were able to master weapons training and radio transmitting so quickly. What was more, with the US not at war with France, she could be sent in openly, under the guise of a journalist accredited to Vichy, researching articles for the *New York Post*. Having decided to set up an advanced F base in Lyons, SOE asked her to become its first 'resident', in order to coordinate and look after their agents in the field.

Calling herself Mlle Germaine Le Contre, Virginia reached Lyons via Madrid in August 1941, the first female SOE field officer into France. She started to write articles about food shortages, about Vichy, about the Statut des Juifs. 'I haven't seen any butter and there is very little milk,' she wrote. 'Women are no longer entitled to buy cigarettes and men are rationed to two packets a week.' Under cover of the bland and innocent articles, Virginia met the SOE agents dropped into her area, found them lodgings and ration books and supplied them with transmitters. When necessary, she hid them in a convent and got them out to Spain. Officially with an SOE circuit called Heckler, she also acted as liaison with other circuits, yet maintained her independence and worked with a local doctor called Jean Rousset. Still pursuing her cover as an American journalist, she held her meetings openly, in cafés and restaurants, and took care to be on good terms with Vichy officials, from whom she learnt many interesting things. To her colleagues, she referred to her wooden leg as Cuthbert, but most would later say they had never known about her accident; they called her 'the limping lady', on account of her slightly rolling gait. From time to time, she used the aluminium puppy to store compromising documents.

Having entered into a secret deal with Laval to send Gestapo officers south ahead of the occupation of the whole of France, the Germans had soon picked up traces of SOE activity. One by one, a third of the 24 agents in Virginia's area were caught; many were tortured, some were shot. 'We age very quickly out here,' Virginia wrote to Buckmaster. 'I and all the others are about a hundred years old. We'll never be the same again.' It was not long before an informer, a double agent posing as a French priest and calling himself Abbé Alesch, got wind of the existence of a female organiser, going variously by the name of Philomène, Isabelle or Diane. Orders went out from the Gestapo to capture the 'woman who limps' and who 'is one of the most dangerous Allied agents in France. We must find and destroy her.'

Dr Rousset was caught and tortured, but gave nothing away. With very little time to spare, Virginia managed to make her way to the Pyrenees. 'Cuthbert is being tiresome, but I can cope,' she cabled to her superiors in London. The man who took her message had no idea who Cuthbert was. 'If Cuthbert tiresome,' he wired back, 'have him eliminated.' Virginia got across the border, but was arrested; having no papers, she was held in Figueras prison for six weeks, until a prostitute with whom she was sharing a cell smuggled out a letter to the American consulate in Barcelona.

On reaching London, Virginia requested to be dropped back into France. Aware that the Gestapo had posted a fairly accurate description of her, supplied by the false abbé, SOE refused and sent her to Spain instead, where, once again posing as a newspaper reporter, she filed stories to the *Chicago Times*, while arranging safe houses for agents and running the network from Madrid. She was bored. 'I'm not doing a job,' she wrote to London. 'I am living pleasantly and wasting time . . . after all, my neck is my own. If I am willing to get a crick in it, I think that's my prerogative.' By 1943, she was back in London.

The Office of Strategic Services, the OSS, the American organisation set up in June 1942 'to plan and operate special services' of intelligence and sabotage in Europe, had entered into a loose partnership with SOE, and was looking for recruits to drop into France to make contact with the Resistance and prepare for the Allied landings. If SOE was a club, full of oddballs and eccentrics, so OSS had also attracted a remarkable mixture of men and women who somehow did not fit naturally into the fighting forces: Wall Street bankers, academics, missionaries, professors, jockeys, philanthropists, big-game hunters and steely and ambitious young women. 'All those first OSS arrivals in London,' wrote Malcolm Muggeridge, who was working for MI6. 'How well I remember them, arriving like *jeunes filles en fleur* . . . all fresh and innocent, to start work in our frosty old intelligence brothel.'

Through a friend, William Grell, former manager of the St Regis Hotel in New York, Virginia was introduced to OSS; they offered her the rank of second lieutenant, and sent her for further training in radio transmission and to observe parachute operations at Milton Hall, near Peterborough. Occasionally, she carried her aluminium puppy in a bag. New recruits were urged not to indulge in prejudice or fads when it came to the food in France, and to eat whatever came to hand, even, if need be, mice, rats, dogs and cats. The best way to deal with a hedgehog, they were told, was to turn it on to its back, tickle its tummy, and when it poked its head out, chop it off.

Unable to parachute into France on account of her leg, Virginia was landed off the coast of Brittany in a torpedo boat. She was accompanied by a second OSS operative, a man going by the name of Artemis, and they travelled up to Paris together by train from Brest. She had reluctantly agreed to age herself, dyeing her hair a shade of dirty grey-black and pulling it back in a wooden clasp. She wore a long skirt to conceal her wooden leg. Posing as Mlle Marcelle Montagne, a Parisian social worker with Vichy's welfare organisation, she went to lodge with an old friend in the Rue de Babylone, Mme Long, taking Artemis with her. Both women soon took against him, Mme Long saying that he was too indiscreet, and Virginia that he was arrogant and physically feeble, always complaining about his health and refusing to carry anything heavy.

Leaving Artemis in Paris, Virginia went off to the Creuse, where she lodged in great discomfort with a farmer and his elderly mother, for whom she cooked meals over an open wood fire and took the cows to pasture, checking out possible parachute sites along the way. She had become, she said, a 'milkmaid'. But she had been instructed to keep moving, and was soon in Nièvre, where she lived in a garret in another farmer's house, tending goats along roads conveniently used for German troop movements. She wore a faded kerchief, a full skirt with a peplum, an ample woollen blouse, and a baggy sweater, and she carried a staff. Delivering goat's milk and messages to her colleagues in the Resistance nearby, she used her attic as a transmission post. When parachute drops were announced, she arrived at the site with a donkey and cart. In one drop came a pair of medical stockings with which to cushion Cuthbert.

And then, in the late spring of 1944, Virginia was posted to the Haute-Loire. SOE had received information about the local groups of *maquisards* from a dealer in lentils, Jean Joulians, whom Virginia had happened to meet before the war in Boston. She was to pose as a Belgian journalist doing research on children, and had an introduction to August Bohny of Secours Suisse. She made her way to le Chambon.

The first that Pierre Fayol and his *maquisards* knew of Virginia's arrival was when he got a message from Bohny to say that there was a strange American woman asking for contacts in the Maquis. He had little opportunity to be wary. When they met, she wasted no time on pleasantries. How many men did he have? What were their weapons? Which were the best places for parachute drops? Desperate for weapons, money and supplies, Fayol fell into line, though he did take the precaution of contacting Algiers, to be told that Virginia was a 'lieutenant colonel' with considerable authority. Later he observed that his first impression of her had been her 'atrocious accent'.

The thinking behind OSS–SOE was that their agents in France would act as counsellors and instructors. Virginia saw herself more as a leader. Next day, despite the awkwardness of her leg, she set off on a bicycle to identify good open fields for drops, covering miles on her own, criss-crossing the high pastures. Unsure at first of Fayol's trustworthiness, she set him a little test, handing over a sum of money and seeing how wisely he spent it. He passed, and she cabled London that le Chambon was 'good'. She had discovered two areas for the drops, one at Villelonge, the other near Tence. In Villelonge, it was the job of the baker, Alphonse Valla, to recharge the batteries for the lamps needed to light the field for the pilots. When they were ready, he hid a message under a tree on the road to le Chambon. Virginia concocted codes of her own. Villelonge was 'bream'. Yssingeaux became a shark and the phrase for transmission '*le requin a le nez tendre*' (the shark has a tender nose).

One day, Miss Maber was visited by two young boys asking whether they might borrow her car, long since sitting idle in the garage for lack of petrol, for 'Diane', also known locally as La Madonne, to carry out a more distant reconnaissance. When it was returned to her a few days later, it came with a packet of English tea and a note of thanks.

Twenty young men – there were no armed women among the *maquisards* on the plateau – were recruited to assist at the drops, announced over the BBC in coded sentences. One of these was Jean Nallet, the orphaned boy who had been taken in by Bohny, and who was doing his baccalaureat under Darcissac while serving with the Maquis. Nallet would always remember Virginia as 'seductive' in her American military jacket and trousers. He told her that he planned to become a doctor, and she enrolled him as her medical assistant, gave him the medical supplies to look after and called him her *'infirmier'* – nurse. The parachute drops started. *'La soupe est chaude'* – the soup is hot – brought 300 kilograms of guns, ammunition, clothes, chocolate, vitamins, radio receivers, money and cigarettes; *'Qui veut noyer son chien l'accuse de la rage'* – he who wants to drown his dog accuses him of rabies – a further 10 enormous containers of provisions. What the teacher Olivier Hatzfeld later remembered was that after a drop, when everything had gone off all right, when the canisters had been retrieved and brought back, and their contents examined, the young Frenchmen felt a sense of recognition, of status, of being brothers in arms with strangers many miles away; they were no longer terrorists, or dodgers of STO service, but part of a liberating army, and recognised as such.

In the canisters there was invariably a packet of English tea with Virginia's name on it, sent by Vera Atkins, assistant to Buckmaster and in charge of the recruitment and deployment of female agents. Jacqueline Decourdemanche and Mme Fayol helped gather up the parachutes, which were much prized by the women in le Chambon, who made them into blouses, and the mottled khaki silk was soon on display all over the village. One drop, code name 'the big Indian smokes his pipe', brought a Scottish captain in a kilt, who, having extricated himself from his parachute and climbed down from the fir tree in which he had landed, solemnly shook everyone's hand, then got out a flask of whisky and passed it around before disappearing off into the night. Another brought German soldiers, who had intercepted the message; they were rapidly killed and their bodies buried in the banks of the Lignon.

Once she thought the structure was securely in place, Virginia decided to move on again, this time in the direction of Burgundy. Fayol and his men, increasingly impatient for more Allied support, afraid that without better weapons they would be overrun by the Germans stationed at Le Puy, sent Jacqueline and the bookseller Eric Barbezat to look for her. They tracked her down and she agreed to return to the plateau with them. When their train was briefly halted by an Allied bombing raid, she told the others to remain calm; the pilots knew that she was on board and would not bomb the train itself. They did the final leg of the journey up the mountain in an ambulance. Virginia went to live with the Fayols, spending her days sitting at the kitchen table working out codes. The Germans had spotter planes and she was forced to keep changing her transmission site. She moved to Camus' former home, Le Panelier, then to a barn near Villelonge close to Valla's boulangerie, which had become the headquarters of the local Maquis. She acquired a helper, a 22-year-old Alsatian teacher called Dédé Zusbach. Virginia bought bicycles for her team, and thought of herself as an elder sister to them. Jean Nallet powered her transmitter by pedalling on a stationary bicycle.

Some of the young Frenchmen found Virginia secretive and distant. As the weeks passed, waiting for messages that did not come and for drops that failed to be made, her temper frayed; she became hard and intransigent, quick to swear at anyone who made mistakes. To keep herself going, she had a small supply of Benzedrine and amphetamines. Later, people would say that they could not help resenting her assumption that she was somehow in charge; they had not much cared for taking orders from a woman, and there was anger when only light weapons were dropped instead of the mortars and bazookas they had requested. Later, too, no one would be able to agree on her accent, how foreign she sounded, how fluent her command of French. For her part, Virginia would say that the young *maquisards*, though very willing, were undisciplined and badly trained, and far too greedy and competitive. In theory, most of the various forces of the Resistance were now united under the banner of the MUR, but fierce jealousies persisted.

All now, *maquisards* and hidden Jews alike, were waiting for a liberation that never seemed to come.

CHAPTER SIXTEEN

Today, I have nothing to say

When Pastor Trocmé came home in the early summer of 1944, le Chambon was not the village he remembered. He had been away ten months. For a man so devoted to his children, so mindful of his responsibilities, his exile had been long and hard. He reached the village towards evening, to find a reception committee of his family and parishioners, and on Sunday he preached to a packed temple. Magda, he thought, looked thin and tired, but Nelly, Jean-Pierre, Jacques and Daniel were lively and affectionate. His parishioners found him quieter, less assertive.

When he had left, le Chambon had been a place of hiding, of silence and waiting and never saying more than was absolutely necessary. Now, the young *maquisards* strolled boldly around the village carrying an assortment of weapons, dressed in bits and pieces of more or less military uniform. Trocmé had no choice but to accept that many of his friends and colleagues, who previously had tacitly accepted his pacifism, had become openly in favour of armed struggle.

He had, he said, no difficulty in accepting Léon Eyraud's belli-cose talk, saying later that Eyraud had in any case long since abandoned his Christian faith; nor did he worry about the over-excited demeanour of the local boys, including his own sons, wielding their new weapons, swaggering proudly down the main street. What he minded was a visit by a group of the student theologians, the *futhéos*, who told him that they were starting a Christian Maquis and wanted to borrow a plate and chalice from the temple, so that they could celebrate Communion every day in the mountains. Trocmé refused. How, he asked them, could they reconcile the taking of Communion with a desire to kill

Germans? We are convinced, the young men replied, that 'God is ordering us to do this'. Later, Trocmé described, not without a certain smugness, that this same group of *futhéos* had stolen a bicycle belonging to the curé of Tence, telling him that they needed it for the 'defence of the nation', and that he had been able to calm the enraged curé before summoning the boys and ordering them to return the bicycle. They obeyed. Even now, his authority could prevail.

Aware that his pacifism – to which he remained fervently committed – was unlikely to win him followers any longer, Trocmé appeared to be relishing a new role as peacemaker. When the volatile Dr Le Forestier refused to hand over the keys to his ambulance to a group of *maquisards*, who wanted it to 'go to the front', on the sensible grounds that as a Red Cross vehicle it fell under the Geneva Conventions, and one of Virginia Hall's agents threatened to shoot him as a traitor, Trocmé was on hand to intervene. If the doctor promised not to stir, would they allow Trocmé to shut him up in the presbytery? The *maquisards* agreed; Dr Le Forestier promised. Later, Trocmé was furious when he discovered that the doctor had not kept his word, but had slipped out of the presbytery and gone home, where Trocmé discovered him surrounded by his wife and two boys, saying that he was through with the Maquis, if that was how they chose to treat him.

The hidden Jews, against all the odds, remained undisturbed. In the ten months Trocmé had been absent, not one had been arrested; there had been no raids on any of the children's homes and no visits by the Gestapo. The German convalescents in le Chambon seemed anxious and unsure; many of them now were boys of no more than 16 or 17, and the girls from Roanne, coming into the village from time to time from their distant farmhouses, laughed at their gauche manners and childish looks. 'We strutted before them,' one of them would say. 'They were like frightened children.' Though some of the Jewish families, grimly fearing the worst, had buried themselves even deeper into their hiding places, the months of inviolability had given them a little confidence. They felt spared. It was now, they told each other, simply a question of holding on. With every reported Allied advance, their spirits rose.

*   *   *

What made their apparent safety all the more extraordinary was that throughout the rest of France, the arrests and deportation of the Jews had not let up. In November 1943, a reshuffle in the Commissariat Général aux Questions Juives had carried off Darquier de Pellepoix and brought in a career colonial officer, Charles du Paty de Clam; when he proved too passive, his place was taken by another staunch anti-Semite, Joseph Antignac, who would later say that he only took the job to 'prevent the worst' for the Jews. How these men chose to persecute the Jews, however, was no longer of much concern. The Germans had decided to take overall control, and a concerted drive, meticulous and efficient, had been launched to find and deport France's remaining Jews in a race against the clock and the arrival of the Allies, now recognised to lie not far ahead. In recent months, they had become skilled at distinguishing forged documents from real ones. Helped by the Milice, the Gestapo redoubled their efforts at identifying schools, convents and families in which children were held, raiding prisons, labour camps and farms for adults. Ever more generous rewards were offered to informers. Letters of denunciation poured in.

On 6 April, Barbie dispatched a party of Gestapo officers to one of the very few OSE homes that remained open, at Izieu, a little village not far from Lyons. The 45 children and their teachers were having breakfast. Most of the children were already orphans, their foreign Jewish parents having been arrested and deported; some had spent months in Gurs and Rivesaltes. It should have been safe: the farmhouse was remote, on a hill, with a long view of the road and any approaching vehicles, and it had been protected by sympathetic Vichy officials. A warning system should have been in place; but it was a beautiful, peaceful morning and it had not been activated.

One child, who was not Jewish, was released. Everyone else was taken to Montluc. The next day they were sent to Drancy, and a week later, 34 of them were put on a train to Auschwitz; the rest soon followed. Only the director, who happened to be away on the day, arranging for a more secure hiding place for the children, remained free; one teacher survived deportation. Several of the children in Izieu had been placed there by Madeleine Dreyfus.

Never had the rescue organisations themselves been in greater danger. Two days after the raid on Izieu, the last remaining OSE office, in Chambéry, was visited by the Gestapo. Seven members of staff, and three others working for the Comité d'Aide aux Réfugiés, were caught. They were forced to walk up and down the street, enabling the Gestapo to pick up anyone who spoke to them; then they were interrogated by Brunner, veteran of the Drancy and the Nice round-ups. From Grenoble prison, the director of the OSE, Alain Mosse, who was a Catholic, managed to smuggle out coded messages to close down every last home and take all the remaining children into hiding.

Two of those arrested were Julien Samuel, the former OSE director in Marseilles, and Nicole Weil's husband, Jacques Salon. Julien managed to get a telegram to his wife: 'Claude gravely ill, take every precaution to avoid contagion'; she had time to disappear into hiding with their new baby. Both men were taken to Montluc and tortured. They were then put on a train for Drancy. However they had with them a file, smuggled to them by a friend, and were able to break through the bars, and when the train slowed down, they escaped. They survived the rest of the war unscathed.

Word reached Garel in Limoges of the raid on Izieu, together with reliable information that the Germans knew every detail of the OSE's hidden children. Within 48 hours there was not a child left anywhere: all had been moved into deeper hiding. Marianne Cohn and Loinger, meanwhile, were ferrying party after party to the Swiss border. There was a feeling, now, that no one would survive unless the Allies arrived soon.

Remarkably, Garel was still free, moving around the country on trains with his bicycle, checking up on the new arrangements, still posing as a salesman in pottery. Andrée Salomon, the OSE woman who had done so much for the children in Gurs and Rivesaltes, decided to get a group out to Palestine via Spain. Selected and prepared by the Armée Juive, 12 children aged between 8 and 14, and 5 adults, started out from Perpignan on a day of thick fog. They made it safely to Andorra, and though it took many months to sort out their papers, they eventually embarked from Cadiz on the *Guinée*.

Joseph Bass was caught while having lunch in a restaurant in Marseilles. In his buccaneering way, he managed to overpower his guard, get hold of the keys to the handcuffs, and free himself; he reached safety in Le Puy.

Loinger too was still free. One day he was summoned by his friend Deffaugt, the mayor of Annemasse, who continued to shelter the Jews while remaining on good terms with the Gestapo, from whom he learnt many interesting things. Loinger, Deffaugt told him, though not yet identified by name, was on Gestapo lists. It was time for him to hide.

He went home, alerted his wife and two children, the younger a six-month-old baby, retrieved the pieces of gold he had prudently hidden for just such an eventuality, and they set out for the frontier. There they joined a party of people waiting to cross. Loinger would later describe how frightened his wife had been, and how he had kept urging her to keep going. As they reached the crossing point, dogs were heard. The *passeur* panicked and fled. The assembled people began to run, but were quickly rounded up by a German patrol. One officer put a gun to the head of Loinger's baby, whom he was holding in his arms, and told him not to move; he set his dog to guard him. The dog ran off. Loinger seized the suitcases and, clutching the baby and dragging his wife and older son, ran towards a nearby house, just inside the French side of the border. Its owner and his wife tried to stop them entering, saying that the house would be burnt down by the Germans. Brandishing a knife and proffering his gold coins, Loinger forced his way in.

Next morning, at dawn, they walked to the wire and Loinger called out to the Swiss guards on the other side. He explained that he needed to get his wife and children across, but that he would be going back. Pushing up the barbed wire, he infiltrated his family through. As a father of two small children, he would probably have been accepted by the Swiss, but he had more work to do. Hastening back down the hill to avoid the next patrol, he returned to Deffaugt in Annemasse, where he learnt that the Gestapo had put out the word for his immediate capture. He left, but it was only to collect more children who needed to cross. 'I was famous,' he said later, 'for being the lucky one.' Between the autumn of 1943 and the summer of 1944, he and his colleagues got 1,069 children to safety in Switzerland.

Marianne Cohn, who had helped Simon Liwerant to safety, was not so lucky. A German patrol with dogs caught her just 200 metres from the border as she was about to cross with 28 children. They searched the children and found their real names and addresses hidden inside the lining of their clothes. Marianne was taken, with 11 of the older boys and girls, to the prison in Annemasse. Deffaugt managed to persuade the Gestapo to release the younger ones into supervised residence in the town. Loinger got word to Marianne that plans were being made to rescue her, but she refused, fearing repercussions against the children. She was tortured. A month later, the Gestapo took her and five other members of the Resistance to an isolated spot not far away and beat them to death with spades. Deffaugt, learning that all of the 28 children were about to be sent to Lyons, into the hands of Barbie, convinced a Gestapo officer, through a mixture of threat of reprisals and promises of post-war protection, to turn them over to him. They all survived. Had Marianne escaped, it was unlikely that they would have lived.

At some point during her days in prison, Marianne wrote what would become one of the defining poems of the Vichy years. She left it with the children.

> I shall betray tomorrow, not today.
> Today, pull out my fingernails,
> I shall not betray.
> You do not know the limits of my courage,
> I, I do . . .
> I shall betray tomorrow, not today.
> Tomorrow.
> I need the night to make up my mind.
> I need at least one night.
> To disown, to abjure, to betray.
> To disown my friends,
> To abjure bread and wine,
> To betray life,

To die.
I shall betray tomorrow, not today.
The file is under the windowpane.
The file is not for the window bars,
The file is not for the executioner,
The file is for my own wrists.
Today, I have nothing to say,
I shall betray tomorrow.

On Tuesday 6 June, 160,000 British, American, Canadian and Free French soldiers were landed by sea and air along an 80-kilometre stretch of the Normandy coast. The battle for the liberation of Europe had begun. With the help of SOE, the French Resistance began to attack railway lines, ambush roads, and destroy telephone exchanges and electrical plants. Four days later, in the space of just a few hours, Yssingeaux was liberated. The plateau was, in theory at least, free; but what followed, as the Maquis took over the area and the Milice fought back, was anarchy. Catholics, Protestants and Darbyists alike awaited the arrival of the Allied forces with a mixture of longing for the Americans and fear of the Russians and what communism might bring.

Just what the Germans would be capable of as they retreated, fighting their way north and east, was brought home when, on 9 June, the SS Das Reich division of the Waffen SS, helped by the Milice and in reprisal for the killing of some 40 of their men, entered the town of Tulle in the Corrèze, rounded up 600 men and boys, some no older than 16, and hanged 99 of them from lamp posts, trees and balconies, so that their swinging bodies lined the streets, while the SS officers watched, drinking, laughing and taking pictures. On the 10th, they drove the women and children of Oradour-sur-Glane into the village church and set fire to it, then herded the men into barns, shooting them in the legs so that they could not run away, and setting fire to them as well, so that by the end of the day, 642 people were dead.

On the plateau, Virginia Hall radioed Buckmaster for more supplies, planned a mission to cut the railway line between Lyons and Saint-Etienne, and welcomed Allied agents, dropped in threes as part of the combined SOE–OSS commandos, known as Jedburgh, to whom she gave schnapps stolen from the Germans.

News had finally come of Daniel Trocmé, whose last message before Christmas had spoken of a transfer to another camp. His brother François had lost both his hands trying to save his factory in a fire the Maquis had started in the hope that it would prevent supplies from reaching the Germans. The German officers who came to see him in hospital to thank him for his efforts asked him if there was anything they could do for him. 'Find my brother Daniel,' François told them. They said that they would do what they could. Towards the end of May came the information that Daniel had died in the camp at Maidanek in Poland. He was 31.

Later, from survivors, it became known that he had been ill all through the spring with heart trouble, and that he had spent some time in Dora in the concentration camp, in a work battalion, but that, growing thinner and weaker all the time, he had been put on a transport for Maidanek with 500 other sick and dying men. Given the length of the journey, some 900 kilometres, and his state of health, it was highly improbable that he had survived the journey. His friends reported the intensity of his pleasure when a parcel had arrived for a fellow prisoner from the plateau and the way that it had been shared out while Daniel described the bands of people protecting the hidden Jews. The tragedies to hit his immediate family did not end with his death. His mother Eve was badly injured by shrapnel when the Americans shelled L'Ecole des Roches, and died soon after; his father was killed in an accident with an American jeep.

And then tragedy came to the plateau itself, in the shape of three unrelated, senseless events. It was, wrote Trocmé later, as if the divine intervention that had shielded them was suddenly lifted, and he understood for the first time how it was that the Romans consulted auguries in search of clues to the future.

The first malevolent act of the gods concerned Manou Barraud, Gabrielle's 17-year-old sister, a cheerful girl who had often been heard to shout 'Nasty! Nasty!' whenever she encountered a young woman in le Chambon whom she considered too friendly to the convalescent German soldiers. At Beau Soleil, Mme Barraud had continued to take in students from the Ecole Nouvelle Cévenol, along with Jewish boys and girls sent to her by Madeleine Barot and Cimade. It was an affectionate, noisy household. Until the Normandy landings, Gabrielle helped Oscar Rosowsky with the forged documents; M Barraud was away in the mountains with the Resistance.

Manou had a boyfriend, a youth not much older than herself, who had got hold of a gun and joined the Maquis. On the afternoon of 5 July, he visited Manou to show off his gun, reassuring her that he had put the safety catch on. Suddenly it went off. A bullet hit Manou in the stomach; she died in Gabrielle's arms. Le Forestier was called, but there was nothing he could do. 'The best,' he said sadly, 'are the ones who die.' Laughing, fearless Manou was buried in the cemetery. All the village attended. Mme Barraud insisted on keeping her daughter's boyfriend by her side for several days, fearing that his guilt and grief might lead him to take his own life. 'It's not your fault,' she said to him. 'It's the world that is mad.'

Running for the hills

The next day, after a shoot-out between the Maquis and German troops not far away at Le Cheylard in which the Wehrmacht killed some 50 people, there were fears that the Germans might reach le Chambon. Emile Sèches sent his Jewish children from

Tante Soly out to the forests. He had built them a hide in the woods, a pit dug out of the earth made of tree trunks covered in moss and leaves, and there they huddled until his piercing whistle – one long, three short, morse for T and S – told them that all was safe. Miss Maber led her own boys out of the village and on to the high plateau.

For all his irritation with the *maquisards* on the plateau, Dr Le Forestier remained very close to the resisters, prompt to treat their injuries, alert to the dangers they found themselves in. Brès, the scout leader, was godfather to the doctor's three-year-old son, Bernard; Le Forestier's brother-in-law ran a Resistance group in the south of France. Le Forestier's nature had always been somewhat slapdash, quick to act, impatient of obfuscation. Whether he had or had not imprudently kept copies of the medical notes on the young men he treated along with the rest of his patient files, and whether they were actually removed in secret one night by Maquis leaders, has long since been lost in the mists of history. But he was certainly on their side, and he was much loved throughout the plateau. He had had to flee le Chambon for a while after the police in Tence told him the Milice were looking for him. He had also taken in and hidden Jews and people escaping the Gestapo, and had insisted on keeping open the door to his house at night in case anyone arrived in need of safety. How far he was a model for Camus' hero Dr Rieux in *La Peste* is also not clear; certainly the two men were remarkably alike: humane, optimistic, tolerant, free-thinking, ever alive to injustice and acts of inhumanity.

At one o'clock on the afternoon of 4 August, the doctor told his wife Danielle that he had to go to Le Puy to intercede for two *maquisards* held by the Germans. She tried to persuade him not to go – and Trocmé would later say that he too had told Le Forestier that it was an act of folly – but he was adamant. The boys were risking death; something had to be done. His assistant and midwife, Lucie Chazot, covered the roof of his car with an enormous Red Cross flag and he set out, taking with him Denise Debaud, daughter of the grocer in Villelonges, who was the fiancée of one of the imprisoned men. Along the way, they took on board Bob, of the Armée Secrète, and another *maquisard*, and also a petrified boy called Jean Rambaud, suspected of being an informer. Le Forestier was told to stop near a disused quarry, where two other *maquisards* were waiting. Jean was led away; shots were heard; the doctor was asked to certify that the boy was dead.

The group resumed its journey to Le Puy, getting there around 3 p.m. Bob went into a bookshop, Denise set off for the prison with some food, and Le Forestier entered a café to talk to two men who, he hoped, might be able to save the prisoners' lives. He left the second *maquisard*, Leroi, to guard the car, but the young man wandered off to talk to two friends. At this point, a group of Feldgendarmerie arrived and rounded up the three young men. When Le Forestier and his contacts, hearing shouts, came out of the café, they arrested them too. Bob and Denise escaped and returned on foot to le Chambon to spread the news.

Meanwhile, the Germans searched the car and found two revolvers left by the *maquisards* despite Le Forestier's repeated reminders about the rules of neutrality governing Red Cross vehicles. Le Forestier spent that night in the prison in Le Puy and was taken next day to the *Kommandantur*. A court martial was convened, under Major Schmähling, who was still in Le Puy, though his command of the Haute-Loire had passed to a harder man, Oberst Metger; Le Forestier was condemned to death. Danielle hastened to Le Puy, accompanied by Trocmé and Auguste Bohny of Secours Suisse. Bohny would later say that Schmähling had been frank and polite and that he had not received the impression that he was 'speaking to a blank wall'. Danielle, who was appalled at the sight of the bruises on Le Forestier's face and the swellings on his 'beautiful hands', was told that the death sentence had been commuted: Le Forestier was to go instead to serve as a doctor in Germany.

Through the air vents in his cell, he was able to talk to a neighbouring prisoner to whom he described his family; for much of the time he hummed, recited prayers and sang snatches of psalms, but there were moments of silence, after torture.

When Danielle returned to see him on the 9th, she was told – in error – that he had already left. But he had written her a letter. It had a curious, somewhat stilted tone, as if there were things that he was not saying. He had spent, he wrote, 'hours, nights and days prey to physical and mental torture, but my soul is calm because, at the peak of my ordeal, my Christian faith has never deserted me'. He told her that he had deliberately asked to be sent to serve as a doctor wherever he was needed, since medicine was something that transcended nations. 'Kiss the children for me every morning,' he concluded. 'Keep your hair in plaits in memory of me, because I like it that way.' At the bottom of the letter was a small list, under the heading of 'suitcase'; it included a pullover, a travelling blanket, under-clothes, soap, a selection of books from the Pléiade collection, a bible and a *'belle photo'*. But it was too late to get them to him.

On 10 August, Le Forestier was put on to a lorry bound for Montluc. It is not clear what he was thinking when he took off his wristwatch, gave it to Leroi, the *maquisard* who made this journey with him, and asked him to see that it reached Danielle. On the 11th – taking the watch with him – Leroi was put on the last train to leave Lyons for Germany, where he was forced to work in an armaments factory.

On Sunday 20 August, Barbie ordered 25 German soldiers and 10 *miliciens* to conduct 120 prisoners to the Fort Côte Lorette at Saint-Genis-Laval, where there was an abandoned house, once lived in by the guards. Among them was Dr Le Forestier. Twelve of them were women; several were priests; most belonged to one of the many Maquis groups in the area. They were taken, hand-cuffed in pairs, up the stairs to the first floor, lined up and shot; when the first floor was full of bodies, the rest of the prisoners were shot on the ground floor. Phosphorus was scattered and drenched in petrol; the building was set on fire. Three prisoners managed to climb out of a window; two of them were caught and thrown on to the flames. Explosions continued to be heard until dawn, when the inhabitants of Saint-Genis-Laval crept out to see what had happened. Only a third of the charred remains were in any way identifiable.

Four days after Le Forestier's murder, Montluc was liberated.

Danielle knew nothing of all this. It was only six weeks later, having looked everywhere for traces of her missing husband, that she caught sight, among the fragments of clothing retrieved from the incinerated house and put into 24 bags, of the distinctive buckle of Le Forestier's belt. She was a widow, at 23. Her sons were five and three.

Most senseless of all, perhaps, was the third and last tragic incident.

Trocmé loved all his children. He loved practical, reliable 17-year-old Nelly, not knowing that she disobeyed his orders and went dancing with her friends, dancing being forbidden to the Protestant students at the Ecole Nouvelle Cévenol as 'immoral and licentious and likely to give rise to unwanted children'. He called her 'Trocmette' when he was in a good mood, and 'Tante Pauline' when she got on her high horse. He loved thin, gangly Jaques, with his bursts of idealism and his constantly changing moods, and little Daniel, wild and canny and always getting into mischief. But the one he loved best was Jean-Pierre. He thought this son was just like him, his 'alter ego', a boy who could not stop thinking and worrying, who visited the villagers when they were ill, who played the piano with the sensibility of someone far older, and who had once said to his father: 'There is something in me which prevents me from being happy.' Jean-Pierre had many friends among the Jewish refugees; his companion after school was often Pierre Bloch, the boy from Lyons, who lived with Mme Roussel just up the road from the presbytery.

On 13 August, returning with Magda from trying to settle a dispute between a warring couple, Trocmé heard Jaques call out: 'Papa! Papa! Come quickly. Jean-Pierre is dead!' They found Jean-Pierre in the presbytery, hanging from a rope tied to the cistern in the bathroom. Dr Riou arrived and pronounced that the boy was indeed dead. Their first horrified thought was that he had killed himself. But then they remembered that a few nights earlier, a celebrated actor called Jean Deschamps had given a recital of fables and poems in the temple, among them Villon's famous 'Ballade des Pendus', and how realistic he had been as he spoke the lines about the hanging bodies swinging and dangling in the wind, swinging and dangling himself in front of the mesmerised audience. Jean-Pierre, his friends told the Trocmés, had been much struck by the poem, and they had heard him recite it to himself several times on the banks of the Lignon. The fact that he had carefully wound his pants around his neck before fastening the noose showed, said Dr Riou, that it had simply been a terrible and stupid accident and that he had never intended to die. Miss Maber, who had seen him that day, testified to how happy and carefree he had seemed.

Jean-Pierre's coffin was carried by his classmates, the older boys wearing their odd assortment of *maquisard* uniforms. He was buried next to Manou Barraud, and both graves were covered with wild flowers from the fields, tied in bunches with brightly coloured ribbons by the village children. From the back of the cemetery, Pierre Bloch looked on, too shocked to cry; the two boys had spent the afternoon of Jean-Pierre's death together. Pierre would later be haunted by the thought that the fault was somehow his, that they had been too close, too emotionally bound up with one another, and that Jean-Pierre, fearing his father's displeasure, had indeed killed himself.

Magda wept, saying over and over again, 'I should have been with him.' But then she stopped and struggled on, throwing herself back into looking after some of the many people still in hiding who needed her. For Trocmé, acceptance was impossible. Looking at his son's body, he remembered that of his mother, after the car crash that had killed her when he was 10. 'An emptiness. A nothing,' he wrote later, 'against which one can do nothing.' He told himself that God would speak to him, but when he walked through the forests, God remained silent. He felt himself to be like one of the tall pines, whose top had been sawn off and which would never grow another. When he preached next in the temple, he took as his text the resurrection of Christ. He and Magda decided that for the sake of the other children, they would get on with their lives, learn to live without Jean-Pierre, as normally as possible. And they took the decision to pay no heed to the 'odious and pathetic rumours' circulating around the village, that Jean-Pierre had been a '*mauvais garçon*', a bad boy.

Walking up the hill from the cemetery on 15 August, Darcissac fell into step with Trocmé. 'I know this is a terrible day for you,' he said, 'but I have to tell you that the BBC has just announced the debarkation of the Allies in the south.'

When at last it came, the end came quickly. On 19 August, the German garrison at Le Puy was ordered to move northwards, falling back on Saint-Etienne. Some 6,000 *miliciens* and their families went with them; those who volunteered to continue the fight were sent to the Pomeranian front, from where not many returned. Pursued by the various Maquis bands of the Haute-Loire, among them Joseph Bass's group of young Jewish fighters, they were cornered near Saint-Geneys; 17 Germans and seven *résistants* died. Bass, now known as '*le Capitaine André*', shouted through a loud hailer to the Tartars, Georgians, Croats and Armenians to lay down their weapons and switch sides. Vastly outnumbered, Schmähling gave the order for his 120 men to surrender.

Before pulling out, the Germans had soaked the buildings they occupied in Le Puy in petrol, but they had not set fire to them. They had left behind 300 of their auxiliaries with TB. Maurice Nizard arrived to help run the hospital. Oscar Rosowsky's mother came from Fay to act as interpreter. Though protected for a while by the Maquis, the Russians were eventually handed back to the Red Army; what happened to them then, how the Red Army chose to deal with these turncoats, no one cared to think about. Rosowsky arrived in Le Puy with Samy Charles, requisitioned a local printing firm, and began putting out a newspaper. On 25 August, Lucienne Ruel, Lulu's daughter from Mazet, was one of dozens of young people from the plateau to join the liberation parade down the main street. They had decorated a cart and filled it with bunches of poppies, marguerites and cornflowers.

The captured Germans were taken to a manor house at the Pont de Mars, on the edge of the commune of le Chambon, to be guarded by the very policemen who just a few days earlier had been doing their bidding. Feelings against them ran high, and there was talk of revenge. Since they were being held in Trocmé's parish, it fell to him to be their chaplain. As scrupulous in this as in all else, heedless of how unpopular it would make him, Trocmé went to visit the prison. He found the German officers arrogant and unrepentant, still convinced that Hitler would win the war, and when they attended the service he held for them on Sunday, they turned out in their formal uniforms, clicking their heels and marching in line, as if they were in their own barracks. Trocmé took the opportunity to see Schmähling to find out more about Le Forestier. The major told him that he was already in Germany. Whether he knew this to be a lie is not known.

Though he spoke good German, Trocmé had written out his sermon in French and asked Mlle Hoefert, the Austrian refugee who taught German at the Ecole Nouvelle Cévenol, to translate it for him. He had decided to preach on the subject of the Ten Commandments, the forgiveness of God, and non-violence. He announced that he absolutely condemned the war that was just ending. He mentioned Oradour and the gas chambers. That morning, he had preached the same sermon to his congregation in the temple at le Chambon, displeasing the *maquisards* who attended by insisting that they leave their weapons outside the door. Neither the German prisoners nor his French parishioners liked what Trocmé had to say. The Germans rejected the stories of the killings as lies and propaganda, and said that the French would be sorry when there was no one to protect them from the Bolsheviks and the red plague; the French protested that the barbarity of the Germans could never be countered by non-violence. Nor did his parishioners like it when, hearing that the prisoners were complaining of hunger, Trocmé took them some of the grapes reaching the plateau from the harvest in the south. There were mutters that the pastor was nothing but a '*Boche*' himself.

There was a curious moment when 50 Jewish survivors of a 'ghost train', one of the last deportation transports sent to Drancy as the Allies landed in the south and the Germans retreated, suddenly arrived in le Chambon. The train driver had surreptitiously rerouted it into Resistance-held country, where it had been liberated by the Maquis. The survivors, ghost-like themselves from their ordeal, were taken in and looked after.

Committees of liberation were established in the various villages and tribunals appointed to begin a process of '*épuration*', the cleansing of those deemed to have been collaborators. Given the numbers of policemen accused of helping the Germans throughout

France, what was remarkable was that not one local policeman was among them. Three young women from le Chambon and its immediate surroundings had their heads shaved, but how guilty they had really been of fraternising with the German convalescent soldiers no one was quite sure. In and around le Chambon, Mazet and Fay, there were no summary executions, but over the border in the Ardèche, there were terrible acts of revenge.

In the war trials that followed, Colonel Metger, who had commanded the Légion Tartar, was condemned to death; Schmähling was acquitted. Several local people came forward to testify to the unwillingness with which he had obeyed orders, and the protection he had provided to a number of Jews. He had thrown, so it was said, many letters of denunciation into the waste-paper basket. The prefect, Bach, was also brought to trial; he too was acquitted. Magda Trocmé and Miss Williamson were among those who gave evidence on his behalf, saying that he had been a '*bon Français*', '*un laissez-faire actif*', that he had played a part in getting Trocmé, Theis and Darcissac released, and that he had warned the plateau of impending raids. When the verdict was handed down, there were cheers. But Bach's prefectorial title was annulled; his career was over.

Once Lyons had been liberated, on 2 September, and three battalions of men had been trained and armed, Virginia Hall requested to be allowed to go to Alsace to continue the fight. She took with her 18 young men who called themselves '*le corps franc Diane*'. Before they disbanded and joined the regular forces of the French army, they had a final gathering in an abandoned chateau. A great deal was drunk, many speeches were made and Virginia sang old naval ditties. A photograph shows her in military uniform, surrounded by a group of boys, many of them teenagers. One of them is a small, stocky French-American second lieutenant, parachuted in by OSS to join her. His name was Paul Goillot. Another is Jean Nallet, who would always remember their journey through France, ordered to flush out pockets of German resisters and lucky enough not to encounter any. Virginia left them, he said, as abruptly and casually as she had arrived, with a handshake and a packet of cigarettes. And then she was gone; he never saw her again.

Virginia Hall and her *corps franc Diane*

On their way north, Virginia and Goillot liberated a chateau and paused to enjoy its magnificent wine cellar. Before she left Paris, Virginia helped hunt down the false Abbé Alesch, who had sent so many agents to their deaths. He was eventually caught, tried and shot.

Pierre Fayol, the engineer who had taken charge of much of the resistance on the plateau, struck north too to join de Gaulle's army. Summoning the *maquisards* who had served under him, he asked those who felt that they had other commitments and preferred not to accompany him to take three steps back. Olivier Hatzfeld, the teacher known as Penguin, who had successfully ambushed a German convoy on the road to Le Puy with no loss of life, was one of those who decided that he had done enough. It was, he would later say, the hardest decision of his life.

On 1 September, General de Lattre de Tassigny, at the head of a convoy of tanks and armoured cars, drove up the main street of le Chambon. From every balcony hung tricolour flags. Shopkeepers came out with bottles of wine and baskets of peaches. The French troops included Africans from the French colonies; many of the Chambonnais children had never seen black people before. M Dreyfus, Madeleine's husband, anxiously awaiting news of his wife, was among the crowds watching the soldiers throw chocolates and chewing gum to the villagers, who both laughed and wept. At first they had taken the soldiers for Americans, and they were pleased when they realised that it was the French, their own people, who had come to liberate them.

Watching them file past, Trocmé wondered whether 'the hardest and most useful years of my life' were not now over. 'As a Christian,' he wrote later, 'I knew that political deliverance is not the Kingdom of Heaven.' But he was not downhearted. Though not entirely successful, as an experiment in non-violence, what had taken place on the plateau was nonetheless such that he 'could imagine an entirely non-violent Europe offering total resistance to Hitler . . . A Europe that the dictator and his police would not have been able to conquer.' It was wishful thinking, but he thought it.

The war was over. The Jewish families hiding in their farmhouses with the Darbyists, the Jewish boys and girls – many now orphans – in Beau Soleil, Tante Soly, La Guespy and L'Abric, the STO evaders, the refugee teachers at the Ecole Nouvelle Cévenol – all were now safe. No one had been caught in the last nine months of the war and none would be caught now. How many had the plateau saved? Many hundreds, certainly; possibly thousands. In ones and twos they emerged from their attics and barns, their children's homes and the presbyteries of the pastors' temples, and tried to take stock of what peace might bring. In the four years of the German occupation of France, 234 people had been deported from the Haute-Loire – 171 men, 42 women, 21 children – to the extermination camps in Poland. Of these, 176 did not return. For France, this was an exceptionally low figure. Even lower was the number of those taken from the plateau – barely a few dozen.

'Liberation,' wrote Trocmé, 'carried away, like a great wave, all those that the war had brought to us.' It took the young *maquisards*, who joined de Gaulle's army to liberate the rest of Europe; it took Oscar Rosowsky, ill with typhoid and jaundice, to finish his medical studies, and his mother to find a job as a *modiste* while she waited in vain for her husband to come home; it took Jacques Stuhlmacher and his brother Marcel, after their unhappy and hungry year with the Francs, to rejoin their parents; it took Rudy Appel to Grenoble, where he found that his parents were still alive; and Simon Liwerant to Paris, where, having left his younger brother Jacques on the plateau, he set about making his fortune in the leather business. The two boys were never friends again. 'Some came to us as children,' remarked Mme Eyraud, watching her *'gosses'* leave Les Ombrages, 'but left as men.' It made Trocmé think of swarms of sparrows, flying away.

In Geneva, Max and Hanne got married.

Emile Sèches, watching his young charges depart, decided to continue to run his children's home in peacetime. Madeleine would later say that the constant presence of so many strange children deprived her and her brother and sister of a family childhood.

Trocmé, 'a director of a factory without a factory', as one of his parishioners put it, turned his attention to larger causes, to anti-nuclear campaigns and reconciliation. Magda's interests led her to follow in the steps of Martin Luther King and Gandhi. 'A curse on him who believes in gentleness,' Trocmé wrote. 'He shall finish in insipidity and cowardice, and shall never set foot in the greater liberating current of humanity.' His pacifism had never been feeble or accommodating. But as he grew older, his face softened and he became more benign. Magda never lost her Italian accent. The Ecole Nouvelle Cévenol continued to flourish, renaming itself the Collège Cévenol.

Alfred Morel, who had sent warnings of German raids to the plateau, was given the Médaille de la Résistance.

The Roanne girls, emerging with their parents from farmhouses scattered from one end of the plateau to the other, went home, borrowing cars from the farmers and piling them high with their belongings. Genie and Liliane's parents took eggs, cheese and butter in canvas bags to see them through the first days.

Rachel Kamienkar, the little girl rescued from Vénissieux, knew for certain that she had lost everyone. She continued to think about her curly-haired little brother snatched by the Gestapo, and for a long time she wanted to become a soldier, in order to kill Germans. She became a nurse instead. A neighbour of her parents had saved some of the things from their house and gave her a photograph she had found. It was taken at her aunt's wedding, for which her mother had sewed all the clothes. Rachel was one of three little girls in long dresses. When she saw it, she thought how like her mother she looked. She later married and had six children, working nights while her husband worked days; she decided that she would never go anywhere, never leave them, never travel.

Miss Maber went to Germany to take part in a programme of reconciliation, and then to Valence to work with mill girls. When, many years later, she returned to England, her English had grown rusty and she spoke with the accent and expressions of her Edwardian childhood. Asked for her enduring memory of the war years in le Chambon, she would say: fear.

Lily Garel saw a man struggling up the road drenched to the skin and dyed blue all over from a coat that was losing its colour. It was her husband Georges; he had bicycled all the way from Pau, 450 kilometres away. They took the baby and went to Switzerland, where Lily bought a cucumber in the market and marvelled at its crisp freshness, not having seen such a thing for many months. Then they set about making their lives.

The Garels in Switzerland

313

Dressed as scouts, Gilbert Nizard and his sister Mireille took the little train down the mountain, crossed the Rhône, hitched a lift on a military lorry to Aix-en-Provence and from there made their way to Marseilles. Everywhere they saw the debris of fighting. The house in the Rue Notre-Dame was intact, but it had been stripped bare. In a depot near the zoo they found a few pieces of their furniture, labelled 'Jüde Nizard'. A school friend of Mireille's, who was engaged to an American officer, got them passes to the buildings that had been occupied by the Germans, and there they found more of their things. Gilbert wrote to his mother and told her that it was safe to come home. Friends lent linen and plates. Bit by bit, they put their business together again. Gilbert went back to school to do his second baccalaureat. Sometimes, in the evenings, they danced. They waited, every day, for news of Armand and André.

While the Allies fought their way north and west, liberating Europe town by town, it was still perfectly possible to believe that many, if not all, of the 150,000 people deported by the Germans from France might yet come home. Nineteen forty-four was a year of waiting.

As the plateau emptied, the villagers felt a little lost. It had been an adventure, a challenge, to which they had risen, they felt, just as they should have done, with resourcefulness and generosity. They had behaved well, bravely. As Miss Maber would later write, looking back on the years of rescue and hiding, of silence and wariness, of listening out for danger and taking in strangers about whom one knew nothing and whose language one did not always speak, with no sense of when they might ever leave, 'it seemed like the *belle époque* – a time when we lived according to an ideal'. What worried her was that now, having lived so long with lies and illegality, 'we might have trouble knowing right from wrong'.

CHAPTER SEVENTEEN

Memory wars

When Rambert, in Camus's *La Peste*, meets his wife again after the town is reopened, he wants to 'be like all those around him who seemed to believe that the plague could come and go, without men's hearts being changed by it'. The Germans had gone, Vichy had fallen, but the French could not forget. Too much had happened, too much complicity, too many betrayals, too much enmity; their hearts were different. The need to put France back on its feet, and de Gaulle's insistence on speed and pragmatism, meant that there was much instant justice, some of it very rough indeed. Even before the courts got down to work sentencing collaborators to various forms of punishment – from execution and life imprisonment for the '*grands responsables*' of Vichy, to '*dégradation nationale*', national indignity and its ban for those deemed less guilty on wearing medals, becoming lawyers, judges, notaries or public school teachers – 9,000 summary executions had been carried out by the Resistance.

On the plateau, Fayol and Bonnissol took part in the tribunals that led to the execution of 144 men in the Haute-Loire. As Pompidou later said, the French had not much liked each other in the years of occupation, and they did not much like each other now. Fresnes and Drancy, once holding pens for the Jews and members of the Resistance, were now full of mayors, prefects and officials who had served the Germans. But as quickly as justice was meted out, so were their crimes forgotten. Amnesties followed.

France itself was in ruins, its rail tracks blasted, its bridges bombed, its factories idle. For five years, wrote the American journalist Janet Flanner in her diary, Europe had been the 'victim of cannibalism, with one country trying to eat the other countries, trying to eat the grain, the meat, the oil, the steel, the liberties, the government, the men of all the others'. The French felt denuded, impoverished, devoured. In that winter of 1944, when it rained incessantly and then snowed, Parisians said that they felt colder than at any other time during the war; they were living on carrots and turnips and there was no coal with which to heat their houses.

It was not until the spring of 1945, however, when trains began to bring home the survivors from the German extermination and labour camps, that the scale of Vichy's crimes became clear. Of the 150,000 people who had been deported from France, 75,721 of them were Jews. While a little less then half of the political deportees came home – 40,760 out of 86,827 – only 2,564 Jews did so. More than 10,000 Jewish children under 18 had been put on to trains for the death camps: 300 survived. The statistics, reflecting Laval's attempt to buy time for the French Jews at the expense of the foreigners, show that while 13.5 per cent of French Jews had died, the figure rose to 42 per cent for foreign Jews.

Even so, the deportation and murder of the Jews would not become criminal offences until 1964, when French law changed to allow retroactive trials for crimes against humanity. Until then, the Germans, not Vichy, were deemed responsible. More heed was paid to the pillage of France – half a million books and more than 400 trainloads of furniture and pictures – and to the crimes of collaboration perceived to have been committed by writers. No one had obliged them to publish. Many had chosen to do so. Over 400 plays had been performed in occupied Paris, among them those by Sartre, Cocteau, Guitry, Claudel and Giradoux. Sartre maintained that he wrote in coded messages for the Resistance; but it was a code few had the key to.

It would be many years before it was acknowledged that, from the very beginning, with their censuses, their revisions of nationality, their Statuts des Juifs, their seizure of property and businesses and their expulsions from professions and jobs, Vichy had effectively paved the way for Hitler's Final Solution in France. By turning Jews into inferior beings, by interning them in camps, where they starved and grew sick and died, by letting loose on them anti-Semitic zealots, by identifying, gathering, earmarking and preparing them, they had made it far easier for the Germans to do their work. The Nazis could have done little of this on their own. But they had given Vichy no military ultimatum, and on the rare occasions that Vichy said no – as with the wearing of the yellow star in the south – there had been no reprisals. Had Vichy, and Vichy's police, not actively helped the Germans, many more Jews would have survived. Nor were the French who did help the Jews in danger in the way that rescuers in Poland or Germany were; penalties for rescuing and hiding Jews were often smaller. Even modest acts would have made a difference.

No other European country had taken such a clear anti-Semitic line: Denmark sent 93 per cent of its small Jewish population to safety in Sweden, Fascist Italy dragged its heels, and even Hungary's dictator stopped deportations towards the end of the war. As the SS officer Helmut Knochen declared at his trial in 1947: 'We found no difficulty with the Vichy government in implementing Jewish policy.' Nor were the Jews themselves deemed by all to be blameless: one of the many bitter legacies was an accusation levelled at UGIF, the umbrella Jewish body, that by trying so desperately to remain on good terms with the Germans, they had effectively turned their children's homes into traps, and thus become complicit in the arrests and deportations.

Many Jews in France did in fact survive: three quarters of the 330,000 thought to be in the country in 1940. This was due to many things: the existence of an unoccupied zone until late in 1942, the presence in France of such a small occupying force, but it was chiefly because of the behaviour of a number of ordinary French people; and of this, the Plateau Vivarais-Lignon was a remarkable example.

Switzerland did not emerge well from the war years. Of the 28,000 people accepted from France, 12,635 got in by crossing the border clandestinely. At least 1,467 – though the number is certainly far higher – were known to have been turned away, to almost inevitable capture by the Germans. It was only on 12 July 1944 – five weeks after the Normandy landings, by which time those Jews still at liberty or hidden in France had no need to get to Switzerland – that the Swiss federation passed a law allowing foreigners in danger to pass freely across their border. The Swiss did indeed take in more refugees than they have been credited with; but they did not do enough. With a little more generosity, a little less xenophobia, they could have saved many lives.

For the plateau, the connections forged in Geneva by Boegner, Guillon and Mireille Philip were crucial, as was the work of Madeleine Dreyfus, Georges Loinger, Cimade and the OSE on the border. And Switzerland did offer sanctuary to Max and Hanne, and to Simon Liwerant, along with at least 70 people who passed through the Coteau Fleuri, 15 from Les Roches, and all the dozens of young children saved by Garel, Moussa Abadi and Joseph Bass.

Altogether, taking into account the 311 who received visas to emigrate, the 100 or so who made it to Spain, the estimated 1,350 who got to Switzerland and those hidden by Aryan families, some 8–10,000 Jewish children in France survived the war. But many of them, in 1944, now had no parents.

Proportionally, their rescuers had not fared so well. Of the Sixième's 88 full-time workers, 30 died, though Liliane Klein-Liebert remained safe. Joseph Bass survived the war, as did his collaborator Denise Caraco, better known as Colibri. Mireille Philip, Piton, Loinger all saw peace arrive. The Abbé Glasberg, weaving and ducking his way through a plethora of Resistance activities, escaped capture, as did Père Chaillet, who was so upset by the seizure of the children of Izieu that he kept a list of their names in the pocket of his soutane until he died. Two other priests who had played a part in the plateau story were not so lucky. Père Louis-Adrien Favre, of the Salesian college, and Abbé Jean Rosay, curé of Douvaine, through whose hands so many of Madeleine Dreyfus's children had passed, both died in the final weeks of the war, Favre shot by the Germans, Rosay in Bergen-Belsen.

Marguerite Pellet, in whose school for deaf and dumb children Madeleine had been caught, was sent to Ravensbrück and died in the Allied bombing of Amstetten*; the body of René, her husband, caught by the Gestapo, was washed up in the Rhône,

---

* Three women from *A Train in Winter*, Charlotte Decock, Olga Melun and Yvonne Noutari, died with her.

covered in marks of torture. The Marco Polo circuit lost 115 of its agents. It would be many months before these deaths were confirmed. Simon Liwerant was one of thousands of anxious relations who went day after day to the Hôtel Lutétia in Paris, where the lists of the returnees were posted, in the hope of finding his father. Aaron never came.

But Madeleine Dreyfus did. She was sent to Belsen at the end of May 1944, and lived in a barracks with 600 other women, feeling humiliated and diminished by her agonised craving for food. Liberated by the Allies on 15 April 1945, she endured an 85-kilometre walk and a 15-day train journey with virtually no food, seeing many of her companions die. When she reached Paris, on 18 May, she was skeletal. She arrived home in Lyons the next day; Raymond and the children were waiting. Twenty-one-month old Annette did not know who she was. Told to kiss her mother, she obediently went over to a photograph of Madeleine and kissed that instead.

Almost at once, Madeleine went back to her work as a child psychologist, with all the determination and absorption that had carried her through the camps; she chose to behave, said Raymond, as if the 'whole nightmare had never taken place'. It made none of her children happy. Later, Annette would say that she grew up resenting the children her mother worked with and seemed more interested in. 'I was jealous. How could I not be?' She dreaded the reunions of survivors, everyone admiring and praising her wonderful mother. She was, says her aunt, 'a very sad little girl'.

Dorcas Robert, the feisty café owner from Yssingeaux, also survived the camps. She returned to the plateau together with her assistant Rose at the same time as Dora Rivière, the doctor from Saint-Etienne, as part of a group of 299 French women exchanged for 600 German prisoners of war. Dorcas was one of a handful of women to emerge alive from Ravensbrück's infamous Jugendlager, where the inmates were sent only to die, and she had been led out twice to the gas chambers before being reprieved. Dora had worked in Ravensbrück's infirmary. Though Yssingeaux feted Dorcas's arrival with bunting and a parade, and she discovered that her children had been well cared for, she did not find what she had hoped for in post-war France. She renamed her café

Le Restaurant du Patriote, and was awarded the Médaille de la Résistance, but ill health and local rivalries kept her from the political future she had dreamt of. 'I am heartbroken at all these injustices,' she wrote bitterly to the authorities. 'We fought, we made sacrifices, but our victory has been stolen from us and we find ourselves in a still more rotten democracy than the one before the war.' She died less than five years later; Berthe, her eldest child, was only 15.

But for one of the rescuers, the end of the war brought contentment. Having fought her way north with the Allies, Virginia Hall went to work for Radio Free Europe, interviewing refugees from behind the new Iron Curtain. Returning to the US, she joined the CIA. She was awarded the Distinguished Service Medal, the first civilian woman to be so honoured, but declined a public ceremony, telling President Truman that she was 'still operational and anxious to keep busy'. She kept her long hair piled up in a bun on top of her head and stuck a pencil through it. She married Paul Goillot. He was considerably shorter than her and much less well educated, but they laughed. When she reached 60, Virginia retired to a farm in Maryland, which reminded visitors of a turreted French chateau. She planted her garden with bulbs, raised five French poodles and several cats, made her own goat's cheese, and became a crossword addict. Her bookshelves were filled with spy stories, but about her own story she refused to speak.

Annette Dreyfus was not the only girl to find post-war France a sad and unsettling place, nor Simon Liwerant the only boy to wait for parents who never came back. There were many unhappy children in France in 1945.

As the war ended, the OSE and the other welfare organisations took stock: they estimated that there were some 5–6,000 Jewish children who were now orphans, whether hidden in non-Jewish homes around France, or over the border in Spain or Switzerland. They needed to be traced, restored to their proper names and identities, and a future found for them. The OSE alone had 4,401 names on a card index of 'abandoned Jewish children'. Some of them had forgotten their real names; others did not even know that they were Jewish. Most of them were not French at all, but Polish, German, Russian, Austrian or Romanian, the children of tailors and leatherworkers, travelling salesmen and tinkers, doctors and businessmen and miners, come to France in the welcoming years of the Front National. Their short lives had been marked by exile, camps, loss of parents, clandestinity. Some had no memory of their families. They had to be taught how to live with the past, to remember and find their childhoods, to be helped to come to terms with feelings of humiliation, hatred, revenge. They had to be given a taste for life; they had to learn to trust.

Soon, the OSE's social workers, Madeleine Dreyfus and Liliane Klein-Liebert among them, were back on their bicycles, visiting and collecting the children they had so successfully concealed in villages and farmhouses. On the plateau, Tante Soly and Faïdoli and the Ecole Nouvelle Cévenol produced their Jewish pupils; the Darbyists those hidden in their attics and stables. Not all the men and women who had taken in children wished to see them leave, and there were battles around France over relinquishing some of them, and accusations of forced baptisms and conversions. And not all the children, happy and safe with the families who had taken them in, wanted to leave. But there was a strong feeling in the French Jewish community that these children needed to rediscover their Jewishness, receive a Jewish education, become, as they saw it 'un homme Juif nouveau', a new Jewish man.

The OSE opened 25 homes to look after them.

From Switzerland came the 1,500 or so who had been smuggled over the border, of whom 569 were known to have lost their parents. The Circuit Garel had 900 hidden children. The liberation of Buchenwald brought a group to France, many of them originally from the ghettos of Poland and Hungary. Reading the files on the children in the OSE's archives in Paris, you get an extraordinarily vivid picture of just what they had been through: the fractured families, the long journeys on foot or by train, the separation from parents and brothers and sisters, the hiding places in barns and lofts, the hunger, and above all, the fear. In these dossiers, kept on every child, are the few facts known about each of them: the names of their parents and siblings, where they were caught, what camps they were sent to, when they were deported. Sometimes there are photographs, grainy black-and-white pictures of grandparents in Warsaw or parents on their wedding day. Some are police photographs, taken in Gurs or from identity papers.

Deciding what to do with these children was not easy. There were questions of guardianship, the tracing of relatives. The US offered visas, then stalled; Australia and Canada volunteered to take 100, South Africa a number of children under 12.

The children themselves were not easy. They were often closed in, secretive, regarding adults as enemies, for adults had crushed their parents. The more disturbed accepted nothing, neither comfort nor affection. Teachers working with the children reported incessant nightmares and crying, lack of initiative, fear of argument, insolence; the older girls were said to be 'neurasthenic', the boys unstable. Most had a terror of abandonment. At an OSE congress held in 1946, there was much talk about how these 'railing, undisciplined, baffling' children could be coaxed back to life. In the homes, the staff did what they could to remain calm and loving, but were constantly ambushed by surprises. When one woman decided to replace the bell that normally woke the children in the mornings with a more soothing flute, four furious 14-year-olds said to her: 'You take us for snakes.'

In 1946, the OSE had the idea of starting a newspaper in its homes, to be written by the children; they called it *Lendemains*, tomorrows. The poems and stories that appeared are about sport, friendship, holidays and sometimes Palestine, and they have a curiously detached tone. Almost none are personal. So it is oddly shocking, looking through the back numbers, to come across a poem about the death camps. It is unsigned. 'My parents went up in the green flames,' it starts. 'I dreamt that their bones rattled in my ears / Dancing and flaring / Vile assassin worm . . . Vile worm with a black soul / Do not expect my pardon.' Another child described himself as a 'suitcase of whom no one has asked their opinion'. Like the adult deportees returning to France after the war, many of these children preferred to keep quiet, mistrusting their listeners. And like the deportees, who felt marginalised in a country now busy celebrating the heroic resisters, they felt, as the children of people who had allowed themselves to be deported, inferior. They were suspicious, wary, guilty; they wanted to be like other children, but for many this was not possible. They found the very concept of Jewishness troubling, since Jewishness had meant death. In order to live, it was better to forget. It was not a question of how, after the Holocaust, to be Jewish, but how to live at all.

In the immediate wake of the war, reuniting these orphaned children with relatives, however distant, seemed to many the best solution. Aunts, uncles, cousins and grandparents were identified and approached, and the children were sent off to Poland, Cuba, America or Canada, wherever Jewish families had survived or been offered refuge. For some this experience turned out badly. Encouraged to forget the past, not talk about what had happened, they found their new 'families' alien. Their own had vanished; it was inconceivable to imagine another one. Paradoxically, the children who, having no one to take them, remained in the OSE's homes, where they lived among other children with the same sense of loss and guilt, did better. They mourned together.

Nor did all the children who rediscovered their parents alive thrive in the new reality of post-war France. Very young when taken away, loved and looked after by kindly, soft women, they found their own gaunt, exhausted, prematurely aged, grieving mothers, endlessly rehearsing the past and incapable of being proper parents again, infinitely troubling, particularly when they themselves now spoke only French, having forgotten their child-hood language. Some would later say that they wished that they had never found them. The title of one child survivor's memoir is poignant and revealing: 'Not everyone has the chance to be an orphan'. Others would say that they grew up feeling that whatever they did, like Annette Dreyfus, they could never live up to their parents, while at the same time often being conscious, as one of the Roanne girls wrote, that in their parents 'there were scorched lands, arid zones, disaster areas'. Their parents were not the people they remembered. They always looked, wrote Carole Zalberg, who had spent a year hidden by a farmer's wife on the plateau, 'as if they were waiting for something, tiptoeing through this life in such a way that death would have no trouble catching them'.

Very quickly, the hidden children from the plateau scattered. By the winter of 1944, when the snows again cut the villages off from the outside world for weeks at a time, many of the houses in which they had sheltered were shuttered, awaiting the tourists they all hoped would return the following summer, to walk in the forests once again and pick mushrooms and blueberries. Le Chambon looked smaller, quieter.

The older children were the ones who went sooner and further. Max and Hanne had a baby daughter and moved to New York. Rudy Appel also went to the US. Not knowing that he would have been eligible for a scholarship to college, he worked as a furrier until his command of four languages got him a good job in an export company. Joseph Atlas and his brother, having studied chemistry, decided that Europe had become a 'cemetery' and left with their mother for Santiago.

It was the girls from Roanne who first decided that they wished to be a part of the new Israel. At a party of young Zionists organised in le Chambon soon after liberation, a '*jamboree Juif*', for which Genie and Liliane's mother made *œufs à la neige*, floating islands, they talked of what they could do as pioneers. So many of their relatives were dead – almost the entire Polish side of the Schloss family, while Ruth Golan had lost 90 members of hers – that they, like Joseph, felt that Europe had become one vast Jewish cemetery.

The 1939 White Paper, with its strict limits on immigration into Palestine, was still in force, so the girls took courses in nursing and teacher training in Geneva, then went to a camp in Provence where Mossad was preparing young Zionists to enter Palestine illegally. They were on one of the first boats, so old and leaky and overcrowded that it nearly sank, and when they did reach Haifa, two British destroyers were waiting for them. They spent a year in a camp in Cyprus, but were back as soon as Israel's statehood was proclaimed, and lived for the next few years in considerable hardship in a kibbutz on the border with Lebanon, where they took their turn as guards and built a village and a farm out of a stony, treeless hillside on which nothing thrived.

Pierre Bloch went back to Lyons with his parents, but he could not imagine wanting to live among Gentiles again. He studied for a while, then, when the state of Israel was founded, he joined a kibbutz and helped to guard the border. He was, he says, a '*Zionist de cœur*', by absolute conviction. He was annoyed when people suggested that after the war, the hidden children, like Trocmé's sparrows, flew off from the plateau without gratitude or regret. It was not so. 'We left like the survivors of an inexplicable and unacceptable nightmare. We felt that our only way forward was to forget – even the good things.' For many of the plateau's hidden children, it would be years before they made their way up the mountain again. But they did come, and when they came, they brought controversy with them.

No European country has been more interested than France in the nature of memory and history, how it is understood, recorded, perceived, written and transmitted. Ever since Marc Bloch and Lucien Febvre founded the Annales School in 1929, the question of how the past is remembered in the present, how it entwines itself around contemporary thought, has fascinated French historians, long given to theory and abstraction. In what have been called the 'memory wars', 'militants of memory' have picked obsessively over the past, ferreting out conspiracies, questioning, accusing. There are said to be some 10,000 'lieux de mémoire', sites of remembrance, a concept particular to France, with their implied suggestion that memory is a fluid, living phenomenon, something in permanent evolution, a structuring of forgetfulness. These lieux are most often places, but they can equally be ideas, things and even people.

In the immediate wake of the war, the French, struggling to find meaning for the occupation years, were encouraged, not only by de Gaulle but by all the political classes, to believe that Vichy had been the work of a small number of traitors, more misguided than evil, drawn into treachery by the Germans. In what Henry Rousso famously came to describe as the Vichy Syndrome, a first phase of mourning – for the calamitous defeat, the 90,000 dead and the two million made prisoner, the humiliating occupation and the purge of the culprits – was followed by a second, more comforting period in which France as a whole was perceived as having been a nation of resisters. When, in 1964, the Resistance leader Jean Moulin's ashes were transferred to the Panthéon in Paris, they were accompanied by a magnificent cortège, complete with bell-ringers, flags and veterans. During these years, almost nothing was said about the fate of the Jews, not least because of the desire of the survivors to reassimilate themselves into post-war French life. Beate and Serge Klarsfeld's monumental work of recording and tracing those deported and killed by the Germans was only just beginning.

This myth of French heroism could not last. May 1968 saw the French young in a mood to question everything. De Gaulle, who above all others had done his best to suppress the role of the collaborators, died in 1970. It was no coincidence that Marcel Ophuls' *Le Chagrin et la Pitié* was released in 1971, with its 280 minutes recording daily life in Clermont-Ferrand under occupation, a city consumed by indecision and selfishness and not at all united in resisting the invader. In 87 weeks the film was seen by 232,000 people, though it would be ten years before it was put on television – for which it had originally been commissioned. Robert Paxton's *Vichy France: Old Guard and New Order*, based largely on German and American archives, since many of the French were closed to him, was finally translated into French and published in France in 1973.

Paxton was not the first to chronicle the lives of the Jews during the war – Raul Hilberg's *The Destruction of the European Jews* and Joseph Billig's *Le Commissariat Général aux Questions Juives* had appeared in the late 1950s and early 1960s – but it was Paxton and his co-author Michael Marrus who meticulously pulled the myth apart, showing exactly how all the major figures in Vichy, and many minor ones across France, had sought real collaboration with the Nazis, in the hopes of carving out a role for France in Hitler's new Europe. Pétain, Paxton showed, had not been a senile old man; there had been no 'double games' intent on shielding the nation from the cruelty of the invaders. On the contrary, Vichy had consistently offered more than Germany asked for, more and also sooner. The debates triggered by Paxton and Marrus on how the French really behaved during *les années noires*, have played a part in French political life ever since.

With Paxton too, after a quarter of a century of neglect, the fate of the French and foreign Jews in France finally emerged from the shadows. Among the remains of the 15 victims of the war symbolically brought around the flame to the Unknown Soldier in November 1945, not one had been a Jew. No one, not even the Jews themselves, had chosen them to be distinguished as a special category. In the years of heroic *'résistencialisme'*, the *déportés politiques*, men and women arrested and deported for their resistance work, had fought hard to separate themselves from the deported Jews. To have fallen into German hands for an act of resistance was noble; to have been picked up as a victim was shameful. Even the dead, guilty of passivity, were not immune from shame, having let themselves be corralled by the anti-Semitic laws. Simone Veil, the Jewish politician and lawyer deported to Auschwitz, spoke of this neglect as a second death, that of being forgotten. Even the many associations of survivors were full of ambiguity, laying much emphasis on the need for their members to have 'conformed to French honour'. *Résistants* were entitled to compensation; the Jews were conceded it.

But now, in the wake of Ophuls and Paxton and Marrus, after the release of *Shoah*, Claude Lanzmann's nine-and-a-half-hour film about the death camps, and after the steady work of the Klarsfelds, a new phase in the Vichy Syndrome opened. It brought with it studies, books, university theses. By 1985, there were 240 scholars working in the field. It also brought enduring controversy, as arguments about the uniqueness of the Jewish experience were batted backwards and forwards, passionate, bitter and quarrelsome, with macabre battles about who had suffered most. And it brought dozens of *lieux de mémoire*, as the sites of Vichy's repression were discovered and honoured. The Commissariat Général aux Questions Juives in Vichy itself is not one of them, and it is not to be found on any map. On the corner of the main square, on the third floor, is a shuttered flat where Pétain once stayed. It remains untouched and has apparently become a place of pilgrimage for the Maréchal's supporters.

One of the *lieux* is Rivesaltes, the camp near Perpignan from which 2,250 Jews were deported to Auschwitz between August and October 1942, the camp from which Rudy Appel had escaped, and where Auguste Bohny had done so much to look after the small children before moving to le Chambon. The idea was to honour not only the Jews, but the Spanish republicans, the Gypsies and later the Harkis from Algeria who had been interned there, with a fine museum and a fitting memorial. But the local commune ran out of money and Rivesaltes today looks much as it must have done when the first Jews arrived in 1940, a sandy, hot plain with a few umbrella pines and olive trees, the majestic, snowy Pyrenees in the distance. A row of stones bars the entrance to where the museum was to have been. There is a wind farm nearby, and some kind of military installation.

At Vénissieux, there is nothing but a small plaque, almost impossible to find, concealed by a trailing plant.

At Gurs, 200 kilometres to the west, greater efforts have been made to recreate a camp, with one of the 382 wooden barracks freshly reconstructed, a short stretch of railway track showing where the trains arrived, a visitor centre and a ring of stones. The cemetery alongside is well tended, with its 1,072 graves, most of them belonging to the elderly men and women from Baden and the Palatinate who did not long survive the horror of the journey that brought them here. Hanne's grandmother Babette, lies here, as does her aunt Berta.

Finally, over 40 years after the war ended, those most responsible for the persecution of the Jews in France were tracked down and brought to trial. Klaus Barbie, thought to have sent some 14,000 people to their deaths, among them Dr Le Forestier, was unearthed hiding in Bolivia, extradited and in 1987 sentenced to life in prison, where he died in 1991. His trial was the first at which 'crimes against humanity' were in the dock in France. René Bousquet, who as secretary general of the Vichy police was the man most culpable, after Laval, for the deportation of the Jews, and who had been sentenced to five years of national indignity after the war for having been part of the Vichy government, was brought to trial again in 1993, but was shot by an unhinged publicity-seeker as the trial began. Darquier de Pellepoix, the third and perhaps most violent and angry of the heads of the Commissariat Général aux Questions Juives, was found in Spain but died before he could be extradited. And Maurice Papon, who as secretary general of police in Bordeaux had deported thousands of Jews and resisters to the Nazi camps, was finally sentenced to jail in 1999. These trials had been a long time in coming, but they did what nothing else had quite done before: they allowed witnesses to tell their stories, and in so doing these now elderly men and women became the heroes of the day, speaking symbolically for the dead.

The timing of remembrance in Israel was different, but its path has been somewhat similar. In the first years of the new Israel, when the girls from Roanne and Pierre Bloch were helping to guard the frontier, many young Zionists blamed the Shoah, the Hebrew word for the Holocaust, on the passivity of the European Jews in allowing themselves to be slaughtered instead of dying with weapons in their hands. The survivors, arriving on boats from Europe in the late 1940s and 1950s, felt ashamed, much as the French survivors did. Then in 1953, Yad Vashem, the memorial to the victims of the Holocaust, was founded in Jerusalem to correct what David Ben Gurion feared was the ignorance of the generation born after the war, and a remembrance law was passed to recognise individuals worthy of the title of Righteous Among the Nations, Justes, men and women who, at risk of their own lives, had saved a Jewish one. If Paxton's book marked a defining moment in France, it was Eichmann's trial in Jerusalem in 1961 that caused a shift in perceptions in Israel. 'I stand before you, Judges of Israel,' the prosecutor, Gideon Hausner, declared, 'but I do not stand alone. I have behind me six million accusers.' Victims were now witnesses. Schoolchildren were urged to memorise his words.

The story of le Chambon and the villages of the Plateau Vivarais-Lignon was known and talked about in Israel in the 1950s, but it was not until the early 1970s that serious efforts were made to identify individual rescuers. One of the first was Joseph Bass. After him came André Trocmé, and a little later Magda, Daniel Trocmé and Edouard Theis and his wife Mildred. 'André was the leader,' Theis would say. 'I was the disciple, the follower. I was second fiddle.' As Justes, they received a medal, and a tree was planted on the Avenue of the Righteous at Yad Vashem in their honour. Since then, a commission continues to sit to determine, as with the Justes of all nations, whether names submitted by local committees did indeed act at risk to their own lives, and disinterestedly, not in hope of gain.

As of 2012, France had 3,513 Justes, 14 per cent of the total number, but the number rises year by year as new rescuers are identified. The two bishops, Saliège and Théas, the Abbé Glasberg, Père Chaillet, Madeleine Barot are all Justes, as is Jean Deffaugt, the brave mayor of Annemasse, and Georges Loinger, who took so many children across the mountains. Fifty-nine of them are pastors, 80 are policemen.

The Haute-Loire has 87 Justes, 70 of them from the plateau: 47 from le Chambon, 10 from Mazet, 6 from Fay and 5 from Tence, making the area the place with the highest concentration in the whole of France. Mme Déléage, Roger Darcissac, Léon Eyraud, Daniel Curtet, Georgette Barraud and her daughter Gabrielle, and M and Mme Héritier are all Justes. But there are omissions: Miss Maber is not one of them.

Afterword

When, soon after the war, Madeleine Barot of Cimade was asked to name people who should be honoured for the work they had done in saving the Jews, she refused. It would be wrong to glorify their deeds, she said, because they had chosen not to glorify them themselves. And she wanted no part in the 'shameful' exploitation of the past. These sentiments were largely shared by the inhabitants of the Plateau Vivarais-Lignon, who chose to remain as silent about their wartime exploits as they had during the centuries of religious persecution. But they did not stay silent for ever. Of all the *mémoires contestées*, a phrase much loved by French historians, the versions of what actually happened in le Chambon, Tence, Fay and Mazet during the years of German occupation are among the most rancorous. And when these memory wars finally broke out, they did so with extraordinary intensity.

During the fifties, sixties and seventies, the plateau returned to its pre-war existence. More Sylvester pines were planted, more tractors were bought to replace the handsome beige and white local horses, the Darbyists retired to their private lives and the summer tourists returned to walk in the forests. Beneath the peaceable surface, however, feelings were stirring. The more the myth of le Chambon grew – the more Pastor Trocmé was honoured, the more there was talk of pacifism and the selfless behaviour of pious Protestants – the more uneasy the inhabitants of Tence, Fay, Mazet and the hamlets of the plateau began to feel.

Then, in 1979, Philip Hallie, an American historian in search of proof that pacifism could successfully counter violence, chanced upon the story. On a visit to Swarthmore College outside Philadelphia, he discovered André Trocmé's autobiography, together with additions by Magda, deposited there, with no plans for publication. It proved to be a small unexploded bomb.

According to Hallie's book, *Lest Innocent Blood be Shed*, André Trocmé, the 'soul of le Chambon', acting more or less single-handedly, so infused his parishioners with his belief in non-violence that his presbytery became the centre of the rescue operation. There is little or no mention of Madeleine Dreyfus, Joseph Bass, Mme Déléage, Miss Maber or Madeleine Barot, or of any of the other important villages, Mazet, Tence or Fay. The Darbyists are nowhere to be seen.

The mayor, Charles Guillon – who had not even been in le Chambon at the time – is credited with having urged Magda to turn away the first Jewish refugee. Pastor Boegner is described as having tried to persuade Trocmé not to take Jewish children. Le Forestier is a '*puro folle*', an imprudent, heedless man who could have ruined them all with his hotheadedness. Schmähling, the German major who presided over the tribunal that dispatched Le Forestier to his death, is said not only to have done what he could to save him, but to have become so imbued with the pacifism of the plateau that he cast his benevolent eye over the villages and saved the Jews hiding there. The local police are described as having been so impressed by the spectacle of non-violence that they ceased to look for the hidden Jews. Eyraud, the Maquis leader whose calm authority prevented many of the young men from performing foolish actions, never features at all. In this version of events – the basis of the myth that endures in some places to this day – the village of le Chambon, acting more or less on its own and steered by Trocmé, demonstrates that non-violent resistance could conquer even the hearts of Vichy and the Germans.

For a while, until Hallie's book appeared in French, little notice was taken of its claims, though Boegner, alerted to various slurs to his character, had four of the most derogatory pages removed. The plateau was quietly basking in pleasure at the presentation of a plaque, largely engineered by Oscar Rosowsky, and written in both French and Hebrew, honouring those Protestants who had 'hidden, protected, saved the persecuted in their thousands', and unveiled at a ceremony in the summer of 1979. By now Trocmé himself was dead, buried in the cemetery near the plaque, but Theis and his family attended.

Then, in 1987, Pierre Sauvage, a film-maker who happened to have been born on the plateau, decided to put together a documentary film on its war. He gave it the title *Weapons of the Spirit*. A reviewer for *Le Monde* at the Cannes film festival called it a 'hymn' to the Protestant peasants who had behaved so selflessly. In the film, Sauvage took up many of Hallie's points about Trocmé's remarkable actions and about the all-pervasive spirit of goodness that shaped and steered the minds of his parishioners. Hallie, meanwhile, still in search of more goodness, gave a lecture in the US in which Schmähling emerged as the protector of the Jews on the plateau, a flawed, compromised man, but ultimately noble. Roger Bonfils, the proprietor of the Hôtel du Lignon, home to the convalescent German soldiers, was heard to describe a meeting between Trocmé and Schmähling, at which only he had been a witness, and at which some sort of agreement to shelter the Jews had been tacitly forged.

What followed was consternation in some quarters. There were letters, reviews, protests. An effort was made to have Sauvage's film banned from an event. In *Le Monde Juif*, which ran the story over several furious weeks, Oscar Rosowsky, Madeleine Barot and Pierre Fayol all put their names to a detailed critique of Hallie's work and what they called a 'mutation of historical truth'. There was talk of 'approximations, inexactitudes and extrapolations'. The claim made by Bonfils was challenged, both because he had been one of the very few suspected collaborators on the plateau, and because there was no other evidence at all that Schmähling and Trocmé had ever discussed the Jews in the village. Schmähling's 'goodness', and what Hallie elsewhere described as his 'passionate compassion', were vehemently denied: had he not arrested and deported 234 people from the Haute-Loire? Had he not referred to the Milice as 'the best French children'? Were the Mennonites, possible backers of a film of Hallie's book, not the very people who had given sanctuary in South America to Dr Mengele after the war?

Dr Le Forestier's widow and his son Jean-Philippe were drawn into the fray and declared that for anyone to maintain that Schmähling had no idea that Le Forestier would be killed was absurd, as was his claim to have persuaded his senior colleagues not to execute the doctor on the spot. Commenting on Trocmé's memoirs, the Protestant writer Jacques Poujol told Piton, the former scout and *passeur* to Switzerland, that they were nothing but the work of 'a poor man who had become paranoid writing far too long after the events to be credible'. Trocmé's words and deeds were picked over, analysed, ridiculed. In the wake of all this came more attacks and counterattacks, reams of accusatory letters, oceans of calumny. Sauvage can be forgiven for remarking that it was all rather excessive, and that Schmähling was not, after all, 'a very dynamic enemy'. Schmähling himself lay low.

The disputes rumbled on. Then, in 1990, a young Protestant pastor, Alain Arnoux, with links to the Ardèche and an interest in the past, was appointed to the temple in le Chambon. He felt honoured. Soon aware of the battles beginning to agitate his parishioners over the various renderings of the past, Arnoux had the idea of holding a colloquium, to which all involved would be invited. He was sick to death of the bickering, the animosities, the films, books, speeches, each one more inaccurate than the last, the ever-inflated numbers of those rescued – 5,000! 8,000! – and of the parade of American evangelical visitors, who had taken this tale of religious non-violence to their hearts, and came to worship at the shrine of Trocmé's house. Over the years, Trocmé and Magda had acquired a kind of sainthood; it made Arnoux deeply uneasy. As did the idea of the myth becoming a tourist attraction.

The colloquium would, he thought, bring peace. It was, he says, the worst thing he has ever done.

For three days in October 1990, the war on the plateau was rehashed. All those previously neglected – Eyraud, Fayol, Bonnissol, the *maquisards*, the people of Tence, Mazet and Fay, the many other Protestant pastors, the Catholics, the farmers who hid the children, the children themselves, now grown into adults – were heard. But tempers were not calmed; animosity prevailed. It was probably not helped by Arnoux's decision to dwell on the fact that the inhabitants of the plateau had never sought and did not want publicity, and that once someone made a profit from the story, 'then the spirit that reigned here would be betrayed . . . If a church, or any other organisation, or any family, seeks to glorify what was done, they would reveal themselves as totally unworthy of those who preferred to remain silent.' Remembering what took place, Arnoux declared, should inspire not pride but humility.

Nor, probably, did he soothe tempers when, in the presence of the Israeli ambassador, come to bestow Yad Vashem's medal on le Chambon after the colloquium, he announced that he sincerely hoped that, since Israel was honouring the people of the plateau for what they had done, they would now undertake to blow up no more Palestinian homes, expel no more Palestinian families, close no more schools to Palestinian children. Not surprisingly, perhaps, anger followed. In an Israeli paper, Arnoux was called a 'Nazi pastor'.

Silence has not returned to this land where silence was for so long the essence of its people. There have been other colloquia, other debates, of a more mollifying kind, but the competing wars of memory have not gone away. The sniping continues, between historians and academics, pacifists and resisters, bystanders and rescuers. Rosowsky and Sauvage, locked in disagreement, have each in their own way become custodians of the plateau's history, recruiting and shedding adherents, endlessly debating the exact hour at which Le Forestier was or was not arrested, the precise tone of Schmähling's words, whether or not Bach and Schmähling were ultimately good or bad. President Chirac's visit to le Chambon in 2004 and his eulogy to the local inhabitants has served chiefly to reinforce the myth, since in the national coverage of the event there were many references to the '5,000' Jews saved, to Trocmé and to the village of le Chambon, where a conspiracy of good shone brightly in a country otherwise plunged in darkness; yet again, the wider picture was not in evidence. Of the 11 most important sites on the Justes in France, Trocmé's name is the only one to appear on all of them.

Nowhere has this spirit of unhappy divisiveness found greater expression than in the interminable and ongoing saga of the museum, an idea first mooted in 1980 by a newly formed Société de l'Histoire de la Montagne, and which only saw the light of day in 2013, having undergone many twists and turns, sometimes emphasising spirituality and non-violence, sometimes the Resistance and the Maquis, with innumerable bad-tempered meetings and accusations of theft of archive material, and complaints that the project had been hijacked by Parisian historians and political cabals. The formidable new mayor of le Chambon, Eliane Wauquiez Motte, whose son held a government position under Sarkozy, resolutely rising above the squabbles, finally forced through a project in which all aspects of the plateau's history are represented. But she did not achieve this without alienating the other villages, who protested that, yet again, they had been ousted from the story, 'dispossessed of their past' by an explosive mix of entrenched interests and ambitious outsiders. The museum is in the old school, opposite the temple in le Chambon. Mme Wauquiez hopes it will draw tourists, along with schoolchildren, who study the Holocaust in their curriculum, and that it will act as a reminder that there were, in the years of Vichy, places where people were decent.

Where does the truth lie? Was Schmähling a hero, or simply a German officer trying to survive the war? Was Bach more humane than collaborationist? Were the local inhabitants peculiarly altruistic? The plateau was not alone, of course, in saving people during the years of occupation. All over France, other villages, other towns, convents, families, Protestants, Catholics, Gaullists and communists, at great risk to themselves, sheltered those pursued by the Nazis. Dieulefit in the Drôme, the Vabre in Tarn, Vialas in the Cévennes, all did similar things. From one end of France to the other, there were civil servants who falsified ration books, policemen who turned a blind eye, telephone operators who warned of impending raids. Parallel to the map of Vichy is a map of decency.

Just the same, there is something different about the story of the Plateau Vivarais-Lignon.

In these 22 communes and isolated farmhouses, more people, proportionately, were saved than anywhere else in France. Saving was what the local people did, silently, acting together, working things out, planning, sharing the burden. They certainly did not save 5,000, the figure bandied around after the war; it was probably more like 800, though perhaps 3,000 more may have passed through, helped along their way to safety. And why this was so remains one of the many questions that continue to feed into the plateau's enduring wars.

One explanation for what happened is that the mayor, Charles Guillon, paved the way with his foresight about the coming war and the need to help the refugees. As Gabrielle Barraud explained, 'We were prepared by Guillon, he told us to get ready to take in people.' Another is the presence of so many Protestant pastors, steeped in the Old Testament and Judaism, in touch with Protestants across Europe and with the persecuted Confessing Church in Germany; and that of the pious, staunch Darbyists, whose habitual modesty and silence has meant that they have never received the recognition that is due to them. Yet another is the fact that the plateau was inaccessible for weeks at a time during the heavy winter snows, and that even in summer its narrow, winding roads through the forests were not easy to follow. Then there is the fact that the plateau, long before the war, was already well known for its children's homes and *pensions*, so that it became a natural place to house the refugees. The links with neutral Switzerland also played their part.

After that is the fact that the garrison of Germans in Le Puy was small, and many of its soldiers were the unreliable Tartars, Georgians and Armenians, by no means certain to do the Nazis' bidding. This in part explains what is otherwise a mystery: just why the Germans convalescing in the heart of le Chambon for the last 18 months of the war made no move to denounce or arrest the many Jews of whose presence they were certainly aware. But they were Wehrmacht soldiers, not Nazis, and certainly not keen to stir up hostile feelings, particularly after the Maquis became active in the area. And Eyraud and Brès were on hand to keep the *maquisards* calm.

To this must be added the fact that neither the Prefect, Bach, nor Schmähling, the Wehrmacht major in Le Puy, was a zealous anti-Semite; and that Oscar Rosowsky was an excellent forger. There is also the long history of the area, with its cult of discretion and silence, the presence on the plateau of a great many liberal and influential refugees, the fact that the policemen in Tence and Yssingeaux were local men, belonging to the very families who were sheltering the Jews. And, of course, there were André Trocmé and Edouard Theis, who, until they left to go into hiding themselves, were strong influences on their parishioners, as were the plateau's other Protestant pastors. Trocmé may not have been the saint he is sometimes portrayed to have been, nor was non-violence anything but one small part of the story; but to him and his family must go much honour in the saving of the plateau's hidden people, as much must also go to the silent and unboastful Darbyists, and to all the modest Catholics, Protestants, atheists and agnostics, who, supporting each other with little heed for their own safety, ensured that of the hunted and persecuted refugees.

It was all these things: a felicitous combination of timing, place and people.

In the summer of 2012, I asked Madeleine Sèches, the daughter of Emile, who looks out so happily from the photograph of Tante Soly's children, to walk with me around the plateau. Madeleine had spent her professional life as a doctor, and returned to le Chambon from time to time with her children and grandchildren. She showed me how the refugees had climbed off the train in the little station at the top of the village, now closed and the tracks grassed over, and walked down the hill to the Hôtel May, where the farmers were waiting to drive them away in their pony traps to be hidden in farms and outhouses. We looked at Trocmé's presbytery, where Le Forestier had made the children laugh with his antics, and at the temple where Theis and Trocmé had preached so many fiery sermons, and at La Guespy, where Hanne and Rudy Appel had lived, at L'Abric, Faïdoli, the Coteau Fleuri and Les Grillons, where so many Jews, children as well as adults, had lived out the war years unharmed, and Beau Soleil, where Oscar Rosowsky and Gabrielle Barraud had worked all night forging documents. In Tante Soly, Madeleine showed me her bedroom with its window looking straight out on to the terrace on which the German soldiers did their exercises.

We walked along the banks of the river Lignon, where a German soldier would have drowned had it not been for the actions of a local boy, and where Jean-Pierre Trocmé and his friends had stolen another German soldier's clothes, so that he had to climb out and walk home naked, and where Pierre Bloch had gone looking for frogs. Madeleine pointed to the house in the square where Praly was shot, and to the Maison des Roches, on the road to Mars, raided by the Gestapo in the summer of 1943.

At different times, I went to Mazet, where Lulu Ruel and her daughter had hidden people in their attic, and Tence, where Pastor Leenhardt had supervised the protection of 163 Jews, and Chaumargeais, where Joseph Bass trained his Jewish Maquis and Itzhak Mikhaëli read the Book of Ruth by his candle and the light of the stars. And I went several times to Fay, as cold and windy as during the war, but empty now of the many shops that once made it the commercial centre of the plateau. In Fay's presbytery, Daniel Curtet had sat writing his coded letters to his father. These places, Madeleine said, are much as they were when she was a child; the people have gone, but the buildings and the plateau look the same. Though not the trees: Sylvester pines now grow where once were open meadows.

Were John Darby to return to the plateau, to preach and wander from village to village, he would find life curiously unchanged. The Ravenists have gone, though there are still small communities of 'les purs', who keep themselves apart from the world. In the Darbyist homes, the Bible is still read with undiminished piety. The war is remembered with some pride, but with no surprise. 'We are morally conscious people,' one man said to me. 'Our families didn't think of themselves as doing good. They did what they had always done, given sanctuary to the persecuted.' This self-effacement has meant that there are very few Darbyists among the Justes.

I went to Marseilles to see Gilbert Nizard, who, when he retired not long ago, built himself a little house above the city with a view across the sea. His six surviving brothers and sisters had, between them, 20 children, and they in turn gave birth to 61 children of their own. Today they live scattered between France, Israel, the United States, Switzerland and Brazil. They remain a close and loving family. It was only at the very end of the war, when the trains returning from Poland had brought all the survivors back to France, that they realised that Armand and André would not be coming home.

I went to New York, to find Max and Hanne Liebmann. In 1948, the TB that both had contracted in Gurs caught up with them, so that they spent 18 months in a sanatorium and were forced to put their baby daughter with a foster family. Far from being bitter about what had happened to them and their families,

Max and Hanne say that they are profoundly grateful that they came across people so committed to their beliefs that they were willing to risk their lives for strangers. Both now in their nineties, they ask: which of us would have done the same? In New York, I also found Rudy Appel, still working with the export firm he joined not long after the war.

Last of all, I travelled around Israel to visit the Roanne girls, living in small apartments in Tel Aviv and on kibbutzes in the north. In the early nineties, they helped set up an Association of Hidden Children, and they meet to remind each other of the days tobogganing down the icy streets of le Chambon, and of the kindness of their hosts. I found Pierre Bloch in a kibbutz on the Lebanese border. He had changed his surname, his first name, his language and his nationality and had become Eli Ben Gal.

Pierre was one of the people who attended Arnoux's colloquium in 1990. He came, he explained at the time, to thank Mme Roussel, in whose house he had lived, 'for my happy childhood as a little Jew during the Holocaust'. He also wanted to apologise to all the villagers for intruding on their privacy, for seeming to suggest that their natural altruism and courage were things that they wished to be thanked for. But, said Pierre, thank them he must, for saving him and so many others, and for 'reinventing' day after day what it was to possess true human dignity. To me, almost a quarter of a century later, Pierre said something else. 'We lived a very big adventure, an exceptional moment of time and place. It was something extraordinary to be young, engaged at a moment when France was so dark. There was something in the air, in the spirit of the people, that none of us ever forgot. All my life I have tried to live up to that moment.'

List of Illustrations

The maps were drawn by Bill Donohoe.

Every effort has been made to trace or contact all copyright holders, and the publishers will be pleased to correct any omissions brought to their notice and the earliest opportunity.

Bibliography

Primary sources

The most important material for this book came from interviews – in France, Israel and the US – with people who spent time in hiding on the Plateau Vivarais-Lignon during the German occupation, or who themselves helped in the rescue efforts. In some cases, I spoke to their children and relations. I was also fortunate enough to be given unpublished letters, journals and memoirs.

Invaluable documents on the Resistance in occupied France, on deportations and on the German occupiers are to be found in CARAN, the Archives Nationales in Paris (series 72AJ45; 72AJ69; 72AJ78; 72AJ142; F715000; AJ383575; AJ383618; AJ38258; F161–1038; F1c111/1162/1137). There is also a large archive on the Plateau Vivarais-Lignon in the Archives Départementales de la Haute-Loire in Le Puy (Series R, Series 12W, Series 173W, Series 562W; Fonds Bonnissol AD120J; Cabinet de la Haute-Loire, Series 1115W, 12W, 173W, 562W; Rapports de Gendarmerie, Series R3 and R4; Rapports des Renseignements Généraux R6828; Rapports du Préfet 526W208/9/10; Fonds Piton AD168J; AD562W170). More papers are to be found in Cimade's archives (Boîte No. 1, Boîte No. 2 and Papiers Violette Mouchon). Papers on individuals – rescued as well as rescuers – are to be found in the Société d'Histoire de la Montagne in Mazet, in the library of Yad Vashem in Jerusalem, in the United States Holocaust Memorial Museum in Washington, in the American Friends Service Committee (AFSC) archive in Philadelphia, and in the libraries of Cimade and the OSE in Paris. The Mémorial de la Shoah in Paris has a certain amount of material on the plateau and its inhabitants (CCXV111–104; DLXX11–7; DLXX11–53; DLX1–103; DLX1–104; CMXL1V; DCCCLX; DCCCLX1–55; DCCCLX1–37). André and Magda Trocmé's papers are to be found in the Swarthmore College Peace Collection.

Secondary sources

The Second World War in German-occupied France, the deportations of Jews and resisters to the extermination and concentration camps in the east, and life inside the French internment camps have all been much written about in memoirs, journals, letters and academic papers. The following is a selection of those most consulted for this book.

Alary, Eric, *Les Français au Quotidien*. Paris, 2006.

Alary, Eric, *L'Histoire de la Gendarmerie*. Paris, 2000.

Alexis-Monet, Laurette, *Les Miradors de Vichy*. Paris, 1994.

Alsop, Stewart, and Thomas Braden, *Sub-Rosa: The OSS and American Espionage*. New York, 1946.

Amicales des déportés d'Auschwitz et des Camps de Haute-Silési, *Marseille, Vichy et les Nazis*. Marseilles, 1993.

André Philip; Socialiste, Patriote, Chrétien. Colloque 13–14 Mars 2003. Paris, 2005.

Annales, 48 No. 3, May–June 1993, *Vichy, l'Occupation, les Juifs*. Paris.

Bailly, Danielle (ed.), *Traqués, Cachés, Vivants. Les Enfants Juifs en France*. Paris, 2004.

Barcellini, Serge, and Annette Wierviorka, *Passant, Souvient-Toi! Les Lieux du Souvenir de la Seconde Guerre Mondiale en France*. Paris, 1995.

Baruch, Marc Olivier, *Servir l'Etat Français. L'Administration en France de 1940 à 1944*. Paris, 1977.

Baubérot, Jean, *Le Retour des Huguenots. La Vitalité Protestante XIX–XX Siècle*. Paris, 1985.

Bauer, Yehuda, *American Jewry and the Holocaust*. Detroit, 1981.

Bédarida, Renée, *Pierre Chaillet*. Paris, 1988.

Bédarida, François, et Renée Bédarida (eds), *La Résistance Spirituelle 1941–1944. Les Cahiers Clandestins du Témoignage Chrétien*. Paris, 2001.

Belot, Robert (ed.), *Guerre et Frontières. La Frontière Franco-Suisse Pendant la Seconde Guèrre Mondiale*. Neuchâtel, 2006.

Bénédite, Daniel, *La Filière Marseillaise*. Paris, 1984.

Bergier Commission, *Switzerland and Refugees in the Nazi Era*. Bern, 1999.

Berlière, Jean-Marc, and Denis Peschanski, *La Police Française 1930–1950*. Paris, 2000.

Bernard, Serge, *Traces Légendaires, Mémoires et Construction Identicaire*. Lille, n.d.

Billig, Joseph, *Le Commissariat Général aux Questions Juives 1941–44*. 3 vols. Paris, 1955–60.

Birnbaum, Pierre, *Anti-semitism in France. A Political History*. Oxford, 1992.

Boegner, Philippe (ed.), *Les Carnets du Pasteur Boegner*. Paris, 1992.

Boegner, Philippe, *Ici, on a aimé les Juifs*. Paris, 1982.

Bohny-Reiter, Friedel, *Journal de Rivesaltes 1941–42*. Geneva, 1993.

Boismorand, Pierre, *Magda et André Trocmé. Figures de Resistance*. Paris, 2007.

Bolle, Pierre (ed.), *Les Résistances sur le Plateau Vivarais-Lignon 1938–1945. Témoins, Témoignages et Lieux de Mémoire*. Roure, 2005.

Bollon, Gérard, *Aperçus sur la Resistance armée en Yssingelais 1940–1945*. Le Chambon-sur-Lignon, 2007.

Boschetti, Pietro, *Les Suisses et les Nazis*. Geneva, 2004.

Boulet, François, *Histoire de la Montagne-Réfuge*. Roure, 2008.

Boulet, François, *Etrangers et Juifs en Haute-Loire de 1936 à 1944*. Cahiers de la Haute-Loire, 1992.

Braumann, J., Loinger, Georges, and F. Wattenberg. *Organisation Juive de Combat. 1940–1945*. Paris, 2006.

Brès, Eveline, and Yvan Brès, *Un Maquis d'Anti-Fascistes Allemands en France 1942–1944*. Languedoc, 1987.

Burrin, Philippe, *France Under the Germans*. New York, 1996.

Cabanel, Patrick, *Histoire des Justes en France*. Paris, 2012.

Cabanel, Patrick, and Laurent Gervereau, *La Deuxième Guerre Mondiale, des Terres de Refuge aux Musées*. Vivarais-Lignon, 2003.

Cabanel, Patrick, and Marianne Carbanier-Burkard, *Une Histoire des Protestants en France XVI–XX Siècles*. Paris, 1998.

Caen, Simon, *Georges Garel: Directeur d'un Reseau Clandestin de Sauvetage d'enfants juifs 1942–44*. Phd thesis, Université de Sciences Sociales de Grenoble, 1988–9.

Callil, Carmen, *Bad Faith. A Forgotten History of Family and Fatherland*. London, 2006.

Calvi, Fabrizio, *OSS: La Guerre Secrète en France*. Paris, 1990.

Camus, Albert, *La Peste*. Paris, 1947.

Camus, Albert, *Carnets: 1942–1943*. Paris, 1962; *Carnets: 1943–1951*. Paris, 1963.

Capdevila, Luc, François Rouquet, Fabrice Virgili, and Davide Voldman, *Hommes et Femmes dans la France en Guerre*. Paris, 2003.

Carpi, Daniel, *Between Mussolini and Hitler. The Jews and the Italian Authorities in France*. New Haven, 1994.

Charguéranel, Marc-André, *L'Etoile Jaune et la Croix Rouge. Le CICR et l'Holocauste 1939–1945*. Geneva, 1999.

Chaumont, Jean-Michel, *La Concurrence des Victimes*. Paris, 1997.

Chauvy, Gérard, *Histoire Secrète de l'Occupation*. Paris, 1991.

Chouraqui, André, *L'Amour Fort comme la Mort*. Paris, 1990.

Coad, F. Roy, *A History of the Brethren Movement*. Vancouver, 1968.

Cohen, Asher, *Persécutions et Sauvetages. Juifs et Français sous l'occupation et sous Vichy*. Paris, 1993.

Conan, Eric, and Henry Russo, *Vichy – An Ever Present Past*. New England, 1998.

Court, John M., *Approaching the Apocalypse. A short history of Christian Millenarianism*. London, 2008.

Courtois, Stéphane, and Adam Rayski, *Qui Savait Quoi?*. Paris, 1991.

Courvoisier, André, *Le Reseau Heckler de Lyon à Londres*. Paris, 1984.

Croslebailly, Berthe, *Dorcas. Héroine de la Résistance dans l'Yssingelais*. Le-Puy-en-Velay, 1999.

Dear, Ian, *Sabotage and Subversion: The SOE and OSS at War*. London, 1996.

Debiève, Roger, *Mémoires Meutries, Mémoires Trahies*. Paris, 1995.

Delarue, Jacques, *Histoire de la Gestapo*. Paris, 1962.

Delarue, Jacques, *Trafics et Crimes sous l'Occupation*. Paris, 1968.

Diamant, David, *Jeune Combat. La Jeunesse Juive dans la Résistance*. Paris, 1993.

Dray-Bensousan, Renée, *Les Juifs à Marseille 1940–1944*. Paris, 2004.

Dreyfus, Raymond, *Une 'Psy' selon Alfred Adler*. Unpublished memoir.

Duquesne, Jacques, *Les Catholiques Français sous l'Occupation*. Paris, 1966.

Durland De Saix, Deborah, and Karen Gray Ruelle, *Hidden on the Mountain*. New York, 2007.

Eychevine, Emilienne, *Les Pyrénées de la Liberté*. Paris,1983.

Favez, Jean-Claude, *Une Mission Impossible? Le CICR, les Déportations et les Camps de Concentration Nazis*. Lausanne, 1988.

Fayol, Pierre, *Le Chambon-sur-Lignon sous l'Occupation*. Paris, 1990.

Finkielkraut, Alain, *La Mémoire Vaine*. Paris, 1989.

Fishman, Sarah, Laura Lee Downs, Ioannis Sinanglou, Leonard V Smith, and Robert Zaretsky, *France at War. Vichy and the Historians*. Oxford, 2000.

Fitko, Lisa, *Escape through the Pyrenees*. Illinois, 1991.

Flaud, Annik, and Gérard Bollon, *Paroles de Réfugiés, Paroles de Justes*. Le Cheylard, 2009.

Flood, Christopher, and Hugo Frey, 'The Vichy Syndrome Revisited', *Contemporary French Civilisation*, Vol. 19, No. 2, 1995.

Foot, M. R. D., *SOE in France*. London, 1966.

Fry, Varian, *Du Réfuge à l'Exil. Actes du Colloque du 19 Mars 1999*. Arles, 2000.

Fry, Varian, *La Liste Noire*. Paris, 1999.

Gallisol, René, and Denis Peschanski, *De l'Exil à la Résistance*. Paris, 1989.

Garel, Georges, *Activités des Organisations Juives en France sous l'Occupation*. 1947.

Giniewski, Paul, *Une Résistance Juive 1943–45*. Paris, 2009.

Giolitto, Pierre, *Histoire de la Milice*. Paris, 1997.

Golnitz, Gérard, *Les Déportations de Réfugiés de Zone Libre en 1942*. Paris, 1996.

Grandjonc, Jacques, and Theresia Gunther (eds), *Zone d'Ombres 1933–1944*. Aix-en-Provence, 1990.

Grynberg, Anne, *Les Camps de la Honte. Les Internés Juifs des Camps Français 1939–44*. Paris, 1991.

Guéhenno, Jean, *Journal des Années Noires 1940–1944*. Paris, 1947.

Guillon, Jean-Marie, and Pierre Laborie (eds), *Mémoire et Histoire de la Résistance*. Toulouse, 1995.

Guirand, Jean-Michel, *La Vie Intellectuelle et Artistique à Marseille à l'Epoque de Vichy et sous l'Occupation*. Marseilles, 1989.

Hallie, Philip, *Lest Innocent Blood Be Shed*. New York, 1979.

Halls, W. D., *Politics, Society and Christianity in Vichy France*. Oxford, 1995.

Halls, W. D., *The Youth of Vichy France*. Oxford, 1981.

Harris Smith, Richard, *OSS. The Secret History of America's Central Intelligence Agency*. Berkeley, 1972.

Hazan, Katy, and Georges Weill, *Andrée Salomon, une Femme de Lumière*. Paris, 2011.

Hazan, Katy, *Les Orphelins de la Shoah*. Paris, 2000.

Henry, Patrick, *La Montagne des Justes*. Paris, 2010.

Hilberg, Raul, *Perpetrators, Victims and Bystanders. The Jewish Catastrophe 1939–1945*. New York, 1992.

Hilberg, Raul, *The Destruction of the Jews of Europe*. Chicago, 1961.

Jackson, Julian, *France: The Dark Years*. Oxford, 2001.

Jacques, André, *Madeleine Barot. Une Indomptable Energie*. Paris, 1989.

Joutard, Philippe, Jacques Poujol, and Patrick Cabanel (eds), *Cévennes, Terre de Réfuge 1940–1944*. Montpellier, 1987.

Kahn, Annette, *Robert et Jeanne: A Lyon sous l'Occupation*. Paris, 1990.

Kedward, H. R., *In Search of the Maquis. Rural Resistance in Southern France 1942–1944*. Oxford, 1993.

Kedward, H. R., *Resistance in Vichy France. A Study of Ideas and Motivation in the Southern Zone 1940–1942*. Oxford, 1978.

Kernan, Thomas, *Report on France*. London, 1942.

Klarsfeld, Serge, *Memorial to the Jews Deported from France 1942–1944*. New York, 1983.

Klarsfeld, Serge, *Vichy-Auschwitz*. Paris, 1985.

Knout, David, *La Résistance Juive en France*. Paris, 1947.

Kott, Aline, and Jacques Kott, *Roanne*. Paris, 1998.

Laharie, Pierre, *L'Opinion Française sous Vichy*. Paris, 1990.

Laharie, Claude, *Le Camp de Gurs 1935–1945*. Paris, 1994.

Latour, Anny, *The Jewish Resistance in France 1940–1944*. New York, 1970.

Lazare, Lucien, *Rescue as Resistance. How Jewish Organisations fought the Holocaust in France*. New York, 1996.

Lazare, Lucien, *Le Livre des Justes*. Paris, 1993.

Lecomte, François, *Jamais Je N'Aurai Quatorze Ans*. Paris, 2005.

Le Goff, Jacques, *History and Memory*. New York, 1992.

Lemalet, Martine (ed.), *Au Secours des Enfants du Siècle*. Paris, 1993.

Levy, Gaston, *Souvenirs d'un Médecin d'Enfants à l'OSE en France et en Suisse 1940–1945*. Unpublished memoir.

Loinger, Georges, *Aux Frontières de l'Espoir*. Paris, 2006.

Lowenthal, David, *The Past is a Forgotten Country*. Cambridge, 1985.

Lowrie, Donald A., *The Hunted Children*. New York, 1963.

Luirard, Monique, *La Région Stéphanoise*. Saint-Etienne, 1984.

Lytton, Neville, *Life in Occupied France*. London, 1942.

Maarten, Johan, *Le Village sur la Montagne*. Geneva, 1940.

Maber, G. L., *Le Faisceau des Vivants. Le Fagot Chambonnais*. Unpublished memoir.

Mabon-Fall, Armelle, *Les Assistantes Sociales au Temps de Vichy*. Paris, 1995.

Maillebouis, Christian, *Un Darbyste au XIXième siècle. Vie et Pensées de A. Dentan*. Le Chambon, 1990.

Marrot-Fellague Avionet, Céline, *Les Enfants Cachés pendant la*

Deuxième Guerre Mondiale. Mémoire de Maitrise. Université de Versailles, 1998.

Marrus, Michael R., and Robert O. Paxton, *Vichy France and the Jews.* New York, 1981.

Masour-Ratner, E., *Mes Vingt Ans à l'OSE.* Unpublished memoir.

La Mémoire, entre Histoire et Politique. Cahiers Français. July–August 2001.

Merle-d'Aubigné, Jeanne, and Violette Mouchon (eds), *Les Clandestins de Dieu. CIMADE 1939–1945.* Paris, 1968.

Michel, Alain, *Les Eclaireurs Israelites de France pendant la Seconde Guèrre Mondiale. Mémoire de Maitrise.* Paris, 1981.

Michel, Henri, *Les Courants de la Résistance.* Paris, 1962.

Mours, Samuel, *Le Protestantisme en Vivarais et en Velay.* Montpelier, 2001.

Munos-du-Peloux, Odile, *Passer en Suisse. Les Passages Clandestins entre la Haute-Savoie et la Suisse.* Grenoble, 2002.

Nicole, G., and R. Cuendot, *Darbysme et Assemblées Dissidentes.* Neuchâtel, 1962.

Noguères, Henri. *Histoire de la Résistance en France de 1940 à 1945.* 5 vols. Paris, 1967–9.

Nora, Pierre (ed.), *Rethinking France: Les Lieux de Mémoire.* Chicago, 2001.

Nossiter, Adam, *The Algeria Hotel. France, Memory and the Second World War.* New York, 2001.

Nouzille, Vincent, *L'Espionne. Virginia Hall – Une Américaine dans la Guèrre.* Paris, 2007.

Oliner, Samuel P., and Pearl M. Oliner, *The Altruistic Personality. Rescuers of Jews in Nazi Europe.* New York, 1988.

Ousby, Ian, *Occupation: The Ordeal of France 1940–1944.* London, 1997.

Pacy, James S., and Alan P. Wertheimer (eds), *Perspectives on the Holocaust. Essays in honour of Raul Hilberg.* Oxford, 1995.

Paxton, Robert O., *Vichy France: Old Guard and New Order.* New York, 1972.

Peschanski, Denis, *La France des Camps. L'Internement 1938–1946.* Paris, 2002.

Peschanski, Denis, *Les Tsiganes en France 1939–1946.* Paris, 1994.

Poliakov, Léon, *L'Auberge des Musiciens.* Paris, 1981.

Porthuis-Portheret, Valérie, *Août 1942: Lyon contre Vichy.* Lyons, 2012.

Poujol, Jacques, *Protestants dans la France en Guerre 1939–1945.* Paris, 2000.

Rayski, Adam, *Le Choix des Juifs sous Vichy.* Paris, 1992.

Riegner, Gerhart M., *Ne Jamais Désespérer.* Paris, 1998.

Rist, Charles, *Une Saison Gâtée. Journal de Guerre et d'Occupation 1939–1945.* Paris, 1983.

Roznanski, Renée, *Etre Juif en France pendant la Seconde Guèrre Mondiale.* Paris, 1994.

Ruby, Marcel, *F Section SOE. The Buckmaster Networks.* London, 1988.

Ruby, Marcel, *La Résistance à Lyon 19 June 1940–3 Septembre 1944.* Lyons, 1979.

Russo, Henry, *The Vichy Syndrome. History and Memory in France since 1944*. London, 1994.

Ryan, Donna F., *The Holocaust and the Jews of Marseille*. Illinois, 1996.

Samuel, Vivette, *Rescuing the Children: A Holocaust Memoir*. Wisconsin, 2002.

Schramm, Hanna, *Vivre à Gurs. Un Camp de Concentration Français*. Paris, 1979.

Siekierski, Denise, *MiDor LeDor*. Paris, 2004.

Stulmacher, Jacques, unpublished memoir.

Teissier du Cros, Janet, *Divided Loyalties*. London, 1962.

Todd, Olivier, *Albert Camus: Une Vie*. Paris, 1996.

Trocmé, André, unpublished memoir.

Trocmé, André et al., *Le Visage et l'Ame du Chambon*. Le Chambon-sur-Lignon, 1943.

Trocmé, Jacques, *Message Posthume du Pasteur André Trocmé*. Unpublished memoir. May 2003.

Unsworth, Richard P., *A Portrait of Pacifists. The Chambon, the Holocaust and the Lives of André and Magda Trocmé*. Syracuse, 2012.

Wellers, Georges, *L'Etoile Jaune à l'Heure de Vichy*. Paris, 1973.

Wisard, François, *Les Justes Suisses*. Geneva, 2007.

Yagil, Limore, *La France Terre de Réfuge et de Désobéissance Civile 1936–1944*. Paris, 2010.

Zalberg, Carole, *Chez Eux*. Paris, 2004.

Zaretsky, Robert, *Nîmes at War. Religion, Politics and Public Opinion in the Gard 1938–1944*. Pennsylvania, 1995.

Zeitoun, Sabine, *Ces Enfants qu'il Fallait Sauver*. Paris, 1989.

Zeitoun, Sabine, *L'OSE sous l'Occupation en France*. Paris, 1990.

Zuccotti, Susan, *The Holocaust, the French and the Jews*. London, 1993.

Source notes

Part One

Chapter One

15 **When Aaron:** Simon Liwerant, interview with author.
15 **To be Jewish:** Birnbaum, *Anti-semitism in France.*
17 **When, in May 1939:** Paxton, *Vichy France*; Callil, *Bad Faith*; Klarsfeld, *Vichy-Auschwitz.*
20 **Forbidding those Jews:** Marrus and Paxton, *Vichy France and the Jews*; Billig, *Le Commissariat Général aux Questions Juives.*
20 **It was perfectly clear:** Lowrie, *The Hunted Children.*
21 **a venomous anti-Semitic:** Rayski, *Le Choix des Juifs sous Vichy.*
22 **'I have been anti-Semitic':** *Annales* No. 3.
25 **Coffee, of a kind:** Alary, *Les Français au Quotidien*; Ousby, *Occupation: the Ordeal of France.*
31 **There was another:** Jacques Stulmacher, interview with author.

Chapter Two

35 **By the late summer:** Laborie, *L'Opinion Française sous Vichy.*
35 **One of them was:** Hanne and Max Liebmann, interview with author.
39 **Gurs was not:** Grynberg, *Les Camps de la Honte*; Peschanski, *La France des Camps*; Schramm, *Vivre à Gurs.*
40 **The ICRC:** ICRC archives B6003–28–02 (Geneva).
41 **It was by pretending:** Jacques, *Madeleine Barot.*
42 **One of the first:** Hazan, *Les Orphelins de la Shoah*; Masour-Ratner, *Mes Vingt Ans à l'OSE*; Zeitoun, *L'OSE sous l'Occupation en France.*
43 **Donald Lowrie, an American:** American Friends Service Committee archives.
45 **OSE, who became:** Hazan and Weill, *Andrée Salomon, une Femme de Lumière.*

55 **By the time another:** Rudy Appel, interview with author.
57 **Every day now:** Samuel, *Rescuing the Children*, p. 47.

Chapter Three

60 **Laval was heard:** Grynberg, *Les Camps de la Honte*, p. 298.
60 **'This is like Germany:'** Laharie, *Le Camp de Gurs*, p. 237.
61 **On 3 August:** AFSC archive.
63 **At Rivesaltes:** Bohny-Reiter, *Journal de Rivesaltes*.
63 **At La Verdière:** Zeitoun, *Ces Enfants qu'il Fallait Sauver*.
68 **Very early on the:** Porthuis-Portheret, *Août 1942*.

Chapter Four

75 **Many of France's:** Callil, *Bad Faith*, p. 239.
76 **In their monthly:** Zuccotti, *The Holocaust, the French and the Jews*, p. 155.
77 **By inclination:** Cabanel and Carbonier-Burkard, *Une Histoire des Protestants en France*.
78 **Socialism being regarded:** Baubérot, *Le Retour des Huguenots*.
80 **Before the meeting:** Jacques, *Madeleine Barot*, p. 76.
81 **Later, his colleagues:** quoted in letter in Oscar Rosowsky private archives.
81 **The Assembly of Cardinals:** Bédarida and Bédarida, *La Résistance Spirituelle*, p. 15.
83 **the local prefect:** Duquesne, *Les Catholiques Français sous l'Occupation*, p. 250.
85 **In the wake of:** Peschanski, *La France des Camps*, p. 351.
86 **For his cover:** Lily Garel, interview with author. See also Zeitoun, *L'OSE sous l'Occupation en France*; Zeitoun, *Ces Enfants qu'il Fallait Sauver*.
88 **As Donald Lowrie:** letter of 17 September to Tracey Strong.
88 **In September:** Rayski, *Le Choix des Juifs sous Vichy*, p. 172.
89 **Delivering Jews, he said:** Klarsfeld, *Memorial to the Jews Deported from France*.

Part Two

Chapter Five

94 **Albert Camus, who arrived:** Todd, *Albert Camus*, p. 149.
94 **He thought of:** Camus, *Carnets: 1942–5*, p. 15.
96 **In the wake:** Bolle (ed.), *Les Résistances sur le Plateau Vivarais-Lignon*; Boulet, *Histoire de la Montagne-Refuge*.
100 **There was Beau Soleil:** Gabrielle Barraud, interview with author.

100 **In the middle:** Madeleine Sèches, interview with author.

104 **Among its inhabitants:** Christian Maillebouis, interview with author; see also Maillebouis, *Un Darbyste au XIXième siècle*.

107 **In 1837:** Coad, *A History of the Brethren Movement*.

Chapter Six

112 **André Trocmé came:** Nelly Hewett Trocmé, interview with author; see also Boismorand, *Magda et André Trocmé*; Unsworth, *A Portrait of Pacifists*; and unpublished memoirs by André and Magda T rocmé.

119 **From the first:** Danielle Le Forestier and Jean-Philippe Le Forestier, interviews with author.

122 **Her students found:** André Trocmé papers, Box 2, Series A.

122 **There was another:** Richard Maber, interview with author. See also Maber, *Le Faisceau des Vivants*.

124 **Burners Chalmer told:** Unsworth, *A Portrait of Pacifists*, p. 164.

125 **It was at this time:** André Trocmé memoir, p. 247.

Chapter Seven

129 **As the Vichy government:** Paxton, *Vichy France*.

129 **Children were to:** Halls, *The Youth of Vichy France*.

130 **To this end:** Capdevila et al., *Hommes et Femmes dans la France en Guèrre*.

130 **As the writer:** Paxton, *Vichy France*, p. 222.

131 **The list was interminable:** Halls, *The Youth of Vichy France*, p. 53.

131 **They would have refused:** André Trocmé memoir.

133 **Robert Bach:** Boulet, *Cahiers de la Haute-Loire*, 2004.

134 **'If, even in France:** *Cahiers de la Montagne*, 2004.

138 **Day after day:** Bolle, *Les Résistances sur le Plateau Vivarais-Lignon*; Boulet, *Histoire de la Montagne-Réfuge*; Poujol, *Protestants dans la France en Guerre*.

139 **Most poignant:** Ruth Fivaz-Silbermann, interview with author.

144 **Two of the new:** Joseph Atlas papers in the US Holocaust Memorial Museum archive, Washington.

147 **Magda, for all:** Lecomte, *Jamais Je N'Aurai Quatorze Ans*.

149 **A boy called:** Peter Feigl papers in the US Holocaust Memorial Museum archive.

Chapter Eight

151 **Swastikas went up:** Burrin, *France under the Germans*.

152 **All were enjoined:** Archives Départementales de la Haute-Loire, 562W51.

208 Except that this oblivion: Riegner, *Ne Jamais Désesperer*; Courtois and Rayski, *Qui Savait Quoi?*
209 In Lyons: Porthuis-Portheret, *Août 1942.*
211 The rest were: Zuccotti, *The Holocaust, the French and the Jews*, p. 173.
211 These arrests only: Hazan, *Les Orphelins de la Shoah.*
213 To clothe: Lily Garel, interview with author.
214 It is now that: Poliakov, *L'Auberge des Musiciens.*
218 And then there was: Favez, *Une Mission Impossible?*
220 'those who have fled': Belot (ed.), *Guerre et Frontières*, p. 299.

Chapter Twelve

225 On the plateau: Piton papers, Archives Départementales de la Haute-Loire; Boulet, *Histoire de la Montagne-Réfuge*; Bolle (ed.), *Les Résistances sur le Plateau Vivarais-Lignon.*
229 Her place was taken: Merle-d'Aubigné and Mouchon (eds), *Les Clandestins de Dieu.*
231 Between February: Ruth Fivaz-Silbermann, interview with author.

Chapter Thirteen

235 The story of the Blochs: Pierre Bloch, interview with author.
238 On Friday 11 June: Gilbert Nizard, interview with author.
239 The Exbrayats: Archives Départementales de la Haute-Loire, 996W232.
242 Precisely why: Gérard Bollon, *Cahiers de la Haute-Loire*, 1996.
245 The Maison des Roches: Poujol, *Protestants dans la France en Guerre*; Magda Trocmé, memoir.

Chapter Fourteen

253 What Madeleine: Jeanne and Madeleine Sèches, interview with author.
258 Simon Liwerant: Simon Liwerant, unpublished manuscript.
264 Just how dangerous: Masour-Ratner, *Mes Vingt Ans à l'OSE.*
265 On the plateau: René Rivière, interview with author.
245 Most upsetting: unpublished paper, Madeleine Dreyfus archive.

Chapter Fifteen

276 By the spring of: Léon Eyraud, interview with author; see also Boulet, *Histoire de la Montagne-Réfuge.*
283 One of the youngest: Itzhak Mikhaëli, interview with author.
284 Her name was: M. R. D. Foot, interview with author; see also Fayol, *Le Chambon-sur-Lignon sous l'Occupation*; Calvi, *OSS.*
286 'I haven't seen': letter of 4 September 1941.

286 'We age very quickly': Peter Churchill, *Of their Own Choice* (London, 1952), p. 154.
287 If SOE: Alsop and Braden, *Sub-Rosa*.
287 'All those first': Harris Smith, *OSS*, p. 149.
289 The first that Pierre Fayol: Maber, *Le Faisceau des Vivants*.
290 Twenty young men: Jean Nallet, interview with author.
291 Some of the young: Nouzille, *L'Espionne*, p. 290.

Chapter Sixteen

296 Two of those arrested: Masour-Ratner, *Mes Vingt Ans à L'OSE*; Zeitoun, *L'OSE sous L'Occupation en France*.
300 And then tragedy: Gabrielle Barraud, interview with author.
301 The next day: Maber, *Le Faisceau des Vivants*; Lecomte, *Jamais Je N'Aurai Quatorze Ans*.
307 On 25 August: *Bulletin de Mazet-Saint-Voy*, 2004.
309 Once Lyons: Elizabeth McIntosh, *Sisterhood of Spies*.
309 She took with her: Nouzille, *L'Espionne*, p. 303.

Chapter Seventeen

315 When Rambert: Todd, *Albert Camus*, p. 210.
316 It would be: Klarsfeld, *Memorial to the Jews Deported from France*; Marrus and Paxton, *Vichy France and the Jews*.
322 When one woman: Hazan, *Les Orphelins de la Shoah*, p. 231.
325 No European country: Bernard, *Traces Légendaires*; Nora, *Rethinking France*.
329 As of 2012: Cabanel, *Histoire des Justes en France*.

Afterword

333 What followed was: Oscar Rosowsky, interview with author.
333 In *Le Monde Juif*: *Le Monde Juif*, 1988/89, Numbers 130, 131, 132, 133
333 Commenting on: Piton papers, Archives Départementales de la Haute-Loire.
334 Then in 1983: Alain Arnoux, interview with author.
335 Silence has not: Alain Debard, Eliane Wauquiez-Motte, Gérard Bollon, interviews with author.

Acknowledgements

This book could not have been written without the help of the following people. I would like to thank them all for their time, kindness and encouragement, and for telling me their stories: Mireille Alkhadet, Rudy Appel, Alain Arnoux, the late Gabrielle Barraud, Serge Bernard, Patrick Cabanel, Carmen Callil, Gérard Chazot, Mimi Cortial, Isabelle Cotting, Alin Curtet, Mme Darche de Maleprade, Annette Davis, Alain Debard, Robert Ebart, Léon Eyraud, Michel Fabréguet, Henri and Hélène Federmann, Pierre de Felice, Ruth Fivaz-Silbermann, Monique and Marcel Fleismaher, the late M. R. D. Foot, Danielle Le Forestier, Jean-Philippe Le Forestier, Lily Garel, Aziza Gril-Mariotte, Patrick Grandouiller, Charlotte Grundman, M. and Mme Guillaume, Liliane Haimov, Nelly Hewett Trocmé, Liliane Klein-Liebert, Jean Laposte, Hanne and Max Liebmann, Simon Liwerant, Georges Loinger, Richard Maber, Christian Maillebouis, Rachel Malafosse, Lise Martinon-Meyer, M and Mme May, Christian de Monbrison, Jean Nallet, Gilbert Nizard, Olivier Philip, Valerie Portuis-Portheret, René Rivière, Nicole Robert, Mme Roussel, Yves and Madeleine Royer, Lucienne Ruel, Jeanne and Madeleine Sèches, Mme Spindler, Jacques Stulmacher, Sylvianne Vinson-Galy, Eliane Wauquiez-Motte, Francis Weill.

In Israel, Schlomo Balsam, Elie Ben Gal, Ruth Golan, Liliane Haimov, Rita Kobrinski, Lucien Lazare, Itzhak Mikhaëli, Mina Sela and Geni Schloss were all kind enough to talk to me about their wartime memories.

Rod Kedward, Laurent Douzou, Gérard Bollon, François Boulet and Serge Bernard are all historians who have written extensively on wartime France. They gave me generous help.

Much of the material for this book comes from private and public archives. I should in particular like to thank the following individuals and the staffs of their libraries: CARAN, the Archives Nationales in Paris; the National Archives in Kew; Judith Cohen and the United States Holocaust Memorial Museum in Washington; Martin de Framond and the Archives Départementales de la Haute-Loire; Fabrizio Bensi and the International Committee of the Red Cross; the World Council of Churches; Fruma Mohrer and the YIVA Institute for Jewish Research; David Rosenberg and the Center for Jewish History; Don Davies and the American Friends Service Committee;

Alycia Vivona and the FOR Library; the Bibliothèque Municipale du Mazet-Saint-Voy; Agathe Marin and Cimade; Marie-Catherine Efkhanian and the Collège Cévenol; Karen Taieb and the Mémorial de la Shoah in Paris; Wendy Chmielewski and the Swarthmore College Peace Collection; Katy Hazan, Jean-François Lamarque and the OSE; the Musée du Desert; the Société d'Histoire de la Montagne; Irena Steinfeldt and Yad Vashem.

I should also like to thank all those friends who through their hospitality and willingness to travel with me made this book happen: Annie Blaber, Virginia Duigan, Janet Savelli and Karen Democrest. Rod Kedward and Anne Chisholm read the manuscript and corrected many mistakes; I am extremely grateful to them.

And, as always, my warmest thanks to my agent, Clare Alexander, and my editors, Penny Hoare, Poppy Hampson and Susannah Otter in London, Jennifer Barth in New York and Pamela Murray in Canada, and to my publicists, Lisa Gooding in London and Jane Beirn in New York.

Index

shortages of food and clothing on 102–3, 145–6, 207, 213, 252, 253, 255–7; silence and discretion, culture of 19, 110, 116, 162–3, 182, 184, 186, 188, 214, 250, 335, 337; terrain and climate of 93–4, 125, 149, 191, 205, 235, 253; *touristes alimentaires* (visitors in search of food) on 145, 163, 178, 202; tourists in 96–7, 178; tribunals, post-war 315; Vichy and *see* Vichy

Poincaré, Raymond 17

Poivre, Noël 193, 243, 245, 246, 247

Poland 3, 9, 15, 16, 24, 27, 29, 31, 42, 52, 57, 60, 66, 70, 72, 86, 89, 90, 133, 139, 144, 148, 154, 158, 156, 181, 184, 185, 188, 205, 232, 238, 248, 254, 300, 317, 320, 321, 323, 324, 339

Poliakov, Léon 215, 216, 353

police, Vichy French 2, 22, 23, 26, 27–8, 29, 33, 39, 43, 46, 49, 50, 52, 56, 60, 62, 64, 65, 67, 68, 70–1, 73, 85, 89, 99, 127, 130, 134–41, 142, 151, 152–3, 155, 158, 160, 162, 166–7, 168, 171–2, 174, 176, 181, 186, 188, 191–2, 193, 194, 195, 196, 199, 202, 203, 204, 205, 211, 214, 217, 218, 219, 220, 221, 228, 232, 233, 236, 238, 240, 242, 249, 251, 252, 256, 257, 261, 265, 266, 274, 278, 279, 280, 281, 283, 284, 302, 307, 308–9, 311, 317, 322, 328, 330, 332, 336, 337

Pompidou, Georges 315

Pont du Cholet 254–5, 256

Portugal 49, 86, 156, 157, 173, 175

Poujol, Jacques 334, 351, 353

La Pouponnière 99

Praly, Inspector Léopold 2, 171–2, 190, 203, 204, 205, 238, 246, 249, 269, 338

Protestant Church/Protestants: belief in salvation of the Jews 106–7; Boegner directs Protestants to save Jews 5, 84–5; failure to speak out against treatment of Jews 75;

history in France 76–80; individuals involved in rescue/hiding of Jews *see under individual name*; *la Désert* 77, 84–5, 106; 'la haute bourgeoisie Protestante' 79; 'les theses de Pomeyrol', 1941 79, 80; number of pastors involved in saving Jews on Plateau Vivarais-Lignon 10; organisations involved in saving Jews on Plateau Vivarais-Lignon *see under individual organisation name*; pastors involved in saving of Jews *see under individual name*; Protestant nature of Plateau Vivarais-Lignon 104–11; Reformed Synod, May 1941 80; 'Reveil' 77–8, 107; social welfare and charity in the tradition of 106; STO, comes out against 195; tradition of defiance in the Ardèche and Cévannes 104–5, 106

Protestant Reformed Church 76, 270

Puritans 106, 107, 108

Le Puy-en-Velay 2, 93, 94, 96, 121, 131, 133, 135, 137, 138, 140, 152, 153, 154, 167–8, 190, 191, 201, 203, 204, 235, 239, 240, 248–9, 277, 278, 282, 291, 297, 302, 303, 307, 310, 337

Quakers 44, 45, 48, 57, 61, 67, 104, 124, 150, 156, 203, 207, 244

Quilici, Anne-Marie (Bonnet) 215

Rambaud, Jean 303

Rambert, Raymond 152

Ravenists 10, 104, 108–11, 339

Ravensbrück 265–6, 268, 318, 319

Récébédou 63, 99

Red Cross 30, 40, 66, 124, 150, 208, 209, 212, 294, 302, 303

Rédmont, Bishop of Nice, Mgr Paul 263

Reiter, Friedel 56, 58, 63, 64

'Relève' scheme 194–5

Réseau Marcel 263

Resistance, French 5, 6, 30, 74, 86, 151, 196, 201–2, 207, 215, 228,